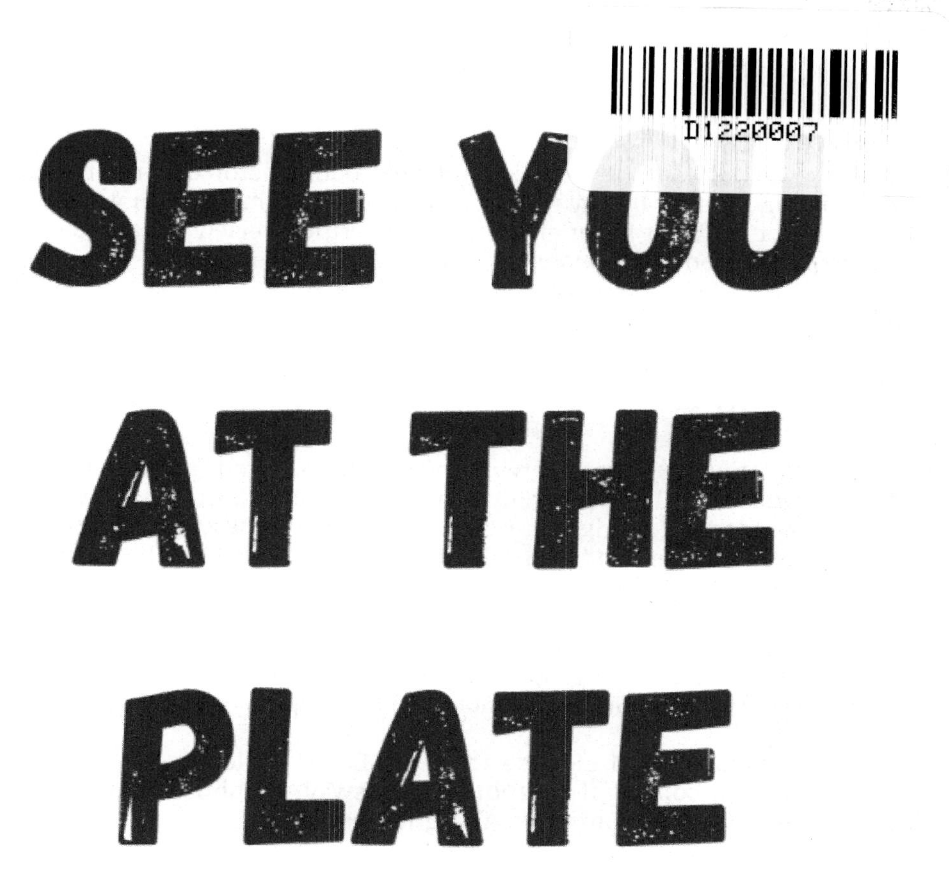

365-day Sports Devotional

Stephen A. Strange

Published by Stephen A. Strange. To request permissions, contact the publisher at steverumc@yahoo.com.

Cover by Stephen A. Strange

ISBN-13: 978-0-578-31427-3

I dedicate this book to all the coaches, ministers, and mentors that have poured into me. I want to especially thank my wife for always supporting and uplifting me in my ministry and sports endeavors. I want to thank my children (Savannah, Lillian, Jackson, and Everleigh) for always giving material to write about and for always allowing their lives to be put on display. I am thankful for every student-athlete that I have been able to work with and how they have touched my life. I also want to thank all the churches I have served for allowing me to coach and serve alongside them. I want to thank Al Sikes for helping me through every step in publishing this book; without his help, you would not have this book. Finally, all the glory goes to God, who took a very average person and has allowed me to do great things for the Kingdom. May this book honor The Father, The Son, and The Holy Spirit and be a blessing to all who read it. I will see you at the Plate.

To Melodie,
May the book bless + encourage you family.
See you at the Plate
Dr. [illegible]
Phil 4:13

INTRODUCTION

I have always loved sports. In fact, I can tell you that sports saved my life and led me into the ministry. I have also been very blessed in life, and I have gotten to do some cool things, and almost all of them have come out of the context of sports. I played every sport as a child that I could. (Whiffle Ball was my favorite.) I was able to play football and run track all the way through high school. I then got the opportunity to play NAIA College Football at Campbellsville College from 1987-1991. In 2012, the team I played on in 1988-89 was inducted into the Campbellsville University Athletics Hall of Fame. I was able to run the St. Jude's Marathon twice, running for a young man that was struggling with cancer. (My time was based more on a calendar than a stopwatch, but I still finished it two times.) I have been able to complete at least three-century rides on my road bike. (I know. Why? Most people do not like driving that far.) I have done over 25 sprint triathlons, numerous 5k and 10k races, and three half-marathons. I have been blessed to complete five half-Ironman (70.3 miles) events, even though I am built more like a professional wrestler than a Triathlete. But the pinnacle of my sports career came in 2007 when I was able to compete and finish Ironman Louisville (140.60 miles). I have been blessed to be a life coach for three different high school football teams here in Alabama. I was also blessed to go with one of those teams to the Alabama 4-A State Championship twice. I have been able to coach travel softball, high school softball, and many youth sports. I have been an FCA Huddle Leader and have gotten to lead Bible studies for coaches and players over the last 25 years. I have also been blessed to be around many Godly coaches in the sports world. (There was none more influential than Coach Ron Finely, my college football coach.) Now the reason I mention these accomplishments is not to brag because I am a struggler, not an overachiever, but in all these things, I have learned more about God and my faith. So, several years ago, I began to write a daily devotional that had to do with sports. Then one day, God gave me the idea to put these in the form of a book and to get them into the hands of people so they might see God in some of the places that I met God. So, I began to put it all together but had no idea how to author a book or get it to print. So, just like in sports, I struggled but persisted, and here is the finished copy. First, a disclaimer, I write like I talk and preach, so this is not scholarly by any stretch, and you may even find some grammar and other literary mistakes. (You might find a lot of those mistakes.)

So, five years of writing and devotions are now compiled into the book you are holding in your hand. So, I want to explain how this devotional book is set up and how you can use it. First, there are 365 distinct devotions, one for every day of the year. They are not dated; they are only numbered because sometimes, when people get a book that starts on January 1, they will not start till then, and by the time that day comes around, the book is forgotten. In this book, you can start the day you get it and then go through 365 days. There are 365 different Scriptures, one for every day. Some days have multiple Scriptures, and some have Scriptures that overlap, but no day is exactly like another day. There are also 365 names for God. You can use these names for God for journaling and prayer. Each day includes a prayer that I spoke over the devotional, and many of them are written in the first person. Some of the prayers are in the form of a song that I was listening to when I wrote the devotion, or I used the song to formulate the premise for the devotional. Not only is the book broken up into 365 days, but the titles are given of each devotional in the beginning so that if you are struggling with something or something that catches your eye, you can go to that day. The other thing is that some of the devotions are combined into series. These devotions are a highlighted on the title pages. They can be used by small groups, teams, or coaches to emphasize an area of growth in sports and life.

I hope that this book will inspire you to be the best athletes and the best followers of Christ that you can be. I hope you will also give copies to athletes so they can hear how God may speak to them through the words on these pages that the Holy Spirit inspired. So, sit down and start reading, and I will see you at the plate!

CONTENTS

Names of God

Day 1

Before "I" Cross the Plate

Exodus 3:5 (NIRV) ***"Do not come any closer," God said. "Take off your sandals. The place you are standing on is holy ground."***

This last week we played in the USSSA World Series in Foley, Alabama. During our last elimination game, I noticed that one of the girls on the opposing team always stepped away from the plate and marked in the ground before stepping back up to the plate. Now, it is not strange for girls to have certain rituals before stepping up to the plate. Some girls twirl their bat; some girls hit themselves in the back with the bat (which I have never understood because it hurts), and some girls push their bat forward like they are going to bunt. But this girl's ritual was different because the mark that she made in the dirt with her bat was the sign of the cross. She was literal, marking the ground that she was standing on as "Holy Ground." She was using every one of her at-bats as a testimony and giving God all the glory. You know I have never thought of the softball infield as Holy Ground, but then again, Holy Ground is where we choose to make it. This girl used the talents and resources that God had given her, and she made it Holy Ground right there at the ballpark. Let me ask you, could you not do the same? What would the world look like if we decided where God had put us, we were going to make it Holy Ground? We would be great ambassadors for Christ. Let me ask you, are you standing on Holy Ground? I will see you at the plate!

Dear Savior,

God let the place that I play, work, or go to school, be Holy Ground. God, by making everywhere I step Holy Ground, I become a vessel for you. Let me share your word in everything I do, and let me always give you the glory.

Day 2

Persevering Through Pain

Romans 5:3-5 ***Not only so, but we also glory in our sufferings, because we know that suffering produces perseverance; perseverance, character; and character, hope. And hope does not put us to shame because God's love has been poured out into our hearts through the Holy Spirit, who has been given to us.***

I saw her grimace in pain as she slid head-first back into first base after the catcher had tried to pick her off. I had no idea what had happened because I was coaching third base; I was just glad that she had got back to base safely. But then I heard her scream with anguish and saw that she was crying. Apparently, the first basemen had jumped up and come down right on her hand with metal spikes. Because she was my catcher, I was able to sub a pinch-runner for her freely. After our bat was over, I noticed that she had put on her catcher's equipment and was headed back out to catch. After the game, I noticed that she was still in a tremendous amount of pain, and I asked to see her hand. It was swollen, and we agreed that we had a 2-hour break between games, so she should go to an immediate care center right down the road and have it examined. She called me right before the next game started and told me to put her in the lineup because the doctor told her she could play. She showed up with a splint on her finger and informed me that she had a small break in her pinky, but the doctor said she could play if she left her splint on. That game, she sat most of the time, but I was shorthanded that day at catcher. So, for the last game of the day, she told me she could catch, and that is precisely what she did. She tagged someone out with a splint on her finger, threw a bunter out going to first, and had a hit with an RBI. The whole time she was playing, you could tell she was in pain, but she stated that she was doing it for the team. Yes, that day, we all learned what it means to persevere and work through the pain. You know that is exactly what Christ did for us on the cross. Jesus continued through the pain so that we would have salvation. In this life, even if we are believers, we will have pain and struggles. But the question is this? Will we persevere so that we can get to the point of faith? You know, faith is the product of long-suffering and perseverance. It is funny what playing through the pain for the team's greater good can show us, but it is a greater testimony when we look at the cross and what good that brought to us. Even if you are in pain, I will see you at the plate!

Dear Father,

God, in this life, we are going to have pain. It is what the result of sin caused but let us learn to play and persevere through it. When we feel we cannot go on, help us to tough it out. God, you went through great suffering so that we could have eternal life, and the suffering we endure is nothing compared to what pain and lengths you went through for us. God, our pain sometimes reminds us of what our salvation cost. Thank you, God, that we sometimes get to suffer.

Day 3

You Are Only As Good As Your Prayer

Philippians 4:6 NLT ***Don't worry about anything; instead, pray about everything. Tell God what you need and thank him for all he has done.***

So, you have taken thousands of swings in the batting cage? You have thrown at least a million warm-up pitches. You have taken infield so many times that you feel you have become one with the dirt. You have caught more fly balls than you care to count. But the question is this, have these things made you the best player you can possibly be? I mean, countless hours of practice are bound to make someone better, but sometimes we miss one secret ingredient. In the book, The Circle Maker, Mark Batterson makes this comment. "Prayer is the difference between the best you can do and the best God can do."[1] You see, the secret ingredient to success is prayer. Sure, you have to put in all the hard work and prepare yourself for every situation. But without prayer, you are only as good as you can be. With prayer, you are as good as God can be. See, you pray as it depends on God, but you work like it depends on you. Prayer is the perfect recipe for success. This is where people see your hard work meeting with fervent prayers. So, let me ask you this. You have spent countless hours practicing, but how much time have you spent in prayer? I will see you at the plate!

Dear Lord,

God, thank you for the opportunity to work hard so I can play the game better. Thank you for surrounding me with people that will push me to make me better. Thank you for allowing me the health and the resources to play the game I love. But help me never to forget that all these things need to be blanketed in prayer. I am only at my best when I ask God for his help and surrender my will to his.

Day 4

Swapping Teams

James 1:1-3 ***Consider it pure joy, my brothers and sisters, whenever you face trials of many kinds because you know that the testing of your faith produces perseverance. Let perseverance finish its work so that you may be mature and complete, not lacking anything.***

There is one thing you can bet when it comes to travel baseball/softball, parents and players will look for greener grass on other teams. There are always people jumping from one team to another. Sometimes it is a legitimate move, and the player is moving up in class. But most of the time, players switch because they have had a run-in with the coach or do not like where they are playing. Most of the time, these moves are initiated by parents that have never made a bad coaching call from their lawn chair behind home plate. But many of those parents have no idea what it takes to run a winning program. They are not really concerned with the concept of a team; they are only homed in on how good their sons or daughters could be if they were playing the right position. So, they are continually switching teams in order to find the team or the coach that will play them all the time right where the parent or player thinks they should be playing. This is one of the reasons that we now live in a world of entitlement. It is sometimes easier to just switch jobs or teams in order to get what we want than it is to stick it out when the going gets rough. The harsh reality is that this is crippling this generation. We are not helping them toughen up and work harder. We are merely saying you showed up, so you deserve it. The reality is that we need not to run when things do not always work out; we need to stand and fight. I am so glad that Jesus did not swap teams. I am so glad that he did not look at the Pharisees and say, you know this religious thing is much easier than this servant thing. No, Jesus stood tall so that we could be saved. He did not switch teams but fully sacrificed everything he had so we could be on his team. So, the next time things are not going as planned, remember that perseverance will build character, and character is really who you are. Stay on the team, and I will see you at the plate.

Dear Spirit,

God, it is easier to throw in the towel than it is to stand and fight, but God make me a fighter. When I am totally exhausted, help me to fight. God, when I think that the grass is greener on the other side, help me to discern the truth. God help me to stay committed to you like Jesus was committed to you.

Day 5

Is Your House Divided?

Matthew 12:25 ***Jesus knew their thoughts and said to them, "Every kingdom divided against itself will be ruined, and every city or household divided against itself will not stand.***

Have you ever played on a team that had drama? A team that had all the talent in the world but could not play together? A team that was not bonded together. You know team chemistry is as important as team talent. I have seen teams that were far less talented but far more unified go on to do greater things than a team full of talent but also full of drama. Jesus knew that a house could not stand divided against itself. When a team becomes unified, they play for one another and not just for themselves. A team must not only work together on the field, but they must work together in the dugout and off the field. Let me ask you, are you the cause of drama on your team? Do you backbite and blame other people for the loss? You see, a sport not only teaches us how to play, but it teaches us how to live. When we learn how to work together on the field, we also learn how to work together through life. A house cannot stand divided, and neither can a team. Is it time to do some unification? Is it time to evaluate whether your team is divided? So become unified; I will See you at the plate.

Dear God of the Universe,

Help me to realize that I am just one part of many moving parts. God, a team, cannot be a team unless they are unified and in synch. God, if I am a drama starter or a pot-stirrer, then help me to quit doing that immediately. God, if there are others on the team that divide the team, I pray that you will give them a cooperative spirit to quit doing those things so that we can become a cohesive, unified team, playing not for ourselves but one another.

Day 6

Failure that Leads to Success

Proverbs 24:10 ***"If you falter in times of trouble, how small is your strength!"***

Have you ever thought that failure was the enemy of success? What would you say if I told you that failure was really an ally for success? Do you realize that every time you fail, you are learning? Every time you fail and continue to get back up, you are learning persistence. During the USSSA Alabama State 16u State Softball tournament this year, I talked with one of the coaches who had just very convincingly beat us. I was stating how well his team played together and that they played almost error-free. He then told me that they had been together since most of them were ten years old and that they had taken quite a few beatings in the past five years. He said, "but over time, the losses and failures had made them into the fine-tuned machine that they were today." See, failure teaches us to try harder, to work harder, and be more mentally tough. It encourages us to put in extra time and to practice harder. Failure ultimately leads to success. Now I will tell you what an enemy of success is, and that is fear. If you fail and quit, then you truly are defeated. My daughter did not make the volleyball team her freshman year in high school. But her sophomore year, after seeing her work ethic in softball, the coach asked her to come to try out again. This time she made the Varsity Team. When I asked the coach why she had put her on varsity, the coach said because she makes a lot of mistakes but never gives up. I want to use her to teach the other girls how hard work can lead to great things. See, my daughter did not allow fear to keep her from trying once again. Let me ask you, have you failed lately? How did you respond? Come on, let's try again, and I will see you at the plate!

Dear God of Second Chances,

This may sound weird but thank you that we are allowed to fail and make mistakes. If we did not fail, there would be no need for grace. God, thank you that we have the ability to learn from our failures and to become better because of the mistakes we make. In our Christian walk, we call mistakes part of our testimony; without failures and mistakes, our testimonies would not be very interesting. The one and only ultimate mistake we could ever make is the mistake of dying without putting our trust in you.

✞

Do Not Forget Where You Got Those Gifts

Colossians 3:23-24 ***Whatever you do, work at it with all your heart, as working for the Lord, not for men, since you know that you will receive an inheritance from the Lord as a reward. It is the Lord Christ you are serving.***

I have heard it said many times that "some teams win on talent alone." It is very true that sometimes you get an athlete that is just a natural phenom. It just seems that everything comes easily to them. But we must remind those people who gave them the ability to perform at that level. Many times, your most talented players are the ones that get in trouble or walk away from the game because they are uncoachable. The reason is that they forget that it was God that gave them the ability to perform at such a high level. The truth is that whatever you do not turn into praise turns into pride. You know the first sin was not eating an apple; it was the sin of pride. You see, it is easy for a talented athlete to get prideful. See, when we are prideful, we need for our ego to be fed. See, ego means "I Am," but the Scripture says that God's name is "I Am." When you think you are above and beyond everyone on your team because you have the most talent, then you are left with an ego. The problem is that there is no "I" in team, so there is no place for ego. Let me ask you, has God given you exceptional talent? Have you let your ego get the best of you? Do you think that you are above and beyond the other team members? Have you allowed your pride to overshadow your talent? If you have allowed your ego to get the best of you, then it is time to give God the accolades for your talent and to praise him for allowing you to do what you do. Give God the praise, and I will See you at the plate!

Dear Gift Giver,

You have provided us all with different gifts and talents. We are the ones that get to decide how we use them. Will we use them for your glory, or will we use them to bring glory to ourselves? Remove from me all the pride of thinking I have achieved this on my own. I know I am not, but I know I am. Let that be our prayer as we strive to put aside ego.

✞

Day 8

My Sense of Entitlement

Psalms 136:1. ***Give thanks to the Lord, for He is good. His love is eternal.***

We are growing up in a time of entitlement. It has been creeping into the sports arena over the past few years. Many young athletes and their parents believe that their kids should play based on who they are or how much money they contribute. This has led to what I call the ***"prima donna attitude."*** It means that regardless of how hard they work, they should start. It means that no matter what mistakes or poor decisions that they make off the field, they should still stay on the team. Entitlement leads athletes to deny what the coach has told them to do, and they have the propensity to do it their way. It leads to not playing till the final whistle blows, the final second ticks off the clock, or the last out is made. You see, the Scripture gives us a remedy for entitlement. It is called having the **"attitude of gratitude."** This is where you give God the glory for all that you have been given and all that you have been able to achieve. Jesus did not have a sense of entitlement, or he would have never gone to the cross to die for our sins. He **humbled** himself and became a sacrifice for us. Let me ask you, do you feel that someone owes you something? Do you do your own thing, or do you follow the coach's instructions? Do you play hard even when you are not in the spotlight? If you feel that you have become entitled, then it is now time for you to humble yourself and give God credit. And after you have humbled yourself, I will see you at the plate!

Dear Humble God,

God help me to realize that everything I am and everything that I have is because of you. God, we can only count on what we earn, and we do that by hard work and determination. God, we cannot rely on our talents alone but must work hard and continue to put you first. God, help the parents who think that their child is better than they are, to be humbled to the reality that it is a game, and it is teaching them life skills. God, to those that think they deserve a position because of their parents and pedigree, help them to realize that it is still going to take hard work and effort. God, if I am the one that is being the prima donna, then I pray that you would humble me and do it quickly.

✞

Excuse Me

Genesis 3:12-13 ***"Then the man replied, 'The woman you gave to be with me—she gave me some fruit from the tree, and I ate.' "So the Lord God asked the woman, 'What is this you have done?' "And the woman said, 'It was the serpent. He deceived me, and I ate."***

One thing that sometimes frustrates me about Jack, my son, is that he sometimes makes excuses. When something is not going his way, or he gets in trouble, he is quick to offer an excuse. He also, without fail, always has someone else's name on his tongue. It is one of the things that we are working on, and he will get better because he does not want to be known as an excuse maker. What is an excuse maker? In explanation, an excuse maker always compares themselves to someone who has made a similar or even worse mistake. Do you know what making an excuse does? It keeps you from having to take responsibility. There is no way that a person can be all that God has called them to be if they are an excuse maker. They will also have a tough time being the team leader because they are always blaming someone on their team and never taking responsibility for their dropped ball, strikeout, or errant throw. A few months ago, right in the middle of a game, I witnessed a player call another player outright in the middle of the field and right in the middle of the game. That then progressed into a verbal altercation in the dugout. Then what was once a three-run lead turned into a three-run loss. You see, that is what happens to a team when you have an excuse maker.

We are also good at making excuses when it comes to sin in our life. When God asked Eve, who had encouraged her to eat the fruit, she blamed the serpent; when he asked Adam, he blamed Eve. You see, the blame game is no more than an excuse for your sin and shortcomings. Listen, if you are always making excuses on the field, then it is time to go to your team or coach and apologize for the excuses that you have been making. Then it is time to cowboy up and start taking responsibility. If you are making excuses for your sins, then it is time for you to repent and start following God's commands. Make no excuses, and I will See you at the plate!

Dear Holy One,

Excuses can only be from the evil one. Throughout Scripture, when someone is caught in sin, we see them deflect the blame onto someone else. God helps me to take responsibility and own up when I make mistakes or fall short. Help me to repent and to turn in a new direction, the right direction. God, when I take ownership, it humbles me to remember that only you are without fault or sin. God, I take responsibility and ask now for your forgiveness.

✞

Day 10

Divine Direction

Psalms 27:11 ***Teach me your way, LORD; lead me in a straight path because of my oppressors.***

Have you ever stopped and thought about the direction of your life? I mean, where are you headed, and is it where you want to go? We often have a strong will and intention, but we have no idea how to get to where we want to go. The truth is that if we are to get to the most prominent place in life, then we have to move in a divine direction. This is the direction that God wants us to take, not the direction we think we should take. Do you know that God charts all of our steps and then allows us to decide if we want to go in that direction? I remember a few years ago, there was a child playing t-ball that had not got a hit all year. Well, finally, in one of the last games, he got up, closed his eyes, and hit the ball deep into the outfield. He then began running, and he was chugging. The problem was that he was running to third, not to first; when he finally reached third, the coach turned him around, and he ran back to home, then he redirected the child again, and he ran to first just as the throw from the outfield was coming in. Then the umpire yelled, "You're out." I know what you are thinking. "I wish this story had a happy ending." But if you start out in the wrong direction, you will never reach your divine destination or have a happy ending. Have you prayed about the direction that you are headed? Are there signs that point that you may be traveling in the wrong direction? Listen, do not head to third when you are supposed to be headed to first. Stop pray, and when you decide to head in God's divine direction, I will see you at the plate.

Dear God of Divine Direction,

God, many times I have learned the hard way that I was heading in the wrong direction. Thank you, God, for helping me turn it around and head in a different direction. God grant me the wisdom to see if I am headed on the road to disaster right now, and if I am, let me turn. I pray that my life will always move in a divine direction, the direction you have charted out for me to take. Give me the discernment and knowledge to know what that divine direction entails. Thank you for your Son Jesus moving in his divine direction for me, the direction of the cross that offers me forgiveness and salvation. Amen.

Day 11

Over in the Twinkling of an Eye

Corinthians 15:52 (KJV) ***In a moment, in the twinkling of an eye, at the last trump: for the trumpet shall sound, and the dead shall be raised incorruptible, and we shall be changed.***

This week is our high school football team's second week in the playoffs, and we understand that now we are on a one-game schedule. If we lose, our season is over, and for the seniors, their football career may just be over. The thing about the playoffs is that when it is over, it is over. It really makes you sit back and put the whole season in perspective. It makes you focus on the brevity of life and how quickly things can change. Sometimes it is an injury that ends it. Sometimes it is that our eligibility runs out. The cold hard fact is that at some point, it will be over, and when we look back, we are going to see how short the time was. So that means we must make the most of every day and every opportunity. It means that you must give it your best every chance you get because it will all be over one day. I recently read a shirt that said: "life is short, so pray hard." A spin-off of the Reebok shirt says, "life is short; play hard." You know we never think of the idea that this could be our last day, but it very well could be. I once heard a wise man say this is how he thought of every day of his life. Live every day like it is your last one, and one day it will be. So let me ask you to approach life just like you approach the one-and-done playoff scenario. This could be the last, so make sure you are giving it your best. You know

Jesus knew in the Garden of Gethsemane that this would be his last night. He knew he had given his all. The next day he looked to God, and he said these words, "it is finished," and in the twinkling of an eye, everything changed. Christ had finished the race for us. He had given his life so that our sins and shortcomings would no longer be held against us. You see, this is important because even though you will play your last play someday and draw your last breath here on earth, if you believe in the power of the cross, you will get to live in eternity with your Father and Creator. So let me ask you this, have you asked Jesus to be a part of your team? Better yet, have you asked him to be the captain of your team? So after you have stopped by the cross to pick up your Life Captain, I will see you at the plate.

Dear Creator of Heaven and Earth,

God, when I take my last breath here on earth, I do not want to be finished. Lord, I ask that your Son Jesus become captain of my team. I give my heart and loyalty to him. God, I know that one day my playing days will be over, but with Jesus in my heart, I will dwell in the house of the Lord forever. Thank you for sending your Son to play for me; he played so hard that he died for me. I accept this with all my heart, soul, and mind, Amen.

Day 12

Core Values: Attitude

1 Thessalonians 5:16–18 ***Rejoice always! Pray constantly. Give thanks in everything, for this is God's will for you in Christ Jesus.***

Attitude is everything! That is what the shirt read. But that statement may be one of the most accurate statements I have ever heard as it relates to sports. You see, you can be the best player on the team, but if your "attitude" is not right, then your performance is not only limited, but it affects everyone else that is playing around you. A few years ago, I was talking with a coach that had left two talented players off of her softball team for the upcoming year. I asked her about it, and her response was talent does not make up for a terrible attitude. You can win the championship and still feel like the season was a failure because the team's attitude was not right. So how do we create in ourselves a spirit of a positive attitude? (I think that spirit and attitude are closely related.)

The verse above gives us the three key components for keeping our attitude in check. The first is "**rejoice always.**" You should consider it a pure privilege even to be able to play. Many people are limited by talent and handicaps that do not have the opportunity that you do to play. You should rejoice that God has given you the ability to play and thank him for the opportunity.

The second component is to "**pray constantly.**" When we pray, we are reminded of how Jesus approached his heavenly Father. Prayer helps us to communicate and receive insight from God. When prayer is absent from our lives, we tend to let our attitude slip. Let it be known that: We can pray through those situations we have with other team members. We can pray through the mistakes that we made. We can pray through that call that did not go our way. You see, prayer is the key to keeping our attitude as "one like Christ."

The third component is to "**give thanks**": Give thanks for the spirit of competition. Give thanks to your coaches and staff. Give thanks for the people that assure you get to and from practice. An attitude of thanksgiving is contagious. An attitude of thanksgiving can change a whole season and even change your teammates. So, let me ask you this, how is your attitude? It just may be time for an attitude adjustment. So please check your attitude, and I will see you at the plate.

Dear Christ,

God, I am the only one responsible for my attitude. I am the only one that can control what I say and how I act when things do not go as planned. God, my attitude directly affects the ones that I am playing with. It also speaks to my witness for you. God, let me continually pray to keep my attitude in check. Let me also give thanks that I even have this opportunity. Also, let me always rejoice, whether in victory or defeat.

Day 13

Core Values: Coachable Spirit

Proverbs 15:2 ***"The fear of the Lord is Wisdom's instruction, and humility comes before honor."***

Jesus picked 12 disciples from a large pool of potential people to follow him and join his team. Why did he pick the twelve ordinary people when he had scholars, religious piety, and great leaders to choose from? Why? I think the main reason is that they had a coachable/teachable spirit. One of the hardest concepts to teach young athletes, especially those who are talented, is how to be coachable. You see, your talent will take you too many places, but when you are talented and coachable, the sky is the limit for your success. What constitutes a coachable spirit?

The first is the ability to listen. Do you know that all of the great heroes in the Bible had to first listen before they could live out the great things that God had planned for them to do? God gave us two ears and one mouth for a reason. When we learn to listen, we take our first step to being coachable.

The second thing is the ability to adapt and change. We all think that our way is the right way. But if that were the case, then we would not need coaches. Coaches have the ability to see something in us that takes us from good to great. But we have to be willing to change the way we have always done something. I once heard a swimmer say, "you can practice swimming all day long, but if you are not using the right form and technique, you are just practicing swimming badly." Bad swimming will never make one better.

The third thing is the ability to put into practice what is taught – being coachable means working hard at what is being taught – not doing it the way you want to do it but doing it the right way. It may mean sacrificing something in order to learn a new technique or play. It may mean that you have to break bad habits that have been formed. It will be a true test of endurance, which is going to be our next core value. Do you have a coachable spirit? Well, if you do, see you at the plate.

Dear Great I Am,

God, let me listen more than I talk. God open not only my ears but my heart to receive what you are speaking to me. God give me the ability to adapt and to move away from obstacles that keep me from reaching my goals. Finally, let me bind your words upon my heart so that I may not sin against you. Ultimately, help me to put into practice what I have been taught.

✞

Day 14

Core Values: Courage

Psalm 27:14 "Wait for the LORD; be strong, and let your heart take courage; wait for the LORD!"

Sometimes we might equate courage and impulsiveness, but today's Scripture tells us just the opposite and then reminds us twice of what we must do. "Wait for the Lord." One of the toughest things for an athlete to do is to wait. Our competitive nature tells us that we must act now if we are an underclassman and an upperclassman is starting over us; this makes us very impatient. Not only do we get anxious and impatient, but this can sometimes lead us to cheer against a team member. You see, it takes courage to be patient.

The Scripture tells us to wait first. This year the University of Alabama won the National Championship with a quarterback that modeled what waiting and courage are all about. He had started his college career at Florida State only to be picked over so that Heisman trophy winner Jameson Winston could start in front of him. Then he transferred to The University of Alabama, where he was projected to be a shoo-in starter his first year but was beat out by Blake Sims and saw very limited time in the 2014-15 season, usually just doing mop-up duty. Then in 2016, no Alabama fan knew going into the first game that the starter was going to be. Coach Nick Saban would not announce a starter, and all kinds of rumors began to swirl. Then that first game, when the starting lineup was read, Jake Coker finally got his chance, as it was announced that he would be the starting quarterback. He had finally got his chance, but many felt that he did not play up to his potential in the first two games, and the third game was benched, and Copper Bateman was named the starter for the Ole Miss game. Things did no go well for Bateman and the Crimson Tide in the first half, and Coker finally got into that game late in the first half. When Coker got into the game, he used his courage to play his heart out. Alabama lost that game (the only loss of the 2015-16 season), but Coker won his starting spot back and kept it the remainder of the year. He also led the Crimson Tide to the National Championship. I loved watching the celebration after the game and watching him hug his mother and other family members. I remember thinking there is a young man whose heart embraced courage, and he persevered when everything looked like it was against him.

Let me ask you, have you waited on the Lord, or have you tried to push your agenda.

You see, courage is sometimes developed as we wait on the Lord, and when your number is called up, you will already know that you are ready, "See you at the plate."

Dear Messiah,

God help me realize that everything is done on your time and not on mine, for I know your ways are not my ways and your thoughts or not my thoughts. God, thank you for giving me the courage not to give up even when things have not been going the way I planned. God, when I get in, let me play with all my heart, all my strength, and all my soul. Help me to persevere to the end.

Day 15

Core Values: Courageous

Joshua 1:9. ***"Have I not commanded you? Be strong and courageous. Do not be frightened, and do not be dismayed, for the Lord your God is with you wherever you go."***

Well, you came into the game today, not thinking you would play very much. Your play has been limited all year long because the person in front of you is just better in all aspects of the game. You have gotten accustomed to playing the role of second team and cheerleader. But then, somewhere in the middle of the game, out of nowhere, it happens. The player that is playing in front of you goes out with an injury, and you are the next woman/man up. Now is your time, and to do good, you will need courage and strength. You are going to need to calm your nerves and do what you have practiced doing. Now is your time, and the question is, "Are you ready for the moment?" Today's Scripture teaches us about the next man/woman up. You see, for a long time, Joshua had played second team to the full-time starter and rock star Moses. But now Moses has died, and it was Joshua's time to lead the people. He had been called to continue the work that was started by a great leader.

How would he respond? If he went into this position with fear and timidity, we would never succeed. So, his prayer to the Lord was that he would not go alone but that God would give him the strength to be strong and courageous. But then he hears God say the words that we must hear when we enter the game in a precarious situation. "I will be with you wherever you go." You see, that is what gives us the courage to step in and be the next player up. Joshua knew that he was following someone who had left a legacy, but he also knew that he would not replace him alone but would have God on his side. So when you are called up, and you feel like you may not be able to fill the shoes of the person you are replacing, remember that it is God that goes with you and gives you the courage to "Step up to the plate." See you at the plate!

Dear Trinity,

God gives me the courage to step up when I am called upon. Let me step up and fill the position with your help. God, I have the courage and heart because I know you are with me and will be with me wherever I go. God, thank you for the opportunity, and I pray for the one whose shoes I am filling. I pray that they will be able to return to action, but until they are back, let me do my best.

Day 16

Core Values: Determination

Philippians 4:13 ***I can do all things through Him who strengthens me.***

"I can do all things through Him who strengthens me." I have this verse along the wall in the room where I hang out and watch all my sporting events. This verse sums up determination. Did you know that Paul was in prison when he wrote this verse and was most likely sentenced to die? But he pens these words in the most adverse situation. You see, a determination is usually constituted when one's back is against the wall when all the cards are stacked against them. Many people have gone on to do wonderful things after someone told them that they were a failure or that they would never make it. We are taught determination very early in life when the book "The Little Engine that Could" is read to us. When we hear the words in that book, we just get the feeling that we are capable of doing things outside of the norm with determination. If one is ever going to achieve their full potential in the sports arena, then one must have a determined spirit. What constitutes a determined spirit?

The first component is **resilience**. This means that when the odds are stacked against us, we refuse to give in. We have resolved that we will fight until we take our last breath. The opponent may be better, bigger, faster, and stronger, but we still believe we can win.

The second component is that of being **unrelenting.** This means that we will not give in even when we are tired and exhausted. We will not stop until we have reached our goals. We will outlast our opponent. We will work longer and harder so that we can fight through fatigue.

The last component is **uncompromising.** This means that there are no shortcuts when it comes to determination. It means that even though it is possible to cheat, it is not plausible. As a team, you must decide that this is the way you are going to do things, and you must do it together.

Teams that are determined will always give it their all and will fight for one another to the end. They will not compromise their integrity, values, or work ethic just to win. So, let me ask, are you determined, and if you are, I will "See you at the plate"?

Dear Omniscient One,

God, give me a spirit of resilience. God, when the devil keeps reminding me of my past mistakes, I need to remind him of who you are and who I am through you. God, give me an unrelenting spirit to keep fighting the good fight even when I want to give in. God, please keep me uncompromised in my faith, devotion, and love for you.

Day 17

Core Values: (Extreme) Determination

Matthew 19: 26 ***Jesus looked at them and said, "With man, this is impossible, but with God all things are possible."***

Tommy Lasorda once said, "The difference between the impossible and the possible lies in a man's determination." I agree with this, but in my opinion, sometimes, a determination is found in God and not always within our minds. Many times, our own minds deceive us because of past failures and shortcomings. Our minds are a lot better at telling us what we cannot do than convincing us that all things are possible. Jesus had just finished telling the disciples that it was virtually impossible for a rich man to enter the Kingdom of God. He said this because a rich man rarely turns to God; they almost exclusively turn to their resources. But then he says, "With God's help, all things are possible." One of the reasons this is possible is that God removes hurdles that we think cannot be removed. He gives us a different mindset, and then he walks with us through our times of challenge. Have you ever thought about how many journeys never started because someone told someone that it was impossible? In our life, we are always going to face challenges that seem insurmountable, but we must remember that our determination plus God's power make "anything possible." I challenge you to believe that with God, all things are possible. And then I challenge you to sit down and make a list of the impossible things that you have dreamed about conquering and then get to work on those things with God's help.

When you feel exhausted, God is there.
When you feel defeated, God is there.
When you feel inadequate, God is there.
When you feel it is impossible. God is there.

So now, with determination and the knowledge that God is there, I will see you at the plate.

Dear Living Presence,

God, you gave me a spirit that says, "I will not quit. I will not give up; I will see the impossible as possible. I will fight until my very last breath, and I will die with determination." I do all of these things because it is the example that your Son set for me as he went to the cross to make all things possible. Christ was born into determination, and he died determined to save everyone that would call upon his name and ask him into their heart. Let my life speak of that same determination. Amen.

Day 18

Core Values: Endurance

Hebrews 10:36 ***For you have need of endurance, so that when you have done the will of God, you may receive what is promised.***

I saw the sign up ahead; it read, "push on." I was at mile 20 of the St. Jude's Marathon; this is the point that they call "the wall." You know it is coming, and then it hits you; your mind says, "push on," but your body says, "You have got to quit." I had hit the wall, and at this point, if someone had offered to pick me up and give me a ride to the finish line, I may have taken them up on the offer. But God had sent me someone else, a little boy that had been stricken with cancer holding a sign that read "push on." That was all the encouragement that I needed to "push through the wall." I thought to myself; that my pain will be over in about an hour and a half and that this 5–6-hour marathon battle is nothing compared to what that young man has to endure daily. Having told you that story, I must also mention that endurance does not always come from what we have chosen to compete in, but sometimes it comes just in the form of life. Sometimes we have to endure illness; sometimes, we have to face an unexpected sudden death or the termination of a lifelong job. We know that none of these things are easy to endure, but with God's help, we can just push on. The Scriptures provide many of those 20-mile markers, signs of encouragement – "push on." Abraham pushed on even when he was in his elder years, Moses pushed on even when he felt he was just walking in circles, and Jesus pressed on even when they hurled insults at him on the cross. If we just "push on," we can achieve things that we never thought were possible. And this includes the things that we compete in and the things that are unforeseen in everyday life. So I tell you what, here is your ninth inning sign: "Push on, and I will see you at the plate."

Dear Holy God of Infinite Wisdom,

When life throws us curveballs, and when the world seems to be pressing hard against us, God helps us to push on. When we feel that we cannot take another step, carry us when we think we cannot get out of bed, lift us up. When we feel that we are at the end of the rope, tie a knot in it so that we do not slide off. God, you have given so many examples in your Holy Word about people that just "pushed on." God, let our life also be that testimony.

Day 19

Core Values: Excellence

---

2 Corinthians 5:9 ***So we make it our goal to please him, whether we are at home in the body or away from it.***

I read a slogan some time ago that made me wonder how one can live up to such expectations. The company slogan read, "Committed to Excellence." This quote caught me off guard because, in my mind, I only know of one person that was excellent in life, and that was Jesus. So, if one had already made a mistake, then how could one be committed to excellence? But in reality, excellence can be broken into smaller increments. To "strive or commit to excellence" means that you know that there is always room for improvement. It means that every day when you hit the field, you are working harder to get better. It means that your commitment never waivers. Every year when your team kicks off another season, it has the possibility of being excellent or maybe even the possibility of being perfect for that season. But what happens when you lose? Is the season lost? Do you give up on the notion of excellence? No, you then break the season into smaller chunks that are attainable. Maybe your goal is to go out and have a perfect game hitting. Perhaps it is to have a game without errors. Maybe it is to make all your free throws for that game. You see, excellence is something that is built upon, not something that is lost after you make a mistake.

You know, the same principle of excellence that we strive for in the sports arena can also be applied to life. We are all going to sin and fall short of the glory of God (Romans 3:23). But we do not have to quit trying just because we messed up. We can push on and recommit ourselves to excellence. You see, that is what Christ did for us on the cross. We have the opportunity to strive for excellence because he modeled excellence. You see, the question to ask as it relates to our spiritual life is, am I pursuing God with the same excellence that he pursued me?

I once heard the story of an outstanding athlete that claimed to be a Christian. This person excelled in everything she did. She worked and strove for excellence every day in sports. Toward the end of her life, a reporter asks her about her spiritual life, to which she responded with this quote. "I am not much on church or worship; I just say the same prayers every day that I learned when I was a kid." How sad is it that someone who strived for excellence on the ball field did not have the same tenacity as her spiritual life? Remember that the things of this earth will pass away, including your athletic ability, but your spiritual life is eternal. So let me ask, are you pursuing your spiritual life with the same excellence as your athletic pursuits? Strive for excellence, and I will see you at the plate.

Dear Lord of Host,

God, you are the most excellent one. How am I even worthy to pray to such a perfect being? And yet, you help us realize the value of perfection as you sent your Son to an imperfect world to perfect it. God, in all things I do, let me be committed to excellence. Help me never to be satisfied with my relationship with you. Help me never to become complacent in my walk with you. Help me to strive for the same excellence in my spiritual life as I do on the field. God, as John Wesley said, "in my life, Lord, I am moving closer to perfection."

Day 20

Core Values: Humility

Psalms 25:9 ***He leads the humble in what is right and teaches the humble his way.***

Oh Lord, it is hard to be humbled when I am perfect in every way and perfect every day. Those were somewhat close to the lyrics of a country song I heard when I was young. The truth is that at times we all feel that way even though we would not admit it. At times we think that we have arrived or that we are the best on the field. But this is not the core value that Christ taught to his followers or what he patterned in his own life. Jesus taught that one should not take the place of honor but must take on the role of the servant. I love when an athlete wins a prestigious award and then gives all her teammates credit. You see, humility comes from the heart, and yet so does pride. You are the one that gets to choose how the world perceives you. Jesus had every opportunity to seize power and to claim his rightful position, but instead, he chose to serve. The truth is that a humble athlete makes those teammates around them better. You see, they push those around them because they encourage them and celebrate the success of their teammates. They also take responsibility when things do not go as planned. They are humble because they also know how to let someone else share the spotlight. You see, the true question is not whether you are the best player, but are you the right player for your team? You may realize that God has given you the ability to do your best, but the question is, do you lead with a servant attitude? See, when you have the right attitude, people are inspired to be like you, so in essence, you are making them better. The counterintuitive of making your team better is when you are full of pride, you may be good, but you are full of yourself. When you are full of yourself, no one is going to follow you. So, you get to make the decision. Will it be humility, or will it be a prideful spirit that you display? If it is humility, then "I will see you at the plate."

Dear Jesus,

God grant me the ability to think less of myself and to think more of others. God, no matter how good I am or become, let me always be humble in spirit. Let me put away pride because pride is what leads to our destruction and fall. God help me to be the teammate that picks others up and encourages them to be the best that God has called them to be.

Day 21

Core Values: Integrity

2 Corinthians 5:17 ***Therefore, if anyone is in Christ, he is a new creation. The old has passed away; behold, the new has come.***

A few years ago, I heard a speaker at a graduation commencement give the graduates some of the wisest words of wisdom I have ever heard. He said, "integrity takes a lifetime to build but only a moment to destroy." One decision can taint a lifetime of achievement. We see this all the time in sports. An athlete can be the most talented and gifted athlete on the field, but if they lack integrity, they cannot truly lead.

Another issue with integrity as it relates to the sporting world is cheating to get an unfair advantage. Some athletes use performance-enhancing drugs to gain a competitive edge over their competition. The problem with this is that all of your accomplishments are tainted once your secret is found out. Your legacy can change in just a matter of minutes. This principle of integrity not only applies to the sports world but can also affect our Christian walk. We can speak lots of religious words, but our actions detour from our testimony. You have heard it said that actions speak louder than words. This is true when it comes to integrity. No one wants you to tell them you are a person of integrity; they want you to show them you are a person of integrity. We recently had a local election in our town, and one of the candidates had the word “integrity” on their campaign sign; it was part of their campaign slogan. The problem was that everyone close to this candidate knew that integrity was not one of the words that best described this person. I had up-close dealings with this person that had even caused me to question his integrity and what he truly stood for. You see, if those words are just on a sign but not really upon our hearts, then they are just words.

At his father's funeral, American Carl Lewis placed his 100-meter gold medal from the 1984 Olympics in his father's hands. "Don't worry," he told his surprised mother. "I'll get another one." A year later, in the 100-meter final at the 1988 games, Lewis competed against Canadian world-record-holder Ben Johnson. Halfway through the race, Johnson was five feet in front. Lewis was convinced he could catch him. But at 80 meters, he was still five feet behind. It's over, Dad, Lewis thought. As Johnson crossed the finish, he stared back at Lewis and thrust his right arm in the air, index finger extended. Lewis was exasperated. He had noticed Johnson's bulging muscles and yellow-tinged eyes, both indications of steroid use. "I didn't have the medal, but I could still give to my father by acting with class and dignity," Lewis said later. He shook Johnson's hand and left the track. But then came the announcement that Johnson had tested positive for anabolic steroids. He was stripped of his medal. The gold went to Lewis, a replacement for the medal he had given his father.[2]

The word “integrity” is defined: to be uprightness of character, honesty. Jesus represented all of these things in his ministry. It is why he was able to say that he was “I am.” He could not be equated with God if he had not truly defined the essence of the word “integrity.” He was absolutely perfect, and therefore his integrity was always intact. Now we are not perfect, and we are going to make mistakes, but each day we should, as John Wesley said, “be moving toward that of being perfected.” You see, our integrity will be far better if we are trying to emulate Jesus daily. So with your integrity intact fully, “I will see you at the plate.”

Dear Lord of Utmost Character,

God grant me the ability to be a person of outstanding moral character. God, let me be who you have called me to be and not just who I want to be. God, when I make mistakes, restore my soul so that I can be whole again. God, if my integrity has been tainted, I pray that I begin today to repair the damage. God grant me the courage to pray for those around me that have corrupted their character and allow me to come alongside them to help repair what damage has been done. Thank you for Jesus, who set the bar of integrity and let me live more like him every day.

Day 22

Core Values: Love

I Timothy 6:10 ***For the love of money is a root of all kinds of evil. Some people, eager for money, have wandered from the faith and pierced themselves with many griefs.***

"For the Love of the Game," I watched this movie a few years ago. I thought about that title as it refers to athletes today. I believe that the love of money has replaced the love of the game in today's sporting world. I have always said that I love Little League through high school sports the best because those young athletes play because they love the game. They love everything about the game. My son loves to practice. Many times, after a 2-hour practice, he will say to me, "we should have practiced longer." You see, he loves the game because he is ten, and otherworldly things have not invaded his world yet. The game is still pure and honest. I often wonder how sports figures, especially pros players, got into the disarrayed shape that we read about today: Players holding out for more money. Players are refusing to play because of a particular style of offense or defense. Players skip practice or mini-camps to do other things. You see, what has happened is that the lure of the mighty dollar has corrupted the pure love that the game once held. The love of money has indeed overtaken the love for the game.

The fact is that these same stigmas that we see in sports can also invade other areas of our life. We lose the focus of why we first started doing the things that we loved. I have met with many people that have fallen away from their faith. They have propped up on the world, whereas they used to prop up upon the Lord. I have met other people who say they are getting a divorce because they do not love the person they married anymore. You know, one example that we see Jesus model is his love for the church. Jesus never let the world corrupt his love for the people that he came to save. I think it is so compelling that we call the final week the Passion Week because that is what Jesus had for us, he had passion. It was that passion that manifested itself for us on the cross. I once read a sign that hung in a pastor's friend's office that said: "It was not nails, but his love for you that held him to the cross." By Jesus' willingness to go to the cross, we see that he genuinely left everything he had on the playing field. So how can we do anything else but give everything we got for the love of the game and the love of life? Love the game for as long as you can play, for it will not be long before you have a love for the game but cannot play. The same is true in life. So do not lose your true love for the game, and I will see you at the plate.

Dear God of Agape Love,

God, we know that the root of all kinds of evil stems from the love of money. God help me to have a pure passion for the game. God let me do things because I am called and love to do them, not because I get paid for it. God, please keep my mind from coveting and my hands from greed. Thank you that your Son was so passionate about me that he went through passion week so that my life could be spared. Let my passion for sharing the gospel of Jesus Christ be evident every day.

Day 23

Attitude

Mark 8:29 (NET Bible) ***He asked them, "But who do you say that I am?" Peter answered him, "You are the Christ."***

It is most likely evident to everyone the sport or sports that you play. It is apparent because of how you dress, and it is the only thing you talk about. It can also be said that it is apparent that you play the game to win. Then the question is asked, what must I do to get better? The "what" part of this is that you must commit to practice and hard work. You must commit to knowing your role on the team and always be uplifting even if things are not going the way you think they should go. You must also commit yourself to doing the right things, not only on the field but also off of the field. This means being a student-athlete and studying hard to be the best student that you can be. It also means that you are above reproach in the community.

Now let's ask another question, why do you play the game? Once again, the answer may be to win, but there has to be more to it than that. Some would say I play the game because I love it. Others would say I play the game because I have the ability to play it. Some would say I play the game so that we can win championships, and others may say I play the game because it is fun. You see, in life, the real question is not what, but why? When defining "why" we play the game, we better understand our purpose and role. Every player on the team knows what they are playing, but some may not understand why they are playing. You see, I always tell the teams that I am coaching that you are not just playing for yourself, but you are playing for every person on that team. This brings us to the last point that we must consider: who are we playing for? If we are just going out to play for ourselves, then we do not have a true concept of team. What if I told you that ultimately you were playing for the One that gave you the ability to play? That you were playing for God. Would that change the way that you play and why you play? It should be because we play to "honor" him. We work hard so that we win for him. You see, athletics has given us the platform to share our faith, and there is no better way to share our faith than to play for the one who created us to play. Let me ask, are you playing for that audience of one? Are you playing for God? If not, then decide that it is Jesus that you are playing for, and I will see you at the plate.

Dear Faith Weaver,

God, I know what sport I am playing, but often I have to ask why I am playing and who am I playing for? Many times, I need to be humbled so that I do not play for my glory but that I play for your glory. God, I pray that my actions on and off the field will always exemplify you. Please help others on the team see that I am playing for you while I am supporting them. Thank you for the opportunity to play, and thank you for helping me decipher what, why, and who.

Day 24

Defeat vs. Being Defeated

Matthew 28:20 ***"…And remember, I am with you always, to the end of the age."***

It is so easy to give up when you feel defeated or looked over. To be honest, giving up and giving in is the easiest thing to do when things are not going your way. You can just call it quits; pack your stuff up, and go home. But it takes a person of character and high integrity to persevere when things are not going as planned. Just this weekend, I was asking about a girl that played travel ball with us the summer before. I knew that she was the catcher for this team playing in the same tournament we were playing in. I approached one of her teammates and asked where she was; they responded, "she quit because she did not like the way things were going and did not like the coach." At that point, I felt so sad for her because if she would give up that easy on a team and a coach, what would the rest of her life look like? She was setting in motion a pattern that would most likely follow her throughout the rest of her life.

Another scenario that makes it easy to quit is when you are regularly losing. I played football on a team in college that went 0-11 my sophomore year. When a team is playing teams that are more talented and more experienced, it is easy to give up and quit. But the game is more than wins and losses. It is about hard work, discipline, learning how to handle adversity, and how to relate to those on your team. Sports were set up to help you with your life, not solely be your life. So even if you are losing by staying to the grind, you are winning. You are learning lessons that will aid you for the rest of your life.

Jesus finds himself in the Garden of Gethsemane, and his spirit is totally defeated. He prays, "Father if it is possible, let this cup pass from me." But then it is gut-check time, and he redirects his prayer and says, "Father, not my will, but your will be done." In essence, he is saying I may experience a defeat, but I will not be defeated. You see, Jesus would not stay down or dead but would be victorious. This is the same lesson that we must carry through sports. We must have this same attitude in life when things seem not to be going our way or when we feel defeated and are waffling back and forth about whether we should quit. Ultimately, you see that because we have decided that Jesus is Lord and Savior of our lives, we cannot be defeated. We may lose some battles with sin. We may have to face earthly rejection, but in retrospect, we win. We win because Jesus faced death on the cross but defeated death at the resurrection. So if you decide that you are not defeated, then I will see you at the plate.

Dear Lord of Lords,

God, we may be struck down, but we are not destroyed. We may be bent, but we are not broke. The Scripture says that "we are more than conquers in Christ." But Father, we must believe these things if we are not to be defeated. God, thank you for your Son's death, and because of his resurrection, we already know that we win in the end. God give me the strength to carry on when I want to quit. God grant me the strength to keep fighting even when I am getting beat. God, give me the strength to pick myself up when I have been knocked down.

Day 25

Stepping Out

Ephesians 3:12 ***"In him and through faith in him we may approach God with freedom and confidence."***

Have you ever felt inadequate? Have you ever felt that you were just not good enough? Maybe someone told you that you were not good enough. Maybe you have tried and tried, and you keep coming up empty. I recently listened to Craig Groeschel preach a sermon about "becoming who God says you are, not who you think you are." He says, "that every time before he preaches, he gets nervous, so when he walks out to speak, he steps forward first." He explains "that this is his way of stepping out from himself and stepping into God." I thought that this was an awesome way to face our fears and obstacles. It is a wonderful way to face the things that make us nervous.

To step away from ourselves and to step into God is precisely what Christ modeled for us while he was here on earth. If we have been struggling at the plate when we come up to bat, what would happen if we stepped out of ourselves and stepped into the power of God? What about when we have not been pitching so well, and when we step up to the mound, we step out of ourselves and into the power of God. What if the next time we had to go in for an interview, we took one step forward and stepped out of ourselves and into God? Do you remember the story of Gideon? He was scared that he did not have enough men; he was afraid that he was not a good enough leader. He was scared of defeat. So, what did God do? Did he send more men? No, he cut the number of men considerably, and then he asked Gideon to step out of himself and step into the power of God. In Judges 7, the Lord tells Gideon, "You have too many men if you were to defeat the Amalekites, Israel would boast against me, 'My strength has saved me.' "You see, God wanted Gideon and the Israelites to step out of their strength and to take the strength of the Lord. You know how this story ends; it ends with Gideon defeating the enemies and God getting the glory. So let me ask you, are you willing to step up to the plate, step out of yourself and step into God? When you are ready and willing to do this, I will see you at the plate.

Dear Sovereign Lord,

God gives us the strength to trust you when things do not make sense. God help me to step outside of myself and to step into you. God, you are the one that provides us with power, strength, and might. You sent your Son to step out of his Kingdom and to die for us.

Day 26

Where Is the Name?

Philippians 2:9 ***Therefore, God exalted him to the highest place and gave him the name that is above every name…***

Recently, it seems like there is a huge trend for some teams not to put names on the back of uniforms or jerseys. At first, I thought this was just a little strange, but then I read an article that stated that Notre Dame was playing for the National Championship, and they voted not to have their names put on the back of their jerseys. You see, for the last six years, they have not had names on the back of their jerseys. The media and others wanted them to put names on the back of their Jerseys for the national championship game, but they voted against it. You know, as a fan, I do not like that they do not have names on their jersey because I want to know who it is that is running the ball or making the tackle. But I have come to the realization that I may care, but they do not. You see, when you have no names on the back of your jersey, it tells the viewers that no one player is above another. It says that they are all a part of a team and that there is a greater goal than their own glorification.

When I was coaching pee-wee football, I always thought it was funny that we ordered jerseys without the names on the back, but parents would take them to the local sporting goods store and have them put on. I mean, I understand that they are proud of their sons or daughters for their accomplishments on the field. Then there is the flip side of that, which begs to answer, are we teaching them that it is all about them and not about the team? I cannot answer that, but I like the concept that without the name, we are a number, and every number on the team counts.

Now I have one more observation about this name on the jersey debate. Two years ago, I watched a University of Maryland football game, and they were playing the game for the wounded warrior project. As I watched the game, I noticed that many of the players had the same last name on the back of their jerseys. But as I looked closer, I realized that it was not their last names on the jersey but characteristics that a soldier upholds. The jersey read courage, service, commitment, country, and freedom. It was then I realized that it is not the name on the back of the jersey that made us the player that we are, but it was what is inside our hearts that made us the player that we are. You see, when you play with commitment, honor, courage, and service, you do not play for yourself, but you play for something so much bigger. You play for your team. So, let me ask you, what characteristics are you wearing on the back of your jersey these days? I will see you at the plate.

Dear Name Above All Names,

Your name is power. Your name is mercy. Your name is faithful. Your name is glory. Your name is humility. Your name is love. Lord, help me to live out these names that you encompass and help me to be just like you so that when people see me, they see you.

Day 27

Is My Name on the List?

Revelation 21:27 ***Nothing evil will be allowed to enter, nor anyone who practices shameful idolatry and dishonesty--but only those whose names are written in the Lamb's Book of Life.***

You know there have been several times since my kids started playing ball that they had to wait to find out whether they made the cut (whether they were on the team or not). You see, many times, the coach would announce that tomorrow, at a certain time, we are going to list the names of the people who made the team for the upcoming season. My children have often had to wait for two or three days to determine whether their name was on the list. Those days leading up to find out if your name is on the list can be filled with fear and anxiety. Now, I am going to be honest, there were a few times, my kids' names were left off of the list, and I can tell you that my heart broke for them. I knew that being left off the list would lead to feelings of rejection. It would also make them question what they could have done better. A few times, I felt like my children may have been better than some of the kids who made it and that politics had somehow played a part in the decision. But to be honest, there were also times when they were left off the list because they did not deserve to make the list. The people that tried out with them were better or more experienced. Now, if you have ever been left off of a list, you have a decision to make. Do I work twice as hard this year to make the list next year, or do I just give up? If you choose the latter, it is an extremely easy way out, but if you choose to work hard to improve, it may reap the rewards. But it will be challenging to improve. You see, when you do not make the team, you do not get the reps that those that made the team get. You also do not get the hands-on coaching or the game-time experience needed to become a better player. But if you are willing to find a coach, put in lots of hard work, and maybe even consider becoming a manager, then you can overcome the obstacles, and just maybe next year, your name will be on the list. You know, as I was working on this devotional, I thought about another list that we all hope to find our name on. That is the list that God possesses that says, "That he knows us and that we have a personal relationship with him." You know this list is easier to get your name on than the team list. You see, you get your name on this list by putting it on the list. It is simple to add your name to that list; you just say these words, "Jesus, I want to be on your team, I want you to be my Lord and Savior, I want to have a personal relationship with you, and I want you to become my best friend." There you have it, your name is now on the list, and you will never have to worry about the anxieties you felt when you checked to see if you made the team because the truth is that Jesus already tried out for you through his death and resurrection. You are on the list because of what he has done, not because of what you have done. I will see you at the plate because your name is on the roster.

Dear Author of the Book of Life,

I have already asked through this devotional that my name be put on the list. I am glad that you have added me to the roster. I pray now that others that have not added their name will do so. I ask that I be bold in telling people about your loving grace and that you showed out for them a long time ago so they could make the team. God, thank you that my name is on the list.

Day 28

Hit the Spot or You Will Miss Your Mark

John 14:6 ***I am the way, the truth, and the life.***

One of the things that are important for a softball pitcher is learning to hit your marks. It is a term used to describe the different places where a ball needs to be placed so that the hitter cannot hit the ball or at least cannot make solid contact with the ball. Recently, one of the pitchers was told to hit the spot on a known homerun hitter low and away. But instead, she missed her spot and threw the girl high and straight across. The pitch resulted in a 3-run homer. You see, when a pitcher misses her mark, terrible things can result. But the same can be said when it comes to our life.

You know the Greek word for sin is "hamartia." [3] This word means to miss the mark. It was developed from the concept of an archer who was shooting and did not hit the target. In our society, we view sin more as carrying around baggage, which may ultimately be the guilt of sin, but sin is defined as missing the mark. You see, just like a pitcher misses the mark and bad things result, the same can be true in our life. When a pitcher misses the mark, it causes the whole team to suffer. Many times, it even derails the whole team because of the devastating results. The same can be said of our sin. When we get off of the path, it not only affects us, but it usually causes damage to other people's life. So, what is a pitcher to do when she has missed her mark? Well, at this point, she has to regroup and get back on track. The same is true of our lives; when we are missing the mark, we will feel the burden of sin. To put this into perspective, the real problem with sin is that we are missing the mark, and we are on the wrong path. The Greek word for repentance is "metanoia." [4] This word literally means to change direction; to move in a different path; to change your playground; to examine your habits.

To burn your ships so you cannot return to the wrong course. You see, we can ask for forgiveness all day long; we can say we are sorry so much that it falls on deaf ears. But until we change our way and redirect our paths, we will continue to miss the mark. Now some of you may be asking, but what is the mark, and what is the way. Well, Jesus told us the way in the Gospel of John. He said, "I am the way." Follow in my footsteps, and you will not miss your mark. So, let me ask, are you willing to change your ways and stop missing your mark? Because if you are willing to follow Jesus, then I see you at the plate!

Eternal Lord and Savior,

I have missed the mark so many times. The result of this has left damaged relationships, hurt feelings, and even alienation. I pray that I can put my life on the track of the "way." You sent your Son to show us the way. He came in truth. He brought us life and showed us the way. Now use my life to help others find their way as I walk in the footsteps of Jesus. Please help me not to miss my spot. Amen.

Day 29

Let's Play the Matching Game

Proverbs 11: 3 ***"The integrity of the upright guides them, but the unfaithful are destroyed by their duplicity."***

Two words are often thrown around the sports world and mainstream media that deal with how a person is perceived. The two words that I am referring to are <u>integrity</u> and <u>reputation</u>. Now at first glance, you think that these two words are the same, but sometimes these two words just do not match. Integrity has been defined as "who you are when no one else is looking or who our dog thinks we are." Integrity is defined as who you truly are every moment of every day. Reputation is who other people think that you are. You see, those who are not close to you have no idea who you are when you are off the field. Often, we are taken back when we learn of an athlete or star living a private life. They may have been giving to charities or even been in the public speaking forum, and then we find out the devastating reality that the whole time they were a fraud. They had a good reputation, but the truth is that they had a default in their integrity. Therefore, their reputation is ruined. We must understand that as an athlete and as Christians, people are watching us. They are playing the matching game. Does our attitude match our integrity? Does our character match who we say we are? Do you know what the first thing we always teach an athlete when they are beginning to play? We teach them how to stand.

By teaching them how to stand, we are helping them build a firm foundation on which to build off. The most important part of any structure is the foundation. If the foundation is shaky, then the whole structure is going to be shaky. Many times, people build their foundation on the shaky ground of deception. It is kind of like playing a "Jenga" game and pulling the bottom blocks out first; when this happens, it is not long before the whole tower comes crashing down. What is happening is that people are living amid duplicity. Let me simplify that by saying, "their integrity does not match what people think their reputation is." I want to challenge people to work just as hard on their integrity and reputation as they do their athletic endeavors. You see, when your integrity is intact, then you are in no danger of ruining your reputation. I will see you at the plate with your reputation fully intact.

Dear Breath of Life,

God, help me to be the same when I am around people as I am when I am alone. God help me always to keep my integrity so I can keep my reputation. God, I know that my witness depends upon my integrity, and ultimately, what defines me is my reputation. Thank you for sending your Son to pattern what my reputation should emulate.

Day 30

Failure Is Not Final

Psalms 73:26 ***My flesh and my heart may fail, but God is the strength of my heart and my portion forever.***

"Success is not final; failure is not fatal; it is the courage to continue that counts." Sir Winston Churchill spoke these words. They were probably not intended to motivate a sports team when they were spoken, but they sure fit. How often have you heard about a team being on top, and then a few years later, they struggle to reach the .500 mark? Then there are those teams that were on top, and now it just seems that they cannot catch a break to help them get back in the "win" column. You see, it is in the best of times when we need courage, and it is in the worst of times that we need courage.

When we are winning, courage comes from trying to maintain a superior level of play. It is also humbling to know that things may not always be going the way they are now. It also takes courage to keep us from becoming arrogant in our winning.

Courage keeps us from being sore winners.

On the other side of that is when we are failing. Courage is what keeps us from giving up. It is what keeps us from throwing away our dreams and aspirations. Courage helps us to face an opponent that outmatches us and has way more talent. Courage is picking ourselves up for the hundredth time, even when it would be easier just to lay down.

But courage does not only exhibit itself in the sports world. We are going to find we need courage in everyday life. When David faced Goliath, he needed courage; when Joshua took over for Moses, he needed courage; when Mary faced an unexpected pregnancy, she needed courage; and when Jesus went to the cross for our sins, he needed courage.

Let me ask you, do you have the courage to continue the race. Do you have the courage to say no because you know it is morally wrong? Let me ask, do you have the courage not to cheat because there are no shortcuts to true success? Where is it in your life that you need courage? Now let me tell you how to get the courage you need. Pray and ask God for it. He wants you to ask him for it so that he can provide it for you. So let me ask, do you have courage because if you do, then I will see you at the plate.

My Rock,

God grant me the courage to stand in the gap for what is right, true, and Godly. God help me to be a good winner and a good loser. Courage is having the ability when I cannot get up to ask you to pick me up and carry me to the finish line. Courage is what Jesus had when he faced the cross for my sin. Now give me the courage to stand up for Jesus, the one that died for me.

Day 31

Do You Have H.E.A.R.T.?

This week we will take the word H.E.A.R.T. and do a series of devotionals on what kind of heart you must have when you step onto the field or step up to the plate.

Everyone knows that in life, it takes HEART to compete. Sometimes it is the heart and not talent that wins Championships. I would rather have a player with a strong heart over a player with tremendous talent but no heart every time. So, this week, let's do a heart check and see how healthy our competitive hearts are.

H.E.A.R.T. - Hungry Heart

Matthew 5:6 ***Blessed are those who hunger for righteousness, for they will be fulfilled.***

In order for an athlete to win, they must have a "hungry heart." This hunger starts in how they prepare and how they manage their time from game to game. I have often said that winning is contagious; once you have experienced it, you continue to hunger for it. Many times, I have heard a coach tell his/her team to "stay hungry." This means that we should not get complacent in trying to get better every time we practice or step on the field/court. You see, when we stop being hungry, we will soon find that we have lost our appetite for winning, and then eventually, we have lost our drive to continue to play the game. A hungry heart keeps us competitive and driven to succeed.

In life, we must hunger after Jesus to stay in the game. You have often heard it said that people have backslid or turned from Jesus, but the fact is what that usually means is that they have lost their hunger heart for Jesus. It may also mean that they are now hungering after the world and no longer have a taste for Jesus. One of the things that Communion does for us is that it reminds us that we must stay focused on what Jesus did for us. The Holy Meal reminds us that we hunger after his love and grace. Often on the communion table, we see the words, "Do this in remembrance of me." That statement alone reminds us to stay hungry for the knowledge that God provides, stay hungry for righteousness, and stay hungry in winning souls to Jesus.

The last part of a hungry heart is staying hungry for the word of God. This means that we should have a steady appetite for the words and instructions found in the Holy Scripture. You see, a week without God's word makes one weak. A hungry heart cannot get enough of what God has to say to us through his living word. So, stay hungry, and I will see you at the plate.

Dear Gamechanger,

God help me to stay hungry so that with every practice, I can get better. May I hunger always to be the best and do the best every chance I get? God help me to remember that you hungered for righteousness and were found blameless so that I might be saved through your sacrifice. Let me hunger after your words and bind them to my heart so that I will never be satisfied until I am with you in heaven for eternity. Lord, let me have a hungry heart.

✞

Day 32

H.E.A.R.T. – Expectant Heart

Acts 3:5 (ESV) ***And he fixed his attention on them, expecting to receive something from them."***

You know that many times our success on and off of the field depends upon our expectations. When I was growing up, I was not pushed in school like I probably should have been. I set my expectations on making a "C." I figured that this was average and that I could squeak by with being average. You know, for a long time, this bled over into other areas of my life. I suffered and lost out many times because I had learned to set my heart in low expectation mode. You see, our expectations are a direct reflection of how hard we work and what we also expect from other people.

We sometimes are not good because we do not expect to be good. You see, we need to set our expectations as realistic, but we also need to realize that most of the time, we have set our expectations too low. "We will achieve what we believe." Sometimes we expect to low because of past performances. Sometimes our expectations are limited due to our perceived resources. Sometimes our expectations are because of our lack of faith in those that are playing around us. All these can limit our expectations, but they can all be overcome by a heart that is set on high expectations. You see, when our heart is full of high expectations, it will become infectious to those around us. When we raise the bar in our own lives, we also raise the bar for our teammates. Let me challenge you to sit down and pray about what your expectations are. Make a list, and then start to look at where you can raise the bar. You see, you are going to get exactly what you expect you are going to get.

One of the areas in our daily life that are affected by low expectations is when it comes to our faith in Jesus. The reason that we do not see more of Jesus is that our expectations of Jesus are so low. We have reduced Jesus to just an ordinary teacher, guide, friend, coach, or mentor in the world we live in. We have such low expectations of what Jesus can do, and most of the time, we pray, expecting that he may not show up. You see, Jesus is not ordinary, he is our Savior, and he is above extra-ordinary; he is equated with God. He is the "I am." There is nothing ordinary in him or about him. What makes Jesus look ordinary is our expectations of him. Let me tell you this; with Jesus, you are going to get exactly what you expect. Let's raise the bar in everything we do, and let's expect great things from an extraordinary God. When you have an expectant heart, you have your sights set on the things that are above. So raise your expectations, and I will see you at the plate.

Dear Host of All Eternity,

God, I have lowered my expectations, and it has cost me to limit the power of the Holy Spirit. God help me to have an expectant heart, a heart that realizes that there is nothing ordinary about you. God help me to raise the bar, not only on the field and in the classroom but also my daily walk with Jesus. God, I will achieve exactly what I believe, so make me believe in the things that man cannot see but are guided by your hand. Lord, give me a heart of high expectations.

Day 33

H.E.A.R.T. – Accountable Heart

Romans 14:12 (NAS) ***Therefore, every one of us shall give an account of himself to God.***

It is common today for people to wear a heart rate monitoring device when working out. This has become an extremely popular trend, with many companies offering heart rate monitoring devices that can be worn on your wrist with no additional hardware. Athletes wear these to let them know just how hard they are working out and how many calories they burn in a workout session. The number of heartbeats per minute tells us what kind of cardio zone we are in. Sometimes we are in what they refer to as the maintenance or warm-up zone (easy). But if we want to get the most out of our exercise, we must get into the aerobic zone (heavy exertion). If we push even harder, we can get into the anaerobic zone, which is close to maximum effort (all-out). Only a few top endurance athletes can stay in this zone for extended periods without giving out. The heart rate monitor is a way of keeping you accountable for your workout. It can tell you if you are slacking or only giving a minimal amount of effort. It is a way of holding you accountable for your workout.

Our spiritual lives also need to have heart monitors so that we can be held up to the standard that Jesus has patterned for us to live. These monitors come in the form of people that we trust to hold us accountable. These people need to be fair and honest and know where to exert more effort or change to live more like Christ. Sometimes these people need to call us on our sinful patterns or shortcomings. In the sports world, the only way to get better is to have coaches and mentors who hold us to a high standard in the hopes that we will one day reach perfection. The same must be true in our lives. Many people say that "Jesus will accept you just as you are," while that may be true; he does not expect us to stay in that spot. A coach does not expect an athlete to be the same on the last day of practice that they were on the first. No, they practice in hopes of not only improvement but mastery. When someone is there to hold us accountable, and our heart is open to receive it, we become **"sanctified."** So, open your heart up to someone and ask them to hold you accountable, and when you have been held accountable, I will see you at the plate.

Dear God of the Living Word,

God, help me to hold my heart accountable for my actions, words, and deeds. Bring someone into my life that will hold me accountable to be better and move on toward perfection. God, thank you for the coaches, teachers, and mentors in life that expect more of me than I expect of myself. God, continue to help me in the sanctification process as I want to be more like your Son Jesus every day. God, thank you for Jesus, the perfector and my ultimate role model.

Day 34

H.E.A.R.T. – Righteous Heart

Proverbs 15:28 (ESV) ***The heart of the righteous ponders how to answer, but the mouth of the wicked pours out evil things.***

Many times, we get the old pep talk that we must play with heart. But what would it mean if we were told to play with a "righteous heart?" Would this statement seem to make us weak or less aggressive toward the idea of winning? I would answer absolutely, "not." You see, playing with a righteous heart means that we play with the utmost integrity. We recently played a game against a team where the running back scored five touchdowns against us. On this day, he was the most superior player on the field, but he also played with a righteous heart. He never taunted our players; in fact, every time he scored, he pointed to heaven and thanked God. So many times, athletes want to taunt or run their mouths on the field. Many coaches just accept that this is part of the jawing that goes on in the heat of the battle. But I would be the first to say that one that plays with a righteous heart does not need to taunt or mouth to get their point across. Their competitive heart and righteous heart will be his true testimony.

We must also have a righteous heart when it comes to everyday life. I cannot tell you the number of testimonies that have been destroyed because someone did not put their heart into gear before their mouth. How many times do we wish that we could just take back the words that we just said? The Scripture is clear that the product of our speech starts in the heart. I often tell my congregation that you do not have a sin problem; you have a heart problem. See, we have taken the word righteous to mean something we hope to achieve, but in Biblical times, the Greek word, "dikaiosune," meant to stand in uprightness. It meant to keep your part of God's covenant. You see, to be righteous in biblical times was a way to show the world how God was and how he is. They believed it could not be taken off and then put back on; it essentially was who you were. I would say that in today's time, it is not different; you either have a righteous heart or you have a corrupt heart. So put on your righteous heart, and I will see you at the plate.

Light of the World,

I am created in your image, and even though I am a sinner, I can still have a righteous heart. God guard my mouth and hold my tongue. Let my actions do the talking and not my words. God, let me never boast because it is you that has given me the ability to play. God, let my heartbeat be in rhythm with you. God, let me stand upright, holy, and true. Never let me dishonor your name on the field of play or in my everyday walk of life. Thank you for making my heart righteous through the death of your Son, who bore my filth and unrighteousness.

Day 35

H.E.A.R.T. – Thankful Heart

Colossians 4:2 (NLT) ***Devote yourselves to prayer with an alert mind and a thankful heart.***

Do you ever just stop and thank God for the talents and ability that he has given you? I have heard it said that the ones that we are closest to, we often take the most for granted. We simply just forget to thank them. I received a letter this Christmas from our head coach's wife. She thanked me for the prayer and support I gave to her husband and the other coaches this football season. It had not been an easy season as the year before; we had made it all the way to the state playoffs, and then this year, we struggled to reach 500. But she explained in the letter how thankful she was that we stood by the team and reminded them that God stood by them. You know, in the world of sports, we have so much to be thankful for. We need to be thankful that God provides for us coaches and mentors. God has supplied us with the resources and support that we need to be successful. We also need to give God thanks for our ability to play this game. You see, when we do things with a thankful heart, it helps to humble us. It helps us remember that our real help comes from the one we should be closest to. Our talent, our help, and our strength come from God. So stop right now and give God the thanks with your thankful heart, and then I will see you at the plate.

Dear Spotless Lamb,

God, thank you. Thank you for my coaches, and thank you for my talent. Thank you for my team(s), and thank you for lessons learned from the wins and from the losses.

God, thank you, thank you, thank you. God, help me always to remember to have a thankful heart.

✞

Day 36

Rough Day

2 Corinthians 4:16 (NLT) ***That is why we never give up. Though our bodies are dying, our spirits are being renewed every day.***

Have you ever had one of those days where nothing seems to go right? Your alarm does not go off, you are late for school, you forgot about an assignment due, and you forgot your workout clothes. Then you get to practice, and you cannot hit the ball to save your life. You almost made a spectacular catch, but at the last minute, the ball pops out of your glove. You overthrow the bag on a routine ground ball. When you have a day like this by the end of practice, you wish you had just never started this day. You are convinced that this day will define your life. And that definition of your life right now spells out L.O.S.E.R. I have a statement for days like these. I call it the drop back and punt day. You know, when a football team punts, they hope to regroup and start all over on the next drive. They are giving up the ball, hoping that the next drive will be better or that maybe even their defense can score. Some days are just rough, and when those days occur, we need to drop back and punt.

The most amazing thing about being a Christian is that with grace, it is implied that we can start over and have a new beginning and a new day every day. It reminds us that our hope lies in that tomorrow will be a better day. That is the promise that God has given us because we know that we will live with him in heaven one day. But we can also experience grace when we have the opportunity to start fresh tomorrow. Grace gives new hope and new opportunities. Grace screams, I know you can, and I will be here to make sure you can. Grace is what picks us up and gives us the fortitude to try again. So now that you are done with that terrible yesterday, pick up the bat today, and I will see you at the plate.

Dear Redeemer,

God yesterday was rough, but with each day, we receive new blessings. God's grace allows us to start over, no matter how bad yesterday got. It helps us to see that we are given chance after chance to get things right. This is only possible through your grace that was established for us at Calvary. God, thank you for renewing my spirit and making me whole again and again, forever.

Day 37

The End of Me

Psalms 61:2 ***From the ends of the earth I call to you, I call as my heart grows faint; lead me to the rock that is higher than I.***

Often, an athlete has the potential, but they allow themselves to get in the way of being great. This week, I read an article in FCA magazine about Rashad Jennings, the NFL star for the New York Giants. The article explains that while Jennings was a Junior in High School, he was failing out of school because of his arrogance. He was also not living up to his potential on the playing field because he was out of shape. He had all the potential in the world, but he could not let go of himself. In his junior year, his brothers helped him to get a transfer to a Christian school where he came to the "end of me." It was there that he excelled, gaining over 3000 yards and scoring 37 touchdowns. He went from there to the University of Pittsburg (Pitt) and excelled. But because of a family crisis, he finished his college career and graduated from Liberty University. He was selected in 2009 as the 250th overall pick in the NFL draft. Rashad Jennings did not start until he came to an end. "The end of me."

How many times have you started and restarted something in your life? It always starts with new promises and new aspirations. It gives you hope, and you consciously think this time, I am going to make it. I mean, you have nothing but good intentions for wanting to change or do better. But the truth is that you need an end, not a beginning. Not all races start at the starting line, especially when it deals with self. No instead, if you are going to change, you need first to visit the finish line. You will learn that you must come to the end of you; to get to the new you. Doing the same thing over and over, expecting a different result, will only reap the same results as before and before that and before that (you get the repetition here). When you want to improve in life, you must first die to yourself. This was Jesus' whole reason for coming to earth, so he could teach us to die to ourselves. The Scripture talks about how he turned this Kingdom upside down for us. We are worried about gaining more, yet he always said: "less was better." We always look to those that are fixed, and he always ministered to those that were broken. In his longest sermon ever, he started it out with a note about dying to self. His statement was, "blessed are the poor in spirit because they will inherit the kingdom of heaven. Here, "poor" is translated from "ptochos," which means "to crouch or cower as one helpless." It signifies the beggar, the pauper, one in abject poverty, totally dependent on others for help, and destitute of even the necessities of life. [5] This leads us to the end of ourselves because it is here that we find our full reliance on God. See, to accomplish something, you must first get to the end of me. Now, this is not going to be easy because "me" does not want to change, and "me" does not want to let go of "me" because "me" has a tight grip on what "me" wants. But when we let go, we come to the end of me, and that is where we meet Jesus. So now you can begin, and I will see you at the plate.

Dear Word of Life,

I am at the end of my rope, I have nowhere else to turn, and this is where I come to the end of me. It is here that I can start anew. It is here that my total reliance is on you. I cannot do it anymore, and that is a good thing. God, I place my whole life in your hands, and now I can live the life you have called me to live, not the life I think that I should live. God, the end of me is the beginning of you. Amen.

Day 38

The Light from Within

Matthew 5:14-16 ***You are the light of the world. A city set on a hill cannot be hidden; nor does anyone light a lamp and put it under a basket, but on the lampstand, and it gives light to all who are in the house. "Let your light shine before men in such a way that they may see your good works and glorify your Father, who is in heaven.***

Last night after the College Football National Championship, Dabo Sweeney (Coach of the Clemson Tigers) used a quote that made me think about why we play the game and who gets the glory when we play. The quote was stated like this, "I have been telling my players all year to let the light from inside shine, not to shine in the spotlight." The more I thought about that, the more difficult it sounded in the culture that we live in today. We live in a selfies and social media culture that allows us to be in the spotlight any time we choose. We can put ourselves in the spotlight. We can brag about our accomplishments or even make them up. (because everything you read on social media is true) This concept of "me" is even more intensified when we are talented in the sports, performing arts, or the music arena. Some schools and programs even lean toward making "you" the center of attention. But the more I thought about this statement, the more I realized that what God wants from us is for him to be in the spotlight and for us to hold that spotlight. He has given us a platform and an audience so that we can show his light. When we play from the light within, we learn to play for each other and not ourselves. We learn that winning and losing is a team concept, and not all the accolades or disappointment fall solely on one individual.

Do you remember when you were young singing the VBS song? This Little Light of Mine. You know the light that you were going to let shine and shine and shine and not let anyone snuff it out. We are his ambassadors, and we are his missionaries. We are the ones that have been called to shine the light. The only way that light will shine is for us to step out of the spotlight and shine our heart lights. Let me ask you this; is your light shining in everything that you do? Are you playing the game to shine your light, or are you playing the game so that you can be in the spotlight? I dare you to be counter-cultural and let your light shine so that the whole world can see it. See you at the plate!

Dear Radiant Light,

You created light when there was only darkness. You sent your Son to be the light of this dark world. God, as this light is upon my life, let it shine for you. God shine your light into the dark places of my life so that they will show your glory. God help me to step out of the spotlight so that people can see that you are the true spotlight. God show me your Glory.

✞

Day 39

One Word

John 1:14 ***The Word became flesh and made his dwelling among us. We have seen his glory, the glory of the one and only Son, who came from the Father, full of grace and truth.***

What if, as a team, your New Year resolution was just one word? I mean, I know we have team goals and aspirations. We have team slogans, team banners, and team chants. We make up t-shirts and window decals to show we are motivated and why we play. But what would it be if it were just one word? What would that word be, and how would you get that word to describe your team and its goals? For some, the word may be "commitment." For others, the word may be "perseverance." Some may choose a catchier word like "ferocious or tenacious." But the truth is that simplifying your goals to one word may lead to a more concerted effort. I do many funerals in my ministry, and sometimes I may not know the person I am doing the funeral for, so I will meet with the family and ask the family to summarize that person's life in one word. It may sound funny, but you would not believe how many people can sum up a life with one word. The problem with this is that sometimes the words used do not represent the person in a positive light. What about you? What is one word that people would use to describe you? What about your team? What is one word that would describe your team?

You know I thought about Jesus, and I thought about my one word to describe him, and that word is "Grace." He encompasses the very meaning of that word, and here is the reason why. I am supposed to get death because of my sin and disobedience, but I receive eternal life because of his death and resurrection. Talk about unfairness; he came into the world sinless and left with my sin because I am a sinful being. Yet, his death justified my sin. That is what grace is all about. It is a hard concept to understand and a hard concept to grasp, but my one word to describe Jesus is grace. Now it is your turn. Give me one word that describes Jesus: ____________________________. Now that you have that word, I will see you at the plate.

Dear Majesty on High,

God, all of us may have a different word to describe you, but you define all of those words. You created the very actions behind those words. God, thank you for the gift of your Son, which brought us peace, love, and Grace. Thank you that he came to this messy world. God, help whatever word we chose for our lives to embrace that and for that word to show through our lives. Amen.

Day 40

Next One Up

Deuteronomy 34:7-9 Moses ***was a hundred and twenty years old when he died, yet his eyes were not weak nor his strength gone. The Israelites grieved for Moses in the plains of Moab thirty days, until the time of weeping and mourning was over. Now Joshua, Son of Nun, was filled with the spirit of wisdom because Moses had laid his hands on him. So, the Israelites listened to him and did what the Lord had commanded Moses.***

One of the major concerns for every coach is player injuries. An injury to any key player or captain of the team can cause the whole game plan to change. It is usually a coach's worst nightmare, but inevitable, we know that it will happen. This year I watched as Alabama lost their key running back in the National Championship game, and from that point on, things were different. I watched this season as Auburn had quarterbacks and running backs injuries throughout the year; this caused them to be very inconsistent at the end of the year. But sometimes, when a player gets hurt, a new star arises. We call this the "next one up" approach. Sometimes there is that diamond in the rough, the one player that may have been overlooked but now has time to shine. Your life can sometimes also be like this, and in that situation, you are called to be the "next one up." Sometimes this happens on your job or in your occupation. Sometimes it happens within your family, and sometimes it happens when God calls you. Many times, the next one up goes into action apprehensively. What usually happens after these people have had tremendous success, they tell the world that something was working within that they cannot explain. Some inner strength that they did not know they possessed. They explain the whole situation as being surreal. When that happens in my context, we call it the power of the Holy Spirit. You see, when you are called to do something outside of your comfort zone, or you are thrown into a situation that you feel you may not be able to handle, that is when the Holy Spirit kicks into overdrive. God promised throughout the Scripture that he "would never leave or forsake us." We have proof of that statement, and that proof comes in the power of the Holy Spirit. The spirit takes the fear and turns it into courage. The Spirit takes weakness and turns it into power. The Spirit takes doubts and turns them into willingness. Yes, sometimes, because of injury, suspension, or unforeseen circumstances, you will be called to be the next one up. When this time comes, remember that you are not stepping up to the plate or walking out on the field alone. You have one that gives you power, the power of the Holy Spirit. So, if you are the next one up, step on up, and I will see you at the plate.

Dear Spirit of the Living God,

I have been on the sidelines for some time, and now I am being called upon. God, I have prepared for this. You have given me the ability, and now it is my time to shine for you. God, please be with the one that is injured or has been making mistakes, but thanks you for the opportunity to now get in the game. God, let me not only showcase my skills but honor you as I step into the limelight. God, grant me the courage to undertake this endeavor. Amen

Day 41

Go Hard or Go Home

Matthew 5:5 ***God blesses those who are humble, for they will inherit the whole earth.***

I recently met with a group of coaches, and they expressed how hard it was to push their athletes to the next level. They were all stumped as to how to motivate their players to get maximum production for maximum performance. They asked me what I thought was causing the lack of heart and drive. I think that they expected me to answer with some type of spiritual statement; I mean, after all, I am a minister, but I just simply said, 'these kids today are just too soft." They do not have the same drive and work ethic that many had years ago. They live in the land of entitlement. They want to put in minimal effort but expect the greatest outcome. The problem is that if you do not go hard, then you are going to go home. You are going to go home without success. The science behind sports has changed over the last decade, but the effort required to succeed has not changed. If you are soft, you will never go hard. When you just expect it without working for it, then you are not only failing yourself, but you are failing your team. You must go all out every chance you get so that you will not go home empty-handed and feeling like you did not leave it all on the field. Last week, I was preaching from the beatitudes in Matthew 5, and I came across the Scripture that says, "Blessed are the meek for they will inherit the earth." This made no sense to me; how could you be meek and inherit the earth? But then I thought about the word meek as being humble rather than weak. I guess another reason I struggled with this verse is that I have never seen Jesus as weak. But the one thing that Jesus exemplified was humbleness. You know humble people are not weak; in fact, they are the strongest because they know where they need help. They work extra hard because they are thankful to have the opportunity. And finally, they give credit to those that helped them get there. When we go hard, we humble ourselves to the point that we know we have not arrived. We subconsciously know that we must put in the hard work. It is what makes us better, and it is what makes the team better. So humble yourself and then go hard or go home. I will see you at the plate!

Lord of Lord and King of Kings,

God humbles me. Make me not so self-reliant but help me to become God reliant. God, let me go as hard as I can go every time I step out onto that field. God, help me to understand that Jesus taught the lesson of humility to everyone around him. God, help me not to be soft but to have a spirit of forbearance and power. God, help me to remember that I am nothing without you. God, help me go hard till the day I come home, home to a Kingdom you have prepared for me.

Day 42

Everybody Gets a Trophy

1 Corinthians 9:25 (NLT) All ***athletes are disciplined in their training. They do it to win a prize that will fade away, but we do it for an eternal prize...***

I have to tell you that the everybody "gets a trophy concept" has ruined youth sports.

I will never forget I had a parent come up to me after a dismal youth football season and say, "let me know when you order the trophies and how much they cost. I want to make sure I pay for my son's trophy." I responded with this, "What are you talking about? We only won two games all year. We did not earn any trophies; we did not even make the playoffs." To which the lady responded, "I know, but we get trophies every year at the banquet no matter how many games we win." As you may have guessed, we did not do trophies that year. One of the main problems within our society is the everybody gets a trophy mentality. This mentality has ruined what it truly means to work for something. I think this concept goes beyond just sports, and I think it is exemplified in our world that says, "You owe me for showing up." It is the very reason why when someone does not get what they think they deserve, they start to boycott, picket, and march against something and everything. They are not marching for a cause; they are marching because they did not get their way. I will never forget that back when I was in youth ministry, there was a girl who did not make the cheerleading squad. Her father, a lawyer, found some loophole in the judging and point system after his daughter did not make the squad, and he sued the school. To save face, the school decided not to let it go to court, and they let every girl who tried out make the squad, so there were like forty cheerleaders. It was the worst year ever, and it sent a statement to everyone on that squad. The message was that your hard work and effort were for nothing. Just show up, and you are on the team. You know, the same thing sometimes happens in our Christian walk. We do not want to put any effort into advancing the Kingdom of God. Our theory is that all we have to do is show up a few Sundays a year. I have long preached against the just show-up to get-in mentality.

Jesus intended more for us and more from us. John Wesley told us that we should be moving toward perfection. The last I checked, the only way to get to perfection is by putting forth effort. Even Jesus said, "Not everyone who calls out to me, 'Lord! Lord!' will enter the Kingdom of Heaven. Only those who actually do the will of my Father in heaven will enter." What do you mean I do not just get a trophy for showing up? No, Jesus loves you way much just to give out participation trophies. See, Jesus gave us a trophy that would never perish and never fade away. He gave us eternal life by giving his life. Jesus did not just show up here on earth, but he gave everything he had so that our sins would be covered. So don't just show up but show out. Now, I will see you at the plate to work toward a trophy that will be earned, not just handed out at the end of the year. Work hard, and I will see you at the plate!

Dear King of Heaven,

Help me to understand that I am in this game to play it to the fullest. It will require effort on my part, but you will be there with me every step of the way. God, please help me to understand the value of hard work. God, grant me the wisdom to understand that life is not fair. Sometimes I get what I do not deserve, and sometimes I don't get what I have worked hard for. Let me understand the full price that you paid for me and my sin. Let me work harder at everything I do to say that I was fully vested for the sake of the cross. God, thank you for giving me the greatest trophy in life, the trophy of eternal life.

Day 43

Total Surrender

Job 11:13-14 ***Surrender your heart to God, turn to him in prayer and give up your sins—even those you do in secret.***

The word "surrender" has so many negative connotations. The word is synonymous with "coward" in the sports world. Even when you are outmanned and less talented, you are told to fight on, to persevere. When you are down by three touchdowns or seven runs with little time left to play, you are told to fight on; to keep playing, and keep believing. If the right coaches have coached you, you have been told to "never surrender" and "never give in." It is the motto of the military and the motto of every successful sports team. "Never surrender and never retreat." I think this is why it may be so hard for athletes to surrender their life to Christ. The rhetoric of that word just seems to deliberate thinking of weakness. To surrender means that you are accepting defeat in the midst of your weakness. So rather than total surrender to God, we hold onto the "I can do this by myself mentality." But surrendering to God is different than giving up. It is more like joining "allied" forces. I remembered a few years ago; we were struggling with pitching on a team I was coaching. Before one of our tournaments, I found out that I would be able to reenlist the pitcher that we had used the year before because we would be playing up an age division. We realized at this point that we had someone who could help us and all that would be joining us. God does the same thing in our life when we surrender our lives over to him; we now have an ally: Someone who will walk with us, and that will help us reprioritize our life and goals. You see, when we surrender to God, it is not a sign of being a coward or weakness; it is a sign of empowerment. It is not waving the white flag; it signifies that we will not fight the battle alone. When we surrender to God, we are not held captive but are set free. So let me ask you, is there something that you are holding on to? Is there something that you are scared to give to God? Do you have the great head knowledge of the Scripture, but you refuse to submit your heart? Then today, stop and surrender your heart to God. You will not be losing control; you will be gaining the **controller** (God). This surrender means that you win, not that you lose. So go into the full surrender mode, and I will see you at the plate.

The One True Mediator,

I struggle to surrender my whole life to you. I have aspects that I want to hold onto too. I have places that I do not want to give you because they are hurtful. I have other areas that I just want to hold onto because of my selfish ambition. God, help me to surrender so that we can join together. Thank you for being my friend and my ally. I am letting go and letting you have total control. Amen.

Day 44

Trust the P.R.O.C.E.S.S.

Proverbs 3:5 ***Trust in the Lord with all your heart and lean not on your own understanding.***

Trust the P.R.O.C.E.S.S. This will be the team motto as we go into the current Lady Tigers season of softball. We have adopted this slogan from Clint Myers, head coach of Auburn University Softball. We will first and foremost have to learn how to trust. This may be a troublesome process because, along the way, things have happened to us that has left us with a propensity not to trust. Trust means that we admit that we cannot do it on our own, that we may need correction or even punishment to alleviate weakness and improper technique. We must first trust ourselves to show up every day, get better every day, and never quit or give up. We must trust in the coaches that have the best interest of the team in mind. Trust means that we give our attention to the coaches that will teach us the process. It means that we get better every day, that we make adjustments every day. It is not just about trusting our coaches but also about trusting each other as teammates. We have to buy into the fact that this is a team. We win as a team, and we lose as a team. We celebrate as a team, and we congratulate our opponents as a team when we win or lose. We trust that no one is bigger than the team. We must trust and remember that team has no "I" in it.

We also must trust in our Lord and Savior, Jesus Christ. We have placed our life into his hands so that he may be glorified through the process. In this process, we play for the applause of Jesus and not for the applause of our parents or the fans in the crowd. We realize that part of the trust process is that the crowd will turn on us in a minute. The process is not necessarily about wins and losses, but it is something that we will carry with us throughout life. But having said that statement, if the process is followed correctly, the wins and success will certainly follow. The process is exactly that it is a process. It will take time, and it will require your full attention and participation. The process is also ongoing, just like our walk with Jesus. It will help a player mature with time and perseverance. The process will also be contagious and start a process that many will want to be a part of. So welcome to the process; now, all you have to do is trust it. So now, we will take a look at what the process entails. See you at the plate!

Dear Creator of the Process,

Thank you for letting me be a part of the process. Many chose not to be a part of this process because it was too rigorous and demanded too much. God, help me to trust myself. Help me trust my coaches. Help me to trust my teammates. Help me to trust you more and more every day. God, help me to trust the process even when I do not understand it.

Day 45

Trust the P.R.O.C.E.S.S. – Prayer

1 Thessalonians 5:16-18 (ESV) ***Rejoice always, pray without ceasing, give thanks in all circumstances; for this is the will of God in Christ Jesus for you.***

Before you embark on any process, the first action must be the act of putting it to prayer. I do not know how many disasters could have been avoided, if someone would have put the prayer ahead of the action and reaction. Let's face it, most of the time, we are compulsive creatures, and we react with our feelings before we ever stop, drop, hit our knees, and pray. We are so reactionary that we move before we even sit down and calculate what this may mean in our life. The first prayer of the process is to pray about what this process will entail. How much time will it take? Am I willing to give it 100% because it does not just affect me, but it affects my whole team? Am I willing to forgo other things so that I can be the best I can be? Yes, it is through our prayer life that we discern these questions. The process is hard, arduous, and requires that we give copious amounts of time. So, before you embark on this process, I beg and plead with you to stop, get still, go to your prayer closet, and bathe this endeavor in prayer.

I had a friend that was considering taking a new job. He said that he had prayed about it but did not feel comfortable about his decision. He asks that some of his friends also pray about it, and I was included in that sphere of influence. I also did not have peace about it, and I told him that I thought he would be better with another option. He refused to listen to his prayers or his friend's prayers, and he took the job because of its financial reward. Two years into the job, he failed miserably, making some moral decisions that would ruin his life. He did not trust the prayer portion of the process. God had even guided him through friends, but he refused to listen to that still small voice that helps us discern the direction in our lives. So, if you want to be a part of this process before taking another step forward, pray, then pray, and then pray some more. Then ask people to pray for you and then pray for your coaches, teammates, and opponents. Pray for your umpires, and pray for those that will cheer you from the stands. After you have prayed, I will see you at the plate.

Partner in Prayer,

The process of everyday life is about the process of prayer. Jesus prayed in the desert, he taught his disciples to pray, and he prayed in the garden. He often withdrew to pray so that he could watch the process unfold. God help me to spend as much time in prayer as all of the other parts of the process combined. God, through prayer, help me to discern what this whole process is about.

✞

Day 46

Trust the P.R.O.C.E.S.S. – Practice

Philippians 4:9. ***Keep putting into practice all you learned and received from me-- everything you heard from me and saw me doing. Then the God of peace will be with you.***

In the first week of the process study, we are going to look at the "P"s. The first word for "P" is **practice.** There is no process without practice. Now, most people will tell you that they do not like to practice. Most people like to play the game, not practice to play the game. But the process includes practice, or when you get to the game, you will not be prepared for your opponent. Practice should be viewed as more than physical preparation. There should be a teaching and a learning side to practice. Practice also has a mental side to it. You are learning concepts and visioning while practicing. Practice is developing muscle memory.

There is a lot of debate over this, but many people say it takes between 1,000 to 10,000 reps for something to become muscle memory. I know that sounds like a lot, but think about how the more you do something, it just becomes natural. A few weeks ago, we were at the indoor batting facility, and the boy's baseball team had just finished up a 2 ½ hour practice. About 30 minutes after practice was over, six boys returned to the facility and spent another hour hitting. Everyone of these young men is already a top performer and one of the best hitters on the team. They are the best because they do not come to practice because they have to come to practice; they show up because they want to improve every day. Let me ask you, how can you get better if you do not practice? Let me give you the answer, you cannot. So, trust the process by showing up to practice, and every time you show up to practice, want and yearn to be better.

Practice can also be applied to our everyday life and living. Did you know that being a Christian takes practice? Ask any person that has matured through their Christian walk, and they will tell you that it was the practice that led them to be the person they are today. Not all of the spiritual fruits came easy for them. Some were rather hard to bear. Take forgiveness, for instance. Most people will tell you this is one of the hardest concepts. But forgiveness comes easier with practice. Discipline is another concept that is learned through practice. When you are disciplined, all the aspects of life seem to fall into place. We know that Jesus was said to have been perfect. We model our lives after Jesus, so our goal is perfection. You have heard it said that practice makes perfect. This means that every aspect of life ought to be practiced. So show up to practice and practice to be the best you can be. Bring with you the willingness to learn and a work ethic to get things done. After you have practiced, I will see you at the plate.

Dear Perfect One,

God, you are perfect in every way. I strive to be more like your Son, who was without sin. God, I practice so that I can be the best you have called me to be. God, thank you for the gifts and talents you have given me. But help me to stay motivated to practice these talents so that I can be the best. God, let me practice things that I need on the field and those and that I need off of the field. Practice makes perfect, and one day I will be perfect because I am in your presence. I am a child of God.

Day 47

Trust the P.R.O.C.E.S.S. – Perseverance

James 1:12 ***Blessed is the one who perseveres under trial because, having stood the test, that person will receive the crown of life that the Lord has promised to those who love him.***

The second "P" word for this week is perseverance. It is defined as a continued effort to do or achieve something despite difficulties, failure, or opposition. The root of the word in Greek is "meno," which means God's permanence. This means that God is always with us even when we feel abandoned and alone.

Let's face it; some days are just too hard. You are just too sore from the day before. You feel stuck that you are not getting any better, stronger, or faster. You have been working, but a plateau has surfaced. We all go through seasons in our life when we feel that we are just going through the motions. We show up, but rarely do we show out. Then we ask the tough question, "why am I doing this?" That is when the doubt creeps in. Should I continue, or is it time to give in and give up? If you play the game long enough, you will always come to a place where you ask this question. After asking this question, some of our greatest strides can be taken if we decide not to let the suffering break us. In those times of doubt, we learn to persevere and push through the pain and the doubt. It is all just part of the process. The process is not just about making you better, but it is about making your team better. It is in the presence of defeat and suffering that we grow the most. Sometimes, the suffering and the doubt lead us to work harder and not give up.

There are times in life when we feel like we are cursed, times when nothing is going right. We search for answers but only get more questions. We just want the pain to stop. We want the struggle just to be over. We constantly ask the question of why me. But the Holy Spirit within us reminds us that I am there for you. We are in this battle together, and then we hear the word that causes us to push on. Persevere. Push on. This test will soon become your testimony. Yes, this is what will define your character. It was your willingness not to give up and to push through the pain so that you can see the hope that is promised in the hope of the resurrection. So pick yourself up, push through the pain, and persevere because perseverance will lead you to one more at-bat. I will see you at the plate.

Dear Chosen One,

God, you are the constant. You are with me. You promise that you will never leave or forsake me. I pray that no matter what trial I am facing, no matter what pain this life brings, I will never give up. I pray that your Holy Spirit will always abide in me to help me to push through. This perseverance will lead to faith, and that is what all hope for.

Day 48

Trust the P.R.O.C.E.S.S. – Purpose

Proverbs 19:21 ***"Many are the plans in a person's heart, but it is the Lord's purpose that prevails."***

I have seen some old movies where someone will approach a door or gate, and someone on the other side will greet the visitor with this summons, "state your purpose." We do not greet people that way these days, but it is interesting to think about. What is our purpose for playing the game? Our purpose for playing the game will always define the process. The ultimate reason you play high-level competitive sports is so that you can win a championship. When you were younger, the process was different; the process was all about learning the game, the basic rules, the basic skills, and how to play with others. It helped you to become part of a team and learn to play as a team player. Now the competitive process does not mean that we are still not homing in and developing better skills. But the process does change because now we are becoming more intentional about playing with a purpose. Every practice and every meeting is done with a purpose in mind. The coach's purpose is to make you better. Your purpose should be to get better every day. The team's purpose should be to play more like one cohesive unit. The ultimate goal is to win and then to win consistently. The purpose is to create a winning environment and a winning legacy.

A few years ago, I read the book "The On-Purpose Person" by Kevin McCarthy. The book asks many questions that made me evaluate where I was in life and helped refine the purpose of my ministry and my personal life. You see, many times in life, it is easy to get pulled away from our purpose. Throughout Jesus' ministry, Satan and sometimes even his own disciples tried to pull Jesus away from his purpose. But he would not have it. His purpose was to win the game for you. Jesus had a purpose, and that purpose was to die for you. His purpose was to become a champion, not a champion of the world but a champion of your heart. This life that God has given us also has a purpose. Many people struggle with purpose and find their life void of significance. They may be surrounded by people and possessions but have no purpose. When our purpose is to be a disciple of Christ, it helps define our existence's true purpose. You have a purpose that is to worship and serve the creator. Now that your purpose has been defined, I will see you at the plate.

Dear Life-Giver,

God help my life to have a purpose. A divine purpose. Help me learn that the purpose of the process is to make me better, not only on the field but also off the field. Thank you that Jesus came to love me and die for me. God helps people to see that the purpose of my life is to glorify you in everything I do.

✞

Day 49

Trust the P.R.O.C.E.S.S. – Repetition

I Timothy 3:16 ***All Scripture is breathed out by God and profitable for teaching, for reproof, for correction, and for training in righteousness…***

I think it is so funny that they have instructions on the back of a shampoo bottle. But a confession is that I never really follow the shampoo instructions. Have you ever noticed it says, Wet hair, apply shampoo, lather, and rinse? Repeat? You know what, the only time I repeat is if I cannot remember if I put it on before I washed the rest of my body. Let's face it; most of us have a hard time with instruction and an even harder time with repetition. We live in a world where we are ready to move on to the next thing. But repetition is a particularly important part of the process. It is what trains the muscles and the mind to do it without thinking. The problem is that most of us get bored with the repetition part of the process. I heard a story the other day that stressed the point of repetition. The article was about a basketball player; it stated that after a recent game, the player went back into the gym and practiced shooting after the game was over. What? Play and then repeat. How can that be part of the process? The game is already over. No, the player was in the process of repeating so he could get ready for the next game. One of the most important parts of the process is repetition.

The same can be true in our walk with Jesus. Our spiritual disciplines involve repetition. Jesus tells the story of a widow who wanted justice, so every day, she would repeat her petitions. It says that the judge neither feared God nor cared for people, and yet because of her persistence, the judge granted her request. (Luke 18:1-8) Finally, the Judge caved, and the lady got what she was so persistent about. Do not stop praying. Pray, ask, repeat. Do not stop reading your Scripture; read, meditate, and repeat. Do not stop journaling; write, reflect, and repeat. You see, our spiritual disciplines come from repetition. You want repetition, then take the 21-day challenge and develop a good habit of spiritual disciplines. So focus on repetition, and I will see you at the plate. Then repeat, and I will see you at the plate.

Dear God of Truth,

Prayer itself teaches us the repetition of spending time with you daily. God, help me to be persistent when it comes to the spiritual disciplines of praying, mediation,

Scripture reading and memorization, and journaling. If I am persistent in these disciplines, then all the other areas of my life will also be consistent. God, thank you for your constant and repeating love for a sinner like me. I hope to be as persistent in my daily walk as you are in your love for me.

Day 50

Trust the P.R.O.C.E.S.S. – Rest

Matthew 11:28-30 (NIV) ***"Come to me, all you who are weary and burdened, and I will give you rest. Take my yoke upon you and learn from me, for I am gentle and humble in heart, and you will find rest for your souls. For my yoke is easy, and my burden is light."***

One of the most important parts of the process is rest. You know, one of the problems with athletes today is that they do not get enough rest. They push and push but see minimal results. Rest is essential for you to get the most out of your workouts. You have to essentially have days when you do nothing but rest your body and your mind. Rest is not being lazy or being a slacker. As a matter of fact, rest allows the body to rejuvenate and to grow. If you overwork a muscle, the muscle will not fully develop. You must also walk away from the sport for just a little while so that you do not burn out on what you love. I have always been a proponent of playing multiple sports and not focusing on just one. You must also have a mental break to let your mind rest and rejuvenate. We have such a tough time resting these days; we pile on more and have more resources to keep us moving all the time. But to be successful in the process, you have to be able to rest. You know, one of the hardest things for us to do is to Sabbath; it has been that way since the beginning of time. I often ask people to name the Ten Commandments, and they get the do not lie, murder, covet, do use God's name in vain. But rarely do they remember about keeping the Sabbath day holy. The interesting thing about this is that God spent more time explaining this commandment than he did any of the other commandments. God knew if we were going to serve him and be effective, we had to have an assigned, isolated day of rest. (Sabbath)

God, the creator of all, created everything in six days, and then he rested. He commanded the Israelites as they fled captivity to rest every seven days. By resting, you learn to listen. By resting, you learn to lean against God and all that he provides. When we rest, we can be in the posture of worship, and through this worship, we are refilled and replenished. Yes, God knew that this thing we call life would be complicated and that we would find ourselves weary and tired. So let me ask you, have you had a Sabbath lately? Have you rested? If not, take a Sabbath, and then when you are refreshed and renewed, I will see you at the plate.

God of Sabbath,

Give me rest. Let me not slumber but let me find my rest in your arms. God fill me again. In this time of rest, let me hear your voice and see your direction. Let me Sabbath so that I can be complete, and I can continue to do what I love to do. Let others who need rest learn to take time to rejuvenate. God, thank you for permitting us to rest.

Day 51

Trust the P.R.O.C.E.S.S. – Resilience

John 19:10 ***"Why don't you talk to me?" Pilate demanded. "Don't you realize that I have the power to release you or crucify you?"***

The Merriam-Webster Dictionary defines resilience as an ability to recover from or adjust easily to misfortune or change.[6] We know that in sports that we must learn to adjust in order to have success. Sometimes everything we worked on in preparation; is different when we get in the game. We have to be able to make changes on the fly. This is a hard part of the process for some because they are rigorous and methodical. This part of the process is as much mental as it is physical. The next part of resilience is moving on from a mistake or error. I once had a coach tell me that if you are going to be a successful player, then you are going to have short-term memory. In essence, what he was saying is that we cannot dwell on our mistakes. One thing I always tell pitchers is that they have to forget it and move on. If you dwell too long on a bad pitch or play, you will ruin the whole game. Resilience is the part of the process that is really up to you. The coaches will quickly forget, but you must also move on from the mistake. You need to remember that some of the greatest opportunities come from times of opposition.

We must also be resilient in everyday life: You have had those days where the alarm did not go off. You got a parking ticket on your lunch break. You spilled coffee on your white shirt. You lost that important email. You cannot let those things define your day, or eventually, they will come to define your whole life. Jesus taught us this resilience when he stood in front of Pilate. Pilate wanted to release Jesus, but Jesus had to remember that he was destined to die for our sins. Pilate said, do you not know that I have the power to release you. Jesus was in pain, and he was in agony. He had been up all night beaten at least twice, mocked, and spat upon, but he responds to Pilate by saying, "you would have no power over me unless it were given to you by my father." This tells us what we need to do when things are not going our way. We need to turn to the Father God, who will help us if we cannot help ourselves. He will get us to the point that we will be able to forget and move on. You have to trust this part of the process if you are going to be successful. To be resilient means that we can encounter all kinds of setbacks, but we move forward to reach the goal set before us. Now let's practice resilience, and I will see you at the plate.

Dear Shepherd,

God, I need resilience in my life so that I can forget what Satan wants to keep reminding me of. I have failed you, but the only way to continue this spiritual journey is to press on. Life will be full of mistakes, but how I respond to those mistakes will propel me to do great things in my life. God, thank you that your Son had such resilience on the cross that he died for me. He chose the nails instead of defending who he was or compromising what he believed. God, thank you for being resilient in your love for me.

Day 52

Trust the P.R.O.C.E.S.S. – Rewards

I Peter 5:4 (NIV) ***And when the Chief Shepherd appears, you will receive the crown of glory that will never fade away.***

We live in a society where there is a huge emphasis put on trophies and awards. We rank teams before the season even begins. We fire coaches because they did not win the National Championship. We give out rings every week at travel ball tournaments around the country like they just won the World Series. We give participation trophies for just showing up. We feel like that at every banquet, every kid that played ought to get something. **But the truth is that the greatest rewards we will ever get are the rewards that we get from just being part of the process.** You see, there are rewards that only teammates will understand. I remember this year in softball; a girl went almost 15 games without a hit. When she finally got a hit, the team went crazy because she had just received that internal award of knowing that she had overcome a hurdle. What about the reward of moving up in the lineup because you have increased your batting average by 100 points? What about when you finally bench 200 pounds for the first time? You see, the process is about small rewards that lead to bigger rewards. One thing that every athlete should ask every day is this, "What did I do today to get better?" You see, people who do not participate daily only have one way of weighing awards: position and rank. But we know that we get rewarded by just being part of the process. In addition, the greatest reward that we can ever receive is knowing that we gave our all and that we left everything we had out on the field.

Jesus, in the Scripture, warned people all the time about relying on earthly rewards. You know, I have a whole drawer full of medals that I won or received from participating in triathlon events. But they mean nothing because the greatest rewards I got from competing were the rewards of knowing that I had improved and that when everyone else told me I could not do it. With God's help, I did it anyway. You see, the same could be true of our walk with Christ. We do not serve other people or live a disciplined life so that people will reward us. No, our reward simply comes from being a blessing to someone that needed a blessing. If you became a Christian only to get a reward, in the end, you are missing out on the process – the process of growing closer to Christ every day. So, ask this question now related to your walk with Christ: "What did I do today to get better?" I will see you at the plate.

Dear Son of God,

Help me to begin to see why the process works. It is not about trophies or individual accolades but about being the best I can every day. God help me get better today. Help me focus on what you would have me focus on and not on what the world wants me to focus on. God, I am simply part of the process, but you are the process. God, if I fail, today then help me to get up and go again tomorrow. God, your trophy was a cross that became my trophy of salvation and grace. Thank you for loving me.

✞

Day 53

Trust the P.R.O.C.E.S.S. – Respect

I Peter 2:17 ***Respect everyone and love your Christian brothers and sisters. Fear God, and respect the king.***

In our society, we use the word "respect" in many different areas of life. We talk of young people having no "respect" for anything or anybody in authority. We talk about how we must "respect" our elders. We talk about the lack of respect for our nation. We talk of how we must "respect" people different from us in their ways and culture. We hear the word "RESPECT" so much that we often are confused about what the word entails. I think that the sports world helps us to show a true definition of respect. The first thing that a player must do is respect their coach. That coach has been placed in a position of authority for a reason. Many times, I have heard players talk back or even yell at their coaches. There is no place for a person like that on a team, even if they are the most talented ones on that team. Another thing we must do is respect our teammates. A team is only as good as its weakest link. A family does not always get along, but they must always mutually respect one another if they expect to remain a cohesive unit. The third thing a team must do is respect the officials. Are the officials always right? Absolutely not! But they have been put in place to keep order and control of the contest. Respecting officials has to start with the coaches and parents. If they have disrespect for the officials, then so will the players that play for you. This will also bleed over into other aspects of a player's life. The last component of respect on the field is that you must respect the other team. Sometimes you will be way better than the team you face, and sometimes you will be inferior to the team you face. Many times, you will be right on par with the team you are playing. But whatever the circumstance, you must respect your opponent and give them credit for showing up and playing just like you did.

Respect starts with self. If we do not respect ourselves, then we will never respect anyone else. In Luke 10, a religious leader asks Jesus, "Who is my neighbor?" The reason that he asks is that he had no respect for people that were from Samaria. But Jesus answered by simply saying everyone is your neighbor. In essence, he is saying everyone deserves respect. But what about those who do not respect us, you ask? What did Jesus do? He prayed for God to forgive them. If we want to be like Jesus, we must respect even when it is not extended to us. So, do you respect the game, your coach, the officials, and the other team? If you do, then I will see you at the plate.

Dear Protector,

I realize that I have often been disrespectful to my peers, parents, and the opposing teams many times in life. Help me to learn how to respect those that may not even like me. Help me to stay above reproach. Help me to respect people when they make mistakes or even the referee when he misses the call. God, thank you for respecting and loving me even when I have fallen short and missed the mark. God, most of all, let me have respect for you. I love you. Amen.

Day 54

Trust the P.R.O.C.E.S.S. – Opportunity

2 Timothy 4:2 (NLT) ***"Preach the word of God. Be prepared, whether the time is favorable or not. Patiently correct, rebuke, and encourage your people with good teaching.***

Have you ever heard anyone say when you get your opportunity, you better be ready for it? We all know that sometimes an opportunity comes because of someone else's misfortune or injury. That is why we must always stay prepared. We may not be a starter, but we must prepare like one because we just may be the **"next one up**." I cannot tell you how many great athletes have been discovered because they were ready when the opportunity came up. They were on the sidelines one game, and the next, they were the MVP. This is not only reserved for the sports world but extends to every area of our life. You must make the most of every opportunity given to you. You know, my football coach in college used to say all the time, "you know what luck is? It is when opportunity meets preparation." What he was saying is always to be prepared when the moment arises. You will never get lucky if you have not prepared for this moment.

Let me ask you, what are you doing to prepare yourself for when the opportunity arises? Are you sulking because you feel like you should be starting or playing a different position? The flip side of this coin is when we are in a starting position or the top of the lineup, and we do not make the most of our opportunities. This is the place where we short-change the team and God. Another awaking experience is when we take for granted our position, and suddenly we find out that we have been replaced. Seize the day, seize today, and look for the opportunity to arise. But if your opportunity does not come today, then keep to the grind and keep preparing; your opportunity will eventually come.

Remember that things can change in the twinkling of an eye, so always be prepared and look for your opportunity. Has anybody ever caught you off guard and asked a question about your faith? I cannot tell you how many times someone has asked me something that I never saw coming. One of the scary things about living out your faith is knowing what to say when the opportunity arises for you to share your faith. The Scripture says, "Study to show thyself approved." This means that we must prepare for when the opportunity arises for us to share the gospel with someone. Sometimes we are so caught up in carnal opportunities that we neglect the spiritual study that it takes so that we can share when the opportunity arises. Let me ask you, are you spending time in the Word daily? Are you having a fruitful prayer life, and finally, are you asking God to allow you to share your faith? Are you prepared to share or even defend your faith? We should be even more prepared for this than we should when it comes to sports opportunities. You see, sports are temporal, but the faith, love, and grace of Jesus are eternal. Make the most of your next at-bat, and I will see you at the plate.

Eternal Loving Father,

Help me to prepare for the opportunity. God then give me the opportunity. God, let me take the opportunity. God let me make the most of every opportunity provided to me. God, please send someone to me so that I may share my faith with them. Please prepare my heart for the opportunities that are before me. For some, it may be my last opportunity to share with them; that is why I must make the most of this opportunity. Amen

✟

Day 55

Trust the P.R.O.C.E.S.S. – Overcome

John 16:33 ***"I have told you these things, so that in me you may have peace. In this world, you will have trouble. But take heart! I have overcome the world."***

You know that anyone that has ever climbed to the top of their game had times when they had to overcome unforeseen setbacks and hurdles. Sometimes these come in the form of injuries; sometimes, they are just a slump in performance. But if you do live long enough, there will be something that comes up that you must overcome to carry on. Sometimes we are born into circumstances that we must overcome. We lose a parent early in life. It may be that our grandparents had to raise us because our birth parents abandoned us. It may be that we do not have the financial resources to sustain even the necessities of life. The truth is that I have heard numerous stories of people that have overcome certain situations to shine.

One of my favorite movies is **"The Blind Side."** It is the story of Michael Orr. A young African American boy born out of wedlock to a drug-addicted mom and left to the streets before a rich white suburban family takes him in and gives him an opportunity. He goes on to graduate college from Ole Miss and eventually lands a contract in the NFL. It is the story of an overcomer. Let me ask you, have you ever had to overcome something that seemed impossible? You see, I once heard a pastor say that your test will soon become your testimony. When you become an overcomer, you become an instrument that God can use to share his story. You see, the Bible is a story about overcoming. It is God's story of how he soon overcame our sin through his death. He also overcame the stigma of death that every individual fear.

You see, Jesus was an overcomer. I heard a song on the radio the other by a lady named Mandisa. It is entitled "Overcomer." Later I watched the video and realized that the song's video surrounds Robin Roberts, who battled and overcame cancer. The words are so catchy but also a promise to live life by. (You may want to listen to the Song) So what is it today that you are going through that seems too big to handle? Hold on and let God show up and help you be an overcomer. And when you have overcome it, I will see you at the plate.

Dear Overcomer,

I am down, but I am not out. I have seen better days, and I will see them again because I know that you are with me. You are with me in the good times, and you are carrying me in the hard times. I am an overcomer because your Son was an overcomer. Thank you that he overcame my sin, defeated death, and set me free. I am an overcomer.

Day 56

Trust the P.R.O.C.E.S.S. – Outwork

Proverbs 13:4 (ESV) ***The soul of the sluggard craves and gets nothing, while the soul of the diligent is richly supplied.***

We all know that we cannot work our way into heaven, so this devotion may seem somewhat awkward. I would suggest that one of the ways we become who God wants us to be is by outworking our opponent. Now, I know what you are thinking; you just said you could not work your way into heaven. So let me explain what I mean. Satan hopes nothing better for us than for us to fail. The Scripture says that Satan is a liar. He came to kill, steal, and destroy, as stated in John 10:10. That is why we must always be on our guard for his plan to trip us up or cause us to fail. What does it mean to outwork? It means knowing your game plan. When you are playing a game, you read the scouting report or watch a film of your opponent. If you are on a scout team, you try your hardest to emulate the other team, and you go full speed to make your starters better. You must put in that extra rep or go that extra lap. You must spend more time in the cage, hitting or on the mound dialing in your pitches. You see, when we put our minds to outwork our opponent, we do not have time for the foolishness that may be lying in wait. When we outwork our opponent, we can sometimes overcome a more talented team than we are. I read a slogan off of a t-shirt the other day that says, "Hard work beats talent when talent doesn't work hard." Every day in life, as well as on the field, is an opportunity to get better. When you come to realize that you will never have that day again, you must make the most out of it. When you work harder, you give yourself a sense of satisfaction, and you always have a chance to win. So let me ask you, are you outworking Satan and his plans to have you fail? The second question is this: are you outworking your opponent so that you will not second guess if you are properly prepared? So get to work so that you can outwork your opponent, and I will see you at the plate.

Dear Mighty One,

Thank you for giving me the ability to work. Now let me prepare with you in mind. Let me work so that I have made the most of every day. Let me outwork the schemes of Satan by turning to you every day in prayer and Scripture reading. Let me outwork my opponent so that I will be victorious in your name.

Day 57

Trust the P.R.O.C.E.S.S. – One Goal

Exodus 20:1-3 ***And God spoke all these words: "I am the Lord your God, who brought you out of Egypt, out of the land of slavery. "You shall have no other gods before me.***

One of the hardest aspects of the team is getting everyone on the same playing field. What I mean by that is not the physical playing field but the mental and physiological playing field. You see, when a team plays with the same heartbeat and the same pulse, you can begin to work for one common goal. I remember one year we had a very talented team. It was full of athletes, but each one of the players had their own agenda. They wanted to know their stats and would pout if they did not get to play when and where they thought they should play. We quickly found ourselves in a one-win four-loss situation, losing against two teams we should have beat. The problem was that the team had not become one. They did not have one pulse, one heartbeat, and ultimately one common goal was absent. Fast forward one year, and we had a team with less talent and not many previous starters from the year before. Many times, we were outsized and outmatched, but we started that season off 4-0.

Why? Because we had a team that had one common goal, and that was everyone playing as hard as they could. If you are going to be successful on the field, then the team has to share one heartbeat and one goal. So let me ask you what you must do to change your demeanor so that you can play with one team goal in mind? The same goal holds in life also. Let me share with you your one goal in life as a Christian.

That goal is to live for Jesus Christ. It sounds simple, but we all know how difficult it can be. We somehow always find a way to put ourselves before Christ. The first command lets us know how to live solely for Jesus. "Thou shall have no other gods before me." You see, anything that you put above God first becomes an idol. Our motivation for everything we do; should come from having no other gods before me. When honoring God is our key priority, then it is easy to have one goal. To honor God in everything I do. So it is time to honor God in your everyday life and your sports. I will see you at the plate!

Eternal God,

You are my only God, and the one God leads to one goal. My goal is to honor you in everything that I do. I must remember that you created me for the sole purpose of honoring you and making your name great through all that I do. Forgive me when I cared more about myself than I did the team and when I cared more about stats than I did win. God, forgive me when I cared more about how I looked than how I honored you. You are my one God and my one Goal.

Day 58

Trust the P.R.O.C.E.S.S. – Outshine

Matthew 5:16 ***In the same way, let your light shine before others, that they may see your good deeds and glorify your Father in heaven.***

The word "outshine" sounds so much like a word that promotes personal accolades and self-achievements. But to outshine is more about who you are internal than the things you can accomplish. To "outshine" in the sports world means to have more character and honor than your opponent. It means that you can turn the other cheek and still stay competitive. To outshine means that people can spot who you are by how you play the game. Wins and losses do not define it. To outshine means that you not only playing hard but that you are also practicing hard. It means that you are a shining example to the younger, less seasoned players. To outshine means you do not care if you get the glory, but the spotlight is shone upon a whole and complete team. Throughout my ministry, I have heard that some people just have a glow that surrounds them, the glow of the Holy Spirit. I have met a few of these people along the way. It is just like Jesus seeps from their inner being. I often explain that they are living out what Christ told us to do when he said we were like a city on the hill, or we were like a light that was not hidden under a bowl. I remember these similar words from a recent Toby Mac hit song: Light Shines Bright.

He says in the song that he wants to reflect the Son (not the sun). And to make this third rock (which represents the earth) glow.

What if that was our goal? To make sure that our light always shines brightly. When you shine, you might just be the light that this dark world needs. Your light shines bright everywhere you go. Hey, it is time to light up, and I will see you at the plate.

Dear Morning Sun,

You are the light of the world. When there was nothing but darkness, you came and let your light shine so that we would have light to live by. Then when the world became dark again because of our sin and selfishness, you sent your Son to illuminate this dark world filled with our sin. Now, God, I ask that you illuminate me so that my light will shine bright for a world to see. Let me be your light, and let the world see your light through me. Let me shine brightly on the field as well as in my everyday life.

Day 59

Trust the P.R.O.C.E.S.S. – Compete

I Corinthians 9:25 ***God's Word Translation "Everyone who enters an athletic contest goes into strict training. They do it to win a temporary crown, but we do it to win one that will be permanent."***

The word "compete" is defined in Merriam Webster's dictionary like this: to strive consciously or unconsciously for an objective (such as position, profit, or a prize); be in a state of rivalry.[7] Sports are all about competing, yet somehow, this has diminished in this everyone gets a trophy world. The truth is that everyone should not and does not deserve a trophy. To compete means that you got into strict training so that you can, first of all, earn your right to a starting position. Then it means that you get to compete against another team that has competed for their starters, and now you compete to see who is the best. When everyone gets a trophy, it not only diminishes the competition but also absolves it. The reason that sports exist is so that we can compete. We can compete against ourselves, pushing to be the best we can be. We compete against our friends and our teammates to hopefully win the starting position over them. Finally, we compete against our opponents. I have seen many times when the team across the field or court has us outsized and outmanned. At times like this, we know we may not win, but the coach says to the team, "I just want you to compete." You see, when we compete against those that are better, then it makes us better. By competing, we show that we are striving to get better, and we are reaching toward a higher goal. It also gives us an upper hand when we are evenly matched with another opponent. When everyone gets a trophy, there is no aspiration to be better.

I knew a retired coach who returned to run the scout team for the high school he had once coached. His son was now the coach, and that is what allowed him the opportunity. Now the funny thing about the retired coach was that he was always a competitor. When I say competitor, I mean he hated to lose more than anything. I am willing to bet that he never played scout team his whole life, and if he did, it would have been such a short stint because he would have wanted to be on the first team, so it was ironic that he coached the scout team. But you know what that coach did for that scout team. He made them furious competitors because he hated to lose. This, in turn, made the starters even better because now they were being pushed by a scout team that was being led by a furious competitor. In the end, everyone got better because one person chooses to push the level of competition.

Now how do we compete in our Christian life? Are we trying to be better than the other person that sits next to us in church or youth group? No, our competition is against the evil one, not against our teammates. It is against the liar, the one that came to kill, steal, and destroy. You see, in the end, everyone does not get that trophy on judgment day. Some will hear the words "depart from me, for I never knew you." Now the sad thing is that this eternal trophy is there for everyone to accept, but it is Satan, our competitor, who does everything in his power to detour us from the trophy. Do not let Satan win; he is competing for your soul, but these words will neutralize him and send him on his way. You simply say, "Jesus, I want to play on your team. I want you to be my head coach. I want you to make me a true competitor in life. Jesus, be my Lord and Savior, I surrender all to you. Amen Now, after you have said this prayer, I will see you at the plate.

Jesus Christ Son of the One True God,

Jesus, I want to play on your team. I want you to be my head coach. I want you to make me a true competitor in life. Jesus, be my Lord and Savior, I surrender all to you. Amen.

✞

Day 60

Trust the P.R.O.C.E.S.S. -Character

Luke 21:19 (NLT) ***By standing firm, you will win your souls.***

We are no more than what our character says we are. Our character is truly what defines us. Sometimes we can fool people for a while; we can be an imposter, a fake, and a fraud. Sometimes we can even fool ourselves into thinking we are someone that we are not. We have this strange ability even to fool our hearts. A few weeks ago, we played a Friday night game against a team known to have low character. At one point in the game, one individual kept hitting our players after the whistle blew. At one point, he started a fight with our players and tried to pick a fight with one of our coaches. I could not help myself, and after the game, I approached him to shake his hand. I said this to him, "you are a good football player, but you have zero character." It does us no good to be a talented player on the field but to have zero character in life. We somehow think that winning or being the best justifies that we can do whatever we want on the field. You see, at the end of the game, the big plays will be forgotten, and most people will even forget the score. But when you have zero character on the field, it will always be remembered. Let me ask you, what kind of character do others on your team say you have? What kind of character do your opponents say that you have?

You realize that who you are to become, you are now becoming. Your character takes a lifetime to build but only moments to destroy. Christian character is one of the hardest concepts to understand in living a Christian life daily. To have a Christian character means that you cannot compartmentalize your life. It means that you are always the same, no matter who you hang around or what circumstance you are in.

It means always being like Jesus. You cannot fake Christian character because you will soon be found out. When you are found out, then you have hindered your witness for the cross. Christian character is something that, as we mature in faith, becomes easier to live out. Let me ask you have you checked your character? What does your life say you are? My prayer is that you, in all things, will be a person of Christian character even when it is not the easiest thing to do. So be a person of character, and I will see you at the plate.

The Truth, The Life, and The Way,

Grant that my whole life might be a shining example for you. My character ought to reflect the character of Christ and the example that he set as he walked the earth. When people see me, let them see you. When I respond to someone, let it be with the utmost Christian character, always taking the high road. Lord, help me not compartmentalize my life but let it be consistent no matter where I am or who I am hanging around. Thank you for your Son and the splendid example of a character he left for us to follow.

Day 61

Trust the P.R.O.C.E.S.S. -Courage

I Chronicles 28:20 (NIV) ***David also said to Solomon, his Son, "Be strong and courageous, and do the work. Do not be afraid or discouraged, for the LORD God; my God is with you. He will not fail you or forsake you until all the work for the service of the temple of the LORD is finished.***

"Courage" almost sounds like an antiquated word because it is so infrequently used. We live in a world where we think of courage as almost a thing of the past. Now, if you want to see true courage, step on any floor of the St. Jude's Children's hospital. It is there that you will see courage in patients who are all children. You will see courage in parents that refuse to give up and let a disease win. You see courage in doctors and nurses that know the percentages are against them. True courage comes when we have to fight against the odds, statistics, and numbers.

A few years ago, a young man from our Church had been diagnosed with neuroblastoma. We had gotten a group together and raised money for this young man through the team in training. We were going to run 26.2 miles for the money that had been sponsored. Now to run a marathon takes a lot of courage and stamina. I finished the race with my training partner, and we came in just a little shy of 6 hours from start to finish. My feet were killing me. My hands were swollen, and I ached in every muscle from my head to toe. But after the race, we got to see the young man that we had just run for. I thought that I had courage because I had run the marathon. But my accomplishment of running a marathon was quickly humbled as I saw this young man struggling every day just to live. It was ultimately he who had the courage. Let me ask you do you have the courage to run this race of life. We get to show courage on the field or in the gym, but we must remember that even to get to play, the game is a gift from God. Many cancer-stricken young people would rather be at practice than sitting in a hospital taking chemotherapy. The truth is that we are on the field to learn courage and how to fight the good fight. We must realize that it is a privilege to do what we do and not a right. Courage is when you feel you do not have any more or that this is redundant. It is then that we think about all of those who would just trade places with us for one day. Do you have the courage to push on even when you want to throw in the towel? So let me challenge you, find your courage, and I will see you at the plate?

Dear Great Encourager,

Dear Father, grant me wisdom to see how fortunate I am. Give me the courage to push through, push on, and never to give up. God be with those that are struggling and fighting for their life. Give me the courage to withstand persecution and the hurling of insults for standing on your promises. Courage only comes through you and the example that your Son had when he went to the cross to die a sinner's death for me. It is in the cross that I find my courage. Amen.

Day 62

Trust the P.R.O.C.E.S.S. -Confidence

2 Corinthians 3:4-5 ***Such confidence we have through Christ before God. Not that we are competent in ourselves to claim anything for ourselves, but our competence comes from God.***

People who have confidence are often perceived as cocky and arrogant, and in many instances, that presumption is correct. The pro sports market seems to be flooded with players that only thrive if they can put down others and parade around every time they make a big play. If this is the example that we take in amateur sports, we will also be seen as cocky, not confident. I would even go as far as to say that many coaches do not like to coach arrogant players because they can be cancer to a team. But I would argue that you can be confident and humble at the same time. Being confident means not that you brag about your accomplishments but that you are prepared to handle situations thrown your way. It means outperforming your opponent on the field and not with a war of words. It means giving God the glory for your accomplishments. Confidence comes from not only thinking you can win but knowing that you can win. Confidence is not confined to only the sports world but bleeds over into every other aspect of life. I would go as far as to say confidence in my faith and security in Christ is the pinnacle of confidence. You see, in faith, confidence comes from things that are not always seen. That is what makes confidence such a key component of faith. In this type of confidence, we believe that Christ is who he was and did what he said he would do for us. Christ offers us through this faith the ability to face a dark world with the confidence of light. It has the confidence that Christ is with us even when things are not going according to plan. Finally, confidence in Christ is knowing that one day we will pass from this world and share eternity with our Lord, Savior, Creator, Perfecter, the One that we have placed all of our confidence in. I challenge you in life not to be cocky and arrogant but to be confident. So, Mr./Mrs. Confidence, I will see you at the plate.

Dear Son of Man,

God, I pray that you give me holy confidence, not the confidence of arrogance and self-reliance. God, please humble me in the areas where I think I am better than I am. Help me put my confidence in the power of the cross and what that sacrifice meant for me. Thank you for giving me the confidence that I will one day live with you in eternity as your beloved heir. Help people see my confidence in the cross so that they will also put their confidence in it.

Day 63

Trust the P.R.O.C.E.S.S. -Embracing the Moments

Isaiah 18:3 (NAB) ***All you who inhabit the world, who dwell on earth, When the signal is raised on the mountain, look!***

When the trumpet blows, listen! I read this quote the other day by Mark Batterson, and I love it so much that I had to share it. It says time may be measured in minutes, but life is measured in moments. Now that quote speaks to the world of sports. We know that each game, no matter what sport, has a time frame, a span of minutes that make up-regulation. I remember during the AHSAA state championship this year (2017), our coach told the boys at halftime. You have 24 minutes of football left, and for some of you seniors, it will be the last 24 minutes of football you get to play ever. Wow, now that will make you want to go out and have some defining moments. The harsh reality is that our eligibility and our tenure will one day run out, but the moments that were created in those minutes will last forever. No one can ever take the moments from you, they are what define you, and they are a part of your story. Let's face it; everyone wants to win a trophy, but trophies are only reminders of the moments. They remind us of the hard work and extra effort that we put in. It reminds us of the lucky play that helped us beat the team supposed to beat us. It reminds us of the walk-off home run or the last strikeout. It reminds us of the stolen base or the last-second heroic touchdown run. See, when we only look at "time" as measured in minutes, we are wasting the opportunities to create moments that take your breath away.

Have you ever thought about Jesus's short life? There is some debate about how old he was when he died, but we know he was between 32 and 34 when he was crucified. Now that seems like such a brief period, as I have already lived way past that age. The significance of Jesus' life was not defined in the minutes or years that he lived, but it was measured by the moments that defined who he was and what his ministry was all about. Jesus walked on water, healed the blind and crippled, multiplied food, appeared out of nowhere, and conquered death. That is a heck of a superhero resume. We may not ever perform such defining moments, but we can make the most of every moment on the field and in life. In the sports world, no matter who you are, you will have some opportunities to have defining moments. What are you going to do when those moments present themselves? Listen, I hope you will embrace this moment, and I will see you at the plate.

Dear Sacred Wounded One,

God, the whole Scripture is filled with defining moments. Moments that define who you are and moments that help us to find who we are in you. God, help me to make the most of every opportunity so that it becomes a defining moment in my story. God, thank you for those most defining moments I will ever have, and that is the moment that I asked your Son into my heart, and I became one of your team members. Amen.

Day 64

Trust the P.R.O.C.E.S.S. -Engage

John 4:7-9 ***When a Samaritan woman came to draw water, Jesus said to her, "Will you give me a drink?"*** (His disciples had gone into the town to buy food.) ***The Samaritan woman said to him, "You are a Jew, and I am a Samaritan woman. How can you ask me for a drink?"*** (For Jews do not associate with Samaritans.)

How many times have you just zoned out because of boredom or exhaustion? In my coaching experience, I have been coaching or teaching my athletes, and they just have that deer in headlights look. Words are coming out of my mouth, but those words are not entering their ear canals or finding their way to the cerebral cortex. If we are going to be the best players that we can be, we need to be hard workers and engage with our coaches/mentors for instruction. We live in a time when social media deters from us engaging with people face to face. When we engage, it shows how much we respect who is talking to us. When we engage with people, we do not only tell them that we are listening, but we tell them that we care about them. We engage with the people we love.

When we disengage, you can bet we will miss the block, assignment, or steal signal. Part of the process is staying engaged. Jesus was great at being engaged with people. I would even argue that people, no matter who they were, had Jesus' undivided attention. The reason that he picked 12 disciples was so that he could not only teach but engage with his Talmid, which is a fancy name for teammates or students. Jesus also loved to engage with the people, even to go home to dine with them so that he could engage in their life. If you are going to be an effective witness for Jesus, you will have to engage with people. It is great to love people from a distance or pray for them, but they feel like you genuinely care about them and love them when you engage in their life. Are you ready to engage? If so, I will see you at the plate.

Dear Friend of Sinners,

We live in a world that tries to disengage us from you and your direction. We have such a hard time getting still and focusing. We have an even harder time truly engaging in people's lives. Help us not only to spend time with people but help us to engage in people. Go, you always engage with us, and we thank you that you sent your Son to engage with us face to face and not just from a distance.

Day 65

Trust the P.R.O.C.E.S.S. -Being an "Encourager"

Acts 4:36-37 (NLT) ***For instance, there was Joseph, the one the apostles nicknamed Barnabas (which means "Son of Encouragement"). He was from the tribe of Levi and came from the island of Cyprus. He sold a field he owned and brought the money to the apostles. -***

Do people around you say you are a complainer or an encourager? Would people label you as arrogant or pompous? The truth is that we live in a world where people read their press clippings or make them up. We love being praised and encouraged, but we rarely reciprocate by encouraging others. I think we do the opposite of encouraging; we almost pray that people fail. In today's world, it is hard-pressed to find an encourager. I think that teammates would play harder if they had more encouragement. I think we see the little league and recreational sports shrinking because of the lack of encouragement. Encouragement not only gives confidence but it also builds self-esteem. When someone believes in themselves, they also believe that they do great things and conquer the giants that lie in wait. I saw a great example of this last year in the college football national championship game. Alabama's quarterback had not played a good game, so they made a switch at half the time. For the rest of the game, the quarterback taken out could be seen encouraging the one who took his place. Most of the time, what you witness is when a player is taken out, you see them sulking over on the bench and just hoping their replacement messes up. Encouragement is a sign of maturity.

In the Scripture, there was a follower of Paul that was known as an encourager. He was such an encourager that the disciples gave him the nickname "Barnabus," which meant encourager. Barnabus believed in Paul when no one else did. He went to bat for Paul; if Barnabus had not spoken up for Paul, then Paul may have never got started in ministry. To be honest, if he had not started in ministry, our Bible would be missing all of the writing that Paul learned on his journeys and the advice that he gave the churches and followers of the way. Yes. Barnabus' encouragement had eternal implications. Just think that your encouragement may change not only the person you are encouraging but just may change the world. So, go out and encourage someone, and then I will see you at the plate.

Dear Awesome in Power,

Help me to be an encourager and not a complainer. Help me to support the player that even takes my place. Let me encourage those that are less talented and even those that are on the sidelines. God's encouragement does not just change a person; it changes the world. Thank you for the greatest encourager of all your Son, Jesus. He not only encouraged but gave his life so that we would have the greatest encouragement of all, the encouragement of eternal life. The promise of eternal life ought to lead us to be an encourager for the sake of the cross.

Day 66

Trust the P.R.O.C.E.S.S. -Staying "Enthusiastic"

1 Peter 4:16 ***"Yet if anyone suffers as a Christian, let him not be ashamed, but let him glorify God in this matter."***

Sometimes when the game or score is not going our way, it is virtually impossible to keep our enthusiasm. I have watched leaders lose their influence over a team because they become deflated and lose their enthusiasm for the game. To be a team leader, we must stay enthused even when we are having a losing season or play a terrible game. Enthusiasm is just a by-product of our attitude. When we can keep our enthusiasm and encouragement in the middle of adversity and turmoil, we can be an encourager to those around us. A good, strong leader does not let the outcome change what they value or their love for the game. Enthusiasm does not come from one's wins and losses but comes from a love of the game. In the Scripture, I am always amazed at how Paul kept his enthusiasm in the midst of persecution and imprisonment. Most of us would have denied our faith if we had just endured some of what Paul had been through. The scripture tells us that the more Paul endured, the more enthused he became for his faith and love of Christ. Paul knew that his suffering would lead people to come to know Jesus. If Paul can endure torture, we can endure when the win vs. loss columns do not add up. Let me encourage you as Paul would. No matter what, stay enthused, and I will see you at the plate.

Dear Heavenly Head Coach,

Thank you for allowing me to keep my enthusiasm amid adversity. Thank you for all the saints that went before me that set this example for me. Help me to be an example to all who witness my enthusiasm. Thank you for being enthusiastic about me even when I am at my worst. It truly shows your never-ending unconditional love.

Day 67

Trust the P.R.O.C.E.S.S. -Empowered by the Spirit

John 14:15-17 ***"If you love me, keep my commands. And I will ask the Father, and he will give you another advocate to help you and be with you forever— the Spirit of truth. The world cannot accept him because it neither sees him nor knows him. But you know him, for he lives with you and will be in you.***

We have often heard that power comes from within, but as Christian athletes, the power comes from even further down. Our power comes from the Holy Spirit. There are times when what we have is not enough; we face a task or situation that is bigger than our strength. It is at that point that we must ask the Holy Spirit to intercede for us. The Holy Spirit is the hidden secret weapon we can unleash when we cannot do it independently. Jesus even tells the disciples at the end of his time on earth that there would be one that was more powerful than he was. One that is known as the paraclete, which means advocate, adversary, or helper. You see, when you step up to the plate with a full count and bases loaded, you are not alone. When you stand on that free throw line with no time left and a chance to tie the game, you are not alone. When you just got the results that it is a torn ACL, you are not alone. See, just like an electrical appliance must be plugged into a power source to work, the same is true when it comes to us tapping into the power of the Holy Spirit. The Spirit never leaves us to face adversity on our own. The Holy Spirit is our main trainer and workout partner. It can not only help us when we are in need, but if we listen to its still small voice, it can also hold us accountable to be better, to train harder, and to become more focused. The Spirit will empower us to move beyond what we can do on our own accord. My prayer for you is that you will grab that Holy Spirit power, and I will see you at the plate.

Dear Training Partner,

Please send your spirit to guide and direct me through all aspects of life. Let me remember that I am never alone that you will always continually pour out your spirit upon me. The Spirit gives me the power that I never realized was possible. Thank you for not leaving me as an orphan but leaving the Spirit to help guide and lead me. Empower me with the Holy Spirit so that others will see where my power comes from.

✞

Day 68

Trust the P.R.O.C.E.S.S. -Sacrifice

Romans 3:25 ***"God presented Christ as a sacrifice of atonement, through the shedding of his blood—to be received by faith."***

Sacrifice: What a word! It is a word that we do not hear very often. The reason is that we are bombarded with a world that is self-serving, not sacrificial. It is what is taught, and for many people, it is what defines their life. Their goal is to get as much as they can while they can. I think one of the most valuable lessons in sports is learning what sacrifice is. To think outside of yourself and to think about everyone else on the team. I used to love to call the sacrifice bunt when I was coaching softball. This meant that a player gave up their opportunity to improve their batting average or hit the walk-off home run for the team's sake. In this scenario, the batter never gets the credit; it is the runner that crosses the plate. Now the truth of this is that without the sacrifice, the run never scores. That is just one example of how one must sacrifice for the greater good of the team. You know, living as a Christian is all about sacrifice. Jesus set that example for us when he willingly gave up his life so that we could have eternal life. If we would just stop and thank Jesus for the sacrifice he made for us right before getting on the field or court, we would play differently. I think it would help give new meaning to what team and sacrifice are all about. Just remember, Jesus did not lay down a sacrifice bunt but a sacrifice of his own life so that we could cross the plate of life and enter into heaven. Now that ought to make you want to be a sacrifice. SO, right now, thank God for sending his Son to be your sacrifice, and I will see you at the plate.

Dear Sacrificial Lamb,

Thank you for sending your Son to give up his life as a sacrifice so that I would not be forfeited at the end of my life. God, let me now seek ways for my own life to be a sacrifice so that others will come to accept you as their Lord and Savior. Make my life a living sacrifice for the entire world to see.

Day 69

Trust the P.R.O.C.E.S.S. - Sweat and Tears

Luke 22:44 (NLT) ***He prayed more fervently, and he was in such agony of spirit that his sweat fell to the ground like great drops of blood.***

One of my coaches that I played for in high school used to say you were not practicing unless you were putting out blood, sweat, and tears. There were some days where I did put out all three of those things. Sometimes to the point where I thought it would just be easier to quit or just tuck it in. Have you ever felt that way? Sometimes we think to ourselves, is this sweat and tears worth the outcome? You know practice is more than just muscle memory; it is also training the mind to overcome when you feel you cannot carry on. We have all known those players that have given in and given up. The sweat and tears not only defeated them physically, but it defeated them mentally. Sports is not just about training the body, but it is about training the mind. Part of the PROCESS is making sure that you are mentally tough so that when the game is online or when life is on the line, you can push through the adversity. Jesus experienced this immense pressure when he went to the garden on the night when he would be arrested and then crucified. I think knowing you were going to be crucified would bring anyone to blood, sweat, and tears. He prayed for three hours, and the Scripture says that he sweat blood. Jesus could handle the physical pain that he would endure, but the mental anguish was overwhelming. So, he set the prayer bar for us when he was broken by the weight of our blood, sweat, and tears; he went to his Father and asked him to walk with him through this overwhelming situation. You know that you have the same opportunity. You have a heavenly Father that will give you the strength to make it through the sweat and tears. So right now, stop and go to the garden and pray, then dry your tears and I will see you at the plate.

Dear Comforting Father,

Sometimes I feel broken by the weight of the world. Sometimes I feel it would be easier to give up and give in. God, I ask that you give me strength when I cannot muster it on my own. God, help me to remember that I am not only training my body, but I am training my mind. Help me to persevere through the sweat and tears. Help me to realize that they are part of the process and that they are making me stronger. I can get through this with your help.

Day 70

Trust the P.R.O.C.E.S.S. - "Sinicism"

Mathew 16:23 ***Jesus turned and said to Peter, "Get behind me, Satan! You are a stumbling block to me; you do not have in mind the concerns of God, but merely human concerns."***

Cynicism is a mindset that is solely set on the negative. It is not easy to sway someone that is cynical. Have you ever been around someone that is cynical?

Cynical people make terrible teammates because they have no trust of the team around them. Even worse than that is when we become "cynical," which leads to "sinicism." This is where we do not trust that God has our best interest in mind; it is that we trust in our abilities more than we trust in God. This will lead us away from God and into sin. Yes, cynicism will always lead to "sinicism." Someone who is "sinical" will only care about their stats. They want to be heroes, and they even have a hard time giving the glory to another teammate if they were the ones that hit the walk-off or made the last shot, or scored the last touchdown. There is an interaction in the Scripture that sometimes takes us by surprise. It is a conversation between Jesus and Peter. In the conversation, Peter scolds Jesus because he shares that he must suffer many things. It is at this point that Jesus turns to him and rebukes him, and says, get behind me, Satan. He tells Peter that he has become a stumbling block. The truth is that Peter's cynicism leads to his "sinicism." He only has his interest in mind and not the interest of the team or, in this case, the world. Jesus came to save all and live the father's agenda, not the agenda of the world. So let go of that "cynicism," and I will see you at the plate.

Dear Almighty,

Please help me not to be cynical, which leads to being "sinical." God help those on my team that are cynical to release their cynicism and give it to you. God, so many times, I want to be the star, but let me celebrate when someone else has the defining moment. Humble me, break me and mold me into your image. And let me say when he steps in my way, get behind me, Satan, because I am all in for God.

Day 71

Trust the P.R.O.C.E.S.S. -Standing Firm

2 Thessalonians 2:15 ***Therefore, brothers, stand firm and hold to the traditions you were taught, either by our message or by our letter.***

When you make the team or join a team, you are surrounded by many different players from many different places. A team is made up of people from different families, races, values, and even morals. This diversity is one of the most challenging aspects of turning individuals into a team. When you are on the field, it is easy to be in harmony and work together. Hopefully, everyone on the team has the same goals in mind. Hopefully, each player is doing their best so that they can make those around them even better. But all those different personalities and people can present a challenge off of the field. Many times, athletes come onto a team with certain convictions and values that have been instilled either through parents, teachers, or coaches. Being around all these other players off the field can lead to our convictions and morals being challenged. We can find ourselves in situations where we are losing ground in what we believe and stand on. There have been many athletes that have compromised rather than stood their ground, and they lost everything. It is sometimes hard to stand our ground when these are our teammates and our extended family. But by standing your ground, you just might be the witness they are looking for. Yes, you will get ribbed, and you will get hammered, but if it is for standing your ground, then you have nothing to be ashamed of. Standing firm is standing on what you believe in and why you believe it. Too many people today are blown like chaff in the wind. They go with the flow, even if it means compromising what they have always believed in. Being a part of a team allows you to stand firm in your convictions for Jesus. Jesus held firm all the way to the cross; he never let his disciples (teammates) get in the way of his goal – the goal of dying so that we could stand firm in our faith. So stand firm, and I will see you at the plate.

My Firm Foundation,

God, first and foremost, be my foundation. Let me stand upon the rock, and that rock is Jesus. God, I have often not stood firm, and I have ruined my witness and opportunity to stand in the gap for you. God, I know even those close to me will try to pull me one way or the other but help me stand firm. God, you are my firm foundation, my rock, my redeemer, and my Savior. Upon the name of Jesus, I will stand, and I will not be put asunder.

✞

Day 72

Trust the P.R.O.C.E.S.S. -Strength Comes in Numbers

Joshua 5:9-11 ***The armed guard marched ahead of the priests who blew the trumpets, and the rear guard followed the ark. All this time, the trumpets were sounding. But Joshua had commanded the army, "Do not give a war cry, do not raise your voices, do not say a word until the day I tell you to shout. Then shout!" So, he had the ark of the LORD carried around the city, circling it once. Then the army returned to camp and spent the night there.***

I have witnessed some teams that only play the best players and rarely give them a break. They have lots of players that just stand by and watch, hoping to get in the game. Many of the players on the sidelines are not as talented as the starters, but you wear your starters out by repeatedly playing them. Then at the end of the game, you suffer a loss because you did not find your strength in numbers. We must learn when to sub and when to coach with the end result in mind. This means we need to look at more than the scoreboard. Sometimes as a starter, it is hard to take a break or allow someone else to play. But we must remember that there is strength in numbers. This concept was even present in biblical times. I recently preached on Jericho's walls and how the people came at the walls with no weapons or battering rams. They simply came to the wall in numbers, and it was in those numbers that they found strength. The same is true in our spiritual life. We need to surround ourselves with people that are believers and prayer warriors. We find our strength to carry on in numbers. Jesus even found his strength in numbers when he surrounded himself with twelve disciples. Remember, the reason that we have a team is so that we have strength in numbers. Hey, guess what? Get off that bench; you are up. See you at the plate.

Dear God of Perpetual Strength,

God, I want to always be the center and in the limelight, but I sometimes just need a break. I need to rest and recoup my energy so that, in the end, I can give everything I have. I need to give others the opportunity to play and give their best, and I need to support them and thank them for filling in. God, help me realize that strength comes in numbers, and that is why I need to surround myself with other followers of Jesus.

✞

Day 73

Trust the P.R.O.C.E.S.S. - Seasoned Veteran

Proverbs 9:9 ***Instruct a wise man, and he will be wiser still; teach a righteous man, and he will add to his learning.***

We are always amazed when we hear of a professional athlete that has been in the league for 10+ years. The press always refers to them as seasoned veterans. It is amazing to see these veteran's wisdom and knowledge of the game that they have learned through the experience of longevity. They not only know what to do on the field, but they also know what to do off the field. As part of a successful process, you know you need seasoned veterans or upper-level students that can lead. I have watched college basketball struggle because of the one-and-done rule. Many teams have talent but have no maturity because they lack upper-level students' leadership. We all know that upper-level students and veterans help to show us the ropes. They help us to mature and teach us the hidden aspects of the game.

The process cannot be successful if we do not have these seasoned players. You know, in life, it is no different. One of the aspects missing in the culture today is the disconnect between the younger and older generations. We learn from those who have been through what we are going through. The most important concept in learning how to be a great spouse is learning from someone with years of experience. The great way to be a great coach is to serve under someone that is a great coach. The great way to be a Godly man or woman is to be mentored by a seasoned veteran. Find someone that has already been through what you are going through and ask them to walk with you. A seasoned veteran in faith has been through many seasons and has weathered many trials and tribulations. They can make you a better player, and they can make you a better person. Do not be scared to ask someone to walk along with you because they may just have been waiting for that opportunity. So, find a seasoned veteran, and I will see you at the plate.

Dear Crucified Savior,

Please line me up with those that will help in my maturation. God help me to humble myself to learn from those that have been where I am headed. Let them teach me even when I do not want to hear what they have to say. Help me to have a receptive heart and to be able to endure the criticism and instruction. God, I am so green and ripe for this learning process. Please send me one to help me on the field and help me in my everyday walk with you.

Day 74

Nothing but Hype

Proverbs 27:2 ***Let another praise you, and not your mouth; A stranger, and not your lips.***

The other day I watched as one of the powers five schools kicked off its football season at home to a sold-out crowd. They had a new coach, were wearing brand new uniforms, and playing a prime-time televised game. They knew that the entire world would be watching as it was the only televised game that night. The team was so excited, and there seemed to be electricity in the air. The team stood in a huddle to kick off, and they danced and shouted; the stadium was going wild, the sidelines were waving towels and pumping up the crowd. It seemed that the team was ready to turn around the dismal year that they had the previous year. Yes, they seemed ready, and there was a ton of hype. But within the first six minutes of the game, all of the hype had given way, and they now trailed by 10 points. The truth is that they were playing horribly. It was then that it set in my mind that they were not different from the year before; there was just a lot of hype. You know we can talk it up, yell and scream, run-through banners with fog machines with cannons going off, but it is just a lot of hype if we are not prepared. You know many years ago, one of my coaches would say to us, "talk is cheap, boys." We need to let our play speak louder than our words. We need to be more than hype. We need to be more than hype. You know our Christian walk can be the same way. It can be a lot of hype with very little action. We love to talk about following Christ, loving our neighbor, and committing to pray, but the truth is that our everyday walk does not match our talk. Talk is cheap, and when we boast, brag, or hype ourselves and do not perform, we ruin our witness. So, forget the hype and glamour, and I will see you at the plate.

Dear Yeshua,

Let my walk speak for itself. Let me only bring the hype to you and not hype myself up. Let me not think too highly of myself, or I will forget to give you the glory. Help me to walk with integrity and humbleness. Let the only hype in my life be the hype of the cross. Talk is cheap, but my actions will show the world why all my hype is found in you.

✞

Day 75

Too Hard on Self

Proverbs 28:26 NLT ***Those who trust their insight are foolish, but anyone who walks in wisdom is safe.***

How many times have you made a mistake, and you got down on yourself in such a way that it changed the way you played the rest of the game? Sometimes in life, we are our own worst enemy. It is alright to strive to be the best we can be, but if we get so focused on our mistakes that we lose focus, we are doomed to fail. I have seen it repeatedly where a player gets so focused on the mistakes that they lose their love for the game. The other day I witnessed a young man come off the field; he had made a great diving catch to keep the ball in the infield but had not been able to get them out of first. When he came off the field, the coach said, great diving stop, his response was, "yeah, but I still did not get them out." It was at that point that his dad turned to me and said, "he is so hard on himself that he cannot enjoy the game." We need to make sure that we are not so caught up in production that we lose the love for the game. In the Scriptures, Peter tends to be the disciple that is hardest on himself. He is the one that got out of the boat when 11 others stayed seated. He is the one that cuts a man's ear off, defending Jesus. He is the one that also denied his best friend three times. Peter then went away broken and feeling dejected. But Peter did not let these mistakes define him. Instead, he preached the gospel to everyone he came into contact with after his Savior's death. If he had been his own worst enemy, the gospel would have never gotten spread the way that it did. We must always strive to do better and be better, but we must also learn to forgive ourselves. We must not be so hard on ourselves that we forget how to love life and the game that God has allowed us to play. So, forget about that last at-bat, and I will see you at the plate.

Dear Lord of the Dance,

God, sometimes I am my own worst enemy. I want to be the best I can be, but when

I fail, it puts me in a funk. Please help me to see that you will never give up on me. That in time of doubt or apprehension, you are with me, and you are for me. And the Scripture says, "That if you are for us then who can be against us." I need to treasure that in my heart so that it becomes part of my DNA. Amen.

Day 76

Playing Favorites

Romans 10:11-13 ***As Scripture says, "Anyone who believes in him will never be put to shame." For there is no difference between Jew and Gentile—the same Lord is Lord of all and richly blesses all who call on him, for, "Everyone who calls on the name of the Lord will be saved."***

This week on SportsCenter, I heard a coach responding to criticism about him picking one quarterback over another. The media was being so hard on him because the one he did not pick to start was transferring, and he was losing a valuable player. His reasoning for his decision was that the one he had named as a starter was just a better fit for the offense. The media's issue was that the other quarterback was older, more experienced, and had led the team to many wins. The truth is that in sports, your job is always being interviewed for, and you are always being challenged. You are always in competition. It is what makes athletics so great. It is what teaches you real life, and that hard work will pay off. We all know some teams play daddy ball and other organizations where politics may keep the best players off the field, but most coaches play the best that have the greatest potential to help them win. So, you may not be the coach's favorite, but keep working hard and doing the right thing, and before you know it, you just may be the one starting.

Now let me shift gears here and tell you a truth about God. God does not have to play favorites. Everyone on God's team is a starter. There is no 2nd and 3rd string. God does not play daddy ball or start the kid whose parents paid for the jerseys. No, Jesus came so that all could have life and life to the fullest. You are number one on God's depth chart. That is such a great promise that Christ came so that all may have a position on God's team. The day that you ask Jesus into your heart, you became a starter. But if you have not asked Jesus into your heart, then let today be the day that you join the starting team, and I will see you at the plate.

Dear Gracious Lord and Savior,

Thank you for putting Christ on this earth to organize the team. To give everyone a chance to be a starter. It is not a sense of entitlement but a sense of sacrifice. You gave everything so that everyone would be included. It was the only way that you could save the whole world by giving your Son to be our sacrifice. God, thank you that I am not the second or 3rd team, but I am number one to you.

Day 77

"Intensity Under Control"

Proverbs 16:32 ***Better a patient person than a warrior, one with self-control than one who takes a city.***

Is it possible to play with reckless abundance and still play under control? I played football with a guy in college that was the hardest-nosed all-out player I had ever seen. He was not very big, but he would wreak havoc on every offense that he faced. His only problem was that he could not control his temper. I remember one game; in particular, he picked a fight before the game ever started and did so without his helmet. The result of that lack of control was him missing the first half while getting his head stitched. You see, there were so many times that his lack of control would cost us penalties and would cost him playing time. He played all four years in college and never did learn how to play with intensity and still stay under control. The sad thing is that this also bled over into his life after college. Somehow, we need to learn how to play and do life with great intensity and passion and, at the same time, be under control. Coaches love players that give all they have, but coaches need players to do this under control. So how do we achieve this? The answer is that we make God our controller. We play for him and go all out, but we do this without bringing embarrassment or shame to the Lord.

There is a funny word that Jesus uses in the Scripture. The word is meekness, and the context he uses it in does not seem to fit. "The meek will inherit the earth." When we look around our dog-eat-dog world, we know that it is intense individuals that inherit. So what could be meant here? Well, Jesus is talking about playing with intensity and still playing under control. The Greek word for this is "praus." Here is how Strong's Concordance translates it. The root (pra-) means more than "meek." Biblical meekness is not a weakness but refers to exercising strength under control – demonstrating power without undue harshness.[8] This example was used to differentiate horses. The "meek" horses were the ones that had been broken and could be ridden. The other horses were wild and were out of control; they were of no use to people. Both had power as they were powerful animals, but the meek ones were not only powerful but were harnessed under control. So, let me encourage you to play and do life with "meekness." That means playing with intensity while under control. So, bring that intensity with you, and I will see you at the plate.

Dear God of Abraham,

Please help me to be meek and strong. Let me be intense and still under control. Let me be under your control and not try to control my own intensity. Your Son set the example of how to be intense and still be in total control. Take control of my life, and you lead me. Help me to never bring shame to you and your kingdom. I want to be the broken spirit that is led by the Holy Spirit. God, I want to be meek. Amen.

Day 78

The Rebuilding Process

2 Corinthians 12:9-10 ***But he said to me, "My grace is sufficient for you, for my power is made perfect in weakness." Therefore, I will boast all the more gladly about my weaknesses so that Christ's power may rest on me. 10 That is why, for Christ's sake, I delight in weaknesses, in insults, in hardships, in persecutions, in difficulties. For when I am weak, then I am strong.***

How hard is it to go to the final round of the playoffs one year and then go 0-10 the next year? The fans turn against you, the administration turns against you, and sometimes even your team turns against you. Have you ever been in one of those rebuilding years? The talent is gone, and the leadership is gone. The DNA of the whole team has changed. We all go through the rebuilding process at some time in our life. Sometimes in baseball or softball, we call it the slump. The truth is that rebuilding and slumps are just part of life. The most important thing to our learning process in a rebuilding season is what God is trying to teach us. He may be trying to teach us how to handle disappointment, as well as success. He is also teaching us that there are victories even when we are losing. The world does not accept or understand loss, but how we handle it will speak to our character and who we are. It is easy to follow Christ when everything is going well. When we are on top, and everyone is singing our praises, we can follow right along, giving God all the praise for our success. But are we able to give God glory during the rebuilding process? I mean, is he still not with us? Is he still not working and walking right beside us? It is so easy while going through that rebuilding process just to give up, "to tucker on in." During these times, we must prop our faith upon Christ and remember that even in failure and rebuilding, Jesus loves us. It is not just in our success that God loves us but even in the midst of our failure that he loves us. The truth is that if you play or coach long enough, you are going to have a rebuilding year. You may be in that season right now, but listen to this, "God loves you right now even in the midst of the struggle." So even though you are in a slump, grab a bat, and I will see you at the plate.

Dear Sustainer,

God, I am struggling. It seems like I am being pressed from every angle. I sometimes feel like I have failed you and failed others. Help me to realize that I will get through this season. Thank you for the success that I have had in the past. Let me give you glory now as I did when we were winning. You are the same God, regardless of my success. Thank you for loving me even when the world is against me. Help me to rebuild but help me to remember that when I am struggling, you are carrying me. Thank you for loving me through this slump. Amen.

Day 79

The "It" Factor

1 Samuel 16:7 ***But the Lord said to Samuel, "Do not consider his appearance or his height, for I have rejected him. The Lord does not look at the things people look at. People look at the outward appearance, but the Lord looks at the heart."***

Have you ever seen a young athlete and just knew that they had the "it" factor? This last week, my son played in a middle school football game, and the other team had a running back that was big, strong, and fast. He had the "it" factor. He was better than any other player on the field. He not only had speed, but he had made up his mind that he would fight through every tackle that was placed upon him. I turned to somebody in the stands, and I told them you would see that kid playing somewhere on Saturdays. The reality is that sports are not the only arena where we see people with the "it" factor. It happens in the academic world. My daughter has a friend that went to a K-12 school – a very small school in a farming town, and he scored just 2 points from perfect on his ACT. Then there are those gifted at music; it just seems that they are in sync with the music. It seems that the notes, chords, and charts have been burned in their being since birth. Yes, if we look around our world, we will see people with the "it" factor. The truth is maybe you are the one with the "it" factor.

What does it look like to have the "it" factor when it comes to our relationship with Christ? The funny thing is that God's "it" factor is not something we see in appearance or even performance. The "it" factor, as it relates to God, comes from the heart. So often, as athletes, we look at size or body language, and we think that this person has the "it" factor. Then we watch them play or perform, and we find out that the outward appearance is merely a façade. You know this is why the "it" factor to God is not the outward appearance but what is in your heart. You can look the part, say the right things, and still not have your heart in the right place. I really think that this is what it means to play with heart. We may not look the part or be the biggest, fastest, or strongest, but we have the "it" factor in our hearts. The Scripture is truly clear that God does not look at the outward appearance but at one's heart. Let me ask you, do you have the "it" factor in your walk with Jesus? If not, I suggest you look into your heart, and then I will see you at the plate.

Dear Heart Mender,

Thank you for not judging me based on size or even my performance. Thank you for looking inside my heart and helping me to see who I am. God, I know that my heart is the hub of my very being. My heart is really who I am. So, God, if you look upon me and see deficits with my heart, then help me to rid them. Thank you once again for sending your Son that helped to pattern how I should align my heart. Lord, break my heart for what breaks yours. Amen.

✞

Day 80

Do Not Fear

2 Chronicles 20:15 ***This is what the Lord says to you: 'Do not be afraid or discouraged because of this vast army. For the battle is not yours, but God's.***

Sometimes we are defeated before we ever step onto the field. We have read the press, and we have listened to the talking heads, and everyone has said you have no chance. We are defeated because, in our hearts and mind, we feel inadequate. The other team is undefeated and is stacked with 5-star athletes. The fact is that we have let fear conquer us. How many times have you lived out this scenario? Did you know that in the Scripture, God tells us not to fear? As a matter of fact, there are 366 references to do not fear; that is one for every day of the year, including leap year. Being scared not only defeats us on the field, but it defeats us in our hearts. The story of David and Goliath is a splendid example of how he should face our fear.

David refused to listen to the talking heads. Eliab, his brother, told him he was too small and needed to get back to the little sheep he tended to. Saul told him he could not win but asked if he would at least wear his armor to look the part when he was defeated. Did David listen to those voices? No. David found his strength in the Lord. He refused to fear because the worst that could happen was that he could lose, but with God's help, he would win. You see, we need not fear because we do not fight this battle alone. Any competition that we go into, we go into with the help of the mighty one, our Lord and Savior Jesus Christ. You may not win every contest, but at least do not fear going into the battle. "Fear not" because God is with you and will always be with you. You are not defeated even when you lose because you did not fear, but you went into the fight, and you did so with the confidence of God. So, fear not, and I will see you at the plate.

Dear Mighty Warrior,

Thank you for going into the battle with me. Thank you for giving me confidence when everyone around me has told me that I cannot succeed. Thank you for giving me strength when no one believes that I can do it. God, thank you for helping me believe so that I can show others on the team that they believe. Thank you that even when I lose, I am not a loser to you. God, I will fear not because you faced death without fear, and you did that for me. I am a confident warrior, and in every battle that I face, you are always with me. The battle is not mine; the battle is the Lord's. Amen.

✞

Day 81

Worth the Pain

I Corinthians 12: 8-9 ***Three times I pleaded with the Lord to take it away from me. 9But he said to me, "My grace is sufficient for you, for my power is made perfect in weakness." Therefore, I will boast all the more gladly about my weaknesses so that Christ's power may rest on me.***

The phrase Endurance sports just brings pain to mind. The hours spent training and pushing your body past the threshold of what is possible. In your training, how many times have you had to push through the pain in order to get the result? It is never easy to push through when your body says, "stop." But we know that when we push a little harder, go a little further, do one more lap, or rep, we are preparing ourselves for the battle that lies ahead. It is often a coach pushing us, and we just wish they would just decide to call it quits or get an emergency phone call. But then, when the game is online, or the finish is in question, we have the ability to push through the pain to achieve the goal or victory that was placed before us. We get to the point where we are convinced that the coach just loves to see us in pain. In life, you are going to have pain. You are going to have situations that you are going to have to push through to get through. Often, the pain in our life is a way of God preparing us for what lies ahead. We often pray for God to take the pain away, and yet it continues. So, we ask why? It is often preparing us for lies ahead or maybe God's way of keeping us humble. There will always be struggles in life, but through those struggles, we become more than conquerors. Paul had a thorn in his flesh that he asked God to remove. Now there has been some debate as to whether this was a physical element or a spiritual element. But what we do know is that the struggle was real. Let me ask you, what are you struggling with? What keeps reoccurring? Now switch your question and rather than ask why, ask what for. What is God teaching me through this? What is it that I am not doing, and finally, how will God use this? So even though you may be in pain, I will see you at the plate.

Dear Perfector of faith,

God, I so often just want you to remove the struggle and the pain. I just want everything to be fine all the time. But in time, our test will become our testimony, and our trial will become our tribulation. God, it is not if or why we are struggling, but the question is, what are you teaching us from this struggle? God, you are constantly preparing me for things to come. Thank you that in my weakness, you give me strength. Lastly, thank you that one day I will dwell in the house of the Lord forever, and there will be no pain at all.

Day 82

On the List

Revelation 3:5 ***He who overcomes will thus be clothed in white garments, and I will not erase his name from the book of life, and I will confess his name before My Father and before His angels.***

Have you ever tried out for a team or position, and they told you that they would post the list of who had made it tomorrow? Now some of the more gifted athletes knew they would be on the list, so there was no loss of sleep or anxiety. Then there are those who are not as gifted or others who may have had a bad tryout, and they are nervous that their name may not be on the posted list. They know that there will only be a limited number of spots for those not as talented, and worry has set in. They often go home from the try-out, fretting what may be the outcome of the list. Will my name be on it? How will I respond if it is not on it? What will people think of me if my name is not on the list? Yes, this can be a very pretentious time in the life of an athlete. It can be a defining moment for some people. If your name is on the list, you can feel that your hard work has paid off; if your name is not on the list, you will have a decision to make. The first thing you will contemplate is if this is the end of your playing career. Is it time to move on? The other thing that this may do is motivate you to work harder to give it another try. (Remember, Michael Jordon, got cut when he was in high school.) The other option is that God may have another direction that he wants to take your life. There may be a spot on another team or event that God wants to use you. It may be a place that lends itself to your specific skill set.

However, there is one list that you do not have to worry about making; you just have to put your name on it. That is God's Team list. It does not have a depth chart or strings; it is just a list of those who have asked him to come into their heart and be their life coach. To sign up for God's team means that you have accepted Jesus as your Lord and Savior and have asked him to be your best friend. If you have made this decision, then one day, you will not have to fret walking up to the list to see if your name is on it. No, when you get to heaven, you will have the team captain, Number 777, Jesus, set up and show you that your name is on the list. Yes, your name is on the list, and it is right next to his name. So now that you know your name is on the lineup, I will see you at the plate.

Dear EL ROI, (seeing)

Thank you for including me on your list. The only list that matters in life is your list. The eternal list. Thank you for sending your Son to put me on that list. I need never worry that I am not included or will that I will be left out. You have written my name in the Lambs Book of Life. You have written it in there with the permanent blood of your Son Jesus Christ. It was by the sacrifice of his life that you opened the book to all who choose to join your team through their acceptance and Baptism. Now help me to share this book with others that have yet to be placed on your team.

Day 83

The Blame Game

Genesis 3:13 (NLT) ***Then the LORD God asked the woman, "What have you done?" "The serpent deceived me," she replied. "That's why I ate it."***

Have you ever made an excuse because you were not prepared? Have you ever had to make an excuse as to why you lost? You had not put in the work, or you had not given your best every day. Some people are habitual excuse-makers. They have a reason for every time they fail or do not live up to their potential. The truth is that in sports, we love to make excuses for why we lost. The number one complaint is that the referees cost us the game. But hold on, you lost by 35 points. The second is that the other team cheated. We blame it on the weather, the field conditions. Yes, we are good at playing the blame game. But I think that sometimes God just wants us to owe up to the fact that we were not prepared, the other team was better, we got outcoached, and we got outplayed. We are so good at playing the blame game, and if we do not change this, then at some point, our life becomes an excuse of what we hoped to do but never worked to achieve it. Excuses have been around since the creation of man. Do you remember when Adam and Eve sinned, and God asked them about it? Eve blamed the serpent, and Adam blamed the woman. The sin aspect was that they both had been told what they were to do, but they refused to follow, so they tried to excuse their behavior. What compounds our sin is when we do not admit that we have made a mistake and need to repent. Yes, repent, that means that we learn from our sins and failures, and next time we do not have an excuse because we succeeded in making a change. Your coaches and God do not want us to play the blame game; they want us to own our mistakes and make changes. So, quit playing the blame game, own it, and then I will see you at the plate.

Dear EL-GIBHOR, (Mighty God)

I have made so many excuses for my behavior and sin. I was just hoping I could excuse it away, but most of the time, this just escalated the sin. God help me to own up to the mistakes I make. Help me to take responsibility for my actions. Help me to realize the only thing I can truly control is myself. God, I am going to own it, and I am going to change it. Thank you that your Son gave his life so I would never have an excuse for not inheriting eternal life.

Day 84

Are You Giving It All You Got?

James 1:7 ***"Every good gift and every perfect gift is from above, coming down from the Father of lights with whom there is no variation or shadow due to change."***

I read a quote the other day when I was doing sermon prep, which stuck with me. It is a quote from Steve Prefontaine, who was one of the greatest American runners in history. This is what the quote said, "To give anything less than your best is to sacrifice the gift." The reason this stuck with me is that as a coach and pastor, I have seen so many people waste the gifts that God has given them. I have watched people with so much talent throw it away because of bad choices. I have watched as people simply did not push themselves to go harder and to be better. I am always amazed at athletes who only give about half an effort and still expect to improve. It shocks me to watch players take plays off and then wonder how they are behind on the scoreboard. What amazes me is that many athletes take for granted that their gifts are God-given gifts. To not use your gifts to their full ability is to not only short-change yourself, but it is also an omission against God. God gave you those gifts so that you could glorify him through your talents and your play. God understands that sometimes you are going to fail but expects failure to be made going full speed. I used to have a coach that would say, "I do not care if you make a mistake; you just better make it going full speed." He wanted us just to put forth our best all the time. How many times in the Scripture do we see someone that decided to waste the gifts that God had given them? I am reminded of Moses, who had prepared his whole life to lead the people out of Egypt. God appears to him, and he immediately makes excuses for why he could not do it. I love God's response to him. God essentially says, you just go all out, and I will do the rest. God just expected Moses to put forth everything he had; God would take care of the rest. I will never forget the day that a top Division One coach came to watch one of our linemen play in the state playoff game. The young man had already verbally committed to this program and would sign shortly after the season. But that never happened; as coaches, we knew that this young man had the speed, size, and talent to play at the next level, but he was lazy and tended to take plays off. This day, in particular, he took lots of plays off and essentially was benched for his lack of effort. After the game, the college coach approached the young man and told him he was resending his scholarship offer. You see, people are watching to see if you are using what God has given you, so are you using your gifts to their full potential? Now is time to go all out, and I will see you at the plate.

Dear Kingdom Come Near,

Thank you for the gifts and talents you have given me. My prayer is that I will not misuse or hold out on giving you my all. God, for me not to go all out is to cheat myself, my team, and ultimately to cheat you. You gave all you had when you gave your Son Jesus, who gave his all and died for my sins. There is no greater example of someone that has given everything they have than Jesus, my Savior, and my friend.

✞

Day 85

F.O.C.U.S.

Proverbs 4:25 ***Let your eyes look directly forward, and your gaze be straight before you.***

This week we are going to focus on F.O.C.U.S. When I am out riding my bike, sometimes, I look down at the computer on my phone, and I have gotten off the course. There is a button I can press that helps me get back on course; it is the re-centering button. This button tells me exactly where I am and how I can get back on course. Yes, it is so easy to forget why we are doing what we are doing? We get so caught up in the outcome that we forget to focus on the now and how we can get better at our skills. Today is the only day that you have guaranteed to get better. So, focus on the now and do not think ahead. When we learn to focus, we are able to see what we are doing wrong. Focus helps others to give us advice and criticism as to how our technique is off. When we learn to focus, we are able to see that there are those around us that are helping to make us great. When we focus, we can see the big picture.

The picture that this is more than a game; it is a time for us to see that this game is going to benefit us in every aspect of life. Yes, the truth is that we are moving so fast that life has become a blur, and now we need to adjust the diopter. The diopter is the adjustment on binoculars that measures the refractive power of lenses equal to the reciprocal of the focal length in meters. Let me break this down for you. It is what brings it into focus. This week will be about tweaking your diopter in order to get you back into focus. Here is what we will focus on:

F = Having **Fun**

O = Desired **Outcome**

C = Call to **Commitment**

U = **Using** your talents to the fullest

S = Handling **Success**

Dear God of Clarity,

Let me use this week to clear my head of distractions. Let me see with clarity and have a renewed focus on what I am doing and what you are doing through me. So often, this world is moving so fast that everything just becomes a blur. God, thank you that even though people surround me, you focus on me and love me. Your Son Jesus had only one focus, and he fixed his gait on it and went to the cross. Let my true focus be the focus of the cross. The instrument that should have been for my death but was replaced with the sacrificial lamb. God, thank you for your provision.

✞

Day 86

Are You Still Having Fun?

Ecclesiastes 8:15 ***So I recommend having fun because there is nothing better for people in this world than to eat, drink, and enjoy life. That way, they will experience some happiness along with all the hard work God gives them under the sun.***

Do you remember why you started playing the game? I hope that it was because it was fun and brought you great joy. There are so many people that lose the main focus on why they started playing the game or even why they chose their specific profession. They did it because they had fun doing it. It did not mean that it was always easy, but even when they were amid the grind, they were still having fun with it. This morning I dropped our sweet foster child off for day school. There was a two-year-old little boy standing there in an Alabama jersey with two yellow flags strapped to his side and a receiver glove in his hand. The lady that works in that room said that he dresses like that every day. There is no pressure on him to perform or worry about the outcome, just a love for the game at the age of two. We so often forget that this game was meant to bring us joy and have fun while we are playing the game. If you are not having fun, then eventually, everything will become a blur. You will put immense undue pressure on yourself that you will burn out on the thing that brought you so much joy.

The same could be said of our walk with Christ. We get so caught up in not sinning that we forget to have fun with our walk with Christ. So often, we only see Jesus as the serious one that never laughed or had any fun. I have a picture of Jesus on my wall in my office. Many people call it the Bob Marley Jesus; it is entitled "Laughing Jesus," a picture of Jesus uncontrollably laughing. I love that picture because it is a reminder that following Jesus needs to the fun. It allows us not to take ourselves too seriously and to sometimes just laugh at our stupid decisions. It does not mean that there are no consequences for things we do, but it gives us hope that grace includes laughter and fun. Jesus loved what he was doing as much as he loved the people that he was ministering to. I bet the disciples loved to sit down and laugh with Jesus as they went about serving a broken world that took things too seriously. Let me ask you, "Are you having fun?" If not, refocus on why you started playing this game in the first place, and I will see you at the plate.

God of Joy and Laughter,

God, thank you for the gift of joy, laughter, and fun. God help me to focus on not taking everything so seriously. Help me to laugh and to learn to laugh with others. God, let me put the fun back in my job, trade, or game. Let me also put the fun back into my walk with you. Let us laugh together as we do this thing called life. Life is Fun, but it is most fun when walking beside you. Thank you for loving me.

Day 87

What Is Your Desired Outcome?

Psalms 118:24 ***This is the day the LORD has made. We will rejoice and be glad in it.***

Part of the focus is what we want to get out of what we are doing. In other words, what do we want the outcome to be? There are different parts of every athlete's season. There is the preseason, the season, and the post-season. The outcome of the preseason is to get better individually and learn how to work as a team. The outcome of the season is to build on what we learned in the preseason so we can win as many games as possible and make it to the playoffs or championship. The outcome of the off-season is to heal up, get bigger, faster, and stronger, and work on where the previous season revealed our deficiencies and shortcomings. In each one of these divisions, we must focus on what is at hand and make the most out of that phase of our season. It is easy to be pulled away from these phases as we either look too far ahead or let the previous season define us. See, focus demands us to live in the now. To take the day God has given us and to get the most outcome from the present. I have seen so many athletes let their success in a previous season make them think they have arrived.

Another thing that will affect the outcome is when we listen to the press. How many times have you heard the press build up a team only for that team to lay an egg in their next competition? You see, if we read the headlines, it will negatively affect the outcome. The truth is that we need to turn off the hype and just go to work. You learned this verse in Bible School or Sunday school, and it has been quoted so much that you probably no longer take it at its value. ***"This is the day that the Lord has made; let us rejoice and be glad in it."*** You see, the glad in it is truly being glad that God has given us today. Today is the only outcome you have control over because you are not promised tomorrow or another season. The outcome you have is the outcome of today. Focus on today's outcome of getting better and what you can do to make a difference in the world right around you. So, you have today to dictate the outcome, so put your mind to it, and I will see you at the plate.

Dear Father of the Past, Present, and Future,

Thank you that there are different seasons in life. Be with me as I prepare, as I compete and as I heal up and grow. God, let me block out all the press that tells me how great I am or how bad I have performed. Let me hear only your voice as you guide me to be the person you want me to be. God, help me to realize that this is the only day I have been promised because we all know that this can change in the twinkling of an eye. God, help me make the most of every opportunity to not feel like life has passed me by one day.

Day 88

Make a Commitment to Commit to the Commitment You Made

I Kings 8:61 ***"Let your heart, therefore, be wholly devoted to the LORD our God, to walk in His statutes and to keep His commandments, as at this day."***

Focus demands that you commit. Without commitment, you will never truly be able to focus fully. One of the greatest deterrents to commitment is that we have way too many choices in life. Sometimes too many choices can cause a lack of commitment. We have seen this in our world today as it relates to marriage; we say I am committed up to the point of for better but cannot commit to the for worse. That is why the divorce rate is over 40%. We have seen it in the church with people not wanting to commit because they may have a better opportunity to come up later. See, the problem with this concept is that we commit up to the point until something better comes along. If we are going to commit to a team, we need to commit regardless of what that team or organization can do for us. I am truly bothered by today's college transfer rule. Many players are transferring because they have been outworked at a position and are no longer a starter. Rather than commit to becoming better, the player transfers out to a new team that they know they are better than the current roster's current talent. The problem with this concept is that we will never get better if we just commit because we are the starter, or we are simply better than our competition. No, when you commit to a team, you are not only committing to get better, but you are committing to be there for your team.

Many people do the same thing in their relationship with Jesus. They follow him right up to a point where it gets difficult. Then when they must make a true decision to follow him or give something up for him, they renege on the commitment they made for Christ. Let me ask you this question. What are you most committed to? Are you truly committed to getting better? Are you committed to your team even when you are not the star or even a starter? Yes. At some point, you committed to getting better, growing in the sport, and sticking in there even when it was not going the way you had envisioned. So, I tell you what: stop right now, make a recommitment to being committed to the thing you committed to, and I will see you at the plate.

Dear God of Centering,

God, let me first and foremost be centered on you. It is from this centering that I get my commitment to follow you no matter the circumstances. I understand that even as a Christian, there will be times when my commitment is challenged. Satan would like nothing better than for me to waiver in my commitment. That is his strategy and his way of getting me out of my peace. God, I thank you for your focus and commitment to the cross. Let me live out the commitment you had for my life in everything I do.

✞

Day 89

Using What You Have Been Given to the Fullest Measure

Acts 5:3 (ESV) ***But Peter said, "Ananias, why has Satan filled your heart to lie to the Holy Spirit and to keep back for yourself part of the proceeds of the land?***

How many times have you had a coach ask if you are giving 100%? The fact is that a coach can tell when a player is not giving their all, or they are taking plays off. Part of the focus process is mentally preparing to use the gifts and talents that God has given you to the fullest. When we use our gifts and talents to the fullest, we not only look good and help our team, but we honor God. God did not give you gifts and talents so that you could use them halfway or at half speed. God wants you to use what he has given you to the fullest. If you give anything less than 100%, then you are not honoring God. God never intended for us just to be average; he wanted us to give our all with what we have been given. One of the problems we run into with this is that sometimes rather than using the specific skill set that God has given us, we compare ourselves to the skillset that others have been given, and we become envious. There is a story in the Scripture (Acts 5:1-10) that illustrates this example of holding out on God. Now the whole community agreed that they would sell their property and give all the proceeds away. They were not forced to do it, but they had all agreed to give it all. But there was one man Ananias who held back some of his proceeds and did not give all. When Peter confronted him, he suddenly just dropped dead. So, this story shows a great example of holding back but still not getting to use what he held back. We will not be blessed when we hold out on our team or God. I plead with you to please use what God had given you to the fullest. See you at the plate.

Dear Giver of Gifts and Talents,

God, I thank you for the Gifts and talents that you have given me. I thank you for the few or the many talents that you have given me. Please help me to use these gifts and talents to the fullest. Help me to use them and use them to the fullest ability so that you can get the honor and the glory. God, thank you for giving me power from above to get through situations beyond my control and out of my reach. Let my life be a testimony as others watch me perform.

Day 90

Handling Success

Matthew 16:31 (NLT) ***Jesus turned to Peter and said, "Get away from me, Satan! You are a dangerous trap for me. You see things merely from a human point of view, not from God's."***

One of the hardest things for young athletes to avoid is getting caught up in the press clippings and media hype. So often, fans love to go online and tell everyone how great their team is and how invincible they are. This can lead to several problems with handling success. The first thing that this can do is take your focus away from getting better every day. You feel as if you have already arrived and are at the top of the food chain. This will get you beat and will also give you a god complex. To get better every day, you must humble yourself every day. The second thing that reading media hype will do is make you think that you are unbeatable. How often have you heard that a team cannot be beaten, and the next week gets beat by an inferior team? You see, to handle success, we must block out the outside distractions. We must focus on the task at hand and get ready for the next competition. So much of the focus involves blocking out the outside distractions of media, press, and family that want to tell you how good you are. When you buy into this hype, you are destined to fail.

Jesus knew how to handle success. The truth is that when Jesus thought that he was becoming too popular or the focus of his mission was becoming on the carnal and not on the eternal, he would remove himself from the stumbling block. On one occasion, as Peter was trying to be helpful, he stood in the way of Jesus and his mission. It was at this point that Jesus says to Peter, 'Get behind me, Satan". He was not calling Peter Satan; he was stating that Satan was using Peter to become a stumbling block to the ministry. Maybe sometimes, when everyone is telling us how good we are and how invincible we are, we need just to stop and say, "get behind me, Satan." When we do this, we keep our focus on what matters. So gather your focus, and I will see you at the plate.

Dear Savior of all Humanity,

Help me to keep my eyes fixed on you and what you have called me to do. Help me see that many times the world wants to tell me how good I am but that Satan uses that to pull me away from what you have called me. I know that this world is filled with distractions, so I ask that you help me recognize these distractions so that I can press on toward my ultimate prize. To God, be the glory now and always.

Day 91

Realizing What Is Important in Life

Philippians 3:13-14 ***Brothers, I do not consider that I have made it my own. But one thing I do: forgetting what lies behind and straining forward to what lies ahead, I press on toward the goal for the prize of the upward call of God in Christ Jesus.***

I read an article the other day on Yahoo. News about a former Alabama Quarterback, Freddie Kitchens. It intrigued me because Freddie played alongside Coach Lance Tucker, who is a friend of mine. The article explained why this past Christmas (2018) was so important to Freddie. You see, Freddie is a quarterback coach for the Cleveland Browns. He is living out his dream as a coach, and he is so thankful for this opportunity. However, this dream almost ended abruptly when he was diagnosed with a rare heart condition known as an aortic dissection. The wall of his aorta had split internally, diverting blood from its intended destinations. The mortality rate was estimated at 80 percent. He survived and said that this incident helped him focus on what is profoundly important: his family and his friends. He realized that there would be many things we had done wrong that he could not fix, but his greatest fear was what he had not done. So, when he came through, he decided to refocus his priorities and make sure he made every day count. What about you? Have you evaluated what is most important in your life? Do you thank God for the ability to do what you are doing? Do you thank your coaches, parents, teachers, professors, and mentors that walk alongside you? One day you will face your mortality, and what will you say was important in your life? After you evaluate that last statement, I will see you at the plate.

Dear Adonia,

Help me to prioritize what is most significant in my life. God, you should be the top priority in my life. You have helped me so much, and no matter what life hands me, you are walking with me, beside me. Let people say at my funeral that people saw you through me, and then my life will be significant.

✞

Day 92

Cheaters Never Win

I Samuel 12:3-4 ***Here I am; bear witness against me before the LORD and His anointed Whose ox have, I taken, or whose donkey have I taken, or whom have I defrauded? Whom have I oppressed, or from whose hand have I taken a bribe to blind my eyes with it? I will restore it to you." They said, "You have not defrauded us or oppressed us or taken anything from any man's hand."***

I remember when I was little, I cheated at some board game we were playing, and a friend of mine said to me, "cheaters never win." Have you ever heard that statement? So, if that statement is so true, why are people always trying to cheat to get the advantage? Why do people cheat rather than put in the work to get better? Why do they cheat rather than run the whole course? The answer is that cheating is so much easier than swallowing our pride. It is easier to cheat and win than it is to lose and admit you were not prepared. Brian Davis was in the final of the 2011 Verizon Heritage Golf classic. He was tied with Jim Furyk, and they were forced into a playoff on the 72nd hole. But before his putt for the win, he called the officials over and told them that he was self-reporting that he may have hit a reed on his backswing. Nobody had seen it or questioned it, but it was against the rules. A slow-motion review showed that it did happen, and Brian was given a two-stroke penalty, causing him to lose the tournament. He lost the tournament because of self-reporting something that no one saw. What would you have done? Not only did he lose the tournament, but he lost about 2 million dollars in earnings that he would have received from the win. Davis went on to explain that in many sports, people cheat. They take performance-enhancing drugs, steal the signs from other teams, and fake getting hurt to slow down the play. But he said, "golf is a gentlemen's game and to even be perceived as a cheater is wrong." He explained that even if he had won, he would not have won because he cheated. He would have to live that he did not beat him fair and square. I love that story because we live in a society and culture that is a win at all costs, even if it costs you your integrity. Sport should teach us how not to be honest and full of integrity, not how to cheat. You can ruin your reputation and your witness if you are labeled as a cheater. The truth is that cheaters "really never win." This is not just true in sports but is true in every aspect and walk of life. Let me ask you, do you believe that cheaters never win? After you answer that question, I will see you at the plate.

Dear God of the Whole Truth,

Help me to be a person of integrity and to be honest in every measure of life. Let me self-report even when my pride tells me not to. Help me to remember that it is always pride before the fall. Let me realize that when I cheat, I mar my reputation and ruin my witness for you. If I must cheat to win, then make me a loser. Because to win by cheating is to lose anyway. Amen.

Day 93

Short Memory

Psalm 145:8 (NIV) ***The Lord is gracious and compassionate, slow to anger, and rich in love.***

Sometimes you will hear a coach say that if they are going to pull this game out, you will have a short memory. Sometimes, they need this short memory when they throw an interception, fumbles the ball, or miss a free throw. If they let those mistakes continue to haunt them, it will not only ruin that moment but will ruin the rest of the game. If you do not have a short memory and forget your mistake, you are most likely looking at a horrible game, and you are probably looking at a loss. I have watched those with a short memory make a mistake to forget about it and then lead their team to victory. I have also seen a player make a mistake and its dominos into a comedy of constant errors. Many times, one error leads to the worst game that they have ever played. The truth is that if you want to be successful, then you must have a short memory; you must own your mistake and move on.

I mean, is this not what we want from God? We want him to have a short memory when it comes to our sin and our disobedience. We want God to forgive us quickly and move on. We want God's blessing right away, even when we are not willing to be obedient. We want God not only to forgive but also to forget what we have done. But do we do the same when people wrong us or sin against us? Are we quick to forgive and move on? I mean, that is our expectation from God, so why do we not follow? You see, when we hold onto our anger, then that is what drives us. If we do not have a short memory, we will allow someone's mistake or sin to dictate the outcome of our life. The sobering reality is that life will work much better when we have a short memory to forgive and move on. So, what are you hanging on to? Well, have a short memory, and I will see you at the plate.

Dear Triune Father,

Thank you that you forgive me. That you are quick to forgive and not only forgive but forget my sins and bury them in the deepest part of the sea. Help me also to be quick to forget when I make a mistake. Help me also to forgive those that are holding me captive. God, let me not make one mistake that leads to destruction. Lord, Give me a short memory.

Day 94

Are You Faking It?

I Timothy 4:7-8 (NLT) ***"Train ourselves to be godly. For physical training is of some value, but godliness has value for all things, holding promise for both the present life and the life to come."***

We all know that sometimes we just do not feel it. We may not have gotten enough rest, or we may have external things that affect our performance. So, what we do is we fake it or at least fake our way through it. We may even pump our arms faster or use body language to make it look like we are working harder than we really are. The truth is that we can only fake it so long before we get caught, and it catches up with us. You must remember that if you are faking it today, someone out there may be working twice as hard and not faking it. Tim Tebow says, "hard work always beats talent when talent doesn't work hard." You can have all the talent in the world, but you are not getting better if you are just going through the motions. You have to keep in mind that out of 100%, only 5% of that is going to compete. The other 95% of your time will be invested in the practice. When you practice that much, it is easy just to take a day off or fake it. The problem with that is that the more you fake it, the more common it gets, and then before long, it just becomes the norm.

The problem with faking it is that it can also creep into our spiritual life. Oh, who am I kidding? It will take over your whole spiritual life. We just try to fake our way through spiritual growth and relationships with Jesus, and then we ask the question, "why do I feel so empty?" We commit to quiet time, and then we feel our lives with constant noise. We promise that we are going to do devotions, but we do so with no devotion. Then we go a whole week without Jesus and then show up to church as the weekend spiritual warrior. If we genuinely want to grow in Christ, we have to quit faking our way through it, and we need to work at it. We need to become a living sacrifice; we need to grasp a plan and show up for our spiritual workouts. There are no shortcuts to godliness. We must do the training, and God will become our changing agent. Listen to me, quit faking your way through it, and I will see you at the plate.

Dear Holy Ghost,

Help me always to be sincere. To always give it everything I have. Even if others on the team are lazy or are faking it, please help me go full speed. God, I have today to get better, and if I am not working hard, my opponent may be outworking me. Please help me never to get beat because I took days and plays off. My hard work does not save me, but it does honor you. Let me go hard or go home.

Day 95

Numbered Days

Psalms 90:12 ***Teach us to number our days that we may gain a heart of wisdom.***

Do you realize that you will walk off the field or the court one day, and you will never compete at this level again? The reality is that our time for competition is limited. There are many undetermined factors that may limit how long you play and how much time you have left to play. One factor is your eligibility will run out. You only have four years of high school and then maybe five years max in college if you make it to that level. Another factor that determines how long we play is injury. You never know if you will have an injury that will end your career forever. Tyrone Prothro, Alabama's star receiver, was going to have a promising professional career in the NFL, but in 2005 he made a play that is so famous it was painted by the artist Daniel Moore. The name of the painting is entitled "The Catch." Now even though it is one of the greatest catches you will ever see, it ended Prothrow's career as he broke his leg on that catch. The break was so severe that he had 11 surgeries in 10 years just so he could walk right, which meant that he would never play football again. His dream of playing NFL football ended with one play. He has since had a rather good coaching career, but he never thought that one play would end his playing football forever. I tell this story because you need to make the most of every opportunity that you get. Do not take for granted the opportunity that is before you.

The same could be said in life; only it is even more fatal than playing your last game. Last Friday, I got a call that one of my church members had gone out to eat with friends, came home, and went to his computer to check his email. A few minutes later, his wife went back to check on him, and he had a mass heart attack and was dead right there at the computer. See, we just never know how many more days we have left. For this reason, maybe the first thing we ought to say when we get out of bed is. Thank you, God, for another day, and let me make the most of this day and the opportunities that lay before me. So, let's use this next opportunity to be the best we can be, and I will see you at the plate.

Dear Bread of Life,

Thank you for today. This may be the last day I have left, so please let me make the most of it. God, you know my days as they were assigned to me a long time ago. I ask your forgiveness for the days I have wasted and the opportunities that I have let pass. God, you did not have to, but many times you have given me additional opportunities that I did not deserve. Thank you for being the God of grace and opportunity.

Day 96

Character Not Color

Philippians 4:8 ***Finally, brethren, whatever things are true, whatever things are noble, whatever things are just, whatever things are pure, whatever things are lovely, whatever things are of good report if there is any virtue and if there is anything praiseworthy—meditate on these things.***

I wish that I could say that racial tension had gone away in my lifetime. But we live in a nation that continues to judge people based on color, race, and speech. The truth is that hatred and prejudice still exist, and in some places, it is even worse than during the Civil Rights Movement. We will celebrate Martin Luther King, Jr. Day this Monday, and I am reminded of this famous quote regarding the judgment of a person's skin color. Martin Luther King Jr. coined these famous words, "I have a dream that my four children will one day live in a nation where they will not be judged by the color of their skin, but by the content of their character." You know God created us all differently, not to be judged by the color of our skin but created as a person of worth and value. One thing I love about sports is that on a team, we all have to work together.

When I was playing ball, I never saw the color of someone's skin. I only saw the color of my teammate's jerseys. All our jerseys were the same color, and we were playing for the same team and the same goal. We all had a common goal and a common purpose: to win the game while also honoring God. We were judged not on skin color or race but on how we played the game and responded to circumstances that transpired during the game. We should always judge a person the same way God does, not by the color of their skin but by the character that they exhibit and live out. **Character matters**: this is a slogan that is often talked about in the sports world. The reality is that character should be the only criteria that we are judged by. The Scripture says, "that man looks at the outward appearance, but God looks at the heart." A person's character is controlled by what is in their heart. You can win every game you play, and still, God judges your heart as losing because of your poor character. Remember to judge a person based on their character and not the color of their skin. See you at the plate.

Dear Father, Beloved Son, and Holy Spirit,

Search my heart and find no prejudice and bias in me. Help me not to see the color of the skin. Help me to judge a person by their character and not by their skin. Help me remember that people will judge me not based on my performance but my heart. God, you see not only in my heart, but you see through my heart.

Day 97

Only Jesus

Galatians 6:14 (NLT) ***As for me, may I never boast about anything except the cross of our Lord Jesus Christ. Because of that cross, my interest in this world has been crucified, and the world's interest in me has also died.***

There is a brand-new song on the radio by Casting Crowns, and the other day, it caught my attention. I want to paraphrase some of the song here: *Make a name the world remembers. I got lost in the lie, but it was up to me to make a name the world remembers. Jesus is the only name to remember. I do not want to leave a legacy; I do not care if they remember me. I just want them to remember "Only Jesus."* Now those words are so counter-cultural as it relates to the sports world. The truth is that we want to be remembered as champions; we want to make a name for ourselves and our team. Now the question is, how do we play the game and give all we have and still honor God? Well, first, I want to make the point that this will not be easy. But I think a few athletes in my time have been able to do this, one being Tim Tebow, Kirk Cousins, and another being Philip Rivers. All these athletes point to "only Jesus" when being interviewed or asked about their performance. If we are going to honor God, we must take the focus off ourselves and say, "do not look to me; only look to Jesus." The stigma of making a name for yourself is not exclusive to the sports world; it can even creep into the church world. Many people in the church setting, including preachers/ministers/clergy, get a messiah complex. They point to themselves and not to the cross. My prayer is that people would not see me and my accomplishments but that they would see Jesus. I hope that when I die, people will say, "his legacy was Jesus." God wants us to do the best we can on the field, he wants us to win and be known, but he wants us to make his name known through our accomplishments. Paul summed this up when he said, "I boast about nothing but the cross." He had become famous, and he would leave a legacy, but his legacy would be the love that he had for his Savior. He even said that compared to Jesus, everything on this earth was rubbish. Let me ask you, when people look at you, do; they see the cross, do they see the love you have for Jesus, or do they just see you and your accomplishments. Stop right now and say, "only Jesus," and then I will see you at the plate.

Dear Holy of Holies,

Only you, Jesus. Let the world not see me and my accomplishments. Let the world see that my strength is found in the cross of Jesus. What can take away the sin, nothing but the blood of Jesus? You loved me so much that you gave your life so that I may live and play the game I love. You make me whole, and the legacy that I want to leave is that I loved you more than I loved my accomplishments, trophies, and acolytes—only you, Jesus.

Day 98

Mental Prep

Mark 1:35 (CEV) ***Very early the next morning before daylight, Jesus got up and went to a place where he could be alone and pray.***

One of the hardest things for many athletes is to prepare for the competition or upcoming event mentally. There are so many outside factors that affect our mental preparation. How do we feel? Have we been sick? How much rest have we gotten this week? Have we eaten right and stayed hydrated? How are my teammates this week? Have they worked together or been fighting amongst themselves during practice? What has the climate in the locker room be like? How is the other team preparing? How well have our coaches prepared us? Have we watched enough films to find tendencies and mistakes? How much have I listened to the outside voices or read the press?

You see, many things affect our preparation and mental aspect of the game. It is also important to take some time to get by yourself for meditation and to pray through your preparation. It would help if you were mentally sharp and cognitive when you entered the contest. This will keep you from making mental errors that may cost you in the long run. You need to be mentally prepared to handle what the other team is going to throw at you. You need to be mentally prepared if the conditions or surface are not what you had planned. You need to be prepared when a call does not go your way. You need to be ready when an opposing team member tries to get in your head. You see, you need to sit down before the contest and ask the Lord to prepare you for what lies ahead. Jesus patterned this for us in the Scripture many times; he would move away from the crowd and the limelight and go to spend time with his Father in prayer and meditation. If the King of Kings and the Lord of Lords needed to prepare mentally, then should we not do the same thing. Do we not need to take time out to breathe, meditate, and talk with our father? You can go into the contest physically prepared, but you may still lose the contest if you are not mentally prepared. So, this week as you prepare to take some time out to focus and get mentally prepared, and then I will see you at the plate.

Dear Kingdom Builder,

We spend so much time in physical training, but we also need to do the physical preparation. Help me to focus and to clear my mind. Help me to connect with my whole heart and my whole mind. Help me to prepare for whatever lies ahead. Help me to get alone with you and to put the distractions of the world in the rearview mirror. Thank you for giving me the capacity to connect with you. Let me be still and know that you are God.

Day 99

Moving On

Acts 15:36-38 ***Sometime later, Paul said to Barnabas, "Let us go back and visit the believers in all the towns where we preached the word of the Lord and see how they are doing." Barnabas wanted to take John, also called Mark, with them, but Paul did not think it wise to take him because he had deserted them in Pamphylia and had not continued with them in the work.***

We are living in a time of free agency in college sports, especially NCCA Football. If a player does not like the coach or is not getting enough playing time, he/she can put in for a transfer and move on to another team. I am not sure how I feel about that because there is some value to hanging in there even when things are not going your way. But on the flip side, there are times when you may need to switch teams or move on. We are often feeling a twitch in our spirit that it may be time to move on. But how will we know? Here are some valid reasons to pray through when you think it is time for a move.

The team does not line up with your values: Several years ago, my daughter was playing on a team, and she came to me and told me that she wanted to quit playing for that team. It was a good exposure team, but the team's values did not line up with my daughter's values. So, we moved on because she was not going to compromise her values just to be on a winning team. Because at the end of the day, you lose in life even though you win on the field.

The team chemistry is all wrong. Sometimes teams are just toxic. You have all the talent in the world, but the makeup of the team does not work. Players are always fighting and backbiting. There is jealousy, and there is animosity towards your teammates. This environment can ruin a winning season or cause one to want to quit playing altogether.

You are not being coached to your potential. You have all the talent in the world, but your coach is not pushing you to be better. Another reason you are not coached up is that a parent spends all the time with their child and puts them in key positions even though they do not fit in that position. The other reason for moving on is when coaches tend to play favorites depending on outside elements. Such as one dad sponsors the team, so his son plays more, or a parent provides new uniforms, so their son or daughter is given special treatment.

You are not being pushed by your teammates. Sometimes we need to switch teams because we are the best, and those around us are not pushing us. I knew a girl that was the best on her high school team. No one could push her, so her father put her on a summer team where she was just another small fish in a big pond. This helped her game and helped her earn a college scholarship.

Sometimes in life, we need to move on from who we are hanging out with and where we are hanging out. We need to ask the question; are the people I am hanging with positive or negative? Does the crowd I am hanging with have the same values and moral character that I want to exhibit? Is the crowd I am hanging out with helping me be the best I can be, or are they leading me down a path that could lead to destruction? Sometimes the most popular thing to do is not the wisest thing to do. Sometimes the only way to fix our play is to change our playground. So right now, stop and ask whether I need to move on from who I am with and where I am hanging out, and I will see you at the plate.

Dear YHWH,

Challenge me sometimes to move on even when it is not comfortable. Help me to see the value in being pushed to be my best. Help me understand that I do not have to compromise my values to stay on a team or in a position. God, there are many times in the Scripture when your Son moved on. Help me to keep my vision focused on the prize, which lies ahead of me. Let the cross-lead me.

Day 100

Lack Luster

Matthew 19:21 ***Jesus said to him, "If you wish to be complete, go and sell your possessions and give to the poor, and you will have treasure in heaven; and come, follow Me."***

Have you ever known a player that possessed every physical attribute that you could have but still lacked something? The other day, I was listening to this color commentator talk about this player that had high aspirations to play in the NBA. The commentator was talking about the player's wingspan, jumping ability, and rebounding ability. He then commented that he was great on the inside but needed to work on his outside shot. And then he said the one thing he needs to work on is his effort and intensity at practice. You see, God had given this young man all the ability in the world, but then he gave him a choice as to how he would develop the skills that had been given to him. So often, we meet someone that looks great, but then we see something that is lackluster (missing). Sometimes, the best athletes feel that they do not have to work as hard as the others. Many times, the one that does not have God-given talent is the hardest worker. This reminds me of a story in the

Bible about a gifted young man that came to Jesus to become a follower. He asked Jesus what he must do to inherit the kingdom of God. Jesus then responded, you go and sell all you have, and then come and follow me. The young man then went away pouting because the one thing he lacked was the ability to let go of his wealth and possessions. He seemed to have it all together on the surface, but when Jesus confronted him with the one thing he lacked, he caved. See, God wants us to evaluate our life constantly, and he wants us to see what we lack. What is it that is keeping us from reaching our God-given ability? What is keeping us from being the best that we can be in life? See, sometimes we need to sell all we have, and then I will see you at the plate.

Dear Creator,

How many times have I squandered away what you have given me? How much have I wasted that could have been used for your glory? God, help me not to lack hard work and dedication. Not because I believe this is what saves me but so that I can be great in your eyes. Let me never give a lackluster performance when it comes to my witness and work for your Kingdom. God, you have given me the ability; now, let me choose to use it to its greatest potential.

Day 101

Bonding Team Love

Romans 12:9 ***"Love must be without hypocrisy. Detest evil; cling to what is good."***

Most coaches will talk of a team becoming one cohesive unit so that they become a family. When you spend so much time with your teammates and coaches, you become family. The truth is that you see your team during the season more than you see your immediate family. The downside of a team becoming a family is that they are a family. Families disagree, fight, argue, and struggle with one another. Families also pray together, love another, and go to battle for one another. These are the dynamics that exist in any family, and they also exist on a team. This family concept can lead to bad things when a teammate is having a bad game or has not lived up to their optimal performance level. One player's action can cause the whole team to run extra sprints or do extra reps. When this happens, the whole team starts to come down on a person because of their poor performance. This can sometimes lead to total team animosity. It is important to remember that a teammate that is struggling is a family member. They may need your unconditional love despite their poor performance. You will have to evaluate and see if these performance issues are internal or external in nature.

Then you must show love to your teammate. As a matter of fact, it may be that unconditional love that pulls the person out of their declining performance or slump. You see, unconditional love is a love that loves even when a person is not at their best. It is the same love (agape) that Jesus has for us. In the Scripture, Peter (one of Jesus's teammates) had messed up. He had turned on his best friend, and he had left the team. But Jesus showed up where he was fishing and loved him back on to the team. You see, when you are the spiritual leader on a team, it may be your job to love someone back onto the team. You are called to have unconditional love for your teammates. You must remember that they are more than just a person in a jersey; underneath, they are a person, and because they wear the same jersey you do, they are family. Let me ask you, who is it today that you need to love unconditionally? Go love them, and then I will see you at the plate.

God of All Nations,

All people are of worth. Thank you for giving me a family and a team. I pray that I will be the spiritual leader on the team and that I will unconditionally love all my teammates. God, you have shown me unconditional love, and so it is my duty also unconditionally to love my teammates even when they fail. Thank you for sending your Son how showed us what unconditional love looked like. But mostly, thank you for your unconditional love, which I am in constant need of.

Day 102

Creating Your Luck

Luke 21:36 ***Be alert at all times. Pray so that you have the power to escape everything that is about to happen and to stand in front of the Son of Man.***

The late Coach Finley, my football coach in college, used to say to us, "*Luck* is no more than when opportunity meets preparation. So, prepare to get lucky, boys." The moral that he was trying to teach us was that you could not just rely on luck to get the win. He stressed that luck might happen, but when you are prepared, you are ready when an opportunity arises. So many people in our world think that they can just pray through a situation without acting, and everything will just fall into place. I grew up hearing this statement, "God helps those that help themselves." That verse is not in the Bible. But throughout the Scripture, we see where people prayed and then got busy doing what God had called them to do. God wants us to prepare; he wants us to be proactive and not just reactive. You cannot pray for God to help you get an "A" on this test and not study. It just does not work that way. You cannot say, "God, let me defeat my opponent," but then not practice to defeat them. If God worked that way and everything was just dependent on luck and prayer, we would be no more than entitled, spoiled rotten children.

God wants us to pray, and he wants us to seek him, but he also wants to equip us, not just give to us. Luck may happen, but to specifically pray for luck alone takes the gifts and talents out of the equation. God will help you prepare to win, but he will not just let you win because you prayed and then showed up. The moral of this devotional is that you create your luck through hard work and mental preparation. I love this quote from Jack Hyles: "There is always a prepared place for a prepared person." So, have you prepared to get lucky? See you at the plate.

The One the Only One,

I pray not for luck but that you would allow me to prepare thoroughly for the contest that lies ahead. Luck is no more than my willingness to prepare, and when the opportunity arises, I take full advantage of it. There was no luck in the cross; it was Jesus' commitment to my sin. Yes, let my preparation always keep what was done for me on the cross at the forefront of my mind. God, thank you that it is not by luck that I am here but by your divine appointment.

Day 103

Holding Back

Acts 5:1-2 ***Now, a man named Ananias, together with his wife Sapphira, also sold a piece of property. With his wife's full knowledge, he kept back part of the money for himself but brought the rest and put it at the apostles' feet.***

Have you ever been accused of holding back? You want to give it your all, but you just doubt yourself and your ability. A few years ago, my daughter would take batting practice in the cage, and she would tear the ball up, but then when she got into the game, she would freeze up. I knew she could hit the ball, but she doubted herself. I finally asked her what was going on, and she responded, "Dad, I am just thinking too much." She was holding back because she doubted her abilities. She could do it in practice, but during the game, she became tense and started to play every aspect of her hitting mechanics through her mind. She just needed to quit holding back, relax, and do what she had trained her mind to do. She finally did that, and her junior year, she hit over .400.

There is something freeing about just letting go and not holding back. The same thing sometimes happens in our faith. We know what the Scripture points out that God will give us opportunities to witness. God lines us up with the people we need to minister to and pray for, but we hold back. We fear the way people will see us or what they will think. One of the greatest tragedies of today's world is that we have all the tools to evangelize and witness, but we hold back. God did not give us a spirit of timidity but gave us one of courage and strength. We have no excuse for holding back because he has given us all we need to be bold. What is holding you back? Is it laziness, is it timidity, is it fear of not knowing what to say? If you answered yes to any of these questions, I want you to bow your head and say these words, God, I am letting go from holding back and letting you take complete control. After you say that prayer, I will see you at the plate.

Dear Giver of Your One and Only Begotten Son,

Give me a spirit of boldness. Let me find my strength in you. I know what to do, but so many times, I hold back. So many times, I let fear guide my heart rather than the strength and power that you provide through the Holy Spirit. God, from this day forward, I am not holding back in any aspect of my life. I am not only going to do it; I am going to conquer it.

✞

Day 104

Live for Today

2 Peter 3:10 ***But the day of the Lord will come like a thief. The heavens will disappear with a roar; the elements will be destroyed by fire, and the earth and everything done in it will be laid bare.***

How many more days do you have left to live? Our creator, God, only knows the answer to that question. So often, we find ourselves living for tomorrow instead of making the most of today. We are sometimes known as the people of procrastination. What you are to become, you are now becoming. I promise you that. You are not going just to wake up one day and be something different. The only day that we are promised is the day we are living right now. The reality is how we live our day is really how we live our life. By life, I mean our entire life. How we live today is really who we are, and if you want to be different, you have to do something different today. You have today to get better. You have today to learn something new. You have today to prepare for the uncertainty of tomorrow. That sounds weird, does it not? We are preparing for what we may not even experience. I was once asked if I thought a lot about the end of the world. Here was my response, "if we live every day like it is going to be our last day, then one day, it will be."

I have a book on my bookshelf entitled "Do Not Waste Your Life." How many people do you know that are wasting today in hopes of tomorrow? How many of you know someone that did not get to see that tomorrow? I plead with you to make the most of today. So, take this day, which the Lord had made and not only rejoice in it but make the most of it. What have you been putting off? What is pressing in your life and cannot wait any longer? Whatever it is, do it now because you are not promised tomorrow. See you at the plate (today).

Dear Creator of Night and Day,

I have procrastinated long enough. I have put it off until tomorrow long enough. I have wasted too many days looking forward to tomorrow. Who am I to waste today when I do not control tomorrow or even know if I will see tomorrow? Let me hold nothing back. God, I am giving you my all and making the most of today.

✞

Day 105

Accepting the Challenge

2 Corinthians 7:4 (ESV) ***I am acting with great boldness toward you; I have great pride in you; I am filled with comfort. In all our affliction, I am overflowing with joy.***

Are you nervous by nature? Do you have butterflies in your stomach and feel like you will be sick before the big game? Many athletes struggle with nervousness and anxiety before a big competition. Sometimes it is hard just to get settled and mentally prepared for the big game. There are several steps you can take to get yourself centered and to calm your spirit.

1. Pray. Pray that God replaces your nerves with confidence.
2. Get by yourself and tell yourself you were made for this moment, and you are prepared.
3. Remember all the hard work and preparation that you have put in. It was not easy to get here.
4. Remember what it took to get here, it has been a hard journey, but you have met all obstacles to get to this point.
5. Finally, say to yourself <u>three</u> times, "give me strength and let me be courageous for you, God."

You know, the Scripture gives us a story that exemplifies a long journey to get to the promised land and the two different perspectives given as to entering the land. You can read the whole story in Numbers 13:1-33, but here is a synopsis. There were twelve spies sent out to survey the land as to whether it was inhabitable. Only two came back with a good report and the confidence that they could move into the land. The other ten doubted and feared and said they would be destroyed if they entered the land. What was the result of this not being ready to accept the challenge? The Israelites got to spend another 37 years wandering in the wilderness. A 37-year setback because of nervousness and fear. They wandered for 37 more years because they did not put their confidence in God. They had walked and wandered a long time to get to this point, but they let fear and doubt overcome their confidence to win. Do not be like the Israelites; get alone and go through the five steps, and I will see you at the plate.

Dear Eternal Flame,

It has been a struggle to get here, but here I am, Lord. Give me a spirit that can conquer my anxieties. Help me to drive out all the fear that surrounds the unknown. Let me not squander the opportunity because of nerves and fear. Let me remember that I am not alone in this battle but that you are walking with me. The opportunity that lays ahead of me is an opportunity to bring you honor and glory.

Day 106

Finding Rhythm

Galatians 5:16: (ESV) ***But I say, walk by the Spirit, and you will not gratify the desires of the flesh.***

You have heard it said that speed kills. The truth is that when you have speed, you have an advantage. But speed without rhythm will eventually catch up to you. I had a girl that played on our softball team that was a great pitcher. She could throw the ball with lots of speed and spin. She was exactly what you want in a successful pitcher. The problem is that if she tried to overthrow, she could not hit her spots. Now you can throw with all the speed in the world, but if you cannot hit spots, you will not be a successful pitcher. She often struggled with rhythm, but once she got into a rhythm, she was almost unhittable. But to get into a rhythm, she had to slow down and focus. She had to not overthrow and focus on what she had prepared to do. You know the word rhythm is rarely mentioned when it comes to sports or even life. I think the reason is that we are so busy. We are busier than we have ever been. We have more resources than we have ever had, but we struggle to find the rhythm. Living in rhythm helps us experience more success, keeps us grounded, and can even help us from injury.

We can also get out of rhythm in our spiritual life. We become so busy doing that we quit being. We quit being in prayer. We quit being in a relationship with Jesus. We quit being in quiet time and the Scripture. See, to find life and live it to abundance as the Scripture suggests, we have to have rhythm; we have to be walking in rhythm with the Lord. When we get out of rhythm, we get out of sorts. So, let me ask, do you feel out of sorts? Today my prayer for you is that you will find the rhythm in your game and your life. When you find that rhythm, I will see you at the plate.

Dear Timekeeper,

Lord of Creation, create in us a new rhythm of life composed of hours that sustain us rather than stress us, of days that deliver rather than destroy, of time that tickles rather than tackles. Adapted from Common Prayer: A Liturgy for Ordinary Radicals.

Day 107

What Can You Control?

Psalms 107:29 (KJV) ***He maketh the storm a calm so that the waves thereof are still.***

In a sporting event, we have many things that we can control as we prepare to play and compete. The first thing that we have control over is how we prepare for the competition. We can also control our mental aspect and focus leading up to the competition. We are also in control of our temperament, and we can control our effort during the competition. But many times, when we are playing, some things are totally out of our control. One thing we cannot control is the other team. We may have scouted them and watched a film, but they may have changed personnel or the game plan leading up to the event. We have no control over how they play or how they respond to competition. The other thing that we cannot control is the referees. They are human beings that sometimes are on their game, and other times they make mistakes. (They are human) You cannot control what kind of game they are going to call. But your attitude can dictate how they will respond and if there is a questionable call, will they favor your direction? But if you leave the game up to one final call, you cannot control that. The last thing that you cannot change is the weather. In today's world, some professionals and some college teams play in domes, which does help some with the weather conditions. Now, in reality, most of us will never be fortunate enough to play in controlled environments. So, many of us will be forced to play in the wind, rain, cold, blistering hot, or even foggy conditions. We cannot control the weather, but we can respond as to how we handle the elements.

The truth is that all these things we cannot control, but we do choose as to whether they will control us. How will we respond to adversity, to a bad call, to driving wind and rain? See, when these elements present themselves as out of control, we reach out to the one in control. We reach out to Jesus to help calm our spirit, and he gives us the strength to keep our attitudes in check. When we are out of control, the way we regain our composure is to go to Jesus. He is the one that calms the storms in our lives. So, get yourself under control, and I will see you at the plate.

Dear Ultimate Controller,

So often, some things are out of my control. Many times, the harder I try to grip the reins, the more out-of-control things get. What I can control is how I respond to what is going on around my life. Help me to always look to you when things are out of control. Calm the storms of my life and the ones that are around me. Help me to see that you are in control and help me to surrender.

Day 108

Keeping Score

Psalm 130:3-4 ***If you, Lord, kept a record of sins, Lord, who could stand? But with you there is forgiveness so that we can, with reverence, serve you.***

Several years ago, I was starting a recreation program in one of my church appointments. The first thing that I brought to the church recreation program was called "Upward Basketball." It was a basketball program that focused on learning the game of basketball without keeping score. It was a program that promised to size people of similar talent and skills against one another. It was a concept to learn the game without the pressure of competing against someone better. Now, I must admit that I have never been one to play without keeping score, and it was difficult for me to not keep up with the score. One particular Saturday, when we were playing, I looked over at the parents, and one of them had a notepad and was writing down the score and who scored. It was then I realized that I was not the only one that had trouble not keeping score. Why do we keep score? Why do we count numbers in church? Why do we take attendance at club meetings and events? It is because we want to know how we are doing. We have this obsession with winning, and that is why we love to play the game. But what if God kept score on how good we were doing? What if he had a scoreboard that had sinned against on the visitor's side and good deeds performed on the home side. What would the score of our life be? What if, at the end of time, we were judged on the score of our life? Would we win eternal life, or would we be the great loser in life? I am so glad that the scoreboard of life does not dictate whether I win or whether I lose. No, the scoreboard was lit up with a win when Christ went to the cross. My acceptance in the cross gives me the confidence that I am saved by grace and not by the scoreboard. The great thing about life is that it is like upward basketball; God is not keeping score; he just tells us to play the game to get better without the pressure of winning. Aren't you glad that we are already winners? So now that you know the score is grace-10 and my sin-0, I will see you at the plate.

Dear Lord of the Harvest,

Thank you for not keeping score and that Love and Grace win. Amen.

Day 109

You Cannot Sandbag Integrity

Galatians 6:9 ***Let us not become weary in doing good, for at the proper time, we will reap a harvest if we do not give up.***

A few years ago, I was coaching a very middle-of-the-road travel softball team. We had some skillful players but had taken a risk on a few other players hoping to help develop their skills. We won some games and, by the end of the year, had drastically improved. We had moved from a C class team to a solid B class. One of the things I would do to challenge our team was to put them in tournaments that I knew had better teams to challenge them. One Saturday, we played a tournament and won the first two pool games, and were placed in the winner's bracket. In one of the games, we had beaten another mediocre team, but in the other game, we beat a team that was better than we were. Another team (the best team in the tournament) had lost their first two games and would now play through the loser bracket, a much easier bracket. We finally had to face this team, and we were exhausted, and our pitching was tired out. The other team had sandbagged to win the tournament. They had intentionally lost so that they could breeze through for a trophy. After we lost to them, one game before the trophy game, I told my team how proud I was of them for the way they had played all day. I told them that they played with heart and integrity. The other team was better than everyone else in the tournament but sandbagged to win another trophy. (Like they needed another one.) I told my team that trophy chasing does not build integrity but that hard work and discipline build integrity. Remember, a trophy sits on the shelf, but hard work builds up oneself. Many times in life, we take the shortcut because it is the easiest thing to do. We avoid situations that tend to bring out fear. We avoid having a tough conversation because it is easier to stay on the surface. We avoid conflict and accountability, even though God has called us to it. The truth is that you can sandbag in sports to get a trophy, but in life, sandbagging just creates a lot of heartaches. You will also miss a lot of opportunities to do God's work when we sandbag. God does not want us chasing trophies; he wants us to formulate character and integrity. I mean, after all, the trophy has already been won; it is the crown of eternal life, and Jesus in no way sandbagged to gain that trophy. No, he considered himself nothing, and he bore for us the weight of our sandbags. So, stop sandbagging, and I will see you at the plate.

My Fortress,

I have missed so many opportunities because of my cowardice and procrastination. But God, I know that you have new opportunities for me every morning. Help me not to seek a trophy but to seek a relationship with you. Let me forget what lies behind and press forward to attain that which you have prepared before me.

Day 110

Huddle Up

Luke 5:15-16 (NLT) ***But despite Jesus' instructions, the report of his power spread even faster, and vast crowds came to hear him preach and to be healed of their diseases. 16But Jesus often withdrew to the wilderness for prayer.***

I know we live in the new world of no-huddle offenses and hurry-up schemes, but sometimes we might need to huddle. We have taken the game to a new level of fast. But there are sometimes consequences for going too fast. Sometimes you need to regroup so that you can pull it all back together. So often, we try just to keep pushing through but may need just to take a deep breath and regroup. How many times have you made a mistake or done something you will regret later because you did not step back and count to ten or at least huddle up? I have a coach friend who got mad playing golf, so he broke three of his clubs. He would later regret that decision because it cost $250.00 to replace the clubs. The wake-up moment was realizing that breaking those clubs did not improve his score.

When you huddle up, it gives you a chance to regroup and to find your focus. Hurry up is good as long as you are in rhythm, but you need to call a huddle and get together if you are not in sync.

The same can be said in everyday life. In life, sometimes we need to call a time out and huddle. I have heard many people say that they just feel that they are running on empty or need to find focus. In the Scripture, Jesus teaches us how to huddle. How to huddle and pray. When life got busy for Jesus, he would find a way to get away. Even if he were at the height of ministry or everyone was looking for him, he would retreat, huddle up and spend time with the ultimate head coach. He would spend time in prayer, finding his strength from the place where all strength comes from. (God) You see, the best thing that we can do when we feel that we are spinning out of control is to huddle up and find time for prayer. I see many people pray before the game or big event and then totally lose their focus during the event. What would it look like if, during the middle of the event, we got by ourselves to refocus and regain composure? In a game or in life, sometimes you need to just get by yourself to huddle and pray. So after you have huddled, I will see you at the plate.

God of Peace,

God, let me just count to ten, breathe, and feel your presence as it calms my spirit and refocuses my soul. To regroup is to be obedient to you and will later keep me from a world of heartache.

✞

`Day 111

Ousted

Luke 10:19 (NIV) ***I have given you authority to trample on snakes and scorpions and to overcome all the power of the enemy; nothing will harm you.***

The University of Alabama went into the game a 14-point favorite against Clemson in the 2019 National Championship game. They had not lost all year. They would be the only team in history to go 15-0. The swirling question was, is this the best team that Alabama had ever put on the field? The fans were confident; the media was confident; this game was in the bag. Just go play it and then hoist up that National Championship trophy one more time. Now, not only did they not win by 14, but they were outplayed, outcoached, and just ousted. The truth is they just quit because they could not get it figured out. The final score at the end of the game was 44-16. No one, and I mean no one, saw that coming. For the next several weeks, talk radio buzzed and asked how the most dominant team in college football history could get beat and not just beat but dismantled. But the one thing that we did not hear about was how Clemson went into that game so well prepared and focused. The truth is that Clemson was the one at the end that got "ousted" by fans and the media. The reason that they got ousted was that no one gave them the credit that they deserved. The truth is, I think they found their focus in their faith. At least I know their coach Dabo Swinny did as he gave God all the credit for the win and the preparation. He did not say God caused his team to win; he just gave credit for God, helping in the preparation and focus of the game. Now, I will be the first to tell you that God does not intervene to help a team win. Some people would even say that he does not care about who won the national championship, but I would argue that God cares because those are his children playing. I think that sometimes God is the hidden weapon behind our focus and preparation. I think that God cares about everything that we are involved in. Will he help you pass the test? No, but he will help you focus, study, and calm the nerves associated with taking the test. Will he change the outcome because you pray for the last-second shot? No, he will not guide the ball in, but he will give the shooter the clarity on why he is playing and who he is playing for. You see, God will not be ousted. No, God will give us the platform and the opportunity to give him the glory. So just remember you will not be ousted, and I will see you at the plate.

Dear Almighty One,

Sometimes we just lose. Sometimes we are outplayed. Sometimes we are outcoached. But God, we are never ousted in the Kingdom of God. Your Son's death made sure that we would never be ousted or set aside but that we would dwell with you for eternity. We may be broken, we may have lost, but we will never be defeated by sin and death because your Son has ousted that from our life. I love you.

Day 112

Ego

Philippians 2:7 (NIV) ***...rather, he made himself nothing by taking the very nature of a servant, being made in human likeness.***

Ego can be the shorter word for the word "egotistical." Egotistical means excessively conceited or absorbed in oneself, self-centered. When I was growing up, we had shirts made up for our football team that said there is no "I" in team. It was a great saying, but only a few on our team lived by that statement. So often, the better a player gets, the more ego they have. I have often said the problem with "pro sports" today is that the athletes have gotten so good that they have a "messiah" complex. An "ego' will create a distance between you and your team. When someone on the team has an ego, they are trying to spell team: with a (t "I" am.) So how does an egotistical player affect the team?

1. Ego separates you from the rest of the team. This separation is not a good thing; it is you against your own team.
2. Ego hurts your team, and many times affects the outcome.
3. Ego brings despair and discouragement to the teammates around you.
4. Ego makes one un-coachable.
5. Ego puts you in the spotlight and takes the focus off of God.

One time, Peter let his egotistical side slip in while he was following Jesus. Well, I bet it slipped in more than once, but this is the example that we have from the

Scriptures. Jesus had just told the disciples that he would give his life up to save the world. He told them that he must die. Peter informs Jesus that he is going to make sure that does not happen. Peter is only thinking about how losing Jesus would affect him. He is not seeing the big picture or thinking about that; this was why Jesus had come to earth. His sole purpose for coming to earth was to die for the forgiveness of sins. Peter says to Jesus; it is not going to happen this way, then Jesus tells Peter that he is not thinking about anybody but himself. It is a quick reminder to Peter that there is no "I" in Jesus either. What a great concept there is no "I" in team, and there is no "I" in Jesus. Jesus set the true example of what a healthy ego looked like by emptying himself of all of himself. It may be time that we empty ourselves and check our ego. Leave your ego in the dugout, and I will see you at the plate.

Savior that Brings Peace,

I am self-centered, self-pleasing, and just plain egotistical at times. Help me to empty myself and fill my spirit with you. There is no "I" in Jesus and no "I" in team, so let me take "I" out of the equation so that the world will see you and not see me. God, thank you for loving me despite me. To God, be the glory now and forevermore.

Day 113

Team Unity

John 17:21 ***...that all of them may be one, Father, just as you are in me, and I am in you. May they also be in us so that the world may believe that you have sent me.***

A team is made up of many different personalities and people. The team is also made up of people that come from different walks of life and live on different sides of the tracks. A team is made of people that come from broken homes, single-parent homes, and blended families. A team is a lot like a marriage, with each player bringing in their invisible baggage. Now mixing all these things can be a recipe for disaster. Because of this unique mix, someone on the team must take the role of a leader and captain. Someone on the team has to promote unity and a sense of direction. A few years ago, I was helping with a team that had phenomenal talents. The truth was that it was more talent than we had seen in quite a while. But we lost more games that year than any of the other years I helped with that team. The reason is that we had no leadership and zero team unity. The talented players brought a lot of baggage in with them, and rather than set it aside, they brought it onto the team. It was a very talented misaligned team. We tried to promote team unity and playing for one another the entire year, but it just never gelled. The result was an early exit in the playoffs and a very frustrating year. Talent without team unity will always present problems.

Throughout Jesus's ministry on earth, he traveled with a team. He chose 12 disciples from very different walks of life. He had Matthew, a tax collector that no one liked or trusted. He had Peter, James, and John, who were rough-cut fishermen that only knew how to fish. Bartholomew was the only one that may have come from royal blood and nobility. Judas was a Jewish nationalist that wanted to start a violent movement. He had Simon, the Zealot, who was also a Jewish nationalist and hated the Romans passionately. Wow! The disciples are diverse, just like a team. So, what did Jesus do? He came alongside them and taught them how to have team unity. His mission was to make sure that they would one day live out their mission. He led by example, teaching them to live outside of themselves and to live for the gospel. He washed their feet, served them, and taught them what it meant to be a servant rather than having the mentality of being served. Jesus was so instrumental in promoting team unity that his disciples carried on his ministry after his death. They carried it out to the point of their death. Let me ask you, are you a leader on your team? Are you promoting unity and bringing them together for a greater purpose? So, rally the troops, set the example, and I will see you at the plate.

Creator of Heaven, Earth and all People,

All Glory and Honor to the Father who created us, the Son who saved us, and the Holy Spirit that sustains us; As it was in the start, it is now, and ever will be, world without end. Amen.

Day 114

Next Level

Matthew 7:24-25 ***"Therefore, everyone who hears these words of mine and puts them into practice is like a wise man who built his house on the rock. The rain came down, the streams rose, and the winds blew and beat against that house, yet it did not fall because it had its foundation on the rock.***

I have a friend that has been working out for several months with no results. The truth is that he has been pretty lackadaisical about fitness with just minimum effort. So, he decided to challenge himself and sign up for the Irontribe training. Now the minute he walked through the door, he knew there was something different: The atmosphere and the ripped to the max guy holding the clipboard told him he was about to experience a whole new type of pain. So often, we push ourselves, but there is nothing like having someone else push us. The truth is that my friend has worked out to the extent of what he knows and may have pushed himself but has not developed a core to get to the next level. Irontribe will make sure that he has a base and a core. You cannot build something if you do not have a core. Those first weeks will be trying, and the truth is he will want to skip or maybe even quit. But if he sticks it out, he will be in the best shape of his life with a great core to build upon. The same kind of thing can be said about our discipleship; the reason that we are no further along in our relationship with our Father than we were two years ago is that we are not building a foundation. We may spend a little time in prayer, read a quick one-minute devotion, and we think that we are building a base, but the reality is that we are just doing maintenance to make sure our temple does not fall apart. What God wants is for us to spend quality time reading, praying, and memorizing Scripture that will build a base so that we will not get knocked over by the evil one. Remember, we are in a constant battle, and we need a firm foundation to stand against the one that came to kill, steal, and destroy. So, win the battle by building a strong base, and I will see you at the plate.

Dear Holy Servant,

In order to have a base, I have to spend time in the Word. Help me make time for you and build a base so that when I am attacked, I can stand firm. Thank you for giving me the Scripture and the availability to talk to you so that I can have a solid core.

✞

Day 115

Base First

Deuteronomy 9:18-19 ***Then once again I fell prostrate before the Lord for forty days and forty nights; I ate no bread and drank no water, because of all the sin you had committed, doing what was evil in the Lord's sight and so arousing his anger. I feared the anger and wrath of the Lord, for he was angry enough with you to destroy you. But again, the Lord listened to me.***

Several years ago, I was coaching a group of 5-6 year-olds in their first year of football. In Alabama, we start them early as this was tackle, not flag football. Now the first practice, we got everyone together, and for an hour and a half, we worked on our football playing position, and that is all we worked on. We drilled it in their head over and over. It is legs shoulder-width apart, knees slightly bent, hands out in front, elbows bent, and the whole time maintain balance. After doing this non-stop for about an hour, one of the players asked, "if we could do something else?" My response was, "You cannot do anything else till you master this." This position is used in so many sports and so many different positions on the field. The truth is that without the proper stance, you will never be able to achieve your full potential. Now I know it seems simple, and some may even say it is a waste of time, but I promise it is the most important thing you will learn. If you cannot get in the proper stance, you cannot bat; you cannot shoot a basketball, make a tackle, or receive a volleyball. You see, the stance is essential to any game you play. Many times, we are hindered from getting better because we do not know the proper stance.

It is also important for us to learn the proper stance for our prayer life. There are times when we just need to hit our knees. I have heard it said, "we do not have far to fall when we are on our knees." The fact is that hitting our knees is a simplified version of how they used to pray in the bible. In the bible, they got in the prostrate position. This is on your knees, hands on the ground, and your face in your hands. The whole position was a way of showing respect and honoring God by humbling ourselves before him. Today we have simplified that by kneeling or hitting our knees. The prayer position is essential for our growth and our relationship with Christ. Let me ask you have you fell prostrate before the Lord; if not, then I encourage you to do so, and I will see you at the plate.

Dear Messenger of Life,

Hear me as I cry out to you. I humble myself so that I can come into your Holy Presence. Just like Moses prayed for the people around him, I pray for my team that surrounds me. Lord, some of them do not know you, some are wicked and worldly, but my prayer is that I would be an example that would lead them to see you for how much you love them. Lord, I fall prostrate and asked for your forgiveness and your mercy and grace. God, thank you that you are slow to anger and abounding in mercy and love.

Day 116

Rest Day

Genesis 2:2-3 ***"On the seventh day God ended His work which He had done, and He rested on the seventh day from all His work which He had done. Then God blessed the seventh day and sanctified it because in it He rested from all His work which God had created and made".***

Many athletes struggle with rest days. They feel that they can push through without rest, and sometimes this can hurt them more than help them. We need rest to let our muscles heal and to let our minds rest. If we continue to push, we are prone to injury, and we will also mentally exhaust ourselves. Many athletes feel that they are not getting better if they rest, but rest is essential. Let me say that again, rest is essential. Having a strong work ethic and being consistent is noble, but overtraining will force one to take time off because of injury and fatigue. You will also enjoy the game more when you get to rest. If you never take time off, you will eventually just burn out. Then the game that you love will feel more like a chore than a blessing.

God intended for us not to just rest from our training but to Sabbath from everyday life. To take time to refocus, regroup and refill. The great God of the universe even rested after he created the world and said it was good. He then mandated that we work six days and take one day to rest. Many times in life, we burn our candle at both ends until we just burn out. The other thing we try is to work very hard and then take a vacation. We think the vacation makes up for the sabbath time we have already neglected. It does not work that way, sure we need a vacation, but that is just a bonus, not the end-all of our burnout. When we Sabbath, it allows us to focus on what is most important, that being our relationship with Jesus. It also helps us to reprioritize our life once again. When we are running nonstop, it is easy to lose sight of our priorities. Let me ask you, are you taking time off? Are you intentionally taking time off so that you will be healthy: physically, spiritually, and mentally? If you are not, then I beg you to take some time to Sabbath, and then after you have had a rest, I will see you at the plate.

Dear God of Breath,

Thank you for the Sabbath. The Sabbath was made for man, not man for the Sabbath. This means that it is our responsibility to rest. Help me to rest in life and athletics. Rest is essential if I am going to be who you created me to be. The Sabbath is not just about rest but about giving you the praise and worship for allowing me to do what I do. Let me rest, let me worship, and let me reprioritize.

Day 117

Home Field Advantage

Hebrews 12:1 (ESV) ***Therefore, since we are surrounded by so great a cloud of witnesses, let us also lay aside every weight and the sin which clings so closely, and let us run with endurance the race that is set before us,***

The other day I was watching Kentucky play basketball against Tennessee. (Kentucky is my favorite college basketball team.) Tennessee was the number one team in the country, yet everyone said that Tennessee was the underdog because the game was in Rupp Arena. And just like everyone thought, Kentucky won the game and won it convincingly. I think what contributed to this win was that it seemed as if they were playing with a 6th man and that 6th man was the crowd. John Calipari's record at Rupp is 136-30 (.819). That is an outstanding winning record, and in fact, they have never lost three games in a row at home since Coach Calipari got to Kentucky in 2009. Now the coach has something to do with this, but the other factor is the fans and the environment at Rupp Arena. The fans help to propel the team and to sway the officials with their noise and enthusiasm. Many people will tell you that

Rupp Arena is the best venue in college basketball. The truth is there is a home field (court) advantage. Besides, the team not having to travel and knowing the lay of the land has its advantages. We do not just have a home-field advantage in sports, but we also have it in life. We are surrounded by this great cloud of witnesses that are praying for us and cheering us on in this race we call life. We have those that went before us that set the example and the standard for what we should try to live up to. Jesus did not leave us alone but left us with a 6th man known as the Holy Spirit. The truth is that we have this advocate and this great cloud of witnesses that help us to push forward when we get down, that cheer us on when we want to quit and still applaud us when we lose. Remember that we have a home-field advantage in this world, and Satan is just the visiting opponent that is going home a loser. So now that you know you have home-field advantage, I will see you at the plate.

Dear Heavenly Abba,

I can feel you surrounding me. Your love encompasses me and sustains me. I know that I have a home-field advantage because your Son left with me the presence and power of the Holy Spirit. Thank you for that great cloud of witnesses and faith that went before me. They are cheering me on and encouraging me to finish the race that you have laid before me. We win, and that is the final word.

Day 118

Maturation Process

2 Thessalonians 3:13 ***And as for you, brothers and sisters, never tire of doing what is good.***

Sometimes a team will graduate many players or be a newly formed team, so they will struggle. Young teams are prone to get discouraged because they lose to more mature and older teams. A young team also makes many mistakes and does not know how to play together yet, but things start to fall into place as time passes and the team grows older. They start to look more like a cohesive unit, and they start to win. Many times, you will hear people refer to this as the maturation process. The problem is that people often want instant success, and they become weary, and sometimes they give up or move on. When I was in college, we were a young team, and we went 0-11 the first year we played together. Four years later, we were ranked in the NAIA top 20 and went 8-3. What changed was that we stayed together and learned how to play with one another. We grew up together, we matured together, and we learned how to lead the younger players. Now there were many players during that time who became discouraged and left. They became discouraged, and they were not willing to persevere because the going was rough. But the players that stayed not only developed a winning attitude but they grew into a family. Some of those relationships continue 20+ years later. Sometimes in life, we go through a season of drought or a season of misfortune. It is easy to let life get the best of you and give up on the faith that you once held near and dear. Discouragement leads to despair, and eventually, it can lead to destruction. The Scripture does not tell us that we won't go through rough seasons and problems, but it does say that we should not despair because God is for us and God is with us. There will be great rewards in our faith when we persevere through life. A battle-tested faith is a deep mature faith that helps not only to persevere but also to lead others. Let me ask, have you been through the maturation process? If not, you will get there, and in the meantime, continue to mature, and I will see you at the plate.

Eternal Provider of Grace,

It is so easy to get discouraged. I hate it when things do not go my way or when life throws me for a loop. Please help me to persevere and to stay close to you and my faith. At the right time, I will mature and reap the harvest that has been set before me. I will never, ever, ever give up because you care for me, and you are with me.

Day 119

Just Show Up

Joshua 6:2-4 ***Then the LORD said to Joshua, "See, I have delivered Jericho into your hands, along with its king and its fighting men. March around the city once with all the armed men. Do this for six days. Have seven priests carry trumpets of rams' horns in front of the ark. On the seventh day, march around the city seven times, with the priests blowing the trumpets.***

This week my son wrestled in a tournament that had the best throughout the southeast coming in from 5 different states to wrestle. We knew going into the tournament that he would be outmatched, as he is new to the sport and has just wrestled for about six months. He lost his first two matches, holding on as long as he could but lost both to falls (getting pinned) toward the end of the first period. He was very discouraged and quickly identified that it was going to be a tough day. I kept telling him that at least he had shown up. Many wrestlers did not show up because they knew how tough this tournament was going to be. I tried to encourage him and said, "just do your best." The time came up for his next match, and his opponent had been injured in a previous match, and he forfeited, giving Jack the win by default. It was Jack's first win for the day. Then Jack's next match, his opponent decided not to wrestle because he was wrestling another classification and wanted to save his energy for that match, another forfeit, and another win by default. In the last match of the day, Jack wrestled the guy that took first in this weight category, and he held him into the second period before he was pinned. Jack had not won a match on his own all day, but because of the two forfeits, Jack came in third and won his first-ever medal in wrestling. After the tournament, Jack's coach told him not to be ashamed of the way he won because half the battle is just showing up." The fact is that you never know the circumstances, and you never know what the outcome will be. But the one thing you do know is that if you do not show up, you have zero chance of winning. The moral for that day of wrestling was that showing up is half of the battle. The same is true in life. Many times, we are paralyzed by fear and trepidation. Other times, we are just lazy, and we decide not even to give it a chance. How many opportunities have we missed because we did not show up? In the Scripture, God tells the Army just to show up and march around Jericho. They knew they were outmatched, and then he told them not to take weapons with them but to take their horns and march around the walls. God was essentially telling them to just show up, and he would work out the rest. Now hear me say this: most of the time, just showing up is not going to be enough, but there is that rare time when showing up is all it takes. So, let me ask you will you show up? If you will, then I will see you at the plate.

God My Father and My Friend,

How many times have I let fear keep me from showing up? Please help me to realize that showing up is half of the battle. That there is no way that I can win if I do not show up. Help me to face the daunting challenges of competition and life head-on. I am reassured that I am never going alone but that you will always be with me and go before me. God, thank you for Jesus, showing up on this earth to eradicate my sins and shortcomings. Amen.

Day 120

The "No Show Fit"

Luke 9:62 ***Then Jesus declared, "No one who puts his hand to the plow and then looks back is fit for the kingdom of God."***

This week, I heard a coach say, "Do not make an excuse for losing if you made an excuse for why you did not come to practice." The truth is that we do not like to lose, but the reality is that if we do not like to practice or if we make excuses for not going to practice, then we cannot make an excuse for losing. The reality is that if you show up for practice but do not go hard while at practice, you cannot make an excuse for losing. You cannot throw a fit if you have not put in the effort. You are acting as if you care, but you were not prepared to win, so you really did not care. To care about winning and losing, you must first care about practice and preparation. Excuses are for what we did not do, not what we did to get better and win. In Scripture, three people are invited to come and follow Jesus. Notice here; I say follow, not believe. All three of those invited make an excuse for not following Jesus. They wanted the benefits of following Jesus without giving anything up. These were all valid excuses. One asked to wait till after the harvest. One wanted to put his affairs in order. The other asked to bury his father. How many times do we make an excuse for not following Jesus? How many times do we make an excuse for not showing up to church? The truth is that Jesus did not make any excuses for us, but he considered himself nothing (Philippians 2:7) and went to the cross for us. The truth is that you do not have an excuse. Quit looking for a way out and look for a way to do it. Does it seem impossible? Not with God. So, quit making excuses, and I will see you at the plate.

Lord, King, and Father,

I am the King of excuses. I make excuses for making excuses. The truth is that an excuse is a lie, so I asked you first to forgive me for my sin of excuse-making. Help me to realize that by showing up and showing out, it will make me better. Let me make no excuses for not following you and loving you because you made no excuses but emptied yourself, becoming one of us so that you could relate to us and save us. Oh, Jesus, how I love you, yes, I do, so let me show up for you. Amen.

✞

Day 121

Stats Matter

Acts 2 38-40 ***Peter replied, "Repent and be baptized, every one of you, in the name of Jesus Christ for the forgiveness of your sins, and you will receive the gift of the Holy Spirit. This promise belongs to you and your children and to all who are far off, to all whom the Lord our God will call to Himself." With many other words, he testified, and he urged them, "Be saved from this corrupt generation." Those who embraced his message were baptized, and about three thousand were added to the believers that day.***

I have heard people say, "stats do not matter." I have heard people say, "it is not about keeping score but having fun." Those statements sound great, but the reality is that it is not how sports operate. There are winners and losers, and stats do matter. You can ask any competitive athlete if it is fun to lose, and I guarantee their answer will be 'No". I would even argue that stats directly reflect the hard work and dedication that an athlete puts in. Stats tell us where we need improvement and what aspects of our game are in dire need. When I helped with high school softball, I found an app called "game-changer." This app kept every stat you could think of. It was immensely helpful to show the players the spray charts of tendencies and the places where they failed. The players could see their batting average and their on-base percentage, their slugging percentage, and their fielding percentage. It counted pitches and let the pitchers know what their strike vs. ball percentage was. It showed if a batter had a habit of doing something verse this pitcher or another. I spent hours looking at stats because they were not only essential to our losing and winning but to a player's development. Stats really do make us better, and they hold us accountable; without accountability, you will never reach your full potential. Some people would tell you that keeping church stats is not important, but that is also not true. The truth is that we want to know if we are reaching our community for Christ and how can we reach more people? A church can never be satisfied with dying from failing to make disciples. We want to be held accountable for living out the Great Commission and winning souls to Jesus. The reality is that every life matters. We should grieve when we have missed the opportunity to share Jesus with someone who does not have a relationship with him. In the Scripture, it is very specific as to how many people Jesus fed. The book of Acts is specific with the number of people who came to be a follower of the Way the day Peter stood up to preach. Yes, stats matter because they show us how much work we have left to do while here on this earth. Let me ask you are you keeping stats? If you are not, then now is the time to start. I will see you at the plate, and I will be keeping your stats.

Dear Sweet Jesus,

I need accountability, and I long for it. I am a mess apart from you. The truth is that apart from you, I can do nothing. I know because of Grace; you do not keep score of my sins. But the place where the score is kept is in the number of souls that we lead to your saving grace. We do not save them; you do that, but we can lead them into your light. Lord, let me lead people into your saving grace and a relationship with you. Thank you that you would leave 99 to come to find me. I was lost, and now I am found; I was blind, but now I see. Amen and amen.

Day 122

"Learning Life Lessons"

John 18:9 ***This happened so that the words he had spoken would be fulfilled: "I have not lost one of those you gave me."***

A lot of times, a coach will be asked the question, "how good is your team going to be this year?" Now many times, a coach's response will be, "we will wait and see." I like a response I read the other day from Joe Ehrmann. He writes in his book "Insideout Coaching" that when he is asked how good his team is going to be that he responds, "I will tell you in 20 years". See, the true essence of a coach is not just to produce wins and losses but to build young men and women of character. The question is not how good are they now, but how good are they going to be? What are they going to take from the game that will help them in everyday life? Sports in schools and universities were originally developed to help build traits that would be used throughout life. They were not the end of all like we sometimes see today but were an addendum to helping build a well-rounded person for life. Here are some traits that I learned while I played.

1. How to handle wins and losses
2. How to work as a team

3. How to respect other teammates and the other teams
4. How to play within the rules
5. They taught me the value of hard work and practice
6. How to persevere through adversity
7. How to care for body, mind, and soul
8. How to balance schoolwork, life, and sports
9. To help us stay physically fit and mentally sharp
10. They taught me to be disciplined

Now stop right here and write down some things that sports have aided you with in life off the field. Make a list of at least 5.

In the Scripture, Jesus surrounds himself with 12 disciples, and he pours his whole life into them. His hope for this is that they will carry his teachings long after he has left to be reunited with his father. Jesus often struggled with whether they were ever going to get it, but he kept being patient and kept teaching. Jesus, like a coach, used every opportunity to teach them the skills that would value them when he was no longer present with them. Jesus modeled for us what the true essence of coaching is all about. At one point, he looks to his Father and says, "look, I have not lost one that you have given to me." How many coaches can say that? He is not saying that they might turn away from God on their own accord, but he said he had not led any astray. Whether a coach or player, we need to be cognizant of those that God has entrusted us to coach and play with. Take a minute now to thank all the coaches that have poured into your life, and I will see you at the plate.

Father of All Nations,

Thank you that your Son came to show us the way. Thank you that he showed us the way to play and the way to coach. We are so blessed to have such a great example. Wins and losses matter; we cannot deny that, but what matters more is what we take from this game. What will my playing and coaching have taught me 20 years from now?

✞

Day 123

In Remembrance of Me

James 1:22-24 ***Be doers of the word, and not hearers only. Otherwise, you are deceiving yourselves. For anyone who hears the word but does not carry it out is like a man who looks at his face in a mirror, and after observing himself, goes away and immediately forgets what he looks like.***

We had the perfect play drawn up. If everyone executed the play right, we score, and we win the game. There was no way they could stop this play because they were not in the right position to handle the formation. We had them outnumbered. But the running back went to the left rather than the right, which left the one man that could make the play unblocked, and he made the play. It was game over, and we lost. When the running back came off the field, I asked him what had happened, and he responded, "I just forgot which way to go." When we forget to do our assignment or when we forget where we are supposed to be, it can have devastating consequences.

The same is true in life. When we forget who we live for and how we are supposed to be living, it is easy to reap drastic consequences upon our life. When I was a young boy, the one thing I remember about our church sanctuary were the words that were inscribed on the altar. "Do this in remembrance of me." The truth is that the altar was the focal point of the sanctuary, and these words were right in the center of the focal point. Of course, these words directly reflected communion, but it was also a weekly reminder of what direction I needed my life to be going. I wish I could say that I always remembered to walk by these words after reading them, but I often got in the middle of the game of life, and I went the wrong way. The result of me going in the wrong direction often brought shame upon my family; other times, I hurt people who did not deserve to be hurt. Did I forget, or did I just think that I knew more than my head coach in the heavens above? God has given us a game plan to protect us from self-destruction and harm to others. "Do this in remembrance of me" is remembering what Jesus sacrificed so that we could live in union with him and not sin against him. Do you need to be reminded of those words today? Do you need to check the direction that you are headed? Stop and do this in remembrance of him (Jesus), and then I will see you at the plate.

Dear Fortress of Salvation,

Help me remember why I do what I do and who gave me the ability to do what I do. To "do this in remembrance of me" is to give Jesus the glory that he deserves for giving his life for me. It seems that I should never forget what he did for me, but sometimes I do. Your Son's body was broken for me, and his blood was shed for me. I remember, and I give him all the glory, honor, and respect that he deserves.

✞

Day 124

Play Like It Is Your Last Game

Matthew 24:42 ***"Keep watch, because you do not know on what day your Lord will come."***

You never know what tomorrow holds. "Carpe Diem" This Latin phrase means "seize the day," and it certainly resonates with the sports world. We must seize each day because we don't know whether tomorrow will come or just how much of this life remains for us. How many times have we heard a coach give the pregame speech and say, "play like there is no tomorrow?" Often, an athlete enters a game, not knowing that they may be sidelined for the next game because of injury or, God forbid, suffer a career-ending injury. That is why it is so important to grasp the necessity of the "now." Many times, you are looking ahead without the promise that there will be another game. How many times did that next game never come to fruition? The reality is that embracing today becomes a habit that carries past practice and truly helps you come game time. You must embrace every day. You must embrace every opportunity. You must embrace the opportunity to practice. Yes, when you embrace the privilege of practicing, you take every event, every game, and every at-bat as a privilege. It is truly a God-given gift. We live in a world filled with distractions that can pull us away from what is important. If we are not careful, we will get lost in the constant bombardment of social media and other distractions. The same can happen in our spiritual life and our commitment to Christ. It is easy to look ahead and not give God thanks for the day he has given us. Today is an absolute gift from God. Let me ask you what you are going to do with this gift? When you lay your head down on the pillow tonight, will you feel as though you have accomplished what you set out to do, or will it have been a waste? Do you lay down more nights thinking about what you could have done or what you accomplished? So, let's make the most of today, Carpe Diem; I will see you at the plate.

Dear Creator of Day and Night,

Today is a gift, and I thank you for today. Let me make the most of today. At the end of the day, let me be able to say that I made the most use of my time and took advantage of every opportunity that was God-breathed for me. Forgive me for the days I have wasted, and let me make embracing today a habit.

Day 125

Quality vs. Quantity

Hebrews 6:11-12 (ESV) ***And we desire each one of you to show the same earnestness to have the full assurance of hope until the end, so that you may not be sluggish, but imitators of those who through faith and patience inherit the promises.***

A few people love to practice. Then there are those players that hate practice. Both know that practice is essential, but how we practice will directly impact the outcome of a game. The more time a player spends on the field or court means they are getting better. At least, this is most coaches' philosophy. But there is a question here as to if that is true? Do the more hours put in equate to you getting better? I would argue that you are only getting better if you are intense and intentional when you are practicing. You will not get better if you get on the field and go half-speed; you are just putting in the time. If you get on the field and are going all out and are focused, you will practice less, but you will gain more. If you do something repeatedly but are doing it wrong, you are just practicing doing it wrong. Practice is a time of learning to get better and a place where we learn our intensity. I see so many players that come out of the locker room hyped-up and ready to play, but they have not had any of that intensity at practice during the week, so they fall flat on their faces. My coach used to say to us, "practice does not make you perfect, but perfect practice makes you perfect." It was a statement that every day we should practice with all-out intensity. Therefore, I would argue that it is not the quantity but the quality that counts as it pertains to practice.

The same could be said in our spiritual disciplines. Are we just throwing up prayer out of habit, or are we hitting our knees and centering ourselves to talk to our creator? Are we just picking up the Scriptures and reading a few verses so that we can check off that we have read God's word for the day? The truth is that how you approach practice will be the same way that you approach everything else in life. You will either do it haphazardly, or you will do it with great intentionality. The choice is yours, and the question is, do you value quality or quantity? Take a minute and ask yourself just how intentional you have been, and I will see you at the plate.

Son of David,

I can do better. I can give more intensity and more effort. I need not focus so much on time but on what I am learning with my time. I want to approach you with a reckless abandonment that connects me in a way that transcends me. God, you gave your best for me, so I ought to, in return for your unconditional love, give my best back to you.

Day 126

For the Love of the Game

Revelation 2:4 (ESV) ***But I have this against you, that you have abandoned the love you had at first.***

Many years ago, a movie came out with Kevin Costner, entitled "For the Love of the Game." The synopsis of the movie is an aging baseball player that must decide his love of the game or his love for a lady. That statement made me think about why we play the game that we love. No matter where we are in the spectrum of the sporting world (amateur, pro, or somewhere in between), we all started out playing because we had a love for the game. The game is what drove us to be the best we could be. We could not wait until the next competition. Sometimes, because of poor coaching, pushy parents, or overplay, we lost the love for the game. I remember one girl in my youth group had an opportunity to play soccer at some pretty significant Division I schools. She came to me toward the end of her senior year, and she told me she was done with the game. She had played so much and had been pushed so hard that she had lost her love for the game. Her worst fear was telling her dad, who had sunk a fortune into travel and lessons. The truth is that the conversation turned out ok, but it still breaks my heart that she lost her love for the game. We must never lose sight of why we play the game and what it is; it is something that we should love and bring us joy. The game should not feel like an end-all or put such undue pressure on us that we cannot enjoy playing it. Sometimes we can get caught up in the same game when it comes to our walk with Jesus. We put so much pressure on ourselves to do good that we forget that we chose to follow Jesus because we loved him. He was the first love of our life. I also see this in churches when they get away from the mission that they were founded on. The mission is to bring people into that loving relationship with Jesus. Maybe it is time to return to our first love – the love that has brought so much joy and pleasure. Yes, my prayer is that you will return to your first love, and when you do, I will see you at the plate.

Dear Son of Mankind,

God, so many times, I have abandoned my first love. So many times, I have thought of following you as a chore and not as a gift. So many times, I have failed you and have not been obedient. I have failed to love you with my whole heart. I have let the world rob me of the joy of the game and the joy of life. I vow today to return to my first love—Jesus Christ, who first loved me and gave himself up for me. Help me to realize that I am Jesus' first love.

Day 127

Are You Fooling Yourself?

Proverbs 10:9 (NIV) ***Whoever walks in integrity walks securely, but whoever takes crooked paths will be found out.***

I read a quote in a devotional the other day that caught my attention. A life coach had used this statement to motivate his athletes. "You can't get where you want to go until you stop lying about where you're at." How many times do we think we are better than we are? How often do we fool ourselves into thinking we are working hard when it is obvious that there are others, even on our team, working harder than we are? You know the one that fools you the most is "you." We have a way of tricking ourselves into thinking that we are better than we are. We have a way of telling ourselves that we are going harder than we are. We have a way of holding back and then telling everyone that is all that I have. We have a way of feeling that we have arrived when we have one victory against a lesser opponent. The truth is that many times we are a "hero" in our minds. A lot of times, there are huge gaps between our desire and our discipline. Many times, there is also a gap between our words and our work. The true problem is that this is an integrity problem. You are who you are when no one else is looking at you. Another way I have heard it said is, "what would your dog say about you?"

See many times; we have an integrity issue because our work ethic does not match our expected outcome. We must live a life of integrity, and that integrity starts with being honest about where we are at and where we are going. This is not just true in the sports world but in life in general. Our integrity crosses into every area of life. Often, we are just fooling ourselves into thinking that we are alright. We need to quit fooling ourselves and realize that we need to be honest with ourselves and God. Integrity is what makes you stand out as a person, but it also is essential if you are truly going to be better in life and on the field. The tell-tell is that your integrity tells who you are. So, I would ask you to quit fooling yourself, and I will see you at the plate.

Dear Lord and Savior of My Life,

Let me quit fooling myself into thinking I am better than I am. Help me to be a person of integrity and honesty. Help me to stand out not because of my performance but because of my integrity. I have not been honest with you, my coach, or myself. I have sinned against myself, and by doing so, I have sinned against you because I am created in your image. Let people never call into question my integrity.

Day 128

Hold Your Head Up

Exodus 17:11 ***As long as Moses held up his hands, the Israelites were winning, but whenever he lowered his hands, the Amalekites were winning.***

We had just lost the final game of the Alabama 4-A State Title Football Championship Game for the second time in 3 years. We were outmatched by a private school that had a lot more talent in every position. They could give scholarships to play sports at their private high school. They had done an outstanding job of assembling the best athlete at every position. After the game, you could feel the rejection of getting to the final game again but not finishing the job even though we were outmanned at every position. After the game, our coach told the team to hold their "head up." It was hard because many knew this would be their last time to play football, and our team had come up short. Once again, the coach told the players to hold their "head up." He was trying to convey the point that they had nothing to be ashamed of because there were over 40 teams that would have liked to be playing in this game, but they had been eliminated weeks before. He conveyed the point to hold your head up because you should be proud to have even played in the Championship game. Hold your head up because you had faced adversity, and yet you were here. The ultimate truth is to hold your head up because this one game does not define you. Your persona is not defined by losing this one game. What you are defined by is the relationship that you have with Jesus. Losing is difficult, and you should never want to lose, but sometimes you are just outmanned and outmatched. "Keep your head up." Many times in life, we face difficulties and things that will leave us feeling discouraged. It is then that we hold our heads up and remember that we are not alone. God helps us lift our heads when we do not have the courage or strength to hold our heads up. There is a story in the Scripture that shows how important it is to hold your head up. Moses was in a battle with the Amalekites, and as long as Moses' hands were raised and his staff was in the air, they were winning. But when he lowered his hands, they would begin to be overtaken. This was God's way of showing Moses to keep his head up and keep his faith in God. We should follow the same example. The world may defeat us, but God sent Jesus to overcome this world. Yes, because of Jesus and the cross, we can always keep our heads up; we may lose a battle here or there, but the war is already won. The war is won because Jesus raised his arms and gave his life for ours. We hold our heads up because Jesus gave his life for us, and we have nothing to hang our heads in shame because our mistakes and sins do not define us. No, hold your head up, and I will see you at the plate.

God of the Cup,

Many times, I have hung my head in shame. Many times, I have failed to finish the game or the job. Help me to remember that even though I may sometimes fail that you always are with me. Help me hold my hands raised to you, giving you the worship you deserve for what you have done for me. You sent your only Son Jesus to stretch his arms out and die for me.

Day 129

Change in Me

Mark 11:24 ***Therefore, I tell you, whatever you ask in prayer, believe that you have received it, and it will be yours.***

How many times have you gone into a game or an event hearing about how good the other team is? You are already filled with fear and trepidation before you ever even start. I have even heard people say, "you just better pray you do not get embarrassed." So, what do you do? You begin to pray for your life, and you pray that the other team forgets what day the contest is on and does not show up. Now you need to pray, but maybe your prayer should not be about changing the other team. You know what I mean by this. We have all prayed that the other team's best player gets hurt or that their coach gets caught up in a scandal, or that the bus breaks down on the way to the game. No, our prayer should not revolve around changing the situation or the other team, but the prayer should revolve around changing you and how you feel about the way we are going into the contest. The observation here is prayer will not change the situation as much as it will change the person. What if we have been praying the wrong way for a long time? What if the outcome of our prayer was for us to be changed? Because we all know that people do not change until they want to be changed, no matter how hard we pray. The same can be said of most situations, but the truth is that most situations are out of our control. The one thing that is a common denominator in our prayer life is "us." We are a common factor in our prayer life. So, what do we pray? Here are some suggestions to help you pray through your situation.

1. Pray for a positive attitude.
2. Pray that God will change your heart.
3. Pray that God will give you perseverance.
4. Pray that God will surround you with strong teammates.
5. Pray that you will remember that this one game does not define you.

The next five devotions will focus on each one of these areas of prayer.

Yes, let's make prayer about changing us and not so much about changing a person or situation. So, stop right now and pray, and I will see you at the plate.

Dear Creator of the Way,

So many times, I have prayed for everything around me to change while neglecting to realize that I needed to change. Many times, I have even prayed for calamity or bad luck to present itself on my opponent. For this, I repent and will change. To win that way is not to give you the glory. I will begin to pray so that it truly is myself that is changed. God, thank you for sending your Son, who changed everything.

Day 130

Praying for a Positive Attitude

1 Peter 1:22 ***Now that you have purified yourselves by obeying the truth so that you have sincere love for each other, love one another deeply, from the heart.***

You may have heard a coach say, "attitude is everything." I had a teacher that had this hanging in his office. It read, "Attitude is everything. Life is 10% of what you make it and 90% of how you handle it." How true is that statement? Do you let the situation dictate your attitude, or do you let your attitude dictate how you handle the situation? The harsh reality is that so many times, the scheme of the evil one is to take us out of our comfort zone. When we get rattled, it puts our attitude to the test of fire.

The other day I was talking to a coach about one of his elite players. He told me that what made this kid so good was how he handled situations and his attitude. The coach said that if things are not going well, he keeps his composure and just keeps on keeping on. Then the coach says that if they win big or win a game that maybe they were not favored in, he stays grounded, does not think too much about it, and starts preparing for the next event. You see, this is a person that has their attitude in check. How often have you witnessed something go wrong, and that player is done for the rest of the game? You see, throwing bats, helmets, or any sports paraphernalia never took back that third strike or erased the error. It never changed the scoreboard or even changed a bad call. The truth is that letting your attitude get out of control usually leads to another strikeout or multiple errors. Throwing a fit only shows that you are out of control and not in check of your attitude. A bad attitude can also be contagious and lead to a whole team breakdown. Yes, the first place to pray for change is our attitude and how we respond to adverse situations. When we have a positive attitude, we bring about positive change, and we change how people see us and how they see the Lord. Let me ask you, have you prayed lately about how God may change your attitude? So now, with a positive attitude, I will see you at the plate.

Provider of Communion,

How many times have I thrown a fit and acted out? How often have I shattered my witness by acting like a child who did not get his way? Forgive me, Lord, for my fits and tantrums. Help me to keep a positive attitude and to have the mind of Christ in everything that I do. How I respond truly is a testimony of how I see you and how I live for you. May my attitude be one with Christ. Amen and amen.

Day 131

Change My Heart

Proverbs 4:23 ***Above all else, guard your heart, for everything you do flows from it.***

I have often heard it said after a valiant effort that an athlete had "played with heart." I have often wondered what made the coach or person come to that conclusion, and what did play with all their heart mean? I wondered if it meant giving everything they had or did it mean pushing through adverse situations? Did it mean that one was in check the whole game even when things were not going right? I would answer that maybe all of those mentioned above had a role in someone playing with heart.

You see, many times, we hear that the brain is the center of our being, but many would argue that the brain only makes choices based on the direction of the heart. I would have to argue that the heart is the center of your being. It is somehow what connects your body to your soul. To play with all your heart, you must first prepare your heart to play the game. You must have your heart in a condition that withstands the good and the bad. Now the question is, how do you do this? How do you condition your heart? I mean, physically, I know that diet and exercise, but I am talking about the spiritual window of your heart and not the physical window of your heart. The one thing that helps condition the heart is praying for your heart. Praying that God would open the windows of your heart to see as he sees, praying that God will give you a right and contrite heart, praying for your heart to be pure and Holy, praying that your heart would be steadfast and upright in the sight of the Lord. I have even argued with people before that they do not have a sin problem but a heart problem. The sins were just symptoms of a wayward heart. I have always said if you show me a person's heart, I can tell you who that person is. See, we have a keen way of talking our hearts into and out of things. Want to play better; change your heart. Want to love better; change your heart. Want to quit sinning; change your heart. Yes, the condition of your heart directly influences whether your heart is bent toward the ways of God or the ways of the world. When the heart is changed, the whole person is changed. So, let's stop right now and say a prayer from your heart and for your heart. When you have finished checking the condition of your heart, I will see you at the plate.

Dear Vine,

Change my heart of God that I may have a pure heart. Change my heart, oh Lord, so that I may see the world with the lenses of my heart and not just my eyes. Break my heart for what breaks yours. Let me play the game of life with heart and when I pass away, let them say that I had a heart for God.

Day 132

Playing through Adversity: Perseverance

2 Timothy 4:7-8 ***I have fought the good fight, I have finished the race, and I have***

remained faithful. And now the prize awaits me—the crown of righteousness, which the Lord, the righteous Judge, will give me on the day of his return. And the prize is not just for me but for all who eagerly look forward to his appearance.

One of the hardest things for an athlete to do is to keep playing through when things are not going the way they think they should. But if we are going to be successful, we should be able to play through nagging injuries and adverse obstacles. Many things that we try to control are out of our control. The true test of a champion is how they respond when things are not going their way. There are two options when things blow up: to quit or to play on. That is why we must be prayed up when we get to a situation that requires perseverance. See, God wants us to pray before we get to the adverse situation. One way to do this is to ask God to go before you and prepare your way. The most important thing that this form of prayer does is let you know that you are not alone. It lets you know that God is right there with you. The other thing that prayer does is that it gives you the power of the Holy Spirit. The Holy Spirit is the untapped power source that goes before and gives us the strength to play through pain, suffering, and adversity. The third element of praying through perseverance is that it prepares you for when you have given your all and still came up short. Paul is a great example of perseverance and praying through situations that would often arise. Here is a list of things that happened to Paul during his ministry, according to 2 Corinthians 11:25-29. "Three times I was beaten with rods, once I was pelted with stones, three times I was shipwrecked, I spent a night and a day in the open sea, I have been constantly on the move. I have been in danger from rivers, in danger from bandits, in danger from my fellow Jews, in danger from Gentiles, in danger in the city, in danger in the country, in danger at sea, and in danger from false believers. I have labored and toiled and have often gone without sleep; I have known hunger and thirst and have often gone without food; I have been cold and naked. Besides everything else, I face daily the pressure of my concern for all the churches. Who is weak, and I do not feel weak? Who is led into sin, and I do not inwardly burn?" Based on this list, would you have given up? But Paul had a greater goal than himself. Paul wanted everyone to know that Jesus came and died for the forgiveness of their sins. Your sins are forgiven, so I will see you at the plate.

Dear Jesus Friend of Mine,

God help me to pray before I get to the crisis, not just during the crisis. God help me to push through when I feel like giving up. Help me to realize that you are with me all the time. Help me to see that I can do things that I think that I cannot do. My prayer continues to be "with God; all things are possible." Let me press on to obtain the prize my Lord has already earned for me through his death.

Day 133

Strong Team Mentality

Luke 11:1 ***One day, Jesus was praying in a certain place. When he finished, one of his disciples said to him, "Lord, teach us to pray, just as John taught his disciples."***

What kind of teammate are you? Go ahead, tell me. Now, what if I ask that question of your teammates? What would they say about you as a teammate? Would they say that you are pompous, arrogant, or selfish? Maybe they would tell me that you are the ultimate team player. (By the way, this is the better option.) In many circumstances, God has given us a great ability to play the game, but he has also given us the unique opportunity to be a part of a team. The team concept has always been important to God; we know this because he set all the tribes up and put people into unique communities. It is also why Jesus chose a team and did not just do ministry solo style. So, let me ask you, do you pray for your teammates? Do you take time to know what they are going through on the field and off the field? A simple prayer can change a player and potentially lead that player into a new and different relationship with Jesus.

Another beneficial prayer is praying that our teammates do not get injured or quickly recover from a recent injury. The next thing that we are praying over teammates is that they will be willing to work together and work for common goals. A team that is bonded together and prayed over can handle adversity better than a splintered team. Do not just be a teammate; be a "praymate." You will be the true captain of the team, well, at least the prayer captain. I think that it is so ironic that the disciples could ask Jesus for anything but what they ask of him was that he teach them to pray. They, at the time, did not realize how that simple prayer would help to sustain them and carry them through tough and trying days. Let me ask you not what kind of team you are but what kind of praymate are you. Hey, stop right now, hit your knees, and I will see you at the plate.

Teacher of Prayer, our Father who art in heaven, hallowed be thy name. Thy Kingdom Come. Thy will be done on earth as it is in heaven. Give us this day our daily bread, and forgive us our trespasses, as we forgive those who trespass against us, and lead us not into temptation, but deliver us from evil. For thine is the kingdom and the power, and the glory, forever and ever. Amen.

Day 134

Not Defined by One Game

I John 5:14 ***This is the confidence we have in approaching God: if we ask anything according to his will, he hears us.***

Have you ever just had one of those days? You have prepared, and you felt ready, but for whatever reason, this day, you just have fallen flat on your face. If you play the game long enough, you will experience a game when nothing goes right. You were better prepared and the better team, but it was just not your desired outcome. This week I was watching the conference tournaments in NCAA Basketball, and Gonzaga was playing. They have been projected a number one seed all year going into their conference tournament. But in the first game, they lost to a lower seed. They were the better team, and they had a lot more talent; it was just that the ball would not go in the basket. Now they will get another chance, and they will still probably be the number one seed.

After their conference loss, I heard one of the sports analysts say, "they cannot let this game define them, or they will go into the next contest behind." The truth is that one game can never define us, but so often, we let one bad game turn into a downward spiral. The same is true in life. So many times, we just mess up because we are messy people. But our mistakes or one event does not define us. When we find our faith in God, we are prepared for that terrible game because we have already surrounded it in prayer. We have convinced ourselves that what defines us is God's love and that Satan is not permitted to remind us of our mistakes. Prayer not only draws us into the presence of God but also centers us on things that happen on the field and in life. Prayer is not an option, as you have seen through this week of devotions. Prayer is essential if you are going to be prepared for life and be the teammate that God has called you to be. Yes, there is immense value to being physically prepared. There is also immense value in being mentally prepared. But I would argue that the most crucial element to the game is being prayed up so you can play up. Hey, prayer warrior, I will see you at the plate.

Dear Sweet Breath of Air,

Make my life a prayer. Let me be in constant prayer with you. Let me pray for my teammates, opponents, and the spectators that give me a lot more value than I deserve. God, I do not want to be just a teammate; I want to be a "praymate." May my knees be sore, and my mouth be open as my words go from my lips to your heart. Lord, teach me to pray.

Day 135

Dream Big, Achieve Big

Ephesians 3:20 ***Now to him who can do immeasurably more than all we ask or imagine, according to his power that is at work within us,***

Do you dream big, or do you think small? The reality of this concept is that it is a mentality. Sometimes one has been programmed to think that they cannot achieve it. Sometimes, they have been told that they are not worthy and will never amount to anything from an early age. If someone has heard this over and over, they are programmed to think on a small scale. The reality is that sports are all about breaking us out of the mindset that one cannot achieve or win it. Sports is littered with stories of teams and individuals that have defied all the odds. Sports is about dreaming big so that we can do great things. You have heard it said, "the sky is the limit, but that is only true if you believe it." But it goes a step further than that; you must also work hard to live out big dreams. So often, even in everyday life, we think small, and we live small. We see life as boring and mundane because we do not dream bigger than life. The truth is that we often see our God as small instead of a big audacious God that he is. You see, God is infinite, and God wants us to dream big; the bigger we dream, the bigger our God gets. You see, God wants you to do the impossible, and with him, all things are possible. I read this quote the other day from an unknown author, but it is a great quote. "Every pro was once amateur; every expert was once a beginner, so dream big and start now." So what are you waiting for? Think big, dream big, be big. See you at the plate.

Dear Infinite, All-Powerful Mighty God of Big Dreams,

Forgive me for shrinking you; forgive me for thinking and dreaming small. Forgive me for settling for the mundane, common life. Help me to dream big and to look at you as a Big God. Let me not put you in a box or limit what you can do with my doubt. God, how majestic is your name in all the earth? There is nothing small about that statement. Amen and amen.

✞

Day 136

Learning to Enjoy the Moment

Psalms 118:24 ***This is the day the LORD has made. We will rejoice and be glad in it.*** 1 Thessalonians 5:16-18 ***"Rejoice always! Pray constantly. Give thanks in everything, for this is God's will for you in Christ Jesus."***

Let me ask you, are you able to enjoy the moment? Have you learned how to just give God the thanks for now? The reality is that in the world we live in today, it is often "a time to move on mentality." A few years ago, someone asked Nick Saban how long he would enjoy this win after he had won the national championship. His response was, "I will enjoy for about 24-48 hours, and then it is time to hit the road to recruit for the next year." Now I understand part of that, but I think sometimes it is good to just breathe. To just enjoy the moment that God has given us. To not always look ahead too far because it robs us of the joy of the moment. We have to be careful that we do not miss the now while looking at the future. The truth is that we do not know what the future holds. Only the Good Lord knows what tomorrow holds. My wife did not know what to get me for Christmas, so she got me an iWatch. Now I did not know what to think or whether I would like it. But so far, it has turned out to be a useful tool for workouts and information. But one thing I like that it does is that it reminds me to enjoy the moment. It will vibrate my wrist from time to time, and it will simply remind me to breathe. It reminds me to stop what I am doing for just a second and take in the now. Sometimes that is what we need to do. We just need to breathe. To breathe in the Spirit of God. To breathe in the life that God has given us; to breathe it deep into our lungs. To just enjoy this moment and not look ahead. We must remember that what we do have is the now and no promise of the future. So, let me ask you this have you stopped to enjoy the moment? Have you stopped to breathe in the very breath of God? If not, do so right now, and I will see you at the plate.

Dear Provider,

You are the very breath that I inhale. You live in me and through me so that the world may see you through me. I would aspirate without your breath filling my lungs. Your breath represents the presence of your being in my life. Breath in me and make me whole. Breath into my soul so that it comes alive. Breath upon my dry bones so that they may live. Amen.

Day 137

Playing with Heart

Colossians 3:23 ***"Whatever you do, do it with all your heart for God and not for man."***

This week we are going to focus on what it means to play with **H.E.A.R.T.** You have heard this stated a million times, but what does it mean? How can you prepare to play with your heart? We have said this before, but the truth is that the heart is the central core of your being. To have a heart means that you never give up even when everything is stacked against you. Playing with heart means that you go into the contest, always thinking you can win. It also means that you understand that some things are out of your control, so you handle what is in your control without letting the things that are not in your control get you out of control. So, what does it meant to play with HEART? Here is what we will cover this week:

H= Hard work always beats talent and skill.

E= Earn it and do not expect that it will be given to you.

A= Your Attitude will always be the outpouring of your heart.

R= Repetition renews our confidence.

T= Being thankful that you have the opportunity to play this game.

See you at the plate.

Infinite God,

This week I am going to open my heart up to you so you can show me how to play from the heart and not from the head. God, my heart is fragile and has been broken so many times, but you are there to restore my heart and my soul. You are there to carry me when I cannot walk. You help me to gain strength when I am weary. God, break my heart for what breaks yours. Amen to all in the name of the Father, the Son, and the Holy Spirit.

Day 138

Hard Work Always Pays Off

Proverbs 18:9 ***"Whoever is slack in his work is a brother to him who destroys."***

We know that the Scripture is very upfront that we are saved by grace and not by works. (Ephesians 2:8) So, you would think that hard work would be futile. But the truth is that hard work is the result of grace working in your life. The Holy Spirit manifests hard work to make a difference in your life and the lives of those around you. Hard work leads to us having a healthy spiritual heart.

The question that many coaches ask now about a player is how his/her work ethic is. You can be off the charts talented, but if you do not work hard, it is contagious to a team. When your most talented player works super hard and does not just depend upon their God-given skills, it causes the whole team to have a strong work ethic. The truth is that laziness and going through the motions are just as contagious as the concept of hard work. The truth is that hard work will always take priority or talent. The truth is that we often see this on the field; the most talented team loses because they did not put in the preparation and the work. Now I bring this to the forefront when we are talking about "playing with heart" because playing with heart is an everyday thing, not a once in a while thing. You cannot have four lazy days and one good day and win championships. You see, when you are used to hard work, your heart can take things that unexpectedly come up. The condition of your heart is a direct reflection of your hard work. In the Scripture, we see where King David refused to go to war. (You may want to pause here and read the story in 2 Samuel.) He refused to go out and fight as he had done in the past. This one decision led to a heart issue, which would change the trajectory of David's life. So, what does he do? Instead of fighting with his men, he sleeps with one of his top soldiers' wives and later has Uriah killed after discovering that he has impregnated Bathsheba.

You see, David traded the hard work that the Kings do in the spring to defend his Kingdom for a lazy way of life. David had all the talent in the world as God had selected him, but he traded hard work for entitlement in this case. Look back upon your competing life at how many times you got caught because you refused to work hard. Now look at your spiritual life and ask the question of how many times you have fallen into sin because you became lethargic and lazy. Yes, your heart condition will be a direct reflection of your work ethic. So, let me ask you, how is your heart, or better yet, how is your work ethic? Check it, and then I will see you at the plate.

Dear Creator of Hard Work,

Let me understand that my heart is a direct reflection of my work ethic. I failed so many times because I have become lazy and become tired of doing good. The condition of my heart will directly affect how I play and how I live my life off the field. God, let me like David, a person that is after your own heart.

Day 139

Reflections of the Heart

Jeremiah 17:9-10 ***"The heart is more deceitful than all else And is desperately sick; Who can understand it? "I, the LORD, search the heart, I test the mind, Even to give to each man according to his ways, According to the results of his deeds.***

Your attitude is always a reflection of your heart. That is a profound statement but one that is so true. How often have you seen a good player ruin the way people viewed them because of their attitude? I was watching an AAF football game the other night. It was Birmingham Iron vs. Memphis Bolts; both teams are new to the AAF league. Now the reason that this game was so intriguing is that Johnny Manziel, the Heisman Trophy winner from Texas A&M, had just been acquired by Memphis. Now what I was hoping to see was a new, refined change of attitude in Johnny Manziel, but instead, I saw the same thing that got him kicked out of the NFL. They saw the same thing that recently got him kicked off a team in Canada. In the second series, he was already cussing other players and started a fight. The fight had to be broken up, and then I watched as hot head Johnny went to the sidelines and even started yelling back at a coach. It is just heartbreaking that here we are on at least three chances and no change. He does not play with the heart; he plays with talent and a bad attitude, and that bad attitude means that he truly does not play with heart. Several times we hear in the Scripture that God looks upon the heart when he chooses. Samuel picked the first King for the Israelites because he viewed him as tall in stature and good-looking. He picked Saul, but Saul failed. The reason he failed was because of his heart. His heart was full of himself. His heart was full of anger. His heart was full of jealousy, and it showed in the way that he led the people and eventually plotted to have David, his successor killed. You see, Saul refused to look inside his own heart and to see the corruption and evil. He was warned and even had his son tell him he needed a heart change, but he refused because of his selfish ambition. Saul led from his strength and mind, not from the heart. Let me ask you to take a look at the reflection of your heart. How does it look? How do other people see it? After you have looked at your heart refection, I will see you at the plate.

Dear King of My Heart,

Please search for my heart. Show me the places that contain anger, self-centeredness, envy, malice, hatred, and jealousy. Create in me a new heart and heart that values love, peace, contentment, mercy, justice, and renewing graces. Let me be of the heart of Jesus. For his attitude always reflected his heart, and that was pure.

Day 140

Repetition Renews Our Confidence

---

2 Timothy 2:15 ***Do your best to present yourself to God as one approved, a worker***

who has no need to be ashamed, rightly handling the word of truth.

Repetition, repetition, repetition. How many times have you heard a coach make this statement? The truth is that repetition is as exhausting for the coach as it is for the player. But we all know in sports, repetition is essential to getting better and being consistent. Constant repetition is what trains the muscles, the mind, and the body. But it goes a step further than that, and it also trains the heart. Repetition trains the heart to persevere through difficult times and adverse situations. You see, repetition in and of itself takes to heart. It has been said that it takes 10,000 repetitions to master something.

You see, when we master something, it means that we are not second-guessing. It means that we can perform at a high level through muscle memory without thinking about what we are doing. It means that deep within our hearts, we believe we will make the shoot, hit the ball, or make the last out. It means that playing with heart had come from reaching deep within while we were repeating the same thing over and over. We may have been complaining over and over about doing the same things over and over, but now the repetition will pay off. Now repetition is not just in our sporting life but also in our spiritual life. Have you trained your heart through prayer, Scripture reading, and memorization of Scripture? The sobering reality is that life can change in the tick of a second. I remember the night that we got the call from my mother-in-law that my father-in-law had just died of a massive heart attack. He was one minute talking with her, and the next minute he was gone. Just like that, in the twinkling of an eye, everything changed. Now in order for my mother-in-law to move on, she will have to play with heart, even if it is a broken heart. When we train our spiritual side, we are ready for whatever happens in life. Train, repeat, and I will see you at the plate.

Sacrifice for Our Sins,

Let me pray: Repeat
Let me read Scripture: Repeat
Let me memorize Scripture: Repeat
Let me journal: Repeat
Let me serve others: Repeat
Let Me Love the Lord: Repeat

✞

Day 141

In All Things Give Thanks

Psalms 116:17 I will offer you the sacrifice of thanksgiving and call on the name of the Lord.

One of the things we will sometimes do in small groups is ask, "what are you thankful for?" The odd thing about this is that people rarely give thanks for tangible things; it is always intangible things like health, employment, education, loving parents, or that they are just glad to be alive. This same thing should be evident in our privilege to play the sports that we play. We have been given the rare opportunity to play something very few get the opportunity to play. The higher the level (high school, college, professional), the more grateful and appreciative we should be. The reality is that what I see is that the higher up the ladder people go, the less they play with heart. I also have realized that they take for granted what God is allowing them to do. The reality is that one day it will be gone. The Scripture says, "life can change in the twinkling of an eye" (1 Corinthians 15:52). The only thing you will have are memories of what you did or did not achieve. If you did not play with your heart, you have more regrets than you do accolades. People that play the game with heart know to make the most of every opportunity. They realize what a gift they have been given, and they need to make the most of every opportunity that presents itself. The truth is that the player that plays with a grateful heart is the player that plays with a love of the game and a love for life. It is common that a player that plays with the heart on the field will also play with heart in every aspect of life. They will give thanks for the intangible things that they did not earn but have been given to them through our Lord and Savior, Jesus Christ. You see, giving thanks starts with what Jesus did for you on the cross and continues to do for you through the power of the Holy Spirit. So, get out there and enjoy the opportunity and play with heart, a grateful heart, and I will see you at the plate.

Good, good, good, God,

I have so often taken for granted the opportunities that are before me. I failed to give you the thanks that you deserve. I have deserted the love for the game for the taste of money, fortune, and fame. I have failed to play with my heart and have suffered the consequences. But today, I am reminded that my thanks come from a hill far away from where my Savior bled and died for me. Let me play this game of life with a thankful heart. I am giving thanks every day for what you have done for me and the opportunities you have given me.

✞

Day 142

Quit Playing Prevent

2 Timothy 1:7 ***For the Spirit God gave us does not make us timid but gives us power, love, and self-discipline.***

The coach took the podium to explain how they had just lost a six-point lead and had lost the game. He explained that against his better judgment, he had dropped them back to play "prevent defense." He said that this allowed the other team to complete many underneath passes, and then on a screen, two defenders ran into each other, allowing for a clear lane to the end zone. The team scored to tie the game and then kicked the extra point to win the game by one and move on to the championship. The coach said these words, "We got beat because I played it safe." The coach offered these closing remarks at the press conference, "To my players and the fans, I apologize because this one is on me." How many times have we been burned for playing it safe? So often, we play not to lose rather than play to win. What happens when we do this, we throw our game plan out the window and hope for the best. The truth is what we start to play with is fear and not confidence. Fear in a game will get you beat just like it will in life. If you operate out of fear, then you have forsaken your hidden weapon. You have forsaken the fact that God is for you, and he wants you to be on the offense. He wants you to advance the kingdom, not withdraw because you fear the world. One of the sad things I see in today's world is people playing prevent. They put their lives and even their children in a bubble rather than playing offense and advancing the kingdom of God. Paul made it pretty plain that he was not going to play defense. He had been beaten and jailed to force him into a prevent mode, but he refused to adhere to fear. No, instead, Paul conquered his fear through the power of the Holy Spirit. Paul's offensive scheme was to share Jesus with as many people as he could. He was never a coward going into a prevent; instead, the more they tried to muzzle his message, the more fervent he was about moving forward. Let me ask you this question, in your faith, have you been playing prevent? Have you been bold, or have you been timid? Hey, we are on offense; I will see you at the plate.

Dear Shepherd of the Flock,

God help me not to cower in fear. Help me to play to win and not play to lose. God, you have given me a spirit of power and might. God, I will fail if I buy into the fear that the world wants to impose upon my life. I will never waiver from the offensive game plan that you have laid out in my life. I face the world the same way that Jesus faced the cross. He faced it with love for me and not a fear of death because death had no power over him, and therefore there was no fear.

✞

Day 143

What Is Your Excuse?

Romans 2:1 ***You, therefore, have no excuse, you who pass judgment on someone else, for at whatever point you judge another, you are condemning yourself, because you who pass judgment do the same things.***

Have you ever met someone that has an excuse for everything? They never achieve or win, but they always have an excuse for why they failed to win the game, make the grade or get the job. The truth is that excuses are the reasons why we did not achieve it. You never hear a winner make an excuse or project the blame onto someone else. A winner does not need to make excuses because they trained, prepared well, and carried out the game plan. You see, excuse makers spent as much time trying to finagle their way out of things rather than just hitting it with passion and the drive to win. Here, let me give you some examples of some excuses I have heard along the way: The referees cheated us; they had it out for us the whole game. The other team had the home-field advantage. The field condition was horrid, so we could not play to our strength. Well, the other team cheats; they have illegal players. The other team had more time to prepare. The other team did not have as tough of a schedule and played easier teams to get here. And the hits could just play on, but I will stop. Now here is a harsh reality, you will keep making excuses if you do not make changes. Here is a great quote for you to put in your toolbox. “Make excuses or make changes; the choice is yours." If you want to quit making excuses for losing, you must change your preparation, team, or coaching style.

An excuse revealed the first sin ever committed by Adam and Eve. God had given Adam and Eve one commandment. I mean, how much simpler does that get? One commandment to live by and live forever. If you follow this one rule, everything will always be good, no sin, no death, no war, no famine, no fear, no loneliness. (No sin, no problem.) But we know that the temptation got the best of them, and then after they sinned, they began to make excuses. The woman blamed the serpent, and the man blamed the woman. If they had just followed what they were supposed to do, then they would not have had to make an excuse. How many times in your life have you had to make an excuse for your sin, for your shortcomings, and for not doing what you were expected to do? Yes, the truth is that winners and overcomers of sin do not have to make excuses. So stop making excuses, and I will see you at the plate.

Fountain of Israel,

You created everything to be perfect, and yet we messed it up. The truth is that under temptation, I would have also sinned and fallen short of the glory of God. I need to quit making excuses for my sin and my losses. I need you to help me to change because without a change in my life. I will just continue to make excuses and try to hide my sin. God, nothing is hidden from you. For you knew me while I was still in my mother's womb. Because of your Son Jesus Christ, I have no excuses because the game has already been won, and Satan has been defeated. I win, no excuses.

Day 144

Daring Greatly

Matthew 25:21 ***"Well done, good and faithful slave!"***

How do you define success? Do you define it by wins and losses, or do you define it by personally giving everything you got? Do you give it your all every time you compete? The world defines success by wins and losses, but sometimes, you can succeed in life and the game even in a loss. At the end of every game, if you can look in the mirror and say that you held nothing back, that you finished the contest as strong as you started, then you were successful. I watched an amazing performance by a young man this week that played for Purdue Boilermakers. Carsen Edwards almost single handily won an elite eight-game against Virginia. He scored 56% of Purdue's points, hitting ten three-pointers and scoring 42 points. (Purdue still came up short, losing the game 80-75). During one of his free throw attempts, I noticed that Carsen had three things written on the white tape on his wrist. So naturally, I investigated and found this is what he had written on his wrist. "Thank God," "Help Mama Out," and "The Man in the Arena." Now I had to do some research on the last quote, and I found out that this quote is from Theodore Roosevelt. He used this quote to encourage completion and giving it everything you got. Here is how Roosevelt explains the quote: "The credit belongs to the man who is actually in the arena, whose face is marred by dust and sweat and blood; who strives valiantly; who errs, who comes short again and again, because there is no effort without error and shortcoming; but who does strive to do the deeds; who knows great enthusiasms, the great devotions; who spends himself in a worthy cause; who at best knows, in the end, the triumph of high achievement, and who at the worst, if he fails, at least fails while daring greatly..."[9] While this quote came long before Carsen Edwards was born. The striking thing to me is that Carsen Edwards had already defined his success with the writing on his wrist. I knew if he gave all he had, and they still came up short, he had still given all that he had. This is the freeing concept of not worrying about the outcome, the other team, or even how your team responds. Simply give everything you have so that at the end you can say, "I dared greatly." Have you ever thought about those in the Scripture that dared greatly? Those that risk their life so that the gospel of Jesus Christ could be shared with us today. Many times, these people dared so greatly that they lost their lives. They died while daring to confront society, the system, and Satan. It is documented that 10 of the remaining Disciples all lost their life while daring greatly for the kingdom of God. Let me ask you not what is written on your wrist but what is written on your heart. I hope you have written there, "The man in the Arena." It is time to dare greatly, and I will see you at the plate.

Dear Ark of the Covenant,

God, the greatest example we have of daring greatly was your Son and the sacrifice he gave to us. He was the man in the arena and the man on the cross. When the world thought that he was defeated, he conquered death and was resurrected so we could dare greatly. God help me to be bold, to be wise, and to give it my all. Thank you for loving me, and thank you for your Son. I love you. Amen.

Day 145

Speaking Truth in Love

Ephesians 4:15 (NLT) ***Instead, we will speak the truth in love, growing in every way more and more like Christ, who is the head of his body, the church.***

Coaches can be rather hard on players, and it seems that they are hardest on those who may not be playing up to their potential. Coaches have a unique way of looking at players and knowing if they are playing up to their potential. When coaches observe this, they have the tough job of speaking the truth in love. They try to balance their coaching between making the player better with constructive criticism or tearing the player down out of frustration. The same could be said in parenting also, but that is for another book. The truth is that when a coach speaks the truth in love, he is helping the player become well-rounded in all aspects of their game. No one likes criticism, but you can never improve without it. You will never reach the pinnacle of your talent without a coach speaking the truth in love. . One of the things I see in the professional ranks of sports today is that players think they are above the law. (Well, at least above the coach.) They cannot take coaching, and they struggle with accountability and criticism.

I have seen several coaches leave the professional ranks to return to college because they said that the professional athletes were uncoachable. Let me ask you, do you believe you are above the coach? Do you think that you have arrived? If you do, then my prayer for you is that you would humble yourself to receive someone to speak to you in truth and love. This is not just for on-the-field but also in life. If we are going to be who God wants us to be, we will need people to speak the truth in love. We need people to hold us accountable and to make us better people and players. You see, God speaks the truth in us through other people. The question is, how do we receive what people are speaking to us in love? Do we listen and then turn and do our own thing? Do we not listen and just act as if we heard what is said? Or do we listen with an open heart and open mind to receive the truth in love? When we do this, we not only listen, but we apply the truth that has been spoken to us. I urge you to listen to someone speaking the truth in love because they truly love you and want you to be better. So, listen intently, and I will see you at the plate.

Dear Sword Of The Spirit,

Speak to me through Godly people so that I can be who you want me to be. Mold me, mend me, break me, and then shape me back into your image. I have often created my own image, the image of me, and who I think I should be. Speak the truth in love to me through your Holy Spirit. Help me to realize that the truth you speak into my life will not always be easy to receive, but it is for my good and the good of others. Word of God, please speak to my heart and let me receive it. Amen.

Day 146

Looking Too Far Ahead

Matthew 6:34 (CEV) ***Don't worry about tomorrow. It will take care of itself. You have enough to worry about today.***

Have you ever got caught looking past the next game? During the playoffs or tournaments, we can often get caught looking too far down the road. This sometimes leads us to overlook the next opponent. The next game up is always the most important game. If we overlook that game, we may not even have the opportunity to play the game we are most worried about or looking forward to playing. So many times, in sports and life, we get too far ahead of ourselves. We begin to worry about tomorrow when tomorrow is not even here yet. That is why the statement, "there is no time like the present," is one to live by and bears repeating every day. The moment you have is now, and the next game is, well, the next game. This game will affect the next game, and in life, this decision will affect the next decision.

It had never happened: a 16-seed had never upset a number 1 seed in the NCAA tournament. But as you know, it was going to happen at some point, and it did. In 2018 Virginia, a number 1 seed and a strong pick to win the whole tournament, got beat by UMBC. The world was stunned, and everyone's bracket was busted. So what happens? Well, the Virginia player interviewed said that they had overlooked the game and that they had focused on the next game up because, on paper, it looked like a tougher game. They had overlooked the immediate opponent, and now rather than playing in the next round, they would be watching someone else play.

The next year Virginia was back in the tournament, and as of me writing, they are playing in the final four. The reason is that they said in this year's interview that they did not overlook any team. They took care of business one game at a time. Now let me ask you another question, do you worry more about tomorrow than today? Do you let the fear of the unknown and the uncertainty of what tomorrow holds rob you of the joy of today? God gave us specific instructions that we should not worry about tomorrow but embrace today because this is the day the Lord has made and given us. Another point to make here is that God is already going before you and is with you now. So, quit worrying about your next time at-bat, and I will see you today at the plate.

Dear Creator of Yesterday, Today, and Tomorrow,

God, help me to embrace today and not to worry about tomorrow. For no worry can change what tomorrow brings. Amen.

Day 147

Unclean Lips

Isaiah 6:5 (NIV) **"Woe to me!" I cried. "I am ruined! For I am a man of unclean lips, and I live among a people of unclean lips, and my eyes have seen the King, the Lord Almighty."**

It seems like cussing and playing sports go hand in hand. I have often wondered why coaches cuss to get the attention of their players. I think that it is no longer effective. The truth is that it was probably never effective. It is so ineffective in today's world because we have become immune to bad language. After all, it surrounds us; it is everywhere. We hear cussing in our music, written in articles, and all over television interviews and programs. It is all over Facebook and social media and is more common in public than ever. I was even at a college game last year where the opposing fans had made up t-shirts that said, _ _ _ _ the Tigers. (You fill in the blanks with any four-letter word you would like.) Yes, we are surrounded by unclean lips, and the truth is it has bled over into our lives.

Now is confession time, and the confession is that I have often struggled with cussing and language when I get angry or when things get out of sorts. But the truth is that cussing and raving mad does not change anything. It has ruined my witness on more than one occasion. I will never forget my senior year of football. I had given my life to Christ, started a Bible study for the team, and had been a keynote speaker at FCA and The Baptist Student Union. I had done a good job that year of really taming my tongue. The truth was that it was easy off the field, but when I got on the field, I would cuss if I got irate, and I mean to say bad – bad words.

The reality was that I would lead a devotion and prayer, and then I would cuss the man across from out of Saturday. I was truly a man of unclean lips. The flip side of this was that I was also ruining my witness with those I played alongside. It was truly an area where my walk did not match my talk. (No pun intended.) As I got older and became a Chaplain, I understood just how bad that language sounded. I will never forget one game when we were losing at halftime, and the defensive coordinator did not use more than three words without using an explicative to explain how the defense was playing. After the game, one of the players came up to me and asked why the coach thought that language would work to motivate the players. He said, look, "No one deserves to be talked to that way." You know what, he was exactly right. When we speak with unclean lips or gossip, we are ruining our witness for Jesus Christ. Let me ask you a personal question, are you a person of unclean lips? If you are, then zip it, change it, and I will see you at the plate.

Dear Balm of Gilead,

I am a man of unclean lips. Please help me to tame the tongue. Help me only to speak the truth in love and things that build up the kingdom of God. Help my words to be my witness, and my hands and feet be my service. I love you, Lord.

Day 148

Pushing Through with Help

Luke 22:42-43 ***An angel from heaven appeared to him and strengthened him. 44 And being in anguish, he prayed more earnestly, and his sweat was like drops of blood falling to the ground.***

It is bound to happen at some point. You feel the fatigue. You are worn out. You have gone so hard for so long, and now you are struggling to do another rep. Sometimes this is called the mid-season blues. Now the mid-season blues can affect you physically, spiritually, and mentally. You must remember that all of your being's components are essential for success in sports and life. But you are exhausted, you are spent, and you feel as if you cannot continue. You look for motivation, but you continue to come up empty. You are told to push through, but you do not have the strength or the drive at this point. Sometimes this happens in the form of an injury. You are rehabbing, but it seems to be going nowhere. You take two steps forward and three steps back. This is where you can find a strength that you may have forgotten existed. You can find the power of the Holy Spirit. The Holy Spirit is the source that many people are keenly unaware of. We often think that the Holy Spirit is solely for the spiritual things in our lives, but the Spirit is also known for helping us overcome our daily battles and even fatigue. The Spirit can help us push through mental and physical hurdles as well as spiritual dilemmas. So often, we forget that the Holy Spirit is like our secret weapon. We neglect the fact that the Spirit is for us and not against us. The Spirit wants to lift us and propel us forward. In the Scripture, the Holy Spirit is known as a "parakletos."

Now the ironic thing about this word is that it means counselor or comforter. This is so good to know that Jesus left us not just a bunch of instructions, but he left with us a Spirit that abides in us and for us. The Spirit is the motivation and the reason that when we are exhausted, we can take one more step. The Holy Spirit is truly our biggest fan because he is directly given to us by the Father and sustains us and propels us to move forward. I know you are exhausted, but do you feel the power of that presence in your life. That is the power that Christ left with us and the power that wants us to tap into and use when we feel that we can no longer push on. So, dig deep and feel the presence of the Holy Spirit in your life, and I will see you at the plate.

Dear Holy Spirit,

I am exhausted. I am spent. I have no strength left. But I know that you did not leave me as an orphan, but you gave me the power of the Holy Spirit. You are a triune God. You are the creator, savior, and sustainer. The Holy Spirit not only counsels me but pushes me through fatigue and discouragement. Thank you that I have power from above, and I can do things through the Spirit that gives me power.

✞

Day 149

Doing It Together

Mark 3:13-15 ***Jesus went up on a mountainside and called to him those he wanted, and they came to him. He appointed twelve that they might be with him and that he might send them out to preach and to have authority to drive out demons.***

Our team would be great if it were not for my teammates. What an arrogant statement, but sometimes it is exactly how we feel. We feel as if we can do it all on our own. We feel like we are the most important cog in the wheel, but we fail to realize without the other cogs in the wheel that the wheel will fall apart. We wear the shirt that says, "there is no I in team," but our thoughts are, "there is an I in victory, and it starts with me." Here is an old ancient African proverb: "If you want to go fast, go alone. If you want to go far, go together." That statement is so true in life. Life was never meant to be lived in isolation or alone. We were meant to be a team. To have people that prop us up when we are having a bad day or game. We were meant to be on a team for accountability. We were meant to be on a team so that we stay humble and not self-centered. God created us to be in a relationship with one another. The truth is that Jesus even chose 12 to walk along with him. He did this because he knew he could go further with a "Talmud" than he could be himself. Talmud is just the fancy biblical name for team. He also used this team concept to pour into the Disciples so that they would know his heart and what his true mission truly was. The Scripture reminds us over and over not to think too highly of ourselves. Working together keeps us humble and keeps us grounded in the common goal that has been laid before us. I think that the reason to attend worship is not to become more holy, even though that may happen. But the true reason to attend worship is so that you can do life with other people. This means that you have someone you are investing in, and you have someone investing in you. You have someone praying for you, and you get to know the prayer concerns of those around you. Let me ask you, do you know what is going on with your teammates? Are you just playing together, or are you truly doing life together? I tell you what, let's do it as we and not as me, and I will see you at the plate.

Dear Jesus Christ,

Thank you for putting aside self and becoming my sin. Thank you for not just doing life alone but teaching us how to do life together. I cannot even begin to thank you for what you have done for me and how you continue to do life with me. Let me do life with my teammates so that it is not just about me but about you and those that you have put in my concentric circle.

✞

Day 150

From Last To First

Matthew 20:16 ***"So the last will be first, and the first will be last."***

As mentioned in an earlier devotion, the Virginia Cavaliers let something happen in 2018 that had never happened in NCAA Basketball history; they let a number 16 seed beat them in the first round of the NCAA 64 team tournament. It was an embarrassing and humiliating loss. They would go down in history as the first number one to ever lose to a 16. Now everyone knew that one day it was bound to happen; it was just that no one wanted it to be their team. A loss like that is a heavy burden to carry around and a burden that can crush your self-esteem. So, what was Virginia going to do about being humiliated? Well, the next year in 2019, they would become the NCAA Men's basketball national champions. They would beat Texas Tech in an overtime thriller to redeem the previous year's loss. They would truly go from the first out of the tournament to cutting down the nets.

After the game, Virginia's coach Tony Bennet said that the loss the year before had called him to re-evaluate the program, his values, and his beliefs. He said it helped to strengthen his faith in the Lord. You see, Tony is a strong man of faith, and the loss helped to highlight what was important in life. You know, as I listened to the press conference after the game and then read articles in the days waning, I could not help but think of the verse that says, the last will be first and first will be last. God's Kingdom is such a paradox. We so often see these same kingdom principles played out in life. You see, one of the reasons Jesus told us to never sit at the head of the table is that he wanted us to stay grounded. Jesus knew that our message would only go as far as our humility. Paul reiterates Jesus' teaching in Romans when he says, do not think more highly of yourself than you should. You see, the truth is that arrogance cannot speak for God. This Virginia victory was so significant because it was done so out of a humble spirit and not out of an attitude of arrogance. I guess this is why so often we pull for the underdog and not the top-tier teams. We love to see the last become first. SO I know you may be batting last in the lineup, but that is ok because I will see you at the plate.

Dear Humble Servant,

Help me to be humble in every aspect of my life. Let me not take a seat of honor but a seat at the end of the table. Let me remember that arrogance cannot present the gospel. Help me remember that it is through humility that we speak the gospel and live the gospel.

Day 151

Prayer: Make This One a Good One

Philippians 4:6-7 ***Do not be anxious about anything, but in every situation, by prayer and petition, with thanksgiving, present your requests to God. And the peace of God, which transcends all understanding, will guard your hearts and your minds in Christ Jesus.***

All we needed to do was win this game, and we would be off to the Class 4A State Championship Game. We were not a favorite to win this game as we had kind of limped into the playoffs anyway. I served as the life coach for our high school football team, and one of my responsibilities was to pray before the game and after the game. Right before we were to go into the locker room, (actually we were in the end zone as the locker room was at the top of the hill – a strategic ploy by our opponents), the coach leaned over to me and said, "you better make this prayer a good one." I nodded and reeled off a pump-you-up prayer for the ages. It would give you the strength and the courage to run through a wall. I had done my part, and there was no way we were losing that game. And as you might guess, we won that game and went on to the final game for the state title but then lost. I guess my prayer on the day of the title game was subpar.

I had not thought a lot about that statement, "you better make this one a good one," until reading a devotion the other day that had a very similar story to mine, only it was a different sport, and it was a player that prayer it. But the Scripture and the devotion brought me back to that day. You know, I think the coach had the best intentions because we truly wanted to win the game, but now as I view it, he was looking more for a lucky charm than asking God to help us do what we had already prepared to do. You see, I was praying for God as if the other team was not praying. I was truly trying to out-pray rather than pray for God to give us the strength and courage to do what we had already prepared to do. The other thing that I realized is that I had been praying for this game all week. I had already been engaged in other prayers and conversations leading up to this game. No, the truth is what I read in this devotion, and that is that we do not pray for the battle because prayer is the battle. See, the truth is that we do not pray to win, but we pray that God will use us and lead us to be his. We pray that we have the strength to do what we already have practiced and are prepared to do. We also pray that whether we win or lose, we give God thanks.

I got to witness this firsthand this week as the Auburn tigers lost to Virginia in the final four on two very questionable calls. The fans were booing the refs. The players and coaches were devasted as they felt as they had been robbed of a victory. But after shaking hands, the team gathered in a circle by their bench, and they went to the Lord in prayer. They gave God the thanks even though they had essentially been robbed. You see, this is what prayer is all about. It is not your lucky rabbit's foot to pull out when you need a favor or extra help. Remember, prayer is the battle, and the battle is the Lord's. So, let me ask you, have you prayed yet, and when you have, I will see you at the plate.

Dear Glowing and Radiant One,

I give thanks to you for giving me the opportunity. Let my prayer be the battle; not my words be a prayer for the battle. You won this battle a long time ago when you defeated death. Win or lose, at the end of my life, I win because I believe in Jesus. Lord makes my life an instrument of my prayer, so I help lead others into the victory of the cross. Lord, you are a mighty warrior, and you fight for me every day.

Day 152

Competitive Drive

I Kings 18:20-21 ***Ahab summoned all the people of Israel and the prophets to Mount Carmel. Then Elijah stood in front of them and said, "How much longer will you waver, hobbling between two opinions? If the Lord is God, follow him! But if Baal is God, then follow him!" But the people were completely silent.***

Some people are just competitive by nature. They hate to lose, and they will compete in anything, and that means anything. They will try to beat their grandchildren (if they are that old) in a game of Chutes and Ladders. They will try to win even if you have made it clear that it is a friendly competition, and you are not keeping score. Believe me, when I tell you this, they are keeping score. Most professional athletes have this competitive drive; it is what helps them stay in a game that is so competitive. The problem with a strong competitive drive is how you handle yourself when you win or lose. When you pout about losing or find a million excuses why you lost, you alienate yourself from those you are competing against. How one handles this competitive drive will be the difference between a God-honoring competitive spirit and a competitive spirit that wrecks their witness.

One way we do this is when we rub it in the other team. I played in a softball tournament a few years ago, and we were getting killed by an "A" class team playing in a friendly fund-raiser tournament. They were beating us (I mean real beat down) and then rubbing it in. They were making a crude gesture as they would get us out. They were hitting home runs and walking around the bases backward. I knew one of the guys on the team and knew that he was very active in his church, yet he participated in the humiliating antics. My prayer was that none of the youth he worked with at church was at the game, or his witness would be tainted. Now, this is just one example of how that competitive drive can kill your witness.

On the other hand, I coached under a coach that never believed in humiliating a team. When he got up by a good margin, he always shut it down. His comment was, "one day, you will be on the other side of this." So, this week we will be looking at the word D.R.I.V.E, what it means to have a competitive drive, and how to be competitive without ruining your witness. How can you be gracious in winning and keep your head when you lose? So, if you have that competitive drive, I will see you at the plate.

Dear Anointing Oil,

Help me to receive your word this week. Help me to stay competitive and not to lose my edge. But on the other side of that help me to stay humble and kind. God, my witness, is more important than wins and losses.

Day 153

D=Desire

Psalms 37:4 ***Delight thyself also in the Lord: and he shall give thee the desires of thine heart.***

Drive starts with a strong desire to achieve. Desire comes from a deep innate feeling that you have to win and be the best at everything you do. It is the belief that second is never an option. We have all known competitive people, and then we know a person who is constantly driven. There is a type "A" person, and then there is an **extremely type "A" person**. This person's desire is so great that they cannot turn it off. These traits borderline on unhealthy because they are constantly thinking about how to get better, and they are also looking at what went wrong when they did not achieve the desired outcome. So, the question here is not what to do with desire but how one handles this desire. One way that this can balance is by having the same desire for God that we have for winning. We must sometimes evaluate the desires of the heart. We must do an inventory with this question in mind.

Do I care more about my accomplishments than I do about my relationship with my creator? It is not that we want to win any less but that we want God much more. The truth is that to desire God is what our hearts were created to do. See, we have to remember that no matter how many wins, victories, or achievements we accumulate, none will measure the same as desiring God. The second point here is that all of our accolades here on earth or temporal, but our desire for God is eternal. To desire, God is to know him in a more intimate way. Sometimes that desire to always win is because we are so self-reliant that we cannot imagine relying on someone else. But God wants you to sometimes prop up against him.

God longs to help us get through things that we cannot handle on our own. Here is a revelation for you. You will struggle in some area of your life, no matter who you are. So, when we desire God, he is ready to share the victories with us. This also gives God the glory and not that we did all on our own. I mean, without God, you would not have the air in your lungs to do anything. The other question here is, where did that competitive desire come from? It came from God, and now he gives you a choice as to whether you give him the honor or tell the world it was your desire that got you through. Yes, you have the desire, but when you desire God, you realize that the desire came from God. So, let me ask you? Are you desiring God, and if you are, then I will see you at the plate.

Dear Worthy of Praise,

God give me the desires of my heart but make those desires be what honors you. I delight in the Lord, and I am thankful for his grace. Jesus had one desire in his life, and that was dying so that I could be free. God, you are the desire of my heart. Desire is the start of a competitive heart, but it is also a heart bent toward you. Amen.

Day 154

R = Resist Being Arrogant

Proverbs 16:18 ***Pride goes before destruction and haughtiness before a fall.***

One thing that comes with a competitive drive is the reality that you are going to outwork most of your opponents. This will often lead to you being better in all aspects of the game. Usually, when you are better at all aspects of the game, this will lend itself to lots of wins and sometimes not just wins, but blowout wins. The truth is that a competitive desire can lead you to crush your competition. This is the point where you must be careful that you do not become arrogant. You must resist the temptation to become arrogant, haughty, or proud. In the sporting world, the devil loves to creep in during your success and let you know that you should make fun of those that you crushed. You should humiliate them now with your words, not just with the score. The truth is that arrogance ruins your testimony and witness. You can celebrate your victories but do so with humility. When we reject arrogance, we actually present ourselves in a Godly light. We win, and then we simply shake hands, thank the other team and officials, and then we move on to our next competition. The other thing that being humble does is that it sets an example for your team.

Many times, there is that person on your team that loves to brag about accomplishments. They are stat-driven, not team-driven; they cannot resist wanting to know how well they performed so that they can brag and rub it in the face of others on the team. Many times, this creates disunity and turmoil on a team. When you set the platform for humbleness and resist arrogance, you have the opportunity to confront this issue and set a great example for the whole team. Recently I heard a country song on the radio by Tim McGraw entitled Humble and Kind. (You may want to listen to it to help with this study.) The song talks about that no matter how good you are or what you achieve, make sure that you stay humble and true. One of the verses in the song speaks volumes to what is presented here. You must resist the temptation to become arrogant and proud and instead become humble and kind, and I will see you at the plate.

Dear Altar of the Tabernacle,

Help me to be humble, kind, and true. Help me to resist the temptations to become haughty, proud, and arrogant. Help me to understand people are watching me in victory and defeat. Thank you for humbling yourself to come here and to die for my arrogance and sins.

Day 155

I = Inventory Your Attitude

Luke 14:28 ***"But don't begin until you count the cost. For who would begin constructing a building without first calculating the cost to see if there is enough money to finish it?***

When we have a "competitive drive," we need to be aware of our attitude and how others perceive it. The first year I was a chaplain for the high school football team, one young man stood out on defense above all the others. I commented to the head coach about how talented this young man seemed to be, which he replied with, "he could be the best on the field every week, but he is a prima donna." The coach went on to tell me that he had an attitude, and his teammates did not trust him. They had not even voted him as captain even though he had led the team in tackles the previous year and had been a 4-year starter. The problem is that he had not taken an inventory of his attitude. He was a hero and legend in his mind, but others did not trust him or want to play alongside him. We are often so driven that we do not sit down and inventory what we might need to change. We are so driven to accomplish that we never sit still enough to inventory our attitude. One of the ways that we take inventory is through prayer. We need to ask God, not for things but to show us things that might hinder our lives. We ask God as David did to search our hearts and to find and shred any iniquities. The second inventory we take is by asking people that we trust how others perceive us. This takes thick skin because the criticism we hear might not be what we want to hear. Finally, we need to take an inventory of self-evaluation. This is where we ask the question as to whether our drive to succeed has gotten in the way of our relationship with others and, most importantly, God. In life, you must slow down long enough to take inventory to know where you are and what needs to happen for you to be who God called you to be. So, take time out right now from your competitive drive and take an inventory, and when you are done, I will see you at the plate.

Dear God of Bethel,

Humble me to see who I am and not who I think I am. Taking inventory brings me to where I really am and also who I have become. I do not want to gain the whole world and forfeit my soul because I was driven that I did not set down to inventory. Let me not be a hero in my own mind but to make you a hero throughout my life. Amen.

Day 156

V = Victory in Jesus

I Corinthians 15:5 (ESV) ***But thanks be to God, who gives us the victory through our Lord Jesus Christ.***

The ultimate drive-in sports are to come out victorious. You can go 14-1 losing the last game, and people will never remember the 14 victories before the loss. That happened to the University of Alabama this year, 2018. They dominated most of their opponents for the regular season, but they lost the last game, and everyone came unglued on what a failure of a season they had. What is ironic is that the year before, they lost two games, barely got in the National Championship game, and won it all. No one even talked about the two losses; they just celebrated the National Championship. Driven people not only want to win, but they hate to lose.

You see, there is a big difference between people that want to win but accept a loss and people that hate to lose. The difference is that the people who hate to lose figure out why they lost and correct their mistakes so that it will not happen again. One thing that I am grateful for is that I do not have to figure out my future after my death. I have the most important victory that can ever be achieved, and no matter how hard I worked at it, I could not achieve it. No matter how much money I have, I cannot buy it. No matter how good I am, I cannot earn it. This victory is the victory I have in Jesus. Have you thought about those words? Not victory by Jesus but victory in Jesus. To be "in" something is to be present with and in it. Victory in Jesus is more than an insurance policy that we receive when we die. Victory in Jesus is to be lived out in our everyday living. Victory in Jesus is truly our driving force. Victory in Jesus is what sets us apart. Victory in Jesus is the ultimate championship. Yes, we are driven by victory in sports, but in our walk with Jesus, we are living more victorious. Death has already been conquered, and the grave is no more. So now that you know that you are living in the victory, I will see you at the plate.

I Am Longsuffering,

Your name is victory. Victory over sin. Victory over death. Victory over Satan. Victory over my foes and enemies. Victory over this world and the dark powers that try to rule it. Yes, there is victory in Jesus, a victory like no other. When I said yes to you, I let out a victory cry heard in the heavens. Oh, yes, there is victory in Jesus.

Day 157

E = Experience the Joy of Playing

Ecclesiastes 8:15 ***So I commend the enjoyment of life because there is nothing better for a person under the sun than to eat and drink and be glad. Then joy will accompany them in their toil all the days of the life God has given them under the sun.***

You know, sometimes you are so driven to succeed that we forget to enjoy the game we are playing. Sometimes the drive can become greater than the joy. Now there will be days that you push the limit; that is how you get better, and you may not enjoy that part of the game. But remember, pain is always part of the process. There comes a time in every athlete's life where they must evaluate whether they still love the game. The truth is that if you do not love the game, then it will affect other aspects of your life. When you do not enjoy the game, then it is time to move on to other things. I am almost convinced that many people stay in the game too long, and they are just driven by wins and awards and not from the sheer joy of getting to play the game. It is amazing that over half of Americans polled hate their job and wish they could do something they love. You know why most work the job or stay at the job they are currently working is because of the pay. I have heard this on numerous occasions, "Well, I hate my job, but it pays the bills." In some instances, that is necessary, but others work at a profession they hate to keep up with their standard of life. But the reality is they are miserable with life, and all the things they are working for they do not get to enjoy because what they are doing daily is robbing them of joy. I recently heard a young lady from the Peace Corp. speak, and she told the group that while she was in Panama, she met a couple in their late 70's and they were serving in the Peace Corp. after retirement. They had retired but were bored with traveling and the beach trips. They had both loved to serve and do for others, so they sold all they had and joined the Peace Corp. They are living out their lives in happiness without doing it in the norm. So, I guess the point here is that do not let the drive rob you of experiencing the joy that comes from playing the game you love. The second point is that if the drive is all that is left, then it may be time to do something else. So, experience the joy of playing, and I will see you at the plate.

Dear Creator and Perfecter of Joy,

Help me to love what you have created. Help me to do my work out of love and not out of routine. Place me where you want me and where my call is. Help me not just to do something because the rewards are great because the truth is that there will only be one prize in the end, which is the reward of eternal life. Your Son Jesus wore the crown of thorns, so one day, I could receive a crown of glory. Thank you for the gift of your Son Jesus, who experienced the joy of life every day while dying for us. Man, I love that paradox.

Day 158

Fruits of the Spirit

Galatians 5:22 ***But the fruit of the Spirit is love, joy, peace, forbearance, kindness, goodness, faithfulness, gentleness, and self-control …***

We have often heard of the fruits of the spirit. Paul mentions them to the Church in Galatians. The fruits of the spirit are different from spiritual gifts. Everyone is equipped with the fruits of the spirit, but it is up to us as to whether we use them or not. The fruits of the spirit can be used as a gauge to let you know how your walk with Jesus is going. They help us to see the areas of our spiritual game that need work. This is like how we evaluate our playing and see where we need to work on our mechanics. Yes, I would say that just like our mechanics in sports need work, sometimes our spiritual mechanics need work. What in this list of gifts comes easy to you? Here is the list: love, joy, peace, patience, kindness, goodness, faithfulness, gentleness, and self-control. When you look at this list, some of these come naturally, but there are others that not only do not come easy, but they need tons of improvement. When you look at that list, there may even be a few on the list that are not even in your life. Now what we are striving for in life is to be a holistic person. So, with that being said, I would argue that if you struggle with these gifts off the field, they directly affect something you are doing on the field. This week we will look at the fruits of the spirit in your life and how they affect your walk with Jesus and your play on the field. So, do me a favor and repeat the fruits of the spirit one more time: love, joy, peace, patience, kindness, faithfulness, gentleness, and self-control. Now that you have read through them. I will see you at the plate.

Dear Dunamis, (power)

I have neglected to look at the areas of fruit where I am lacking. Forever I thought I had a choice in which ones to use and which ones not to use. You have given me these gifts so that I can be a holistic person. You have instilled in me these gifts so that I can be your light. You have given me these gifts so that I can practice being Christ-like every day.

Day 159

Love of the Game and Love of Life

I Corinthians 13:1 ***If I speak in the tongues of men or of angels but do not have love, I am only a resounding gong or a clanging cymbal.***

"I play for the love of the game." I heard the player respond as he signed his 5 million a year new contract with his new team after a year hold-out on his previous team. I thought to myself, for the love of money, not the love of the game. He was getting the opportunity to do something that every athlete dreams about, but only a few ever get to do. I would argue that if you love the game, you play it for free, and if you got paid, it would just be a perk. The sports industry has been ruined with people trying to get rich off of the game. It is no longer a game that is played because of the love and fun of it. It is now a business that is driven by people trying to get rich quickly. That begs me to ask this question, do we play the game because we love it, or has it become such a drive for us to succeed and get paid that we have lost the true love for the game? Anything that we do in life that we do not love becomes a burden. So often, we start with the love of something, but then someone else comes along and ruins it for us. Sometimes it is the parent that is living out their dreams through a child and burns the athlete out from playing them too much. For others, it is a coach that overplays them and gets them injured so that he can win a dust collector. Sometimes it is an agent that comes along and convinces us that we are a demigod, and we need to be paid like a god. (Which we know there is only one God, and he owns everything.) Yes, Satan is out to ruin our love for the game, and he may be using those closest to us to rob us of the love and joy that the game brings. The same concept is true in life. The first fruit listed is the fruit of love. The spiritual truth is that everything we do for God should come from our love for God. When we love ourselves more than we love God, we do things for ourselves and not for God. All the other fruits of the spirit come from our love of Jesus and the love for others. I have often heard it say that it was not the nails that held him to the cross, but his love for us held him there. So, let me ask if you play the game because you love it? And do you follow Jesus because you love him? Yes, the first fruit is the foundation for all the other fruits. So now that I know you love God and love the game, I will see you at the plate.

Author and Crestor of My Life,

I follow you, Jesus because I love you. Why do I love you? Because you first loved me. I also follow you because I love life. Now I know there are difficult days in life, but when we love something, it calls us to sacrifice and push on. God, keep writing my story as the story of love that you have for me and the love I have for others.

Day 160

Got Joy?

Isaiah 61:10-11 (GW) ***I will find joy in the Lord. I will delight in my God. He has dressed me in the clothes of salvation. He has wrapped me in the robe of righteousness like a bridegroom with a priest's turban, like a bride with her jewels.***

Some people may have a hard time labeling sports as joy. This is a paradox because of the rigorous practice and training it takes to accomplish your goals. Now I know there are those anomalies out there that love to practice, and pain brings them great joy. But then there are the rest of us normal folks. So, when we refer to joy, we refer to the attitude you exhibit as a teammate and friend. Joy comes from doing something that you love and something that you are passionate about. Sometimes I hear people refer to someone who is burned out, to which I always respond if they burned out, then they are spending most of their time doing things that they do not want to do or are not good at. The games we play and the competitions that we compete in should bring us great joy. If they are not bringing us joy, then we need to evaluate why we are doing them. Now on a greater scale of life, I heard someone say that they had no joy in life. Sometimes this is because of tragedy or loss. Sometimes it comes with age and the loss of mobility. I try to remind people that our joy is found in the promise of the empty tomb. The promise that this is not all we have. I also remind them that death never has the final word for a Christian. This promise is where my joy is found. I am not saying that we should enjoy this world, but the next has so much more to offer that all our achievements will be nothing but rubbish. Joy cannot always be thought of as something we receive; maybe it is our job to be someone else's joy. Our missions committee always says that serving brings them such joy. Wow, here is another paradox serving without the intent of receiving anything back brings true joy. What a Jesus idea! So, let me ask you, "got the joy"? If so, grab that joy, and I will see you at the plate.

Dear Lord of My Life,

Today, Lord, I choose joy. I choose joy over fear. I choose joy over anger. I choose joy over doubt. I choose joy in all circumstances, and I will have that joy down in my heart and soul. I will also be a joy to other people as they see Jesus in my life.

✞

Day 161

Peace Makers

John 14:27 ***Peace I leave with you; my peace I give you. I do not give to you as the world gives. Do not let your hearts be troubled, and do not be afraid.***

Let me ask you, are you a peacemaker? You know there are two kinds of people in the world, peacemakers and protagonists. The sports world is the same way. So, answer this question, are you the one breaking up the scuffle, or are you joining in the scuffle? Many times, sports bring out the worst in people because they are so passionate about their team. I am not a soccer fan, but I understand that soccer fans are the most passionate of all fans. They will riot when another team beats them. At times, there have been such ruckuses that they have caused riots in the stands. Sometimes it has been so bad that the police dressed in riot gear had to end the unrest. It happened recently in South Africa, where several were injured after fans rioted and rushed after the final whistle.

One of the things that we must pray for daily is a sense of peace. In the Scripture, peace was so important that people would say it as they greeted someone and then again as they departed. This is very similar to the way that we say hello and goodbye. The way they said it was "Shalom." Peace I bring with me and peace I leave with you. Shalom was a way of saying I have made my peace with God. This is the starting point of peace. The second is that you are at peace with yourself. When we are at odds with others, it is because we have not made peace with ourselves. Finally, we need to be at peace with other people. This means accepting that they may not agree, believe or hold the same values that you do. The reality is that you can be a peacemaker and be competitive. It is all in how you handle yourself in challenging and adverse situations. Peace is something that you must constantly pray for and seek. Peace comes from within and is one of those things that only you have control over. Jesus came so that we would have peace. This peace comes from knowing that Christ died for us, and because of his death, we have been set free. So, let me ask you, are you at peace with God, yourself, and others? If not, take time right now to make peace, and then I will see you at the plate.

Dear Peacemaker,

Lord, give me peace that passes my understanding. Give me an inner peace that the whole world can see. Lord, instead of being a protagonist, let me be a peacemaker. Blessed are the peacemakers, for they will be called children of God. God make me an instrument of peace.

✞

Day 162

Forbearance?

Colossians 3:12-13 ***Therefore, as God's chosen people, holy and dearly loved, clothe yourselves with compassion, kindness, humility, gentleness, and patience. Bear with each other and forgive one another if any of you has a grievance against someone. Forgive as the Lord forgave you.***

Now I know some of you are scratching your head and asking what in the world is forbearance? It sounds like something went wrong financially. Merriam-Webster defines it as refraining from enforcing something (such as a debt, right, or obligation) that is due.[10] In Scriptural time it would also be translated as long-suffering. But in today's society, we would call it being "patient." Now, most of us know the prayer that we so often pray. "God, give me patience now and hurry up because I am losing my patience." Most of us are not, by nature, patient people.

The truth is, since the invention of the Microwave and fast-food drive-thrus, we have become less patient. Another reality is that the sports world is even less forbearing. A coach has a bad season or two, and everyone wants them fired. That pressure on coaches leads to coaches not being very patient with players or player development. When this type of behavior is modeled for us, then we also become impatient. Being impatient will cause us to give up on things that have delayed gratification or take time to develop. People often give up on their dreams just because someone has been impatient with their progress and development. I think about this young man that was in one of my churches. He was always tall for his age but was quite awkward and skinny. He looked awkward, playing football as a young man. He would often get manhandled by the boys that had reached earlier maturity and outweighed him. Between his sophomore and junior years, he grew 5 inches, making him 6'7, and he put on over 60 pounds. He got serious about the weights, nutrition, and workouts. This led to his senior year being chosen as a three-star defensive lineman and being recruited by many D-I schools. He finally signed a full athletic scholarship to a team in South Alabama.

He often thanks his coaches for not giving up on him and being patient with God's timing. I think that we could all use a little more patience and forbearance. I think about how patient God has been with you and with me. We keep doing the same thing over and over after we tell God we will stop. We have not been patient with other people, yet we expect God to be patient with us. We give up on people when they disappoint us, and then we expect everyone to be patient with us till we get it together. The reality is that God has been forbearing since the original sin in the garden. He has never given up on us and has been so patient with us. Though we have turned our backs on him, he has turned his face toward us. Let us practice being forbearing, and in doing so, we may be able to extend some of the grace that has been given to us. So you of forbearance, I will see you at the plate.

Dear Root of David,

Thank you for being patient and forbearing even when I refused to extend the same to someone else. Help me to practice patience in every aspect of life. Help me also to be patient when my timing does not match yours. God, thank you for your Son, who exhibited the utmost patience with the disciples and his followers.

✞

Day 163

Can One Be Kind in Competition?

Ephesians 4:32 ***Be kind and compassionate to one another, forgiving each other, just as in Christ God forgave you.***

How many times have you heard you must have a little rough edge to be one up on your competition? You must be mean and hungry. You have to beat your opponent on every play. Not once have we ever heard this, "I need you guys to go out there and be kind." So, the question is, where is the place for kindness in the midst of competition? The answer lies many times with how we are off the field and not necessarily how to handle things during competition. I love that every Bowl Game now offers the teams the opportunity to do a philanthropy project and mission work.

Sometimes it is visiting a hospital, and sometimes it is visiting a community center or school. Many athletes are now encouraged to find ways to serve and build community off the field. How does this lead to kindness on the field? Well, it helps to put into perspective what is important. It also helps people see that athletes are just normal people with exceptional gifts. It also helps the team to build a sense of community within the community.

Practicing random acts of kindness should be a daily goal. What can I do today to show kindness to someone else? Practicing random acts of kindness helps us learn humility and what an honor it is to play our chosen sport. During a high school football team's spring game, I recently saw where they let their manager, who has Down syndrome, suit up and run the ball. They helped him score his first-ever touchdown, and he got a standing ovation. I love that story because it takes what one learned off of the field and how they are now applying it on the field. Can kindness and competition be woven together? The answer is "absolutely." Kindness can be extended in any place that we have been placed. The Scripture even says, that sometimes when we practice kindness, we just might be entertaining angels. Today, before you take the field, go out, and practice a random act of kindness, and after you have finished, I will see you at the plate.

Dear Holy Loving Lord,

Help me to practice random acts of kindness. Help me to be kind even to those that may not deserve it. God, you have been so kind to me. Your kindness can never be repaid, but I can be kind to others created in your image. Your Son encompassed kindness to everyone that he met. Let Jesus be my example of how to exhibit and practice kindness.

Day 164

Oh Goody!

Romans 12:21 ***Do not be overcome by evil, but overcome evil with good.***

Now at first, it seems that kindness and goodness might be the same thing. But the concept of kindness is that it involves caring and being benevolent to others, whereas goodness is more about being obedient and doing what is right. Goodness comes from a deep desire to please God and others that have been placed in authority above us. It comes from not just doing things but doing things the right way. Goodness is not just doing it to get it done but also taking great pride in what we are doing. Goodness is the exact opposite of evil. It means striving to be righteous and set apart. The Scripture refers to this as being "above reproach." That means that no one can hold something against us. Goodness is not the act of trying to earn our way into good graces because we have already been covered in his grace. Goodness is being obedient because we love God and want to do great things for his Kingdom. Goodness also extends to the field as we want to do things the right way. So many times, we try to practice goodness so that we can earn a starting position, but after we have earned that spot, our goodness now comes from a sense that we can even be better. It comes from the sense that goodness helps us to set the standard and the bar for those teammates that surround us. Goodness is related to our character. You see, people only see us in one of two ways. We are either good, or we are bad. Now even the good make mistakes and sin. The Scripture says In Romans 3:23 that "all have sinned and fallen short of the glory of God." But someone that practices goodness does not continue to live in that sin. They seek ways in which they can defeat the evil one. So, let us continue to practice goodness, and by doing so, we will become Godlier in our walk with Christ. So, you are good, and because of that, I will see you at the plate.

Dear Prophecy Fulfilled,

God, you are the good, good Father who loves us despite who we are and what we have done. Goodness should always follow us all the days of our lives. May we extend your goodness to others. Goodness should not be seen as being weak but should be one of the fruits of the Spirit that comes from us patterning.

Day 165

Are You Faithful?

Ephesians 4:14 ***Then we will no longer be immature like children. We won't be tossed and blown about by every wind of new teaching. We will not be influenced***

when people try to trick us with lies so clever; they sound like the truth.

Being faithful in our society has taken a back seat to being successful. Some people have found a way to intertwine the two. But for most people being successful has nothing to do with being faithful. Faithful means that you are loyal to your team, company, or profession. I have been appalled at the frequent transfers in college football. When someone realizes that someone is better, they transfer to a team they can play for, even in a lower division. It seems that there is no team faithfulness. I fear that this will have a systemic effect on the rest of their life. I also think that this lack of faithfulness leads to an attitude of entitlement. The reality is that there can be more learned by being faithful than being blown like the chaff in the wind. We must be careful that we do not lack faithfulness in our relationship with Jesus. So often, we pick and choose when we want to be faithful to Jesus. If we are hanging out with this group of people, then it is alright to talk about Jesus. But if we are with this crowd, they may look down on me if I stand up for Jesus. The truth is that this lack of faithlessness has caused people to see no difference in those that confess to being Christians and the non-professing world. Most of the time, we are faithful to Christ right up until the point that it becomes inconvenient. But that is not being faithful that is being tossed by the direction of the wind. Our lack of faithfulness to the cross is also why almost 66% of marriages end in divorce. I would say that lack of faithfulness leads to us not being able to finish what we have started on many occasions.

Faithfulness has to be an intentional action. It must be something that we commit to putting to prayer and then diligent work to achieve it. Faithfulness is what Jesus showed when he went to Calvary for a sinner such as I. Jesus could have put stipulations on my life for me to qualify for his grace. He could have said that I must not sin this many times, must attend church 75% of the time, pray so many times a day, and the list could go on. But his faithfulness to me put no qualifications on it. He was just faithful. The reason we should be faithful is that he has been faithful to us. See you at the plate.

Dear Perfect, Spotless, Blameless Lamb,

Help me to be faithful in everything that I do. It is through my faithfulness to the cross that people will see Jesus in my life. Your Son set the bar for faithfulness when he died for someone like me. I did not deserve it, but he was faithful to me, and he eradicated the sin of the world. Faithfulness is what I long for.

✞

Day 166

Gentleness? How in the World Can That Be a Sports Attribute?

Ephesians 4:2-4 (ISV) ***Demonstrating all expressions of humility, gentleness, and patience, accepting one another in love. Do your best to maintain the unity of the Spirit by means of the bond of peace. There is one body and one Spirit. Likewise, you were called to the one hope of your calling.***

Gentleness, there is no way that can be a sports attribute. If I am gentle, then I am going to get beat and beat bad. So, let me explain how you can exhibit gentleness in sports. Gentleness can be translated as "meekness," this does not mean weakness. Rather, it involves the act of humility and giving thanks to God. But it even goes a step further than that; it also means being polite and having restrained behavior toward others. The opposite attributes of gentleness are anger, malice, a desire to get revenge, and self-aggrandizement. Gentleness is not toward the other team but is directed at giving God thanks for the ability to play the game. It also gives God the glory when we win the game. Gentleness is the same as being humble in spirit. Gentleness is giving God control of our life. It is being tough as nails on the field but having a broken heart toward the less fortunate or sick off the field. I was thinking about a great display of gentleness in college sports. It takes place every week that the Iowa Hawkeyes play football at home. Hawkeyes fans stop at the end of the First Quarter at Kinnick Stadium. They then turn to wave to the children being treated at the adjacent University of Iowa Children's Hospital. The children who are severely ill or terminally ill wave back to the fans. It is one of the most touching displays of affection in sports. The children call this act of gentleness the highlight of the week. Now the players have even taken their gentleness to another level, and that is going to visit the ones they wave to on Saturday. You see, you can be a winner, you can be tough, and you can also be a person of gentleness. The truth is that success on the field will give you more opportunities to exhibit your gentleness. So, now that you know how gentleness can be fit into the sports world, I will see you at the plate.

Dear Rock of Redemption,

Help me to play hard - to be rough and to be the best I can be. But also help me to exhibit gentleness. Help me display the attitude of humility and the attitude of meekness. Not so that I am weak, but I am grateful for all you have done for me.

Day 167

You Must First Control Self

Proverbs 19:11 ***A person's wisdom yields patience; it is to one's glory to overlook an offense.***

Today we get to the last fruit of the Spirit (sports). Out of all of them, this fruit is the hardest to master, but it is essential if you will be a witness on and off the field. The question is, how is your self-control? When we think of self-control, we think of it in terms of these self-components: our mouth and words, our attitude, and our actions. The first question is, do we have control over our mouths? Do we tend to yell back at the referee when there is a bad call? Do we tend to curse when something does not go right? Do we tend to brag and taunt when we win? Do we yell at a teammate when they mess up, or do we pick them up with our words?

You see, the Scripture says that what comes out of your mouth is just an overflow of what is in your heart. (Matthew 12:34) For the mouth speaks what the heart is full of. Your words are who you are and what is in your heart. The second self-control component is our attitude. How do we respond when we win or when we lose? How do we respond when the coach gets on us, or we get taken out of the game? Do you see the world is watching you because you are on the big stage? The other issue with this is your attitude will dictate how you play when things are not going your way. Only you can control your attitude. The last aspect of self-control is our self-actions. How do we respond when being taunted and antagonized? How do we respond to adversity? Our actions speak even louder than our words. We can tell people who we are every day, but they will never believe our words until they see who we are. The adage, "You cannot just talk the talk; you must walk the walk." How about this one, "your actions speak louder than your words?" So now the question is this, how do we develop this self-control? The answer is through prayer and the power of the Holy Spirit. We pray through the areas where we are lacking, and we let the Holy Spirit guide us rather than being guided by our own thinking. When we show self-control, we show the world that our obedience lies in Jesus Christ and lets the Spirit guide our actions.

So, let me see that self-control, and I will see you at the plate.

Dear Patient Father,

Let the meditations of my heart be what comes out of my mouth. Let my actions be pleasing to you. Let me exhibit self-control so that others can see you through me. Help me with restraint, even when everything is chaotic.

Day 168

Trouble Will Come and Go

Philippians 1:29-30 ***For it has been granted to you on behalf of Christ not only to believe in him, but also to suffer for him, since you are going through the same struggle you saw I had, and now hear that I still have.***

Sometimes you just need God to speak to you because you are amid troubled waters. You may be in a place where the world seems to be crashing down on you, and you need to hear God speak into your life. Now, I have always said God speaks to us in three ways. The first is that God speaks directly to some people. They hear his voice loud and clear. Now, I do not know why he does not just speak to everyone, but then again, my thoughts are not his thoughts, and my ways are not his. The second way that he speaks to us is that he speaks through his word. The Scriptures give us all we need in order to hear the voice of God. The last way is that God speaks through other people. This means it is important that we learn to listen. So, this week I, after about six months of prayer, had to make a staff change. The truth is that even though I feel it is the right decision, it comes with many hurt feelings and people scathing mad at me. It is one of those weeks when you feel the weight of being in charge and having to make a decision that hurts a few so that greater gain can be achieved. So, this morning as I am having my quiet time at Edgar's Bakery, I come across this verse and immediately know it is God speaking to me. It was the last three words that spoke to me: "faith develops perseverance." The reality is that when we pray for God to take some hurt away, he will not immediately wave a wand, and it magically disappear. The reality is that he may allow the testing to continue so that we increase our faith in him. See, my definition of perseverance is this: Perseverance is faith that has endured the pain of the test. If you are never tested, then there is no way that you can develop perseverance, but more than that, you cannot develop your faith unless you go through times of trouble. The truth is that it is the same in sports as it is in life. Remember that you may struggle for a season, but next season because of your perseverance, you may look back and thank God for that test. Troubles will come, and troubles will go, but our faith will always persevere because of the cross. So even in the midst of a test, I will see you at the plate.

The Hearer of my Prayers,

You are a bridge over troubled water. You continue to keep me safe, even amid my struggles. You help me to understand that this test will only be for a season. I am reminded that this too shall pass and that I will be better for it. The cross was a struggle, but it was a struggle that was well worth it.

Day 169

What Really Ruins a Team?

Proverbs 26:20 ***"Without wood, fire goes out; without a gossip, conflict dies down."***

This week we will look at advice from Solomon, the wisest man to ever live. We will be getting all of our devotional Scriptures from Proverbs, a great book of wisdom.

The greatest curse to the world as well as to the sports world is "gossip." Everyone is looking for the next big news story. You often hear someone say they were the first to "break the story" when referring to a news outlet bringing the top story. But then the question becomes, is the story reliable, or is it just secondhand and partially made up. Being a pastor, I can honestly say that gossip is the worst sin in the church, hands down. Now with email and social media, you not only can gossip, but you can broadcast gossip. You can triangle people and get people to join your side solely based on whatever is said. We often think of gossip as harmless, and we may even ask if the Scriptures say anything about gossip. But it is in the Ten Commandments. "Do not lie" is a loose translation of the ninth commandment; the actual translation is that we should not bear false witness (gossip). This is sharing something without first finding out whether it is true or false.

How often have you seen gossip ruin an athlete or a person in the limelight? When we bear false witness, we are killing a person's credibility and character. I will never forget a few years ago the scandal that took place at Auburn University. The story revolved around Cam Newton's father taking money for his son to play football. Now I will never forget the countless news stories and articles written, all of them containing different opinions of who paid who and who was holding the money bag. Now I am not saying that there was no truth to the story, but there was so much gossip and slander. The truth was that they were on a witch hunt and were out to ruin a young man's life. It seems that the media in situations like this want someone to fail, and they want them to fail, even if they bear false witness. Let me ask you, do you spend time gossiping about your teammates or classmates? Would you even hope they fail so that you could take their place on the team or in the starting rotation? You see, being a teammate is more than playing alongside someone. It is willing to go into battle with someone. Being a teammate means that you have a teammate's back, not another teammate's ear. When you gossip, you not only hurt that person, but you hurt the whole team. Do not bear false witness, and I will see you at the plate.

Dear God of Triumph,

I have been a gossiper—a liar. And I have hurt other people with my words. I ask that you tame my tongue. I ask that you search my heart and make it pure. Let me build my friends and teammates up, not tear them down. Thank you for sending your Son, who had no deceit in his mouth and died for the deceit that has come from my mouth.

Day 170

All in the Name

Proverbs 22:1 ***A good name is more desirable than great riches; to be esteemed is better than silver or gold.***

What is in a name? How did you get your name, and what does it mean? In biblical times a name had significant meaning. People were not just named after a city or football coach. No, names had significant meaning as to what a person may become or achieve. Sometimes it foreshadowed what was to come, and sometimes it was a direction they would now be sent. Sometimes God would even change a name, or Jesus would give a new name. Such was with Peter, one of the twelve disciples. Peter was given the name Simon, but Jesus changed it to "Petros" which meant rock. Now the reason that Peter was given this name was because of what Jesus saw in him and what he was going to do with his life. Peter would start the first church, and upon his name, the church would be built, and it would become a firm foundation.

Jesus said to Peter in Matthew 16:18. "And I tell you that you are Peter, and on this rock, I will build my church, and the gates of Hades will not overcome it." So often we associate a name with success; some examples are Kardashian, Trump, Clinton, or Bryant. These names are important because of what they did in the business, sports, or political world. Now, if you are reading this, you will probably never be associated with one of those names unless that happens to be your name, and you are reading this. The truth is that even though we may never have such a famous name, our name can still be famous as it relates to what we have done for the Kingdom of God. Our hope and prayer are that people will not remember our name but will remember the name of Jesus because of our witness and platform. God has given us a great opportunity to make his name great and famous in the sports world. We do this in two ways; the first is that we commit our playing in a way that honors him. That means we give it our all in everything we do and that we carry ourselves above reproach. The second way we honor his name is to give him all the glory for our ability and success. Do we want our name famous, or do we want to use our name to make him famous? Hey, I think they are calling your name, make him famous. See you at the plate.

Dear God, How Majestic is Your Name,

God, you have the name above all names. Holy is your name in all the earth. May the name of Jesus not just be on my lips but be on my life and my heart. It is my prayer that when people say my name, they will think of you.

Day 171

Training for Return

Proverbs 22:6 ***Train up a child in the way they should go, and when they are old, they will not depart from it.***

In college, I had a football coach (Coach Ron Finley) often say this to us, "Boys, what you are to become, you are now becoming." What he meant by that was that what we were learning, what habits we were involved in, is the compilation of who we are. You will not wake up one day and suddenly be something you have not been training to be. This is why it is important that you are coached and mentored by positive, Godly people who believe in you. If you are reading this and are a parent, coach, mentor, or teacher, hear me say this. You are a role model, and you are an example. Your words have the power to either change a life or lead young people astray. Remember that kids listen to everything you say, but more importantly, they watch everything you do.

I was recently sitting with a young lady that had gotten to college and made some terrible choices. She said she knew it was wrong but went along with it anyway. I asked her how she turned it around. Her response was this, "I remembered my teaching throughout the younger years of my life, and I wanted to be the person that those people thought I could be, not the person the world wanted me to be." This example is just one example of a person turning back to the foundation that was laid for their life. Let me ask you this question, what are you becoming? What are you taking from those around you that believe in you? Listen, you are being trained up so that you will know which direction to turn when you get older. Where is that direction? Just look to the cross. So now that you have received this training, I will see you at the plate.

Dear Heavenly Trainer,

God, surround me with Godly people. Help me open my ears and heart to the teachings I need to become the person you want me to be. Help me when I stray from the path to remember the instructions I received as a young person to find my way again. Forgive me of my sin and iniquity that so often binds me to the ways of the world and let me look to the cross of Jesus.

Day 172

Words of Anger and Wrath

Proverbs15:1 ***A mild answer calms wrath, but a harsh word stirs up anger.***

The question for today is, are you a hothead? Do you argue with every questionable call? Do you allow your opponent to get it to your head and cause you to lose your temper? Practice builds character, but competition reveals character. The reality is you are who your words say you are. When you are in the heat of a battle, the question is, how will you respond when things seem to be spinning out of control? So often, because of our competitive nature, we are quick to anger, and very rarely do we give calm answers. We tend to be reactive, not proactive, during battle. You see, our mouths can overload our witness. People listen to you because of your platform, and people wait for you to make a mistake.

The word "wrath" in Scripture today is a word that is rarely used today. The word in the Scripture is used to describe another person's wrath. But how we respond to that person's wrath will define who we are and how we respond to another's anger and wrath. The word used here in Hebrew is "chemah," which can also mean poison.[11] Is it not funny that the word for wrath equates with poison? If we allow anger to constantly drive us, then it is like poison to our soul. It will not only affect us, but it will affect all those around us. Could you imagine if God unleashed his anger on us for the way we treat him and the way we treat the people he created? I am so glad that God does not send down his wrath on me because you know I deserve it. So, if he does not exhibit his wrath, why should we exhibit our wrath in our speech and how we treat others? "A mild answer calms wrath." When you feel that thermometer rising deep down in your being, take a deep breath, count to 5 and then give a mild answer. Remember, if you try to fight fire with fire, you only get more fire. So this is a no wrath zone, and I will see you at the plate.

Dear God of Mercy and Kindness,

Help me to tame my tongue. Help me to practice giving mild answers and not driving anger and wrath with my anger and wrath. Because of my competitive nature, I am quick to be reactive, so help me breathe the breath you breathed into my lungs before responding. The truth is, do not fight fire with fire but fight fire with kindness and compassion.

✞

Day 173

Which Way Will You Go?

Proverbs 14:12 ***There is a way that appears to be right, but in the end, it leads to death.***

So, another week and another report of an athlete being suspended for performance-enhancing drugs. This has become so common in the sports world. A few years ago, a whole team in the Olympics was suspended for testing positive for PED drugs. Some athletes are taking shortcuts by using illegal substances, and this gives young athletes the false impression that PED's is the right way or, better spoken, the easy way to achieve success. But the reality is that this is a dead-end road and can lead to real health issues later. Success does not come easy, and if it does, then there is no satisfaction in getting through the struggle. My daughter recently told me about a girl that made it into the top ten of her graduating class, but everyone in the class knew she was a cheater and took the easy classes she could to achieve that honor.

The truth is, I want to follow her for the next few years of college and see how this ends. The truth is that if you have to cheat your way to the top, then you are better to be middle of the pack. You know the same shortcuts apply to our walk with Christ. Many times, sin is very appealing. Sin is even fun for a minute, but it always leads to death and destruction not only of yourself but of those around you. One night of wrong choices by a dating couple may be fun but can lead to an unwanted pregnancy. One night of partying can lead to a DUI or even the death of you or someone else. One night of deciding to get high off of the new drug can lead to death or a life of addiction. Yes, every day, you stand at the crossroads and must decide which way do I go. The Scripture says that "the wages of sin are death" (Romans 6:23). Now think about this verse as it applies to our discussion of cheating or taking the easy way out. The wage in this Scripture is what you are being paid or what you have earned. So we all deserve death, but then Jesus Christ stepped in and said those that "believe on his name would be saved." Now following Jesus is not the easy way. It is not the popular way. It is not an optional way. Yes, the truth which is Jesus the only way. Jesus said I am the way, the truth, and the life. See, the wages of sin is death, but the wages for following Jesus Christ is life. So let me ask you whether you have chosen the right direction. If not, then pause right now and ask the question, which way will I go? Then I will see you at the plate.

Dear Holy GPS,

I always have a decision to make as to how I will do it. I can take the easy way, or I can take the road less traveled. God, many of my choices have been about comfort and fun. God, my prayer is that I will not take the easy way but choose the way that leads to eternal life. Lord, I surrender to your direction right now. Thank you, Jesus, for being the way the truth and life, and upon your name, I am saved.

Day 174

Always Pride Before the Fall

Proverbs 29:23 ***Pride brings a person low, but the lowly in spirit gain honor.***

One of the hardest things to fight in the sports world is being prideful. Now, most coaches and players will tell you that you need some self-pride to compete at a high-winning level. But the problem stems from when we let pride take over our whole being. I would say that the first sin ever committed by Adam And Eve was not as much about the act of eating a forbidden piece of fruit as it was pride. How we win and how we lose speaks to how prideful we are? But even more than that is the question as to whether we are coachable. A prideful person is very hard to coach. They often have the mentality that they already know everything, which makes them arrogant, a first cousin of pride. During the Battle of the Wilderness in the Civil War, Union general John Sedgwick inspected his troops. At one point, he came to a parapet, over which he gazed out in the direction of the enemy. His officers suggested that this was unwise, and perhaps he ought to duck while passing the parapet. "Nonsense," snapped the general. "They couldn't hit an elephant at this distance."

A moment later, Sedgwick fell to the ground, fatally wounded.[12] Pride keeps us from seeing what is approaching and what we need to do to dodge the consequences of making bad decisions. Pride makes us pump up and feel better for a minute, but it also makes us lose our focus on the task at hand. Consider this saying by David Rhodes, "Pride is the dandelion of the soul. Its root goes deep, only a little left behind sprouts again. Its seeds lodge in the tiniest encouraging cracks. And it flourishes in good soil. The danger of pride is that it feeds on arrogance. Put aside your pride, and I will see you at the plate." [13]

Dear Prince of Peace,

I have allowed pride to defeat me more times than I can remember. I have often said pride always goes before the fall, and then I find myself wrapped up in my own arrogance. I will never lead someone to Christ through my arrogance. Please help me to put away my sinful pride and my self-reliance. Self-reliance leads to pride, but God's reliance leads to humility. Give me a humble spirit.

✞

Day 175

Playing with a Scar

Proverbs 20:30 (JUB) ***The scars of past wounds are medicine for evil, and living reproof reaches the most secret places in the inward parts.***

The other night I watched the defending NCAA Softball Champions from 2018, the Florida State Seminoles play in the super regionals of the 2019 season. When the camera panned in on the dugout, I noticed a young girl in the dugout wearing a toboggan. She looked to be about 11 or 12, and I immediately realized that she was struggling with cancer. I heard the announcer tell the little girl's story; he said that her name was Hayden Stone. This is the story that followed the announcer's introduction. At 11 years old, Hayden was diagnosed with rhabdomyosarcoma, a rare form of cancer found in the soft tissue; this diagnosis occurred in December 2018. It was at that point that, through connections, she was adopted as an honorary member of the Seminoles softball team. She is what they call an "incredible distraction." One thing that she does before every game is that she takes a yellow marker, and she draws a smiley face with a marker on the player's neck. She does this because she has a scar on her neck that resembles a smiley face; the scar is from a recent surgery. This scar for her is a reminder of what she is battling. The mark on the players is a reminder of what they are battling to do. They are reminded that they are playing for someone besides themselves. See scars tell stories and can be a great motivation for us to push through the pain. The Apostle Thomas had heard what Jesus had been through at the crucifixion, but he found it hard to believe that Jesus was alive. He then said to him, "Here, put your hands here and feel, and then you will believe." I heard a new song on the radio this week that helps remind us of the scars that Jesus bore for us. It is by "I am They," and it is entitled "Scars." The song talks about the scars are the reason that we know Jesus's heart. His scars also represent the covenant that he made for us. Let me ask you, are you thankful for the scars? Do the scars inspire you? By his stripes, we are healed. Hey, give thanks for the scars, and I will see you at the plate.

Dear Bearer of My Scars,

Thank you for the scars that represent the sin that entangles my life. The scars are a reminder of how much you love me. The scars remind me of who you are and how much I needed you to die for me. I could not earn my salvation because I bear so many scars upon my heart. I am thankful for the scars. Amen.

Day 176

Can I Hit the Reset Button?

Isaiah 43:18-19 NIV ***"Forget the former things; do not dwell on the past. See, I am doing a new thing! Now it springs up; do you not perceive it? I am making a way in the wilderness and streams in the wasteland.***

Sometimes what we need as an athlete is a reset button. Many times in the sporting world, we wish we could take back what we just said. There are other times where we find ourselves less than ready to play because we slacked on our preparation. Then some coaches wish they had made a different call or adjusted quicker. The one thing that is always true in sports is that you will make mistakes no matter who you are. This week I was watching the SEC tournament, and Auburn was playing LSU. It was tied in the 9th inning, bases loaded, two outs, and Auburn led by a run. All they need is one out game over, and they go to the semi-finals. The next throw, the pitcher threw a pitch in the dirt. The catcher blocked it perfectly, but he kicked the ball and could not locate it when he got up. Then the first baseman made a wild throw as the runner came in to score, and then the runner from second scored on that error, and the game was won with a walk-off error.

The catcher would do anything to have a reset button on that chain of events. But in sports, we cannot rest on what has already happened. The reality is that the only thing we can reset is ourselves to be better and do better. Now, having said that, what is more important than having a reset button in sports is having a reset in life because of the grace of Jesus Christ. You see, God's reset button is for all. God can reset your attitude, he can reset your purity, he can reset your relationships, and he can reset any sin you have ever committed. If you are going to experience reset, what is required of you is that you will have to not just say sorry, hit reset, and keep going down the same path. You must repent as you hit reset. That means reset, but do not do it the same way. Repent means that we decide to go in another direction. It does you no good to hit the reset button over and over without changing who you are and how you are doing it. So here is what I want you to do hit the reset button, and I will see you at the plate.

Dear Alpha and Omega (Beginning and my ending),

God, you are always doing new things even though you are always the same. I so often hit the reset button but then head down the same way again. I need not only hit the reset button, but I also need to go down a different path. Thank you for sending your Son to die for my sin so that I can reset, refocus, and repent. It is through the blood of Jesus Christ that I am allowed to start over.

Day 177

Do I Know How to Communicate?

Jeremiah 1:6-8 ***"Alas, Sovereign LORD," I said, "I do not know how to speak; I am too young." But the LORD said to me, "Do not say, 'I am too young.' You must go to everyone I send you to and say whatever I command you. Do not be afraid of them, for I am with you and will rescue you," declares the LORD.***

Is one of the biggest hindrances to team play these days is communication? As I look around the world, I see people communicating, but I often wonder what they are communicating. A few years ago, we went out to a Japanese steak house to celebrate one of my kid's birthdays. We were seated at a table with four girls, one of which I recognized from softball. She had been a pitcher on an opposing high school team. I spoke, and she looked up from her phone and spoke back then went right back to the phone. It was then that I noticed that all four girls were at dinner together, but none even looked up from their phones long enough to make eye contact with one another. They had come to enjoy the entertainment of a chef who cooks in front of you but barely looked up from their phone to watch the cooking shenanigans taking place. The truth is that they went out to enjoy one another's company, but they never engaged in communication. The reality is that I think the whole world is this way. They have a hard time letting go of the communication device in their hand so they can communicate. I think this can lead to a lack of communication on the field and on the court. The harsh reality is that if we are not careful, we will not know how to communicate. One of the qualities of a strong team is communication. Communication teaches us to play as a team and identify the signs and gestures of a fellow teammate. To know how to communicate what play or shift, we need to adjust into. Another thing is that we need to communicate that we are invested in people if we are going to be a witness for the Kingdom of God. How can we become better communicators?

One way is when you go to lunch with a friend and leave your phone in the car. I have a lawyer friend who requires you to leave your phone in the car if you go to lunch with him. Make sure that you listen as much or more than you talk. Sometimes the best communication on our part comes from listening and not from talking. Take a fast from social media. Do not use your communication to gossip or dress down a teammate or friend. Finally, the most important is to be careful what you post on social media and remember the whole world is watching. It takes a lifetime to build a reputation, but only one post to severe it. Finally, remember to speak your faith loudly and only when necessary to use words. Your communication is not just about what comes out of your mouth. You know the statement: actions speak louder than words. See you at the plate.

Dear Lord of Goodness and Mercy,

Help me listen. Help me to take a social media break. Help me to listen. Help me to put my phone down and look someone in the eyes. Help me to listen. Help my actions speak louder than my words. Help me to listen. Help me to speak the truth in love. Help me listen.

Day 178

Radical Change

Ephesians 4:17-18 ***So I tell you this, and insist on it in the Lord, that you must no***

longer live as the Gentiles do, in the futility of their thinking. They are darkened in their understanding and separated from the life of God because of the ignorance that is in them due to the hardening of their hearts.

Sometimes we need a radical change on our team or in our life. The thing that makes change so hard is change. You see, we get so locked into the way things are that change creates anxiety. The truth is that comfort comes from not having to change. Anytime you have to change, it is uncomfortable, and you know we love comfort. But sometimes, we cannot fight the power of the Holy Spirit, prodding us to make a change. So, the question is, are you willing to make a change so that your team can be better, or your life can be better? You know, one of the things I hear all the time in the church today is that what this world needs is a "radical change." I agree with that statement, but I think we do not see radical change because even as "Christians," we are only willing to follow God only part of the way. I read a quote from Mark Hall the other day that made me think about this. "How can we expect a radical change from God if we are not willing to live radically changed lives?" So often, we are willing to talk about change, but we are not willing to adjust our lives to reflect the change. So often in the bible, when someone was destined to change and was truly going to change, God gave them a new name. Abram had to change addresses and his plan, so God gave him the new name Abraham.

Sari had to learn to be patient and to get with the plan the Holy Spirit had laid out for her life. So, what did God do? God changed her name to Sarah. Saul had a Damascus Road experience and is called Paul throughout the rest of his ministry. And Simon is given the name Peter because, upon his name, the Lord will build the Church. All these individuals went through radical change to get to the place where God wanted them to be. The question is, are you willing to not just talk about a radical change, or are you willing to be the radical change? Listen, it is not going to be easy, but nothing worthwhile or lasting is easy. So do not just talk about radical change; be the radical change that you talk about, and I will see you at the plate.

Dear God of Change,

God change me and then make me a change agent for this world. I often talked about radical change and then kept doing things the way I had been, yet expecting a different result. Give me a new name representing not how I am but who I am in you. Change my heart of God; let me see through the eyes of the Holy Spirit. Change me, make me, and mold me.

✞

Day 179

P.O.W.E.R.

Luke 10:19 (KJV) ***Behold, I give unto you power to tread on serpents and scorpions, and overall the power of the enemy: and nothing shall by any means hurt you.***

So, this week we are going to focus on the word P.O.W.E.R. We live in a world where we are fixated on power. The more power we have, the better we are. We can go to the sidelines in the middle of a contest and replenish with a drink called **Power**ade. When we feel we are bonking, we can eat a Power Bar or have a Protein Shake packed with the power of protein before a contest. But where does real power come from? So often, we have this misconception that we are like the Power Rangers, and we can just transform into a superhero. But the truth is that power comes from dedication, discipline, and hard work.

Now power drinks and power bars may help to sustain you, but they will not transform you. They are not a super potion that turns you immediately into a superhero. No real power comes from knowing how to tap into power before you need it. This week we will cover the tools you need to tap into your inner power. Now before we delve into that, let us first focus on what gives us power in life. Our power comes from the resurrecting power of Jesus Christ, our Lord and Savior. Jesus is our ultimate power source. Did you hear what I said, "resurrecting power?" Now that combination of words sounds so funny, "resurrecting power." The reason that sounds so funny is that our power comes from the death of Jesus Christ. But it is not power only found in his death but also a power that is found in the Resurrection. Death is the one thing that drains every ounce of power. But the grave could not hold Jesus because he is life. He even states that he is the way, the truth, and the life. So this power is not something we wait around to die to receive. No, this power is available to us every day. The power of the Holy Spirit keeps us and sustains us, but it does so much more.

So, this week, we help to equip you with what you need to have the power to play and the power to live out the call that God has a place in your life.

P Pursue Purity
O Obey the Call
W Worship Daily

E Engage Others
R Reject Apathy

Now read through that list again and then say to yourself, I have the power, and I will see you at the plate.

Dear Great Power Source,

God give me the power to tap into the Holy Spirit. God, you are the greatest supply of power. God, through you, comes to strength and the might to conquer our fears. God, through your power, we can push through trials and temptations. Thank you for the resurrecting power of Jesus Christ. It is through the power of the cross that I find how to not only push forward but to push upward. You have given me the power to conquer sin.

Day 180

Purity Paves the Way

Psalm 119:10: ***"How can a young man keep his way pure? By living according to your word."***

Now you may be thinking to yourself, what in the world does purity have to do with sports? The truth is that sports are what you do but what we are most worried about is who you are both on and off the field. You must also remember that you represent a name and what that name stands for when you play for a team. Purity is a way to guard your heart against the pain that is associated with not practicing purity. When I was in youth ministry, one of the seven checkpoints that I wanted my students to leave my program having was a sense of purity. This also meant that by practicing purity, you could leave high school whole and complete. Practicing purity helps you save a whole lot of regrets. One of the statements that I would frequently use was from Andy Stanley. He stated that "purity paves the way to intimacy."[14] Athletes must pursue purity in all things. This is especially true in sexual purity. How many times have you heard of a player being accused of sexual assault? The cold hard fact is that Satan knows that he can wreck your dreams through sexual temptation. It is a lot harder and nobler to stay pure. But staying pure will take a lot of work, which will mean that you have people who hold you accountable.

Now one of the top ten decisions you can make after surrendering your life to Christ (this, by the way, is number one) is deciding to be an athlete that pursues purity. In 1 Corinthians 6:18, Paul warns us to "flee from sexual immorality." Flee does not mean hanging out to see what might happen. It means to move as fast as you can from the situation. Do you remember the story of Joseph in Genesis 39 when Joseph fled from Potiphar's wife after she attempted to ensnare him into sexual sin? When we are pressed to make an impure decision, we need to "pull a Joseph" and Run! Sprint! Flee!

Pursuing purity stretches beyond sexual purity. It means having the right actions, attitudes, motives, and thoughts in all areas of life. It means protecting what you put into your mind through music, television, and media. Purity is not as much a decision you make as it is who you are as a person. Purity comes from the overflow of the heart. An Athlete of Power understands that there is spiritual power in purity and that purity paves the way to intimacy. So, let me ask you, are you seeking purity? See you at the plate.

Dear Your Righteousness,

God, I need you to make me whole. I need you to create and give me a heart that seeks purity. I am truly fighting against the world in this area. We are bombarded by the world telling us what feels good and to do it. But what we need is to do what is wise and not what feels good. God, take my regrets and bury them in the deepest ocean. Create in me a pure heart on God and renew a right spirit in me. Amen.

Day 181

Obey, Obeying, Obedience

Jeremiah 17:7-8 ***But blessed is the one who trusts in the LORD, whose confidence is in him. They will be like a tree planted by the water that sends out its roots by the stream. It does not fear when heat comes; its leaves are always green. It has no worries in a year of drought and never fails to bear fruit."***

When I was little, we used to sing a song entitled "Trust and Obey." The second part of the verse is what really got me thinking this week. Here is a paraphrase, but you can sing the original right now. You must trust and obey, for it is really the only way; no other way will make us happy when it comes to Jesus. So what must we do? We have to obey and trust. See, to be happy in our walk with Jesus, we have to learn to trust, but then we have to take it one step further; we have to obey God in his leading. Often, we find ourselves in unhappy places, and it is during these times, we realize that we got there because we chose our way, not God's way. Part of having power is found in obeying. Obeying is more than listening and shaking your head that you agree. Obeying is truly following the direction of God, even when it is not the easiest course of action. Zig Ziglar nailed it when he said, "You are the only person on earth who can use your ability.[15] You cannot give your ability to someone else. You can help teach someone how to use the ability that God has given them, but you cannot transpose your ability to someone else. An Athlete with Power is willing to obey the call in his or her life, not just the call to play sports, but the call to play sport for a higher calling. Obeying is more than just being good. It means going the extra mile to make sure you are doing what is right. What are the benefits of obeying? First, it assures that we are in control of what we can be in control of. Secondly, it sets an example for our teammates and our opponents. Thirdly, it leaves no doubt as to what our motives and intentions are. When we trust and obey, there is no other way to be happy because we have now moved into obedience by obeying. So trust the obedience that gives your power, and I will see you at the Plate.

Dear Voice in the Wilderness,

Teach me to listen to, so I will learn to trust. Teach me to trust so that I can follow your direction. Teach me to follow so that I can obey. Teach me to obey so that I can be obedient. Teach me to be obedient so that I can be a disciple. Teach me to be a disciple so that I can lead others to Lord. Let me trust and obey, for there is no other way – Amen x 2.

Day 182

Worship Daily

Psalms 95:6 ***Oh come, let us worship and bow down; let us kneel before the LORD, our Maker!***

How often do we find ourselves waiting for Sunday to get here so we can go to worship? Somehow, we have bought into the misnomer that worship only happens on Sunday morning in the confines of a stained glass, steepled church, or contemporary auditorium. When we think that way, it causes us to spend the other six days a week drifting away from our most important relationship. Unlike any other relationship, our relationship with God is built solely around our worship of him. What can we tell him that he does not already know? What can we try to turn him into, he is not already? What can we convince him of that he is not already knowledgeable of? See, the way that we communicate with God is through our worship of him. The truth is that to have power, we need to worship daily. Our God is worthy of our worship and praise; he longs for it and loves when we commune with him this way. He never leaves or forsakes us, so we must not abandon our worship and try to make it all up in an hour on Sunday. So, how can we worship God during the week? One way is to unplug from all our devices and distractions so that we can just be with him. Another way that we can worship with him is to just get alone with him. Another idea is to go on a walk where you listen to praise music and pray. You could also find a solitary place to pray and meditate on his word. When we worship, we ignite the Holy Spirit in our life. When we spend time in worship, we realize that our strength comes from within and not on our own accord. Yes, the truth is that worship is our lifeline to God and what he is doing in our life. Our power comes through our worship to him and in him. An athlete with power realizes they won't thrive without worshipping Jesus daily. So, go and worship, and then I will see you at the plate.

Dear Almighty Powerful Supreme God,

Make my life worship to you. Let me realize that my power comes from my worship and adoration for what you are doing in my life. Help me to realize that six days without worship make one weak, not powerful. My power comes from within. Give me the power to overcome and give me great power. A power that comes from on high and not from this world. Amen.

Day 183

Engage Others

Romans 12:16 ***Live in harmony with one another; do not be haughty, but associate with the lowly never be conceited.***

It has often been said that players play up to the talent level that is on the field. The truth is that a team full of good players challenges one another to be better players. In essence, they engage one another and then push one another to be better. Sometimes, a team has a prima donna; this person solely wants all the attention cast their way. They want the ball, and they want to be the hero. Often, this player seems to always be by themselves; their attitude keeps others from wanting to get close to them. They do not want to engage with other players, and even worse, they do not play as team players. When we do not engage with our team, we are relinquishing the power of the "whole team" for the power of just "me."

I think of Jesus and his ministry when I want to see an example of a team. He did not want to keep his ministry to himself, so he engaged 12 apostles to share in his ministry. The outcome of his engagement is still felt today as each one of the disciples went on from his death to engage other people in the way. If we are going to live out the great commission and commandment, we will have to engage people. One of the problems in today's world is that we engage people through social media or text but have a hard time engaging people one on one. The truth is that very few people now know their neighbors or even they know the people they work with. Jesus' whole ministry came from his engagement with people. There is power in engaging people. It helps to identify what they are going through and lets them know that you care for them. So, go and engage with teammates, and then I will see you at the plate.

Dear Great Rabbi,

Please help me to engage others so that I can share the gospel with all those that I come into contact with. God, help me to realize that power comes through engaging others. When we engage with others, we have the opportunity to show others who you are, mighty God. God, thank you for sending your Son to engage in 12 apostles so that those 12 could engage the world. It is because of their engagement that I can pray this prayer today. Thank you for loving me enough to send your Son to engage me through the power of the cross.

✞

Day 184

Reject Apathy

Ezekiel 2:4 ***"I am sending you to them who are stubborn and obstinate children, and you shall say to them, 'Thus says the Lord GOD.'***

I do not know how many times growing up, I heard the words, "quit feeling sorry for yourself." Most of the time, this had to do with my attitude or how I handled something that did not go my way. I would pout and begin to feel sorry for myself. I would clam up. And rather than engage, I would disconnect. This week my son was at a football camp, and after the camp, I asked him how it went. He told me that it was good, but he got in trouble for his attitude after making a mistake. He said the coach told him to quit feeling sorry and to do it right next time. What great words from a coach. When you are filled with apathy, you are constantly feeling sorry for yourself.

You develop what I call a "victim mentality." Let me; let you in on a secret: the world is not out to get you. Part of sports maturation is learning how to handle disappointment or defeat without feeling it was ever one else's fault. Apathy comes from our blaming everyone else for our lack of preparation and mistakes. Did you know that apathy and evil work hand in hand to destroy? They are the same in reality. Evil wills it. Apathy allows it. Evil hates the innocent and the defenseless most of all. Apathy doesn't care as long as it's not personally inconvenienced.

You see, apathy in life lets the devil sneak into your ear and tell you what you think you need to hear. You must always remember that Satan is a liar. He is not able to tell the truth; it is not in his nature. Everything he says is a lie and a scheme to pull you away from what you were called to do. This is not only in sports but in every aspect of your life. Satan tells you why you are not what you can be, but God tells you that everything is possible. When apathy starts in a team, it is like cancer; if it is not eradicated, then before long, it will take over the whole body. Apathy not only kills the body, but it kills the spirit. Apathy and evil play together, and they are sure to make you fail if you buy into the lie. There is no power in apathy. So, rid yourself of all apathy, and I will see you at the plate.

God of Love, Power, and Might,

Rid my body and soul of all apathy. Let me turn off the voice of Satan. Help me to remember that he is a liar and cheat. He comes to steal, kill, and destroy. He is a destructor of dreams and a robber of self-esteem. Thank you for sending your Son Jesus, who removed apathy when he took my sins upon his back.

Day 185

Actions Greater than Words

Proverbs 4:18 NIV ***In the same way, let your good deeds shine out for all to see so that everyone will praise your heavenly Father.***

I saw a shirt the other day that I loved. It was on the back of Hewitt Trussville's girls' softball practice shirts. (On a side note, they won the Alabama 7A State Championship in a spectacular comeback from coming out of the loser's bracket and beating a team twice to eliminate them.) The slogan had two words; On the top, it had the word "Action," and on the bottom, it had the "Words."

ACTION
WORDS

The slogan represents that your actions are greater than your words. I cannot tell you how often I heard that when I was growing up. Let your actions speak louder than your words. It is such a true statement in sports and life. I recently saw a boxing clip from the '90s where a challenger was taunting Mike Tyson. Mike Tyson never said a word; he never responded to the challenger's taunts; he just got up and knocked him out in the first round. You see, we can tell the world how good we are all day long, but they will never believe us until we prove it with our actions. The same is true in our witness for Christ. Many people say they believe in Jesus, but their actions are contrary to a follower of the way. See, it is not about believing as much as it is about following. Jesus never said to the disciples, just believe in me. No, he said, let me see if you want to act upon your faith. If you do, "Come and follow me." Let me ask you what your words are telling the world? No, scratch that. What are your actions telling the world? Hey, actions trump words every time. So, it is time for some action. I will see you at the plate.

The Blood Atonement,

Make me a person of my word. I want to move from believer to follower. Let me witness, and only when I must use words. Let my actions speak for my soul and my soul speak for you. You sent your Son who said very little but let his actions speak for his love for us. Let my actions always be greater than my words.

✞

Day 186

Courage Under Fire

Acts 4:13 ***The members of the council were amazed when they saw the boldness of Peter and John, for they could see that they were ordinary men with no special training in the Scriptures. They also recognized them as men who had been with Jesus.***

A few years ago, Casting Crowns came out with a song called "Courageous." The song is a reminder that we are made to be courageous, not timid. I was thinking about the story in Acts, where Peter and John are thrown in jail for speaking the truth about Jesus Christ. When they are confronted about their witness, they muster the courage to say that salvation is only found in one person, and that is Jesus Christ. Their boldness came from their personal relationship with Jesus Christ. They were bold because they realized how bold Jesus had been for them as he walked with them for three years and then went to the cross to die for them. The cross is where we find our boldness because nothing else has ever made such a statement on behalf of humankind. So how does this boldness relate to us on the field? It is not so much in our play as it is from the lessons we learn on the field. These lessons are what will take us through life. See many times; we are put in situations on the field that test our courage. The reality is that competition puts our "courage under fire. When we are under fire, we can make one of two decisions. The first is that intense pressure can break us. The second option is that the fire can refine us. I mentioned, in the beginning, the song Courageous; now, I want you to pause and think about the words in the song. (Listen to the song if you can.) You were made to be courageous, and it starts with you. You have to lead the way. You have to pray that your courage comes from the Lord. Will you stand up, be courageous, and take back the fight? Those are the questions that are asked in the lyrics. You see, when you are on the field, there are people in the stands that envy you. Some hope that you win, and others are cheering against you to lose, but no matter what they are cheering, you can be the example that helps them see Jesus. Through your play on the field, you can be an example for Jesus. You can point the way to the cross, and you can show the world that courage under fire has persevered through the power of the cross. So even though your courage is under fire, I will see you at the plate.

Dear Bold and Courageous Lord,

Help me to realize that the cross is where I truly find my courage. You have put within my being the Holy Spirit that helps me when I come under fire. You have refined me under pressure so that others can see the boldness that I have for Jesus Christ, my Lord and my Savior. Help me realize that the only way we will ever stand is to pray on our knees with high lifted hands. Amen.

Day 187

Short-sighted?

2 Peter 1:9 ***The person who lacks these things is blind and shortsighted and has forgotten the cleansing from his past sins.***

I was working on a sermon the other day about self-discipline, and this quote came up from Craig Groeschel. "The reason that we are not self-disciplined is that we are so short-sighted.[16] As I thought about that quote, I realized that we live in a society where everything is so on-demand that we do not want to work hard to achieve great things. The truth is that this thinking leads us to be short-sighted. We see the immediate but have such trouble looking down the road. We want it now, and Amazon and other online companies offer not only having it now but getting it delivered within hours. We have been programmed to be short-sighted and impatient when things do not happen immediately. The drawback of being short-sighted is that we will abandon our hopes and dreams if it does not pay immediate dividends. The great thing about sports is that it causes us to think about longevity and not just a short-sighted vision. The same could be said in our walk with Jesus. Our walk will be one of the peaks and valleys. Let me add that the Christian life is a marathon and not a sprint. We must think about the concept of grace. Grace is not a shortsighted concept; it was a gift given to all generations and all people. The problem with some people being short-sighted is that they feel they have blown it and are no longer worthy of living within God's grace.

You cannot be short-sighted and experience the grace that Christ has given you. Coaches and teachers can also fall into the trap of short-sightedness when they bail the athletes or students out. Many of these leaders are woefully short-sighted when they try to protect students or players from their mistakes when they turn a blind eye. They are more concerned with winning than the student/athlete's journey for knowledge and peak performance. For what is not learned within the concept of self-discipline cannot be given by another. By letting your students or players take shortcuts, you lead them to be short-sighted. So, quit being short-sighted, and I will see you at the plate.

Dear God of Vision,

Help me to fight the good fight. Help me focus on fighting and looking down the road at what you want me to be and what you want me to do. Keep me from thinking that the immediate will satisfy me because only the eternal will satisfy me. Jesus, thank you for seeing way down the road and going to the cross for me and my sins. I give my heart to you once again today. Amen.

Day 188

Temple Body

I Corinthians 6:19-20 ***Do you not know that your bodies are temples of the Holy Spirit, who is in you, whom you have received from God? You are not your own; 20you were bought at a price. Therefore, honor God with your bodies.***

Have you ever thought about the fact that your body was given to you? We talk a lot about being a steward of our money and our talents, but we also need to think about how we might be a good steward of the body that God has given us. The truth is that I was an athlete; that could have been so much better if I had treated my body as a temple. The fact is that we will be good to no one if we are not around to share the love of Jesus with others. Maybe that is why our bodies are compared to a temple. They are sacred and are worthy of being not only maintained but well-taken care of. Do we know that we are what we eat and drink? Now, this is especially true when we are young. How we take care of our bodies when we are young will dictate how our health looks when we are older.

I read an article the other day that was talking about that vaping was going to ruin athletes. The U.S. Surgeon General calls it a public health crisis. A 2018 Surgeon General advisory noted that one in five high school students and one in 20 middle school students vape. In 2017, the Massachusetts Risk Behavioral Survey reported that about 20 percent of high schoolers use vapes, and 41 percent reported using e-cigarettes.[17] Kristin Beauparlant's son, Cade, was captain of the hockey team until he got caught using e-cigarettes in school. He started undergoing treatment for nicotine addiction and learned he had developed lung disease after at least four years of using nicotine products.

"He was a good kid, very smart, very athletic, kind of had everything going for him, and then things just changed," said Beauparlant, a nurse and a mother of three from Newburyport. You see, when we put drugs, tobacco, or alcohol into our bodies, there are consequences and a defilement of the temple that God has given us. We cannot be in peak performance shape and defile our bodies. So, what are some things we can do to make our temple the best witness that it can be for God? The first is to give up your addictions. Remember, you can do all things through Christ, who gives you strength. What are you addicted to? The answer is anything that you cannot give up for ten days. The second is to eat right and eat often. The third is to stay hydrated. Most of the people around us walk around dehydrated yet have a water source around them almost all the time. The last thing is that we should stay physically fit. If you are young, act now on that so that it does not lead to catastrophic health issues later. So, bring your temple out of the dugout, and I will see you at the plate.

Dear Creator of Body, Soul, and Mind,

God, help me to be a great steward of the body you have given me. Help me to remember that choices today will affect my tomorrow. Help me to get rid of the addictions that hold me captive. Help me remember that my body is a temple, which means that it is a witness to my faith and love for you.

✞

Day 189

Some Value vs. Eternal Value

I Timothy 4:8 ***"Physical training is good, but training for godliness is much better, promising benefits in this life and in the life to come."***

We all know the sacrifices that must be made to play sports. We sacrifice rest, time with friends, and even major events to play the game we love. Now sometimes, we even sacrifice our worship and discipleship. This sacrifice teeters a fine line related to our eternal goals and our relationship with the most important one. It is so important that we have balance in our life. I have seen some athletes sacrifice everything for the sport only to get injured, and it all ends in the twinkling of an eye. We want to make sure that sometimes we self-check our temporal goals and dreams to ensure that they are in line and balanced with our eternal goal. So how do we keep our eternal goals in check? The first is to make sure we are not neglecting significant relationships. Make sure you take time out of your constant practice to spend time with people who need you and that you need. Sometimes we get so focused that we forget that God made us relational; it is the very reason he sent his Son. The second is to make sure we are making time for worship. The other day, I read a funny quote on a church sign that said, "seven days without worship makes one weak." We must spend time with our creator and the one that we are going to spend eternity with if we will remain strong. If you play a tournament on Sunday, this may mean that you lead the team in worship or a devotional. Another option is to find a service online and watch it between games. There are so many ways to worship in today's world. The truth is that worship needs to be habitual. Worship is not something you go to; it is something that you constantly do. Your life is worship to God. Sports give you a platform to promote the eternal things that are important to you and your faith. Use the platform that God has given you.

Finally, remember that physical training is of great value, but we will not be whole or complete without the spiritual side of training. For we know that one day the game will end, and the competition will cease, but we know that because of our relationship with Jesus Christ that we will live in eternity with our God and our Father. Now, remember to do your eternal training, and I will see you at the plate.

Dear Soulmate,

God, help me to know that I have an eternal home because of Jesus. Help me to develop a balance in life. Help me to train my soul as well as my body. It will do me no good to reach all my goals here and yet forfeit my eternal trophy of salvation.

Day 190

Rule Follower

Romans 13:1 ***Let every soul be subject unto the higher powers. For there is no power but of God: the powers that be are ordained of God.***

Most of us detest and fight against rules, yet we play sports defined by the rules. Without rules in sports and life, chaos would ensue. Rules set the boundaries and make sure that both opponents have an opportunity to win. Just recently, my son and I were playing cornhole at the beach. I can honestly say I have only played a few times, but this was an intense game. I scored three bags on the last toss, and my score went to 22. At this point, I declared myself the winner, to which my son then said, "you have to go back to 15." He then told me that the rule they play with at school was that you bust if you go over 21; you have to go back to 15. So you know what happened next? An argument ensued. We argued, but I finally decided to be the adult and went back to 15. (I still won the game.) After the game was over, I did what anyone would do that was unclear about the rules. I went to google to search cornhole rules. What I found out was that there are two different ways to play the game and score cornhole. One association does have the bust rule, but the other says first to 21 or over wins. So, what has to happen is that you have to agree before you start on which rules you are going to play by. Now with life, you do not get that opportunity. God has set up a list of laws for us to follow, and then he sent Jesus to summarize those laws. Here let establish the playing rules for you. "'Love the Lord your God with all your heart and with all your soul and with all your strength and with all your mind," and "Love your neighbor as yourself." (Matthew 22:37) That is the formula for following all of the other rules that have been set for us to follow. So, write that rule upon your heart, and I will see you at the plate.

My Supplication,

Thank you for simplifying the rules so that I can understand what it means to have a heart like yours. Thank you for loving and protecting me from myself and others through the rules you have established in how we should live in harmony. You have blessed me and continue to keep me in all of my days. Amen.

Day 191

The Heart of the Matter

Psalms 139:23 ***Search me, God, and know my heart; test me and know my anxious thoughts.***

This week we will spend a few days looking at the condition of your heart. Now many of you may be saying, "I have already had a physical, and my heart checked out fine." A fact is that if you are regularly practicing and taking care of yourself, then your heart really should be strong. But this week, we are going to look at the spiritual window of your soul, the "spiritual heart." Most people may not know this, but the heart is the central processing unit of your whole being. Like a computer has a CPU, your heart is your CPU. You see, what comes out of your mouth comes from the heart. The way you play the game comes not from your skills but from your heart. The way you handle victory and defeat is really just an expression of your heart. How many times have you been encouraged or heard that you must play with heart? Throughout the Scripture, we are cautioned above all things to "guard our heart." I tell people who are stuck in habitual sin or keep doing the same thing repeatedly that they do not have a sin problem, but they have a bad heart condition. So, this week we will examine what kind of heart you have and how you can give all your heart to God. This means that the heart of the matter this week is the heart of the matter. So, let me begin by asking you this question, what condition do you think your heart is in? Not your physical beating heart but your spiritual heart. So right now, stop and ask God, as David did, to examine your heart. What is it that needs to be transplanted, and what needs to be changed? Now that you have checked the vitals of your spiritual heart, I will see you at the plate.

Dear Lord Jesus,

Test me and know my thoughts. Test me and know my intentions. Test me and know my heart. Show me what it means to have a heart transformation or even a heart transplant. Let me put in my life a heart like you exhibited while you were here on earth. Renew me, Lord, and make me pure and holy. Amen.

Day 192

The Scarred Heart

Luke 24:39 ***Look at my hands and my feet. It is I myself! Touch me and see; a ghost does not have flesh and bones, as you see I have."***

You know, if you play sports long enough, you will eventually have some scars to show for your play. Now no one wants scars, but they are just a by-product of hard play and hustle. (Sometimes, they are from overuse or injury.) Scars tell stories and leave a mark that helps us remember what happened. Scars are deep flesh wounds that heal, but the tissue looks different when it heals. Now all of us could show scars of things that happened to us when we were playing. For some, it is a scrapped-up knee from sliding on the floor to retrieve a ball. For some, it is an elbow scar from surgery that we had to repair a tendon.

Some have a scar on their chin from hitting the top of someone's head in a soccer game. I will not even try to explain the scars a boxer or wrestler has. But Webster's has another definition for scars. It defines it as "a lasting moral or emotional injury." The truth is that some of us have scars on the inside. These are known as scars on the heart. Now scars on the heart can cause us to play and function in life negatively. Some of us have been hurt by abuse, neglect, and abandonment. Many have scars because of broken relationships and the situations that life has handed us. Now, if we let those scars of the heart dictate us, then we will struggle through life. So how can we manage the scars of the heart? The only way I know to do that is to give those scars to Jesus. The reason that reason came was so that he could take on my scars through his scars. He bore them as a reminder of what he did for us and that we can give him the scars of our hearts. Because of his scars, we do not have to bear our scars.

God can help put a new heart in us, and he can help us deal with the scars that have been placed upon our hearts. I heard a song the other day that may help you work through the scars placed on your heart. I have mentioned this song before, but it has so much visual imagery in the words that it needs repeating. The song is "Scars" by "I am They." The line that stuck out for me is the line that says, (paraphrase) because, without the scars that you bore on your body, I wouldn't be able to tell Your heart." The reason that I do not have to have a scarred heart is because Jesus has a heart for me. Jesus is why I do not have to focus on the scars that have been placed on my heart. No, his scars are a replacement for my scars, and his heart is a replacement for my heart. Now with your scars present, I will see you at the plate.

Dear Heart Healer,

Thank you for going to the cross for me and bearing the scars of my sin. God, I have scars on my heart, and I have placed scars on other people's hearts. Help me realize that these scars tell stories, but they do not define who I have to be or who I am going to be. Jesus, I trade my scars for your scars and my heart for your heart. Be my Lord and Savior Jesus.

Day 193

Calloused Heart

Psalm 51:17 NIV ***"My sacrifice, O God, is a broken spirit; a broken and contrite heart you, God, will not despise."***

Blisters and callouses are just a part of sports. So often, when working out and lifting weights, we will get callouses upon callouses. We sometimes have so many that we forget that they are even there. Callouses are a way of the body protecting the skin by hardening and thickening the tissue. Now sometimes, we hear people refer to someone having a calloused heart. This means that the heart has thickened and hardened to a point where it is impenetrable. Now I must tell you it is hard to love if your heart is calloused. A calloused heart is one that has little or no compassion for others. If we are going to have the heart of Christ, then there is no way that we can have a calloused heart. So, the question is, how do we remove the callouses that have formed because of the way we have been treated, neglected, or abused? See, our hearts harden over time; we stoically handle things so that we act as if things do not bother us but really, what is happening is that the heart is forming a callous so that you will not feel the pain. But if left long enough, you will not feel anything. Sometimes, we form callouses when we hold a grudge against people or have unreconciled grief and anger. So, what is the remedy for a calloused heart? The remedy is to let go of the pride and allow the heart to practice humility and sometimes experience pain. David was the King appointed by God, yet his family and the people turned on him at one point. So, he had a decision to make. He could have a calloused heart, or he could have a contrite heart. His prayer was that God would examine his heart and renew his heart. So often, as an athlete, we feel as if we cannot be real. We put up guards so others cannot see that we are hurt or that we are struggling. Listen, a team is a family, and when one hurts, we all hurt together. A team is more than wins and losses. A team is a band of brothers/sisters that help one another on the field and in life. So, do not be afraid to be real and to trust those teammates around you. It is through prayer and being transparent that the callouses on your heart will be removed. I know you have tons of callouses on your hands from batting practice, but you do not have to have them on your heart. So, come on with your calloused hands, and I will see you at the plate.

Dear Heart Renewer,

Break my heart. Remove the scales from my eyes and the callouses from my heart. Teach me to let go of grudges. Help me to have a heart like the heart of David. Let me put aside all of my malice, hate, and discord so that I can have a heart that cares about living in harmony.

Day 194

The Hardened Heart

Mark 8:17 ***Aware of their discussion, Jesus asked them: "Why are you talking about having no bread? Do you still not see or understand? Are your hearts hardened?***

So often, I hear talk of people that had been incarcerated as being hard people. I have even heard people refer to someone that was deceased as living a hard life. It is like, at some point, these people just quit worrying about what is going to happen to them. They put up walls and would not allow anyone to get close. They push away those who try to get close, and they feel that if they keep everyone at an arms distance, they can just live in their own misery. If we are not careful, we can develop a hard heart. A heart that is one of stone and not of the flesh. There are various reasons why the heart hardens, but it is usually because of previous situations that cause us to guard our hearts for fear of getting hurt again. A heart that has been broken too many times will soon become a hardened heart. The other reason that hearts get hardened is that we only see things one way, which is their way. They think they must be right, and essentially the world revolves around them.

I think of the Scripture where Moses told Pharaoh what God was going to do to him through the plagues. The plagues that he was going to send would be rememberable. When the plague started happening, Pharaoh would relent just for a minute, but every time his heart would harden again because of his huge ego and his illicit pride. A hardened heart refuses to let God have control. See, a hardened heart is a person that has been hurt. Now we have a saying in counseling, "hurt people hurt people." We have all had that teammate that can play like no other, but something in their past has hardened their heart. The truth is they are great players but terrible teammates because they do not allow anyone to get close. A hardened heart of a key player can devastate a whole team.

So, there are three signs that someone may have a hardened heart. The first is they have no **conviction**. They feel that they are always right even when they are caught in the act of wrong. The focus is on them and not on the greater good of the team. They also ignore the conviction of the Holy Spirit to make a change.

The second sign is that they have no **contentment**. Nothing makes a person with a hardened heart happy or satisfied. They are always longing for something new or the best to make them happy. But they will never find contentment in things.

The third is that they have no **compassion**. They can think of only themselves and what the world owes them. They cannot notice that there are those around them that are hurting and suffering.

Now the only way to get rid of a hardened heart is to allow God to soften it. So first, you must deal with the things that have hardened the heart, and you have to allow

God to cover the hardened heart with his love and his grace. Next, you will receive God's teaching on the places in your heart that need work. God will also show you how to be content with just his presence in your life. And finally, you will see with clarity through the lenses that God gives you to see the world as he sees it. So check your heart, and I will see you at the plate.

Dear Heart Changer,

Soften my heart. Convict me to make a change in my life. Help me to be content and teach me to see with a heart of compassion. All these things will soften my heart and restore my soul. Amen.

Day 195

The Broken Heart

Isaiah 61:1 ***The Spirit of the Lord GOD is upon me Because the LORD has anointed me To bring good news to the afflicted; He has sent me to bind up the brokenhearted, To proclaim liberty to captives And freedom to prisoners;***

If you live long enough, you will surely experience a broken heart. The truth is that you will probably experience many broken hearts in your lifetime. Some broken hearts will come from broken relationships. Some will come from the death or loss of a loved one. Some will come from how someone treated you, and some will come from extreme disappointment and loss. We all must deal with a broken heart, but we do not have to deal with it alone. Jesus came so that he could help us to mend a broken heart. In athletics, a broken heart comes from a few different circumstances. The first is when one is injured and cannot compete. The second is when we could have played better or done more, but we just were off our "A" game. The last broken heart stems from when you were defeated and eliminated. We will have the opportunity to redeem some of these events, but some may not be redeemable. A serious injury could sideline us forever. God forbid this to be the case, but it happens. A loss in the last game of our career could leave us feeling unfulfilled and trying to mend a broken heart. The last game of our career could be the worst game we have ever played. All of these things could lead to a broken heart, but even in these situations that cannot be redeemed, Jesus can redeem us. You see, Jesus wants us always to give our best, but he does not define us by our wins and losses. Jesus defines us by who we are in him. Jesus came to mend the broken heart. Our sin broke Jesus' heart to the point that he paid the ultimate price and gave his life for us. His death on the cross paid for our sins and shortcomings. You see, many circumstances lend themselves to us having a broken heart, but there is one remedy for a broken heart, and that is Jesus. So grab ahold of Jesus, and I will see you at the plate.

Dear Healer of the Lonely and Brokenhearted,

Heal my heart and make me whole. Revive my spirit today so that I might see your healing power. Your heart broke for the sin of this world, and so you did not leave us alone but sent your only Son to die for my sins and to heal my broken heart. Jesus was a friend to sinners and the healer of the broken heart. Amen.

Day 196

A Contrite Heart

Psalms 51:17 ***My sacrifice, O God, is a broken spirit; a broken and contrite heart you, God, will not despise.***

The word contrite is a word that is not a familiar everyday word. But if we are truly going to have the heart of Jesus, it has to start with a contrite heart. Like so many people in the limelight, King David allowed his power and popularity to get in the way of his walk with God. When the Kings were out warring, David decided to stay home, and that is when all "hades" broke loose. David then tries to hide an affair from one of his men who had been out at war. He tells lies upon lies and finally has Uriah killed. He then finds himself knee-deep in sin and struggling with a corrupted, hardened, broken heart. So what does David do? The first thing he does is humble himself. This is the first thing that must be done if you want a contrite heart. You must **humble yourself and give God his title back** (God All-Mighty). The second thing that David did was that he went to worship. We often think about worship as being a time when we got it all together, but worship is truly a bearing of our soul so that God can come in and change our hearts. A contrite heart is mentioned as something God likes, and it is connected to humility, brokenness, and a healthy fear of God's Word. When we have a contrite heart, we go through the Act of Contrition. Here is the definition for the Act of Contrition: "the act of where the consciousness of guilt has completely humbled natural pride and self-sufficiency.[18] This is not the unhealthy guilt that people place upon us to pressure us but the guilt that we feel from the weight of our sin and corrupt heart. A contrite heart does not take the forgiveness of God lightly, and it does not take for granted the sacrifice that Jesus paid for us. A contrite heart is being refined and purified.

Now the reason that this is so connected to sports is that a contrite heart reminds us that we are not God. It also helps us to see our teammates and even our opponents in a different light. It humbles us to play for God and not solely for self-related accolades. A contrite heart is easier to coach and respects correction and feedback. A contrite heart, however, does not come easy. It is only achieved through humility, prayer, and sacrifice. So, let me ask you, do you have a contrite heart? If not, let's start the process, and I will see you at the plate.

Dear Listener of the Contrite Heart,

Put in me a humble spirit and a contrite heart. Let me put aside myself so that I can see you in all your glory. Help me heal my heart of its brokenness and help me rid my heart of the selfishness that is filling it. Help me to see with the eyes of the heart. As the song says, "Open the eyes of my heart Lord, open the eyes of my heart." It is only when I open the eyes of my heart that I will truly see you.

Day 197

A Pure Heart

Matthew 5:8. ***"Blessed are the pure in heart, for they will see God."***

Now in the competitive world of sports, you would think that the concept of having a pure heart would be something that seemed timid and neutered. But the truth is that a pure heart leads to playing a pure game. The greatest athletes are the ones that play hard and pure. A pure heart is hard to achieve in today's world because so many things vying to corrupt your heart. It is not coincidental in the Scripture that it says, "above all other things guard your heart." The Greek word for "pure" in Matthew 5:8 is "katharos." It means to be "clean, blameless, unstained from guilt.[19] Think about those words as it refers to the competition.

To play a clean game and to be clean in your training and preparation. To be blameless in your preparation and mental attitude before the game. The hardest part of the definition is the concept of unstained from guilt. The reason is that we all have things in our life that we regret and wish we could take back. A pure heart lets God cover the stains of sin that so often taint and discolor our hearts. To have a pure heart toward God will mean that you have a pure heart toward those created in his image. To be pure in heart means that others will see how you have grown close to God and how you play the game. The pure in heart will see God. This is not in reference to just seeing him when we die. This reference is the way that we see the world and the way we conduct ourselves. I know you cannot add or take away from Scripture, but I would even suggest that this Scripture could be reversed to say that blessed are the pure in heart because others will see God in them. Do people see God through you and through your pure heart? I sure hope so, and now I will see you at the plate.

Dear Song of My Heart,

Give me a clean heart so that I can play a clean game. Give me a clean heart so that I can show the world how much you loved them. Give me a clean heart so that I can also have clean hands. Search my heart and rid it of all impurities and sin. Create in me a pure spirit that is shown by a clean heart.

Day 198

Read the Playbook

Joshua 1:8 ***"This book of instruction must not depart from your mouth; you are to recite it day and night, so that you may carefully observe everything written in it. For then, you will prosper and succeed in whatever you do."***

Have you ever got a new coach, and they handed you a brand-new playbook? What do you think they expect you to do with that playbook? They want you to learn it from cover to cover. Not just look at the playbook and pick what you wanted to learn and leave what you did not want to do. No, they expected you to write it on your heart so that you could perform it when you were called upon. The playbook was ultimately the coach's philosophy and what he/she thought would result in wins. The coach would not give you a playbook that s/he did not believe in or thought did not give the team the greatest advantage to win. You know, the head coach of our life (God) has also given us a playbook. It is the playbook for our life. It is the BIBLE, and that is the book for me. The Bible is not just a good plan, but it is truly God's promise to help us in every situation in life. The problem that we run into in most situations is that we have not read the playbook. Lifeway Research did a study that people in the United States do not read the Scripture regularly. Only about 13% admit to reading the Bible regularly. How can we know what God wants us to do or what plan he has for us if we do not know the playbook? Not only did he tell us to read the book, but he told us to write the playbook on our hearts. God knows we cannot go through this life without a game plan, and that is why he gave us the playbook. So, take a moment and read your God-given playbook, and then I will see you at the plate.

Dear Life Coordinator,

Thank you for giving us your playbook, which you spoke into word, and that word became the words of life. This playbook was written down by man but was breathed by you. May your word be a lamp unto my feet and light for my path. May I meditate on the words of the paybook and write them on my heart so that I may not sin.

Day 199

Can You Hear Me Now?

James 1:19 ***"My dearly loved brothers, understand this: everyone must be quick to hear, slow to speak, and slow to anger."***

You have all probably seen the commercial for Verizon with the guy walking around, saying, "Can you hear me now?" This is the question that a lot of coaches ask when they are coaching their players. We know that coaches all have a unique way of getting their coaching points across. Some yell and cuss at their players and others. Some use stories and examples to get your attention. Some use motivational speeches from Braveheart or Gladiator to hopefully challenge one to go, fight, and win. But no matter how the coach tries to motivate, it will not matter if the player is not listening. I watched a few weeks ago a coach giving a player instruction as they stood on third base.

You could tell that the player knew words were coming out of the coach's mouth, but none of those words connecting to the ears were processed in mind. Then a fly ball was hit to the outfield, and the player took off toward the plate. Then the left fielder caught the ball, and then the player was thrown out at third without tagging up. I am sure that the third base coach had just told the player what to do, and he did not hear it. So instead of a run and tying the game, the player got doubled up, and now his team had to play defense. In James 1:19, our Scripture for today, the word "quick" can be used to illustrate a runner racing as fast as he can to beat his opponents to the finish line. The runner is absolutely focused on what he is doing; nothing else will hinder him or occupy him. He was one goal and mind, and he is doing everything in his power to get to the line first. So, in the Scripture, James is saying we need to be quick to listen. This means that our sole focus before we even put our bodies into motion is listening and focusing. Then he uses the opposite of quick in the next sentence to say that we must be slow to speak. He is saying, before we respond, we need to process what is being said and why it is being said. A coach, just like God, has your best interest in mind. They are helping you to be the best you can be. How many times do we make a comment that we wish we could take back? The reason is that we were quick to speak, not slow to speak. Not being slow to speak can even have greater ramifications in that it can lead to penalties or even ejection from the game. Finally, he repeats the slow process by saying if we listen, it will slow our anger. Most of the time, when we understand the rationale and the reason, it helps us from becoming angry. Anger in sports will always come back to haunt you. Listen, listen quickly, slow down, and process what is being said, and I will see you at the plate.

Dear Spirit of Wisdom,

Let me be still and listen to your still, small voice. Speak to me, and I will listen. Let me be slow to speak so that I do not ruin my witness. Keep me and guard me against anger as it will only have negative consequences in my life and will detour me from my witness. Let me be quick to listen.

Day 200

What Type of Player Are You?

2 Corinthians 13:11 ***Finally, brothers and sisters, rejoice! Strive for full restoration, encourage one another, be of one mind, live in peace. And the God of love and peace will be with you.***

I was at a football meeting the other day, and the head coach talked to the parents about what type of player he wanted the players to be. He listed four different types of players on the slide. The first was the "just show up player." This player just shows up, puts in very little effort, and does not care about getting better; he just wants to wear the uniform for show. This player is more of a hindrance to the team than he is a help to the team. The second type of player that was mentioned was the "common player." This is the player who shows up, and some days work hard, but he goes through the motions on other days. They only do what they have to do to play, but they never go the extra mile. If you have a team of common players, you will lose more games than you win. You will also have a team filled with apathy.

Then you have what he called the uncommon player; the uncommon player is the player that goes the extra mile every day. They show up on time, and they are ready to listen, learn, and get better. They will stay after practice to get better. They will make sure that they handle their business off the field as much as they handle it on the field. If you have a team of uncommon players, you can win championships. The final player that the coach mentioned was the "legacy players." These are the players that not only want to be uncommon, but they want to leave a legacy. These are the players who stay after practice, but they stay after to help the younger players develop. These are the players that are looking at playing at the next level. These players lead because they want people to remember their names and what they did to enhance the program and win championships.

You know the same comparisons can be made to our spiritual life. I think that most professing Christians are just common players. We skate by just hoping to get the approval of God. What God needs is legacy players because these are the people who leave their mark on the world and change the Kingdom of God. These are the people that will be remembered, not for what they had or earned but for what they gave to magnify the name of Jesus. God does not need the just show-up players or even common players; God needs uncommon players that work hard to be legacy players. So, let me ask you, what type of player are you? Answer that, and I will see you at the plate.

Dear Divine Judge of all Things,

Help me to move past apathy and into compassion. Help me not just to show up but to show out for you and your kingdom. Help me know that I can leave a legacy, but that legacy will be based on what I did for you and not what I achieved on my own. Move me from uncommon and make your name a legacy through me. Amen.

Day 201

Run When You Cannot Walk

Isaiah 40:29-31 ***He gives strength to the weary and increases the power of the weak. Even youths grow tired and weary, and young men stumble and fall, but those who hope in the Lord will renew their strength. They will soar on wings like eagles; they will run and not grow weary; they will walk and not be faint.***

I heard Alabama's head coach Nick Saban give an update on the football team's first week of fall practice 2019 this week. He reported that he felt that the young guys needed to push through adversity and keep up their intensity. This is a familiar statement for the perfectionist Coach Saban to demand perfection and push the athletes through the pain associated with Alabama's summer dog days. But what caught my attention in the press conference was the slogan that he said they have come up with for this week. He said, "that he told the team that they needed to learn to run when they could run no more." He said, "it is that simple if you want to win." If you have ever been pushed to your limits in sports, you know what he is referring to. You know those days when you hurt so bad that every step reminds you that you are pushing your muscles to the max. You know what it means to practice when you are tired. You know what it means to give maximum effort when you want to quit. You know those first few weeks when there is no game insight, and you wonder if this is worth the effort. We have all been there. This relentless grind is not just in the sports world, but it is really how life operates. There are many weeks that we are pushed to the limit. There are weeks when the events in our life paralyze us. It is then that we have to learn to run when we cannot even walk. At this point, we need to realize that Jesus was serious when he said he would not leave us as orphans but that the Holy Spirit would come and give us strength and power. The only thing we need to do is call upon the Spirit and then believe that he will give us the strength to push through adversity. He will give us the strength to mount up on eagles' wings and not walk but run. We will not be faint or weary but will gather the strength to run when we feel we can run no more. So, call upon that Spirit, and I will see you at the plate.

Dear Eye in the Sky,

Help me to run when I cannot walk. Give me strength when all of me has been depleted. Help me to soar when I am feeling totally drained. Send your Spirit to take hold of all the aspects of my life. Thank you that when you soon could not find the strength to take another step toward Calvary, you sent him an aide to help carry out his destiny. It is in the cross that I find my strength and salvation. Amen.

Day 202

Motivating Slogans

John 5:14-15 ***Afterward, Jesus found him in the temple and said to him, "See, you are well! Sin no more, that nothing worse may happen to you." The man went away and told the Jews that it was Jesus who had healed him.***

You know that every team has some kind of slogan or saying that helps to motivate. Sometimes these slogans are all over the locker room or even printed on shirts. The slogans hope to motivate the team and get the team to realize that they are playing for something greater than themselves. A team slogan is trying to help the team to work together and keep unity among diverse teammates. Therefore, I decided to take a team's slogan for the next two weeks and see how it may relate to us. You may even want to adopt one of these slogans not just for your team but how you live your life. Jesus, believe it or not, had many slogans to help motivate people to be better and do better. One slogan used twice in the Scripture is the phrase, "go and sin no more." Now we all know living in this broken world that Jesus was given an impossible task. But what Jesus was saying is that now you have met me go and be different. He was encouraging the person not to return to their old way of life. His words both extended the concept of mercy and demanded a new call to holiness.

Jesus was always the perfect balance of "truth, love, and grace." Think about some of the slogans in the sporting world; they may seem impossible, but the truth is that they are there to set the bar so that we do not settle with just being ordinary. Jesus was great with setting the bar so high that it was unachievable, but he set the bar so that in our attempt to reach perfection, we would be morphing into a more Christ-like character. If you want some examples of these bars read, the beatitudes in Matthew 5:1-12. As we look at team slogans this week, think about what slogans you have played under or play under now. It will also help to think about a slogan for your life and how that challenges you daily. Now here is a slogan that you have heard before, "I will see you at the plate."

Dear Author of all Words,

Help me to live life by your slogan and not by the slogans of the world. You are the author and creator of all. You know the words on our lips before we speak them. You have given us the words of life, and may I write them upon my heart so that I can live and speak for you. Thank you for the greatest slogan that Jesus left with us that we live by faith alone. Amen.

✞

Day 203

Attitude Is Everything

1 Peter 4:1 ***Since, therefore, Christ suffered in the flesh, arm yourselves with the same way of thinking, for whoever has suffered in the flesh has ceased from sin.***

I have seen the slogan "attitude is everything" so often that it has become a staple saying in my sermons. Did you know that there are even books entitled "Attitude is Everything?" You could study what this slogan means for years. But in short, what does it mean? I mean, it is easy to talk about an attitude adjustment. But it is another thing to change an attitude. The truth is that the older you get, the harder it is to change an attitude. This is one reason why youth development is more than teaching skills; it is also about teaching how to play the game and respond to it. If you read the definition of attitude, you will see that it is all about posture, alignment, and positioning. The truth is that if you do not have a positive attitude, then you will eventually fail. The proper attitude helps to center you and helps to align you for learning and developing. Now, these are some examples of why attitude is everything. A positive attitude leans itself to being coachable.

In coaching, you are either going to receive positive or negative feedback. You have to be able to receive the negative with an open mind and without taking it personally. The second thing is that attitude is contagious. How many times have you seen a team with one bad attitude in leadership lead to a team full of attitudes? I watched an Auburn football game last year, and I heard the announcer say that the coach needed to get a hold of the locker room. What he was essentially saying is that the attitude of the team had gone south. Good attitudes are infectious, but so are negative attitudes, and that is why the slogan attitude is everything that has been adopted by so many. The last thing to mention is that attitudes are habit-forming. I will be transparent; when growing up, I was labeled as one with a negative attitude. I was a hothead, and it hindered me. When I came to know Jesus as my personal Lord and Savior, this attitude changed. It went from being that of a negative attitude to being one that served as a life coach to help others with their struggling attitudes. In my life, I can truly testify that attitude is everything. Sometimes, people blame their life situations on their attitude, which does affect them but should not cripple them. You may not be able to control your life situations but what you can control is your attitude. So, check your attitude because it is everything, and I will see you at the plate.

Dear Holy Heavenly Father,

Let me have the mind of Christ and the attitude of Christ, who considered himself nothing and gave his life so that I would not perish but have eternal life. My attitude should reflect one of gratitude. Help me control what I can control and how my attitude responds to the world around me.

Day 204

Life Is Short, Play Hard!

James 4:14 ***Yet you do not know what your life will be like tomorrow. You are just a vapor that appears for a little while and then vanishes away.***

Well, today, I hit another milestone in life as I dropped my son off on his first day of high school. I have no idea how I got to this day so fast. One of the things that I told him as I dropped him off was that this would be over before he knew it, so make the most of these four years. The realization is that in sports, most kids will never play past the high school level. So, to say that time is limited is certainly a reality. Our playing eligibility only goes for a short period. That is why it is so important to make the most of every day and every opportunity. Life is short compared to eternity, and the truth is that we only get so many opportunities. I often think that is why Jesus was so diligent in his earthly ministry. He knew that he only had so much time to spread the good news and establish his ministry. Jesus warns us over and over to make the most of every day and every opportunity. The one thing you really cannot be certain of is your existence or opportunities. The Scripture warns us that life can change in the "twinkling of an eye."

Just listen to sports radio, and every day you will hear of an injury that may sideline someone for the rest of their career. When I hear that, I often wonder if that person has regrets in the effort they gave. I wonder if, like so many, they would do it differently if they could do it all over. I wonder if this quote ever comes up in their mind. "Life is short; play hard." Now, what about you? Are you ready to play hard and to give it your all? Remember, the only promised moment you have is this moment, so make the most out of it, and I will see you at the plate.

Dear Father of Time,

I do not know how many days I have, but I know I must make the most of every day that has been given. God, I also realize that this is not all I have, but I have an eternity to spend with you. Thank you for sending your Son that did not deviate from his sole purpose of dying for me and my sin. Help me to embrace today and now put off till tomorrow what I can achieve today.

✞

Day 205

One Spirit, One Team, One Win

Ephesians 2:18 ***For through him we both have access to the Father by one Spirit.***

Part of playing as a team is playing as if everyone has one heartbeat, beating together. The idea of the team is that everything is shared, and everything is cohesive and fluid. A team cannot have many players who go in different directions and expect the team to surround them. A team is a body, all with different parts but all operating together. A team is more than the players: it consists of managers, coaches, and the scout team players. A team could not operate without all these parts. Therefore, the key concept in being a great team player is never to think of yourself better than those you surround yourself with. I heard an adage in bible study one time that said, "behind every good man is a great wife." I love that because, in my life, my wife and I see ourselves as a team and not as two individuals trying to trudge through life. Now we are not only operating as one team, but we are also operating as one spirit. To be like-minded and to have the same common goals and aspirations is so important to winning. To be of one spirit is even more important than being one team. Being one spirit means that we pray for one another and forgive one another and love one another. We pick each other up as we sometimes fail. Jesus taught us the concept of team as he chose 12 disciples to be part of his ministry. His soul purpose with this motley crew was to help them understand that they were of one spirit, the Holy Spirit. They were one team, even though Judas went rogue on the team. Jesus also wanted them to realize that the one win they all had in common seemed like a loss. The one win was his death, and it was that death that saved us and secured us. When we play as one team with one spirit and with the concept of one win, we become one. So let me ask you, is your team playing as one, and are you doing your part to ensure that you are one in spirit, one as a team, and have that one important win in the forefront? So as one part of many, I will see you at the plate.

Dear Three in One,

We are one, and why are we one? We are one in the Spirit, and we are one within the Lord almighty. And we know that unity will one day be re-established in this world because of our oneness in the Spirit and our oneness in the Lord. We will be unified because we believe in Jesus Christ and his birth, death, and resurrection. Make us one with you and one with one another. Let us be one in the Spirit of the Lord.

Day 206

Practice with a Purpose, Play with a Passion

I Corinthians 11:23-24 ***For I received from the Lord what I also passed on to you: The Lord Jesus, on the night he was betrayed, took bread, and when he had given thanks, he broke it and said, "This is my body, which is for you; do this in remembrance of me."***

The truth is that few people like to practice. This past week in Alabama, it has been over 100-degrees with heat indexes above the century mark. I know many players are dreading that afternoon practice. It is way too hot, but the other team is practicing, so what choice do you have? The real reason that practice is even tolerable is that there is a prize on the other side. We practice so that we get better, but we also practice so that we will be able to perform at our highest level when we are tested. But the truth is that during practice, whether we dread it or are one of the few who love it, we must practice with purpose. We must have a reason why we are doing what so few are doing. When we practice with purpose, we know what we want our desired outcome to be. When we practice on purpose, we get better. When we practice on purpose, we gain confidence. So often, we wish we could just show up and scrimmage. But the first thing that we need is the fundamentals of the game. We need to be purpose-driven, and that is the reason that we set goals and have aspirations. People often find themselves in trouble because they live life, but they live without a purpose. The truth is that we were all created for something, and God has a purpose for our life. The Scripture says that our purpose was crested even before we were born. The other reality to this is that we may be the only person that can complete this purpose. That is why we must pursue this purpose with passion. When we practice and are confident that we are prepared, we can pursue our purpose with passion. Playing with passion is more than playing to win; it is a concept that we play with the desire to reach perfection. John Wesley was huge on this concept that we practice life with passion every day and move on toward perfection. You see, nothing is achievable unless you believe that it is attainable. Passion comes from what we think is attainable. So, the question is, are you practicing with purpose, and are you playing with the passion for being the best you can be? I hope so, and I will see you at the plate.

Dear Lord and Perfecter,

Lord, you are the perfector of all things. You are with me even on those days when I do not want to practice. You give me passion when my tank is empty. You give me a great purpose for life and competition. God, I know that you have created me for a purpose and that I need to be an on-purpose person that does it with the passion that your Son had for me.

Day 207

Actions Speak Louder than Words

Mark 15:2-5 ***Are you the king of the Jews?" asked Pilate. "You have said so," Jesus replied. The chief priests accused him of many things. So again, Pilate asked him, "Aren't you going to answer? See how many things they are accusing you of." But Jesus still made no reply, and Pilate was amazed.***

"Actions speak louder than words." I have heard this statement since I was knee-high to a grasshopper. (I have always wanted to use that statement in a devotional.) Maybe, I have heard it so much that I have taken for granted what it means. I will be honest I was one of those growing up that loved to talk smack. I loved to try to get into your head. I do not know why I was made this way, but my mouth overrode my skills many times. So many times, my words spoke a lot louder than my actions. Maybe that is why I loved to talk smack to compensate for where I felt inadequate. I recently watched a movie with Kevin Hart entitled "Ride Along." Kevin Hart wants to be a police officer in the movie, but he is gripped by fear. So, what does he do? He runs his mouth to intimidate people but always winds up cashing checks his body cannot pay. How many times have you known a team that yelled, screamed, cussed, and disrespected the other team before the contest ever began? Then that team comes out, and they get killed. See, a lot of times, we try to compensate for our lack of preparation with intimidation. One of the things that I love about Jesus is that he always let his actions talk. During his trial right before his death, he is standing in front of Pilate. Pilate has the power to let him go. The truth is that Pilate is trying to get Jesus to talk to defend his actions and to admit who he was. But Jesus did not take the bait. Jesus will let his actions speak louder than any words and died for the unholy words we often speak. Pilate asks Jesus, "Are you the King of the Jews?" To which Jesus simply says, "You have said so." Jesus did not need to defend who he was because he was confident in who he was. He did not need to take the bait that would have him defend his purpose. No, Jesus just simply let his actions speak louder than his words. Will you let your actions speak louder than your words? If so, I will see you at the plate.

Dear Speaker of Life,

Help me to tame my tongue. Many times, it is my words, not my actions, that have gotten me in trouble. Let me be a man of my word, and let me carry through what I have promised. Let me follow Jesus's example of speaking the truth in love. Help me to understand that what comes out of my mouth affects my witness. Let my actions speak louder than my words every single day.

Day 208

Pain Is Temporary; Pride Is Forever

Psalms 30:5 (NIV) ***For his anger lasts only a moment, but his favor lasts a lifetime; weeping may stay for the night, but rejoicing comes in the morning*.**

One thing we can be sure of in life is that, at times, there will be pain. Pain comes in many forms; physical pain, mental anguish, and pain that stems from rejection. Pain is real, and we have all experienced it in unique ways. We all know the pain of losing the game that we let slip away. We know the pain of being looked over. We know pain is inevitable, but the important thing is how we respond to the pain that we experience. Can we experience pain and keep a sense of pride about us? We know that the reason that pain exists is that sin is prevalent in this world. We live in a fallen world. We also know that people that live in pain love to inflict pain on others. You heard me say it before, but "hurt people love to hurt other people." So, our pride does not come out of deflecting pain but how we handle the circumstances that surround our pain. Many times, in sports, the pain comes from losing a game that we should have won. To handle this with pride, we do not make excuses for why we lost; we just go out and get better so that we can win the next time we face this opponent. If the pain stems from hard practices and the struggle to get through it, then we need to get ourselves in better shape. Yes, we know if we are going to win championships, we will experience the pain of hard, arduous practice sessions. But pride comes from when you hoist that trophy in the air that you worked so hard and endured so much pain to achieve.

Now the harsh reality is that pain extends into everyday life. The truth is that life is hard, and it is filled with pain. But our pride comes from knowing that this is not all that there is. Jesus went to prepare a place for us that is free of pain. Jesus tells his disciples that he would not orphan them or leave them alone but that he would send the Spirit to help them get through the pain. He also assured them that he was going to prepare a place for them. He told them these things, knowing the pain they would experience as they took a stance for him and carried out the mission he had started. Our pride comes in knowing that the cross conquered the eternal pain we would have endured had Jesus not given his life for our sin. Yes, our pride came from Jesus' pain and suffering. But Jesus thought you were worth the pain. So, he laid his life aside so that he could rid the pain that the sin of the world had inflicted. Yes, the pride of Jesus truly is forever. Now amid all your pain, show your pride and, I will see you at the plate.

Dear Pain Taker,

Hold on, my child; your joy will come in the morning's bright light. You may weep but remember morning is fast at hand. Hold steady, my dear child, because joy will be revealed in the morning. You may be in your darkest hour, but with the dawn of a new day, there will be joy and rejoicing. Hold on, my child; morning is near.

Day 209

All It Takes Is All You've Got

Ecclesiastes 9:10 ***Whatever the activity in which you engage, do it with all your ability because there is no work, no planning, no learning, and no wisdom in the next world where you're going.***

"All it takes is all you've got" is quite the statement. Is it really possible to give all that you have got? I mean, surely you keep some in reserve. Now the fact is that every coach is trying to get the most out of their athletes. As a matter of fact, it is the coach's job to pull out one more rep, one more sprint, one more up/down. There is a special feeling about giving more than you thought you had. You know we are really capable of pushing harder and going further than we ever imagined. My son started wrestling last year, and I was perplexed by how hard wrestling practice can be. The coaches try to get every ounce of energy and effort out of the wrestlers. The reason is that at the end of an evenly drawn match, the one that can give it their absolute all will win. You know God created us with a mind and the capacity to push through even when we think we have zero left in the tank. When you look back on your playing days, you will never remember the easy days. The days that you pushed through when you wanted to die. Those are the days that you will remember. It was those days that made you who you are or who you are becoming. Those practice sessions made you a champion, but not only that, they helped you develop a character of perseverance. Life can also present us with challenges that seem impossible. In ministry, I have witnessed people that have pushed through and conquered some of life's most difficult situations. I have seen some overcome the death of a child; I have seen others overcome physical limitations. I have seen people that have overcome the abuse and the neglect that was pressed upon them as a child. The reality is that we can push through many things even when we feel that we have nothing left. We can do this because we have a secret weapon, and that weapon is the Holy Spirit. The Holy Spirit will help us to push through when we want to give up. The truth is that God designed us to give more than we have. So, go ahead and prepare to give your all, and I will see you at the plate.

Dear Jesus is Lord,

Thank you for giving me the ability to give more than I think I can give. Help me to push through even when I feel like giving up. Help me to understand that Jesus held nothing back but pushed through the pain to give every ounce of his life for me and my sin. Jesus, you are my all and all. Amen.

Day 210

Are You Going to Get Up?

Judges 16:28-29 (NLT) ***Then Samson prayed to the Lord, "Sovereign Lord, remember me again. O God, please strengthen me just one more time. With one blow, let me pay back the Philistines for the loss of my two eyes." Then Samson put his hands on the two center pillars that held up the temple. Pushing against them with both hands,***

"It's Not Whether You Get Knocked Down, It's Whether You Get Up." – Vince Lombardi

So last week, I watched as my undersized son got mowed down by a lineman that outweighed him by at least 70 pounds. I knew it was a hard hit and one that would take him out of the play, but then I watched as he sprang to his feet and continued to try to get into the play. After the game, we were talking, and he asked if I saw that he had gotten trucked. My response was, I did, but I was so proud that you got up and did not give up. As a young man, I remember sitting in a packed theater, cheering for Rocky Balboa to get up off the mat just one more time to fight Apollo Creed. Look, life will knock you down, but we must decide if we will get back up or if we are going just to lie down. I have met so many people that have thrown in the towel way too early in life. They have given up on their dreams. They have chosen to stick with addiction rather than get help. They have chosen to walk away rather than fight for the relationship. I have seen players give up because of loss and have seen people in business quit because they made one bad deal. I have seen so many people get so close to earning that degree only to give up because they struggled in one area. The truth is that everyone has been knocked down, but those that you see on the platform or in the winner's column are the ones that choose to get back up. There is a character in the Bible that makes lots of poor choices but, in the end, decides to get up one more time. His name was Samson, and a lot of the time, he got knocked down because he had serious issues with pride and women. But Samson ends his life by getting up and giving all he had to the Lord. One thing that we can always remember is that God will help us get up off of the mat. Remember, you will get knocked down at some point, but you must decide to get up before you ever get knocked down. So, what are you waiting for? Get up, get off the mat, and I will see you at the plate.

Dear Blessed Rock,

Lord, I do not know how many times I have been knocked down, but I have gotten up every time with your help. There have been times when it would have been easier to quit, but then I think of Jesus. There have been times when it would have been easier to walk away, but then I think of Jesus. There have been days when it would have been easier to stay in bed, but then I think of Jesus. Jesus is my reminder that he got knocked down on Calvary but got up in paradise. See, death cannot even knock me down because I will be resurrected one day, and I will get to look Jesus in the face and say, "Thank you."

Day 211

Refusing to Let Failure Overtake You

Luke 18: 3-5 **A *widow of that city came to him repeatedly, saying, 'Give me justice in this dispute with my enemy.' The judge ignored her for a while, but finally, he said to himself, 'I don't fear God or care about people, but this woman is driving me crazy. I'm going to see that she gets justice because she is wearing me out with her constant requests!'"***

"Failure Will Never Overtake Me If My Determination to Succeed is Strong Enough." Og Mandino

Failure is not an option. How many times have you heard that statement? The truth is that you are going to eventually fail at some point in your life. This week, I listened to an interview on the Marty and McGee show with the University of Alabama's quarterback Tua Tagovailoa. The questions being asked surrounded his playing badly and losing the National Championship to Clemson. I love what he said; he basically said that losing (which was failure) taught him how bad losing feels. He explains that they had not lost up until that game, so he explains that winning had just become so natural that it was taken for granted. What happens sometimes is the exact opposite of that scenario: you lose so much that you begin to believe that you cannot win.

You allow failure to overtake you to the point that you become numb. So, this is where you have to search for the inner strength of the Holy Spirit. Through the power of the Holy Spirit, you find your determination when you want to quit. It is through the Holy Spirit that you find the strength to reach deeper inside to push harder. There is a story in the Bible about a lady that refused to take no for an answer. She continually went to the judge even though it could have cost her life. Finally, her determination paid off, and she got what she had continually asked for. Here is some good advice: Let a loss help you remember what losing feels like, but do not let losing become a habit. The Holy Spirit will give you the power and strength to never quit and to never surrender. So, listen, you are not a loser; now it's time to prove it, and I will see you at the plate.

Dear Great Overcomer,

I refuse to lose. I refuse to give up. I refuse to give in. I refuse to let the devil win. I refuse to let negative voices in my head. I refuse to give in to the ways of the world. I refuse to not walk in the ways of Jesus. God, I am the winner even when I lose because your Son gave us the ultimate victory. Victory in Jesus, my Lord, My Savior, my coach.

Day 212

Preparation Trumps Pressure

1 Corinthians 13:11 ***When I was a child, I spoke as a child, I understood as a child, I thought as a child: but when I became a man, I put away childish things.***

Preparation alleviates the pressure of a big moment. Patrick Nix

This week, I listened as coach Gus Malzahn (Auburn Head Coach) announced that Bo Nix, a true freshman, would be the starting quarterback for the Auburn Tigers. Auburn has not had a true freshman starting quarterback since 1946. Almost immediately after the announcement, sports talk radio blew up, talking about how this moment was too big for a freshman. Many callers alluded to the fact that he would fail because of his youth and inexperience. Many callers and analyses talked about his youth and the mistakes he would make because of playing in the SEC. One said, “the bottom line is that the stage is just too big for someone this young.” Later that night, Bo got to face the media and defend all the statements that were made about him being named the starter. He spoke from the podium with great poise and maturity. He talked like a young man who was wise beyond his years. The one thing that he said that truly resonated with me was when he said, "my dad always tells me that preparation alleviates the pressure of the big moment." Let me be honest, as a preacher, that statement preached right to me. In athletics and life, preparation is certainly the most proactive way of handling crisis and pressure. In life, we need to learn to be proactive and not reactive to precarious situations. This Sunday, I gave Bibles to 10 young people in our church. (We give Bibles to third graders every year.) As I handed them their Youth Adventure Bibles, I realized that I was handing them God's Word and everything that they would need to face the life they were now holding in their hand. But the truth is, I also asked myself how many of them would open and study God's Holy Word? Listen, God gave you what you needed before you knew you needed it. The Bible contains all that we need in order to live a Godly life. It also gives us insight into how to handle the big stage or life's pressure situations. Oh, and by the way, Bo Nix also referenced his faith many times during the grueling press conference. Now, if you want to know a secret, that will be the secret weapon to his handling the pressure. Now go ahead, all you naysayers and doubters, say what you will, but Bo's preparation has already spoken to your pressure. So, are you prepared, and if you are, I will see you at the plate?

Dear Great Provider,

God, let me read your word to be prepared with wisdom and be armed with the power that comes from your word. God, let me be prayed up because I know that the pressure will heat up at some point. God give me wisdom that leads to maturity. When I was an infant, I spoke as an infant, but now I am maturing in Christ, and I speak as one prepared.

Day 213

"Man Up" (Woman Up)

I Corinthians 16:13-14 ***Be on your guard; stand firm in the faith; be courageous; be strong. Do everything in love.***

I have heard this statement so much in my life that it is written on my heart. The truth is that just yesterday, I heard one of my church members talking about a situation with one of her kids, and she said, "I just wish he would man up." To man, up really means to take responsibility. It means doing the right thing when the right thing is the hard thing. To man up means to push through even when you feel like giving in. To man up means that you become a team player and that you stand in the gap for what is right. There is even a Christian book entitled "Man Up." The book talks about a man once again being the spiritual mentor of the household. I am often saddened by the lack of spiritual leadership that is evident in men these days.

To man up also means to prepare for the battle that you are in for. You may not realize this, but every day, Satan wages battle against you. To man up means that every day you must prepare to face that battle. Think about it; you do not go into a game unprepared. You study the other team, film, tendencies, and weaknesses that you can exploit. Well, we must do the same in life. We must be ready to face the evil opposition that Satan is going to throw our way. We must man up and prepare for battle. Now here is the thing you may be female and reading this devotion. Well, the same is true for you as it is for the men. When you are on a team and in the limelight, Satan wants to take you down. Do not let it happen. So, man or woman up, and I will see you at the plate.

Dear Creator of Visible & Invisible Things,

God help me to be the man my dog thinks that I am. God help me to protect my team, my family, and my friends. Help me to man up even when it is easier to play the victim and coward. Help me to man up so that I can protect those that are under the evil attacks of Satan. Thank you that your Son manned up and went to the cross to die for my sin so that I can now man up – amen up.

Day 214

Remembering Who We Are and Whose We Are

John 1:12 (NLT) ***But to all who believed him and accepted him, he gave the right to become children of God.***

Have you ever heard a coach say you do not play for the name on the back of the jersey but the name on the jersey's front? This statement is pertinent because we often forget that we battle with our teammates and are not fighting alone. We are truly not an island. We often listen to our parents, friends, and media tell us how great we are. The truth is that if we listen to those voices constantly, we will begin to think we are the team instead of that we play for the team. We must remember that we represent our team and our program. This representation is not just on the field but off the field. Many times we ask athletes this question, how are you carrying yourself on and off the field? It could be said that we leave a legacy, but we want to leave a legacy for the program we represent. Sometimes in my prayers, I will say these words, "Lord, help me to remember who I am but, more importantly, whose I am." Do you realize that the most important title you will ever have is the title, child of God? You are who you are because of who you are. God has given you gifts and talents that you can use not to become famous but to make him famous. During Jesus' 33 years here on earth, he never forgot who he was. He always gave God the glory. His sole purpose here was to bridge the gap that sin had created. He knew that he was the Father's only Son and his purpose was to point to his Father. He never forgot whose he was and to who he belonged. This same principle of playing for the team and not for oneself can be applied to everyday life. We are ultimately here to point people to the Father. We remember who we are and that we belong to him because, at some point, we prayed that he would be the center of our life. We do not try to bring God into the center of our selfish life, but we bring life to center around God. This creates for us the concept of not only who we are but whose we are. So, remember not only who you are but whose you are, and I will see you at the plate.

Dear Son of the Living God,

Help me to find my identity in you and not in anything else. Help me to see that I am a child of God. Help me to remember that I am never apart from you. Help my life to point to you and not to only my accomplishments. I am only who I am because of who you are. You have made me who you want me to be, now help me realize who that is and what my purpose is.

✞

Day 215

Who Is Watching Me?

Ephesians 6:6 ***Don't work only while being watched, in order to please men, but as slaves of Christ, do God's will from your heart.***

In college, our coach used to always say to us, "that the person you really are is the person that you are when no one else is watching you." You have also heard the old adage, "If these walls could talk." The question that we must ask ourselves is, "are we really transparent?" When people see us, is this really what they are getting? We often hear those horrifying stories about what people do when no one else is watching them. There have even been people close to us that, when their true life comes to the surface, we cannot believe that they could have possibly been involved in that type of behavior. Have you ever noticed that we tend to work harder when the coach is watching us? Often, coaches give summer workouts so that they will be ahead of schedule when players return to campus. Now some players take these workouts very seriously while others haphazardly put in any effort. The truth is that the top athlete and top performers in life perform the same whether a coach is watching them or not. The true sign of a champion is being who you say you are, no matter who is watching you. A person of integrity operates at the same level, whether they are being held accountable or not. You know, in life, we somehow think that we can hide our performance from God. I had a guy one time tell me he could not go to church because if God knew what he was really like, the roof would cave in on him. I thought to myself, are you kidding me. God not only knows what you have done, but he wants to forgive you for what you have done and help you to move forward with your transparency. We cannot hide our life from God, but we can admit to God that we are not the person he has called us to be. Then we can repent and begin to be the same person of integrity and character all the time. See you at the plate.

Dear Overseer of All,

God help me to be the same all the time. God, we know that nothing is hidden from you and that you know the very words on my lips before they are even spoken. God, you created all, so that is how we know you know all. God help me to confront my hypocrisy of being one way in front of people and another way when I am by myself. God put light into those dark places of my life where I try to hide. God hold me accountable so that when I stand before you at the end of my life, you will be pleased by my transparency.

Day 216

You, Will, Reap What You Sow

Galatians 6:7 ***Do not be deceived: God cannot be mocked. A man reaps what he sows***

This week in my sermon, I mentioned a statement that almost everyone has heard, and many have probably used it. The saying is, "you reap what you sow." Most of the time, we use this statement negatively and direct it towards people we wish would get what they have coming to them. It is our way of directing God's holy wrath upon others. Now the truth is that we use this statement, but we somehow think it does not apply to our lives. We think that we are exempt from the sow and reap process. So, what do we do?

I can lie without getting caught.
I can let my temper fly without damaging my relational life.
I can have a bad attitude at practice and get away with it.
I can have addictions without them taking a toll on my performance.
I can cheat through the test without it catching up to me.

See, you truly do reap what you sow. Here is the truth. There will always be a harvest time. There will be a time when you put into harvesting all that you have sown. The consequences of a person's behaviors are not immediately apparent, the same as when a farmer has to wait for a crop to mature.

Nevertheless, the crops eventually show up. In school, harvest time is the test that we were supposed to be studying for. In sports, it is the game that we have been preparing for. In our spiritual life, we will one day stand in front of God with the life we have lived. It is at that time that we will reap what we sow. So, let me ask you, what are you sowing/planting? Are you sowing goodness, mercy, righteousness, kindness, and self-control? So, it is time to reap what you have sown in practice so that I will see you at the plate.

Dear Covenant of Promise,

Thank you for allowing me to sow and harvest. Thank you for all the opportunities that you have laid before me. Help me to make the most of every day so that I can add to my story. God, I know at some point in my life, you will demand my soul. It will be laid right before, and I pray that what you see is a crop well planted and harvested.

✞

Day 217

How Devoted Are You to What?

Colossians 3:17 ***And whatever you do, in word or deed, do everything in the name of the Lord Jesus, giving thanks to God the Father through him.***

Two questions for you today: first is how devoted are you, and the second is what are you devoted to? This is a question that will never go away. Our first act of devotion should always be to our Lord and our Savior, but our devotion is often to the world. Satan's ploy in the world takes on one form, and that is to divert our devotion away from God. Satan muddles our devotion in two ways: the first is by keeping us busy, and the second is to make things look like they demand our devotion. Satan presents things in the form of idols. Modern-day idolatry looks very different than the idolatry that existed in biblical times. Our idolatry comes in the form of belongings, habits, and addictions. There is an old saying that was eventually turned into a song. The saying is, "you have to stand for something, or you will fall for anything." Really this saying leads us to ask the question of what we are devoted to.

You know the truth is that God created us with a soul shape that will and only can be filled by our devotion to him. Our devotion to God also leads us to be devoted to our team, profession, and family. See, devotion is always intentional and is never accidental. You decide what gets your attention and what you prioritize. So, this week we will look at the **3 D's of Devotions: Drudgery, Discipline, and Delight**. We will look at these in a way that will hopefully draw you into a deeper devotion to your Lord and Savior, Jesus. Do you remember how devoted he was to you? If not, here is a reminder; think about the cross. See you at the plate.

Dear One and Only Way,

Help me to remove the Idols that stand in the way of my devotion to you. Help me to stand for mercy, justice, and serving the least of these. My devotion to you will lead to devotion to my other significant relationships. Help me be devoted to my teams no matter what role I play. God, you deserve all my devotion because of the sacrifice you made because of your devotion to me. Jesus was devoted to one thing, and that was his devotion to me. I was not deserving, but I sure am thankful. Amen.

✞

Day 218

Drudgery Divergence

Luke 16:10 ***"If you are faithful in little things, you will be faithful in large ones. But if you are dishonest in little things, you won't be honest with greater responsibilities.***

"Drudgery" Webster defines drudgery as dull, irksome, and fatiguing work, uninspiring or menial labor. Now the question is, how in the world does devotion come from that? But this is where devotion starts; it starts with the mundane and menial. Being devoted to something means trudging through the tough times. I have done a lot of weddings in my ministry. One of the things that I often think about as the couple takes their vows of devotion is, are they serious about the backside of the vows? It is easy to be devoted to for better, for richer, and in health. But what about the backside of the vows for worse, for poorer, and in sickness.

Sometimes when things like this happen, we drudge through them because we are devoted to them. Everybody looks forward to that first practice in the sports world, but three or four weeks into it, everyone is just trying to get through it. The reality is that most people do not like to practice because it is drudgery. Sometimes it is hard to see the result of our practice till we get a chance to play the game. See, in the Scripture, it says these words, "he who is trusted with little can be trusted with much." When we live in drudgery, we do not feel that we will ever get to the prize. But practice teaches us how to perform so that when we are trusted with the big stage, we will not fail. To me, drudgery and perseverance are very similar in nature. It is those that get through the tough times that are truly devoted. It is so easy to have the inclination that if things are tough, we need to get out. But by giving up, you are diverting your devotion. So, I know that you have drudged through it, but hey, now it is time to show your devotion; I will see you at the plate.

Dear Sovereignty,

Life is sometimes tough. The climb is sometimes overwhelming. God, so often, we get bogged down in the minute and mundane. Help me to see the light at the end of the tunnel. Help me to realize that drudgery leads to victory. Help me to realize that even in the midst of drudgery, you are with me. God, help me to move from being trusted with little to be trusted with much. Amen.

Day 219

Demanded Discipline

Hebrews 12:11 ***"For the moment, all discipline seems painful rather than pleasant, but later it yields the peaceful fruit of righteousness to those who have been trained by it."***

Discipline is a word that we throw out a lot, but we rarely master the concept. We like to talk to other people about discipline more than we like to engage in it ourselves. I will go ahead and say this, "discipline is hard and is somewhat arduous." Discipline requires sacrifice, and it means giving up things in order to achieve it. Discipline is really what separates those that do from those that try and fail. Discipline is an art and requires drive, patience, and self-control. If you do not have self-control, you will never be disciplined. See, the truth is that discipline shows your devotion to something. What are you willing to give in order to achieve what you want to achieve? This is the question that surrounds discipline.

One way to explain discipline is that it is so repetitive that it eventually becomes part of your DNA. Last week, I watched one of the sloppiest football games I have ever watched. It was the first game of the 2019 college football season against the Florida Gators and the Miami Hurricanes. It was the first game for both teams, and they were starting a week earlier than everyone else, so you expected that there would be tons of mistakes and miscues. But the truth is that there were a combined 23 penalties, which is a sign of an undisciplined team, in this case, two undisciplined teams. The reason that Jesus chose disciples is that he wanted them to see what a disciplined life looked like. Now I have always said sports were so important because sports teach you how to be disciplined. They teach what it means when you mess up, and the whole team is penalized. Sports teach you that to play together and win together, you must be devoted to one another. The coaches also need to exhibit discipline in the way they coach and how they live their lives. Sometimes coaches expect their athletes to live a disciplined life, but the fruits of the coach's life do not line up with discipline. See, Jesus not only spoke of discipline, but he patterned it in everyday life. See, Jesus did not just teach discipline; he lived out of discipline. Now is the time to quit talking about being disciplined, and it is time to devote your life to Discipleship, and I will see you at the plate.

Dear Abundant Grace,

God, where I spend my time and my energy, tell me what I am devoted to. So often, my devotion is to things that will never build upon my walk with you or make me a better person. Many times, I talk to others about discipline without really wanting to do it myself. God, let me be devoted to you and to everything that you present to me. God, thank you that Jesus was so devoted to me and to my salvation that he died so that I might live. Help me to be devoted, disciplined, and drastically changed because of Jesus.

Day 220

Delight in the Devotion

Job 22:26 ***Surely then, you will find delight in the Almighty and will lift up your face to God.***

How do we delight in devotion and discipline when they are so tough to follow through with? The answer lies within the devotion that becomes part of your moral fabric and DNA. The truth is that you will delight in the fact that you get to do something many others will not take the time to do. Delight comes from the achievement of hard work and discipline. Delight comes from winning and knowing you won because of the process that you followed. When you look at this Scripture, you immediately go, so if I delight in the Lord, he will give me everything I want. David was writing this Scripture because he felt that his enemies were prospering greater than those that followed the Lord's commands. See, David is giving us the command not to give thanks for the carnal and material things of this world.

What he is saying is that we should delight in spiritual things. We often find it hard to delight in the Lord because we envy others and feel that God holds back on us. But God's greatest concern is that we delight in him for the gift of His Son Jesus and not because he can give us things here on earth. The truth is that even the things you were devoted to earning will all look like rubbish compared to the riches and graces of eternal life. Our delight comes from pleasing God through our accomplishments, not the accomplishments alone. Delight comes from knowing that someone cared for us so much that he spared nothing to give up his Son for us. The truth is that even though Jesus died a painful death, he did so with delight because he knew that his life would pay the ransom for our sin. No trophy, championship, or accomplishment will ever outweigh the gift of Jesus. So, let me ask you, does your devotion lead to delight in the Lord? If not, take this opportunity just to say thank you, Lord; I delight in you. Now I will see you at the plate.

Dear Everlasting Priest,

Lord, I delight in you not because of what you can give me but who you are. You are the provider of the spiritual things that will last forever. The carnal things of this world will pass away. So often, I pray for things that are going to corrupt me or cause me to sin. What I must focus on is the delight that comes from you providing the spiritual things in life.

Day 221

Just a Little Compromise Will Not Hurt

James 4:17 ***So whoever knows the right thing to do and fails to do it, for him it is sin.***

Today the headlines are filled with student-athletes that will have to sit out this year, have been kicked off the team, or have been arrested. Almost every day, you can go to the search engine sports tab and find athletes who have compromised. We never expect these little compromises to catch up with us. Most of the time, we get into that angel on the shoulder argument. On one shoulder is an angel that says, "do not throw away all that you have worked for. Do not start this, and you will never have to quit. Do not do this because what seems to be harmless will lead you down the road to destruction." On the other shoulder is a little demon. He is so cute and has such a way with words. He says, "go ahead and try it; a little will never hurt. You have worked so hard you deserve to be able to take a break. Do not worry about what has happened to others; it will never happen to you. This will not lead you down the road of destruction; it will lead you down the road that rocks." Now you have to make a decision, and the truth is that you are conflicted. But you truly know the answer because you have seen it and experienced it before. You know that just a little compromise can lead to huge consequences. This is where God gave you the gift of the Holy Spirit to help you with fighting the temptation of compromise. Most of the time, our lapse in judgment and propensity to compromise comes from the absence of these things: faith in Christ, commitment, and accountability. Just like not compromising on the field, you have to focus so that you do not compromise off of the field. The truth is that every decision that you make affects the next decision that you make. The other way to make sure that you do not compromise even a little is by surrounding yourself with like-minded people who hold you accountable so that you do not compromise. Remember that your team needs you, so do not even compromise a little bit. Step up, and I will see you at the plate.

Dear Morningstar,

Never Compromise
Friend, let us never compromise God's Word,
But stand firm on the message we have heard;
Though Christians are in the minority,
We hold the only Truth that sets souls free.
Let us lift the Lord's Holy standards high,
That the lost would hear His Word and comply,
Bowing their knee to the Father above…
Coming to know Jesus and His great love.
Never Compromise!
We're in spiritual warfare, my friend,
Let us be faithful to the very end;
March on in the battle, with hope in your heart,
Wearing the Lord's whole armor – not just part.
Oh, may we be good soldiers of the cross,
And never fear suffering, trial, or loss,
Lifting God's banner for this world to see…

The Truth that sets the captive free.
Never Compromise!
When the forces of evil attack us,
The hand of God is there to protect us;
The battle is won by His Spirit's sword…
As we rest ourselves in our loving Lord.
May God help us to never entertain
Sinners on their way to Satan's domain,
But always stand firm on God's holy ground…
That lost souls would hear His call and be found.
Never Compromise![20]
(A poem by Connie Campbell Bratcher - June, 2005)

Day 222

Excuses, Excuses, Excuses

John 15:22 ***They would not be guilty if I had not come and spoken to them. But now, they have no excuse for their sin.***

"I. Hate. Excuses. Excuses are a disease." Cam Newton

This week we are going to look at excuses that we make in sports and life. I have always told those I coach that you never have to make excuses when you do the right thing and win. Excuses are nothing more than a scapegoat to cover what you did not do. Now granted, sometimes the other team is just better and more talented, but when we are equally matched, if we do the right thing and work our game plan, we should come out of the top. So many times, I have heard people make excuses for loss and poor play. Some people blame it on the referees, but if the game were not close, then the referees would not be able to decide it. I have heard some people blame it on field conditions. Both teams play in the same field under the same conditions. I have heard other people say that the other team cheated. Look, most of the time, losses occur because of players failing to execute and perform. I have also heard coaches make excuses, and this sets your whole team up for failure. Sometimes the best thing that we can do is to admit that it was our fault. I remember Auburn playing in the final four basketball tournaments last year. Auburn lost a very tight game by a questionable call. After the game, Auburn's coach Bruce Pearl was interviewed, and many thought that he would make an excuse for why they lost, but he did not. He complimented the other team and then said, "it was a tough break, but if they had made a few more shots down the stretch, then a call would not have dictated the outcome." He made no excuses and pointed no blame even though everyone around him, including the color commentators, was making excuses. You know, when you own up to something and do not make excuses, you gain the respect of those around you. When you make excuses, people turn you off and no longer listen to you. Excuse makers lose their witness for Jesus Christ. Let me ask you, are you an excuse maker, or do you own up and move on. See you at the plate.

Dear Yahweh,

Help me to own up to my mistakes. Excuses are a disease and a disease that will run rampant in my life. God, something is freeing about owning up to our mistakes and going in a different direction. God, help me not play the blame game but take responsibility for my sin and shortcomings. Excuses are just a way of continuing in my sin and excusing my behavior. God, if I continue to use excuses, I will lose my witness. No excuses, no excuses, no excuses.

Day 223

I Was ... "I Can't Say It"

Proverbs 24:16 ***"Though a righteous man falls seven times, he will get up, but the wicked will stumble into ruin."***

I was wrong are some of the hardest words to say. No one likes to admit that they messed up. So often, what we do is play the blame game. Now the blame game is nothing new; as a matter of fact, it dates back to Genesis 3. Adam and Eve both played the blame game when God confronted them about their sin. Adam was confronted first and blamed Eve. Eve was then confronted and blamed it on the serpent. I often wonder how God would have responded if they had just said, "I was wrong. It was me."

I would say 90% of our excuses are lies that come from us not wanting to confess our sins. How many times have we heard someone in the sports world or news play the blame game? What is it that makes owning up for our behavior so hard? It is not as if we can hide our sin from the one that created us. The reason that we cannot own up is that we have a selfish nature. We have been trained to think that we are always right and that someone else is to blame. When we blame someone else, we deflect the issues and, most of the time, never deal with them. Then something comes back up, and once again, we blame someone else. A popular statement that many people use is that the devil made me do it. I really do not use this statement because I do not want to give the devil any credit. Yes, the devil may have put the temptation in front of me, but I decided to follow through. When we admit that we are wrong, we have the opportunity to now move in a different direction. When we say I am wrong, it brings us to a place where we can grow and experience the readily available grace. It does not mean that there may not be consequences, but we are maturing in our faith by taking responsibility for our actions. So, go ahead and use those hard words, I was wrong, and I will see you at the plate.

Dear Lord God of Mount Sinai,

Help me to see that I must take responsibility for my actions. The Scripture says that we must repent of our sins and turn in a different direction. Lord, I cannot go in a different direction if I do not first take responsibility for my sin. Help me remove the pride in my life that keeps me from saying I am wrong. God, thank you that when I am wrong that you have already covered that with the death and resurrection of your Son. Amen.

Day 224

Excuses Lead to Failure

Luke 14:18 ***But without exception, they all began to make excuses.***

"Excuses are the nails used to build a house of failure."[21] Wow, did this quote speak volumes to me? Most of the time, the reason that we fail is because of our lack of preparation. In my family, we have a saying that goes like this, "your lack of preparation does not constitute an emergency on my part." The truth is that excuses not only affect you, but they affect the whole team/family. You say, "I am tired, so it is easier to stay in bed than it is to get up and train." It is easy to say, "it is too hot or too cold outside, and to say I will just wait until tomorrow." It is easy to say, "I have done enough today even when you know you have not pushed at all." Yes, all these excuses are a recipe for failure. The truth is that getting beat does not necessarily constitute failure; not showing up or giving up leads to failure. Excuses are usually made when we know that we did not prepare. Excuses we think will help us to feel better about not being prepared, but excuses rob us of maturing and owning up to our deficiencies. You will never get better when you use excuses to cover your deficiencies.

In the Scripture, he tells the story of three different people who made excuses for not following him. The first one says that he must go first to bury his father. Now the truth is that his father was not dead. It was just if he was not there; he might not get his inheritance. The next one says that he just got married and that he did not have time to follow until he got his family affairs in order. Jesus was not necessarily asking this guy to be the 13th Disciple; he was just asking him to follow his teachings and share the gospel. The last guy says that he had just made enough money to be blessed with some oxen, and now he needed to try them out. All three had an excuse for not following Jesus. How often do we make excuses for not following Jesus? I mean, we literally have a world of excuses. We have jobs, hobbies, bank accounts, and large houses to maintain. We do not want Jesus to get in the way of our carnal life. So, what we do is make excuses for not following Jesus? Now here is a secret if you do not have any excuses for not following Jesus, then you usually will not have any excuses for the rest of your life. Remember this: you do not get to use excuses for why you did not follow the Holy Spirit's lead when you get to heaven. So, no more excuses, and I will see you at the plate.

Dear Elohim,

Most of my failures have been built with the bricks of excuses. I have built a wall of failure because of my laziness, stubbornness, and selfishness. Help me to see the error of my ways and not use excuses to cover my lack of preparation and sometimes my lack of caring. Lord, you take my failures and make them victories because of the cross. I not only believe in you, but I want to follow you. Amen.

✞

Day 225

Mutual Respect

Hebrews 5:12-13 ***In fact, though by this time you ought to be teachers, you need someone to teach you the elementary truths of God's word all over again. You need milk, not solid food! Anyone who lives on milk, being still an infant, is not acquainted with the teaching about righteousness.***

I heard someone repeat the other day a saying that I had not heard in quite some time. Someone said, "respect is earned, not given." The first thing that I thought about was do people even know what respect looks like in today's world? Do we respect our authority figures? Do we respect our coaches and our teachers? Do we respect life in general? Last week, I was over in a shopping center when the school next to the shopping center let out. I watched as a police officer politely told a young man that was loitering in the parking lot that he needed to move toward home. The boy ignored the police officer. Finally, the police officer got a little gruffer with the boy, and the boy began to walk, but the whole time was shouting profanities and calling the officer all kinds of names. He then crossed the street, where he stood for a solid minute, just cussing in the direction of the officer. Now, this boy had a pretty athletic build, and I began to wonder why he was not practicing with the football team instead of loitering in a parking lot? It then dawned on me that it may be because if he does not respect a police officer, he certainly will not respect a coach. But more than that, a person that lacks respect will never respect what the game can truly do for them. See, in life, we must respect other people by how we treat them and how we respond to their direction and correction. See, sports were invented to aid in the development of young men and young women. It was developed so that kids could not only stay physically fit but so that they could learn mutual respect and teamwork. Now, this term is not just exclusive for players, but the same is true of coaches. You cannot disrespect your players and, in turn, expect them to respect you. I think that sometimes this becomes a double standard in sports. The truth is that everyone must be treated with mutual respect until that respect is severed. The reason that Jesus traveled with his 12 disciples was so that he could teach them respect. Not just respect for those that were like them but respect for all human beings. A local youth pastor surveyed his youth to identify the reason they respect others. The number one answer and the only answer was, "Because of the way they treat me; right and with love." He then asked, "Why do you not respect some people?" The answer will not shock you, but it was, "They do not treat me right or with love." See, respect comes in two forms and is not just one-sided. We must learn what mutual respect means as we relate to others. To earn respect means that we do what Micah 6:8 says... *To act justly, love mercy, and walk humbly with your God.* So now that we have that mutual respect, I will see you at the plate.

Dear Authority over all Authority,

God, may I respect those that I may not even agree with? May I show mutual respect for those that are under my guidance and my care? God, help me earn others' respect even when their beliefs and values do not match mine. God, by gaining the respect of others, I will have the opportunity to share the gospel with them. God, let them see the gospel in my life and not only in my words. Thank you for the respect that your Son had and for his life gift so that I could live the life I live. Amen.

Day 226

Living a Lie

2 Corinthians 7:1 ***"Dearly beloved, let us cleanse ourselves from all filthiness of the flesh and spirit, perfecting holiness in fear of God."***

Have you ever been shocked when you read the headline of one of your favorite athletes and found out they had some secret life? There was a very successful high school football coach in my area. He had taken a program and turned it into a powerhouse in high school football. He had won several state titles and had them nationally ranked. But then the bombshell was dropped that he had been involved with another lady besides his wife. The reality was that he had another family in another state. To say everyone was shocked is an understatement. So many times, we hear stories like this, and we are shocked, but the truth is that sometimes people are just living a lie.

In the Scripture, we have a commandment against this, and it is called bearing false witness. The verb "to bear" implies the act of carrying or transmitting something, while the adjective false describes the untrue content. The speaking of an untruth renders what is said as unreal, thereby rendering it artificial and invalid.[22] When you speak as if you live one way, but really live another way, you are bearing false witness in relation to your own life. You can certainly bear false witness on someone else by blaming them when you know it is not true, but so many forget that they can bear false witness related to their witness for Jesus Christ. The question is, "are you who you are?" Do you have a secret life? The other thing to ask is, do you expect from others what you are not willing to do yourself. In the Scripture, it would often refer to the Kings as putting heavy weight on the people. The problem was that the Kings were not carrying their weight. In the New Testament, Jesus made it clear to His disciples that false testimony was a key indicator of an unclean heart (Matthew 15:16-20). It will do you no good to win everything but to bear false witness in your soul. So be true to yourself and do not live a lie, and I will see you at the plate.

Dear Pure and Holy Lord,

Let my life be transparent and open. Let me be the same at all times. Help me not to expect more from my sphere of influence than I am willing to give myself. Let my life be a witness to you and for it not to bear false witness against you. Let me never bear false witness against others as to harm them or to deflect blame. Let me own up to my mistakes and move to a place of holiness.

Day 227

Speed Kills

Ecclesiastes 4:6 ***Better is a handful of quietness than two hands full of toil and a striving after wind.***

In sports, we always talk about speed. We have even named formation and plays that focus on the word speed; we have speed option, the speed sweep, we have the slap hitters in softball that can use their speed to reach first from the plate's left side. The truth is that speed is essential if you are going to have a good team. It is so important that some people have coined the phrase "speed kills." Yes, the truth is that we want to be fast. The high school team that my son plays on has adopted a slogan. "HuskyFast." When you try out for a team, they want to see how fast you are, so the coach times you in the forty-yard dash. Yes, it is very apparent that for a team to be successful, they must have some speed. A well-balanced team will have speed in all aspects of the game.

Maybe we are so accustomed to speed that we do not know how to slow down in life. You see, we must have a separation of speed on the field and speed in our personal life. If we do not slow down in life, we will miss some very important things. If we do not slow down in life, we will never reach our full potential spiritually. Dallas Willard is quoted as saying, "that if you are going to stay spiritually healthy, then you are going to have to ruthlessly eliminate hurry from your life." If you ask him what else is, he will answer nothing and reiterate that eliminating hurry is the key to spiritual health. You see, when we become so accustomed to speed, we have a hard time slowing down enough to hear the direction of the Holy Spirit. I hear people often say, "that they do not hear the voice of God," and then I ask them if they ever slow down enough to hear what he is saying? You see, hurry in life is the enemy of peace. Hurrying in life is the enemy of solitude. Hurry is the enemy of divine direction. Hurry in life says it is about me and what I can do. The reality is that because we are so in tune to speed that we think that we need to hurry. Now be as fast as you can but on the field but slow down in life and listen to what God is saying to you. You know that prayer you have been praying; have you slowed down enough to receive the answer? Slow down, and I will see you at the plate.

Dear Creator of Kairos,

Help me to slow down. Help me to remove hurry from my life. Help me realize that I can only hear you when I take time out of my noisy world to connect with you. God, you created Kairos time, which is a time to be with you, but we have made everything about our time, and that is the "Kronos" time. God help me to realize that the more hurry in my life leads to more distance from you. Jesus patterned for us what it looked like to slow down and to spend time with you. Now let me follow that same pattern. Amen.

Day 228

Can You Predict the Future?

Psalm 32:8 ***I will instruct you and teach you in the way you should go; I will counsel you with my eye upon you.***

So often, we hear about people predicting the outcome and future success of a team. People make their living off of predicting the outcome of a game or series of games. They have often done their due diligence to know as much as they can about the team, and many times, they are right. Most of the time, they look to the past to predict the future. They looked at the areas where the team performed good and identified where there were deficiencies. Now a team can change the outcome and the perception by changing the future. But the only way a team can predict the future is to create it. The good thing is that every day you have the opportunity to create history and your future by what you are doing in the present. You are writing history, or at least your history right now. Some questions to consider as you write your future and leave your legacy follows:

What are you doing right now to get better than you were yesterday?

Are you letting your past define your future?

Are you listening to others and letting them define who you are?

Are you working hard to change what you have done before?

See, you must answer these questions and stop regretting the past if you are going to learn from it. We often get into this frame of mind that this is who we are, who we are always going to be. We often have let people define us rather than us charting our own course. The next thing is that we must stop dwelling on our failures. By dwelling on your failures, you will never be who God has called you to be. Your failures do not define you; what you do when you fail defines you. Listen, the only way that you can look toward the future is by picking your head up and looking ahead. You will never see the future with your head hung and a defeated spirit. I have mentioned this story before, but it is a great example of someone that could not see the future. A rich young man came to Jesus and asked what was demanded of him. Jesus told him to sell all he had and come follow him. The young man hung his head, and rather than walking into the future with Jesus, he returned to his past. Look, the future is ahead, and you are the one that is creating it so that I will see you at the plate.

Dear Holder of the Future,

You have given me today so let me make the most of it. You have blessed me with this moment, but I am not promised another. Help me carve my future and not let others tell me who I am or who I should be. Even though my ways are not your ways, direct me in your ways. Help me to realize that my future is dictated by how I handle today. Thank you that no matter what happens here on earth, your Son dictated what my eternity looks like. Amen

✟

Day 229

Next Man Up

Deuteronomy 31:7-8 ***Then Moses called Joshua and said to him in front of the people, "Be strong and brave, because you will lead these people into the land the Lord promised to give their ancestors, and help them take it as their own. The Lord himself will go before you.***

No one likes to see a teammate get hurt or go down with an injury. Last week, The University of South Carolina Gamecock's highly rated quarterback went down with a season-ending injury. They will now have to start a true freshman quarterback for the rest of the year. I must also mention that South Carolina has the third hardest schedule in the FBS. This will mean that this young quarterback being the next man up, will be under trial by fire. He will be asked to do things that he is not yet equipped to do. But he is the next man up. Now no one wants to hear the news of the star player being injured for the season, but the truth is that injury is just part of a team's attrition. Sometimes one key player's injury can change the whole outcome of the season. We always pray that no one ever gets injured, but sometimes players go down. Many times, when a player in front of us goes down, it now becomes what is coined as "the next man/woman up," and we are inserted in the lineup. Some players have waited a long time for the opportunity to be on this stage. Now the question is, what are you going to do with this opportunity? You are young, inexperienced, and scared, but you are not alone. In the Scripture, Joshua takes over for Moses after his death. Now Joshua was going to lead the people into the promised land. He was going to take them beyond the point that Moses had led them. Now God told him that it would be a huge endeavor but that he would not be alone. Like in sports, Joshua was the next man up, but he would not be alone because God would be with him. You see, one of the prayers of the next man/woman up is that God will go before us. We pray that God will lead us and that God will calm the nerves and anxieties of maybe not being totally prepared. So, guess what, you are the next man up, so I will see you at the plate.

Dear Baptizer,

Many times in life, I have been the next man up. I was not prepared for the situation, but I knew I did not go into it alone. You were with me, and you were for me. God, we pray for our whole team's protection, but we realize that sometimes when an injury occurs, we must step up. Give us the ability to be strong and brave. Thank you that your Son was the next man up and took the place of my sin. I not only want to believe in him, but I want to follow him. Make me like Jesus. Amen.

Day 230

Grand Entrance

Matthew 21: 9-11 ***And the crowds that went before him and that followed him were shouting, "Hosanna to the Son of David! Blessed is he who comes in the name of the Lord! Hosanna in the highest!" And when he entered Jerusalem, the whole city was stirred up, saying, "Who is this?" And the crowds said, "This is the prophet, Jesus, from Nazareth of Galilee."***

I am amazed these days at the great lengths teams go through as the players enter the field or the court. There is smoke, video introductions, blaring music, cannons going off, fireworks, horses, and buffaloes leading the team in, bands marching in time, and teams running through inflatable mascot heads. The truth is that there is something really special about running through that tunnel or coming out of that locker room to compete in a game you love. A lot of that pride comes from playing for a team that you love and in front of the fans that love you. I remember when we started "upward basketball" at one of the churches I served, the favorite thing for the kids was to run through a fog machine's haze as the player's name and nickname were called out. The truth is that these kids made a grand entrance, and they loved hearing their name called. The grand entrance is also used to get the fans pumped up and ready to cheer us onto victory unless you are playing upward because they do not keep score. I remember another grand entry. It had no smoke or fireworks, but it did have fanfare and music. The people had gathered to usher in their Messiah. The grand entrance was aided by people waving palm branches and singing the song of hosanna. But soon, just as the fans welcomed the team with such great fanfare, the voices changed. They went from hosanna to crucify him. What a change in just three days. The truth is that Jesus' grand entrance did not rival the other entrances that took place during Passover. Just across town, there would be another grand entrance. Entering Jerusalem at the same time, from the west, was the Roman governor Pontius Pilate. Like the Roman governors of Judea before him, Pilate lived in Caesarea by the sea. He entered as one with power and one of arrogance. Jesus entered on a colt and not on a stallion. Jesus entered to palm branches, but Pilate entered to the noise of hoofbeats and saluting swords. Both entered with a different fanfare, but one would come out victorious. Jesus would come out as finishing the work that he had started. Jesus' grand entrance was not so that he could win but so that he could win for us. He came into town so that we could find our victory in Christ. Listen as you hear your name called and as you run through that tunnel filled with smoke, remember that someone else made a grand entrance for you long ago. His name was Emmanuel. Hosanna is in the highest, and I will see you at the plate.

Dear Emmanuel,

We enter the game with great fanfare and pride. You entered the city humbly and with one thing in mind, and that was dying for our sin. I cannot thank you enough for your grand entrance. All I can say is Hosanna Hosanna is the highest. Amen.

Day 231

The Big Letdown

Ephesians 5:16 ***New Living Translation (NLT) 16 Make the most of every opportunity in these evil days.***

Sometimes the hardest games to get up for are the games immediately following a big game played just hours or days before. Sometimes, we have what I call "win fatigue." This comes from exerting a great amount of energy to win a big game. Now the problem with win fatigue is that it can lead to a big letdown, and there is a chance that you could struggle with a lesser opponent or even get beat by a team you were supposed to beat. This big letdown can also come from overlooking your opponent or not taking your upcoming event's preparation seriously. The truth is that we must view every day and every opponent as it may be the last contest that we ever get to participate in. We should give thanks for the opportunity and this immediate opportunity because we do not know if this will be our last. So often, another way that the big letdown occurs is when we look ahead to the next big game. This happens a lot when we read clippings or look at the opponent's record. We know that on paper, there is no way this team can beat us, but any team can beat anybody on any given day. This means that we must prepare for every contest and competition with due diligence and a sense of urgency. The truth is that this concept should be practiced every day in life.

We are notorious for looking down the road for tomorrow. We sometimes waste precious opportunities looking for a different opportunity. The same can be true of life as we look toward the second coming of Jesus. I often ask myself the question of what will I be doing when Christ returns? It is not that I am not sure of my salvation; it is just that Jesus has given us the Great Commandment and the Great Commission to live out. The good thing about this is that every day we are around people who need to experience the love of Jesus. The question then is, what are we going to do with those opportunities? Are we going to look down the road, are we going to be satisfied with the work we did yesterday, or must we get busy with this opportunity? Because, after all, we do not know if this is the last opportunity we may have. So it is today, and I will see you at the plate.

Dear God of Eternity,

God help me not to look down the road but to take every day as it is. God, help me to realize that when we take things for granted, bad things happen. The big letdown is sometimes when we realize that we have taken you for granted. God, never let me overlook my opponent in life or on the field.

Day 232

In the Desert, In the Storm, In the Slump

Isaiah 43:2 (ESV) ***When you pass through the waters, I will be with you; and through the rivers, they shall not overwhelm you; when you walk through fire you shall not be burned, and the flame shall not consume you.***

You know it is easy to praise the Lord when things are going our way. It is easy to praise and give the Lord thanks when we are winning. It is easy to praise the Lord when our shots are going down and our batting average is soaring. But what do we do when we are losing, or we are in a slump? Is it easy to praise the Lord when the storms of our life pop up? We all know that many times our praise comes out of our selfish motives to perform well. But the true test of faith is when things are not going as we have planned. Faith comes out of perseverance and suffering.

In a sermon I preached last week, I had a quote from John Ortberg's book, Soul Keeper; here is the quote: "If you ask people who don't believe in God why they don't believe in God, the number one reason will be suffering. If you ask people who believe in God when they grew spiritually, the number one answer will be suffering."[23] The truth is that we must praise God even during our struggles and suffering. It is during those struggles that we will see God amplified. See, God is the Alpha and the Omega; he sees the beginning and the end of our life. God knows that even in the struggle, there will be glory. He knows this because what looked like a tragic end to Jesus' life turned out to be the most glorious event in history. A true test of our maturity in the faith is when we can praise God amid a 0-10 season or a 2 for our last 20 at-bats. We have to learn to praise God during the storm. No one ever expects to go through life without trials and tribulations, but we are still surprised when they happen. We live in a fallen world, and because of that, there will always be struggles in life and struggles on the field. So, listen, you may find yourself in the desert, but God will be there to give you what you need. Give God the praise even in the midst of the storm, and I will see you at the plate.

Dear Precious Stone,

Help me to praise you when I am in a slump. Help me to praise you when things are not going well. Help me to praise you when the storm is overhead. When I praise you in the storm, it makes it that much easier to praise you for the goodness and mercy that you apply to my life every day.

✞

Day 233

Honor System

Proverbs 21:21 ***"Whoever pursues righteousness and kindness will find life, righteousness, and honor."***

Honor is something that is noble, but few possess this character trait. This week we will look at what it means to be a person of honor and how to play with honor. This will be a five-day mini-series on honor.

Just down the street from the church is a guy who has a tent out in front of his house; in the tent, he has vegetables for sale, and he has a box out there to collect money. He tells the prices for the vegetables on the box, and then he says, "please pay on the honor system." I think that it is great that someone still believes that honor exists. You know honor is a word that rarely gets used anymore, and the reason is that our world is filled with voided promises and little honor. I once had a businessman tell me that he was getting out of business after 50 years of being very successful. I asked him why he was giving it up, and he responded, "because a handshake on agreement does not mean anything anymore." What he was saying was that people used to honor their commitments, and they would follow through. There was no need for contracts and negotiations. When a person told you something, they meant it, and there was honor in their word. Today, we live in a world of distrust instead of trust. People's word really just does not mean much. We also live in a world today where people give up on one team and move to another. It used to be that the honor came from the name you played for on the front of the jersey, not the name you were trying to make on the back of the jersey. In sports today, if someone does not start or gets beat out for the starting position, they just go back on their word and commitment and go somewhere else. I wonder how that is going to play out for the rest of their life. I wonder if they are going to stay committed to their job when sales are slow. I wonder if they are going to stay committed to their marriage when things are tough. I wonder if they are going to stay committed to Christ when it seems as if the world has more to offer. You see, your character and your commitment are all directly related to your honor. Honor is truly doing what you say you would do, no matter how hard or inconvenient it is. You see, honor is a noble quality and is a Christ-like characteristic. Jesus had the utmost honor as he committed to give his life for my sin. His honor replaced my dishonest spirit. So, let me ask you this, are you a person of honor? If so, I will see you at the plate.

Dear Rejected Stone of Builders,

Help me to honor my team. Help me to honor my faith. Help me to honor my commitment. Help me to honor my relationship with Jesus Christ. Help me to be a person of integrity and honor. God, my word is more important to my honor than being comfortable.

Day 234

Honoring One Another

Romans 12:10 ***Be devoted to one another in love. Honor one another above yourselves.***

Did you know that God wants us to honor others above ourselves? Wow, that is a crazy concept. Most of us, since birth, have been taught to take care of ourselves – to hold ourselves in high honor. We have been led to believe that the most important person in our life is "us." We have been pushed to make the best grades so we can get the best job. We have been primed as an athlete to strive for the next level. No one ever had to teach us the word "mine;" it just somehow found its way into our vocabulary when we were a year old or so.

Then God, like he always does, gives us the instruction to think outside of ourselves and to honor others. God states that we find honor when we pursue kindness in love. The Bible says, "Whoever pursues righteousness and kindness will find life, righteousness, and honor." In team athletics, when we are kind to our teammates, we show them honor. Sports gives us the prime opportunity to learn how to show honor to our teammates, our coaches, the officials, and the other team. God knows it is important for us to honor others, and he tells us that honor is good! How do we honor our teammates? The first is by treating each one of them with the same respect that we would require. The second thing is that we honor them if they play in front of us or play behind us. The third way is that we honor them is when we celebrate their achievements when their achievements are greater than ours. When you honor your team and your teammates, you shine the light of Christ among the whole team. A team that honors one another is a team that becomes a family. When we honor one another, there is mutual respect for one another. To honor your teammates will also go a long way in the rest of your interactions and relationships. So, honor the guy that is now at-bat, and I will see you at the plate.

Dear Noble One,

Honor can be hard to achieve in a world that teaches us that it is all about us. Humble me so that I can show honor to the lest, the last, and the lost. Help me to honor those around me in higher regard than I honor myself. I know that sounds crazy, but it is what a servant leader looks like. Jesus honors me more than he honored himself, and he gave his life for me. Amen

Day 235

Caesar vs. the Referee

1 Peter 2:17 ***"Show proper respect to everyone, love the family of believers, fear God, honor the emperor."***

It needs to be stated that referees and officials have the hardest job of all. They are called upon to make the best calls they can make, yet one team's fans will always disagree. They are called on to be non-bias and put up with fans, coaches, and players questioning their every move. I have heard people say that to be an official, you have to love punishment. An official, to be effective, must have thick skin and not take anything personally. The reality is that there are officials out there that are just not good or may not call fair, but that number is so minimal. The truth is that the officials are there to do the best they can do and keep order in the game while assuring fair play. Do they make mistakes, absolutely but so do you when you are playing? Now one of the requirements for sportsmanship is honoring and respect for the officials. In the Scripture, Jesus gives us an example of honoring those that are in places of power. Jesus is presented with a coin that has the face of Caesar on it. Now the truth was that the people that handed Jesus the coin had no respect for Caesar, and they were baiting him in how he would respond to his notion of loving and honoring everyone. Jesus responds by saying, *"give to Caesar what is Caesar's."* (You can read the whole story in Mark 12:13-17.) In this statement, he says that you may not agree with the taxes, but you have so much more than Caesar will ever have. He also ends the statement with the part that many people do not quote "Give to God what is God's." Jesus is saying that you do not have to agree with someone to honor them. You may disagree with a call, but it does not give you the right to dog cuss the referee and to belittle him/her. Coaches must set the bar when it comes to honoring other coaches and officials. We must also remember that everyone in the stands is watching how we interact. I have said it before, but I will continue to preach this. It takes a long time to build up your witness but only a minute to ruin it. You know there is one standing there behind the plate, so honor him, and I will see you at the plate.

Dear Tabernacle,

Help me to respect those that are in authority. Help me to realize that people make mistakes. Help me to realize that the officials are not out to get me. Help me to love those even when they make mistakes that affect the outcome. Help me to realize that all people are worthy of honor. Lord, keep my mouth shut and my heart pure.

Day 236

Honor the Opposing Team

Luke 9:54-56 ***When the disciples James and John saw this, they asked, "Lord, do you want us to call fire down from heaven to destroy them?" But, Jesus turned and rebuked them. Then he and his disciples went to another village.***

I watched as the players went through their pregame walk-through. The visiting team had gotten off the bus and walked the field, which is a very common practice. One of the visiting team players stopped in the middle of the field and began to cleat and tear up the home team's 50-yard line logo. It was a tasteless, disrespectful move. Now, I understand the spirit of competition, but we must also respect and honor our opponents. The concept here is that they are all children of God. A few years ago, we beat our rivals from right up the road in a game they had been picked to win. They responded to that loss by using the bathroom on the floor of the visiting locker room—a very classless move. When we visited their locker room the next year, I told our team that we would respond with honor by ensuring that the locker room they put us in was cleaner than when we arrived. The truth is that we must respect and honor our opponent no matter the situation. The truth is that we need to leave the battle on the field, and when we are done with the competition, we need to shake hands and walk together as brothers and sisters in Christ. Jesus did not agree with the religious people of his day, but he still respected them. There was one time when his disciples asked him to disrespect a town that had shunned them. Jesus was heading to Jerusalem, and the people refused to welcome Jesus and his disciples, so James and John, two of the disciples' team captains, asked Jesus if he wanted them to call down fire from heaven and destroy them. Jesus rebuked them for their dishonor and said, "no, let's just move on." Jesus knew that he would ruin the effectiveness of his death and resurrection if he had shown disrespect. Instead, he chose to honor his rivals by moving on. Listen, disrespect for the other team will never lead to a win. What will lead to a win is playing your guts out and honoring your opponent for what they are; they are your opponent. See you at the plate.

Dear Father to the Fatherless,

God, help me to respect and honor others. Help me to stay positive amid competition. God, help me love others who are different and may believe differently than I do. Help me to be an example so that I can disciple someone else.

Day 237

Honoring Self

Job 40:10 (NAS) ***"Adorn yourself with eminence and dignity; And clothe yourself with honor and majesty.***

Now the Scriptures say that we must honor others above ourselves, but it does not say that we should not have any honor for ourselves. The truth is that we must honor ourselves in order to love ourselves. You cannot love others until you love yourself. How do we honor ourselves? Well, we do so by making wise decisions. When we honor ourselves, we look at how our decisions will affect our image and witness. When we honor ourselves, we care about what our image looks like to the world.

This is not so that we get the world's approval but so that we are a witness within the world. See, love is developed from within and not outside, so often we seek the crowd's approval, and when we do not get it, we feel as if we have failed. When we honor ourselves, we learn to love ourselves and quit looking for the world's approval. You live in a world that is obsessed with image. Social media and an ever-ready camera allow us to share where we are and what is going on with the world. Some people take multiple "selfies" a day looking for approval. They base their worth on the number of likes or comments that are made about their postings. The truth is that you can be the best athlete on the field and still feel inadequate and suffer from self-esteem issues.

We have all heard about the athlete that had everything going but was found dead. See, when we honor ourselves, we realize that we are wonderfully and fearfully made by a God who loves us and who wants an intimate relationship with us. We honor ourselves when we realize how much God loves us and that he is for us and not against us. Another way to honor self is by forgiving self. The truth is that we have all made decisions that we wish we could do-over. But at some point, we need to forgive ourselves, or we will never learn to forgive others. The last thing we can do to honor ourselves is, to be honest with ourselves. The most deceptive thing within us is sometimes our hearts. We are good at convincing ourselves of things that are not true. We also have to come to grips with where our weaknesses and our strengths lie. We have to be honest with ourselves so that we can be honest with others. So, honor thy self, and I will see you at the plate.

Dear Host of Honor and Dignity,

Help me to respect myself and love myself. Please help me to be true to myself and honor myself. I am fearful and wonderfully made in your image, and that is what leads to my honor.

Day 238

Strong Tower

Psalms 18:10 ***The name of the LORD is a fortified tower; the righteous run to it and are safe.***

Sometimes when we are strong, talented athletes, we think that we are invincible. We think that we cannot show emotion or show hurt. The truth is that we are human, and there are times that we find ourselves weak and helpless. The truth is that because we live in a fallen world, sometimes things are just out of our control. There will be things in our life that we cannot conquer with brute strength or strong willpower. There are going to be things that are out of our control. Last week one of my son's teammates who had already committed to a Division 1 school went down with a season-ending knee injury. As I watched from the stands, I just prayed that God would be his strong tower. When something like this happens, we can begin to feel hopeless. We have been taught that through strength, we can conquer everything. But sometimes, we find ourselves helpless. It is here that we must find God as our strong tower, a tower that helps to guide our way. A tower that leads us back to him when we have wondered or strayed so far from him. A tower that leads us through the desert and leads us back home. A tower that gives us hope and refuge when we have lost our way. God is also a strong fortress for us when we are weak and are trying to find our way. Even at the height of our winning, we can often lose our way and feel like we are trudging through the desert. It is here that God is a shelter over us and a strong tower that leads us to the face of Christ. It is in times like this that we can say, all I need to see is the face of Jesus. I sometimes think about how Mary must have felt as she was looked into the face of Jesus as he hung there with the world's sin upon his back. I wonder if she saw him as a strong tower, not a defeated man? She knew that one day that face would be all that she would need. Listen, Jesus is your strong tower. You can get through this, and you do not have to do it all on your own. He is your strong tower, and I will see you at the plate.

Dear Mighty Fortress,

Thank you for being my fortress. Thank you for protecting me. Thank you for being like that lighthouse that warns me of danger. God, you are my strong tower and a fortress that guides my steps. God, let me also be a fortress in this dark world.

✞

Day 239

Glory Transformed

2 Corinthians 3:18 (NIV) ***And we all, who with unveiled faces contemplate the Lord's glory, are being transformed into his image with ever-increasing glory, which comes from the Lord, who is the Spirit.***

Here is a great question: Did you make sports, or did sports make you? One of the things that we will gain from sports that we do not often recognize while we are playing is how to live life. We will learn how to deal with difficult people. We will learn teamwork. We will learn how to deal with the agony of defeat. We will learn that commitment and hard work pays off. See, sports make us more than we make sports. You may leave a legacy on the field, but what you carry off the field will be more valuable. Sports also help to pull the veil back on who we are and how we carry ourselves.

The truth is that we will become aware of God's glory as we play. When we play for God and not solely for ourselves, others can see the glory of God revealed through us. See, sports will help to transform us into who God is hoping we will become. Now, if you are playing solely for yourself, then people will never see the glory of God; as a matter of fact, the veil will never be removed from your face. You see, in the Scripture today, it says God's ever-increasing glory. We think that God's glory ended with the death and resurrection of his Son but that his glory should always be ever-increasing through our testimony and our witness to the world. When we make his name greater than ours, he receives the glory that is deserved. When you play, you do not play alone. You are surrounded by the Holy Spirit, which should be your driving force. Let me ask you if his glory is being transformed through your play. Did you make the game, or did the game make you? See you at the plate.

Dear Thy Staff and Comfort,

Remove the veil from my eyes so that I can see your glory. Let my life reveal your glory so that your glory will be ever-increasing. Help me to be Holy Spirit reliant rather than self-reliant so that the world will recognize the glory that your Son brought when he came to dwell among us. Lord, I give you my heart again today.

Day 240

Input = Output

Luke 19:17 ***Well done, my good servant!' his master replied. 'Because you have been trustworthy in a very small matter, take charge of ten cities.***

Several years ago, Gatorade came out with a commercial, and in the commercial, they ask the question, "Gatorade, is it in you?" Then they showed a person sweating drops of Gatorade. This commercial made me think a lot about how we get to our maximum output. It then dawned on me that output is a direct reflection of input. What you put into anything is what you are going to get out of it. If you halfway go through practice, then come game time, you will halfway go through the game. The same could be said for all aspects of game-ready preparation. You see, maximum input leads to trust, and that trust leads you to determining the outcome because you trusted your input. When you have prepared by focusing on your input, you will be trusted when the game is on the line. The coach will put the ball into your hands in hopes of getting the desired outcome. The coach will do this because they know that the desired output is directly affected by your input preparation. If you want to be the star player, you will have to focus on input every day. That leads to this question; if you are not given the opportunity when the game is on the line, then you must ask the question, "Is it in you?" Not Gatorade, but the preparation to win by the input that you worked on all week.

In the Scripture, Jesus tells the story of three men that receive money to invest. Two double their money, but one goes and hides his in the ground and makes no return on the investment. How many times is our spiritual life void of output because we have not focused on our input? God has blessed you with not only athletic talents but also with Spiritual gifts. What are you doing with the gifts that God has given you? Are you preparing for the output when the opportunities arise? Once again, remember that those trusted with little will also be trusted with the ball when the game is on the line. The game is on the line; I will see you at the plate.

Dear Precious Lord,

Help me with my input so that I can resist my output. Help me to be trusted with a small amount so that I can be trusted with eternal things. Help me to realize that when the game is on the line, I have it in me. I have the power of the Holy Spirit so that my output will match the output that your Son gave. What did he give? He gave it all to me.

✞

Day 241

Our Strongest Muscle

Proverbs 12:18 ***"There is one who speaks rashly, like a piercing sword; but the tongue of the wise brings healing."***

Many times, as athletes, we work with different muscle groups to strengthen our core. We are fully aware that we are stronger in some areas than we are in others. Some have impressive bench presses, while others have massive squat totals. Some have abs that you could wash your clothes on, and some have arms that look like legs. Now, we may not realize that the strongest muscles we have are the ones that control our mouth. The Scripture says, "that the tongue is as sharp as a two-edged sword." I do not know about you, but there have been several times when as soon as the words left my mouth, I wish that I could get them back. But I knew that I could not get them back. I have even used an illustration in children's sermons to illustrate that you cannot get them back once words are gone. I take out a toothpaste tube and have the kids squeeze it all out, and then I tell them to put it back in the tube. We all know that it is impossible to get the toothpaste back in the tube. This illustration gives us a great example of what happens when we speak. The words are out, and we cannot put them back.

We all know that in sports there is a lot of jeering and cutting-up. For some reason, it just comes as second nature to make fun of one another. We know that nicknames are frequently given to players. Some of these nicknames will stick for the rest of that person's life. We also must realize that sometimes the jeering and the nicknames are meant to cut down and hurt. If you have ever been on the other side of the jokes, then you know that words can cut a person to the core. I had a youth minister in one of my churches that used to preach to the kids that their words had "power." She used to say, "do not speak it into existence." The truth is that we are either building someone up with our words, or we are tearing them down. The truth is that many times after someone has heard cutting words repeatedly, they begin to believe that those words have power over their lives. So, how are you using the most powerful muscles that you have? Are you using them to build up the team or to tear it down? Here is another question in the Kingdom of God; what are you using your words to do? Are you using them to build up or tear down his Kingdom? Hey, here are some words for you. You are wonderfully and fearfully made by God and for God. See you at the plate.

Dear Son of the Virgin Mary,

God, I continue to say things I wish that had never left my tongue. Help me to remember that my words have power. Help me realize I can either be an encourager or be a person who cuts down others. God, help me to deal with my insecurities so that I do not exploit someone else's. Forgive me for the words that I have used in the past that have helped define someone negatively. Keep your hand on my tongue as I keep my hand on my heart. Let me speak life and truth. The truth of your Son Jesus Christ and his kind words spoken for me, "it is finished." Amen

Day 242

Please, God, Speak

I John 5:15 ***And if we know that he hears us in whatever we ask, we know that we have the requests that we have asked of him.***

Have you ever anticipated an answer or direction for your life? What do we do when we are living in that anticipation? We say, "Please God speak," and speak right now. Sometimes it seems that our prayers never make it higher than the ceiling. We have asked and asked over again, but we have yet to receive an answer. The truth is that we are not patient, even with God. There have been many times in my life when I questioned God as to why he was taking so long. There have even been times where I asked God if he was even listening to me. Most of the time, I think I know what is good for me, so I tell God rather than ask God. Many times, rather than wait on God to act, I act on my behalf. The truth is that sometimes God is slow to speak because we are in constant process, and he wants to teach us patience. Maturity and faith are both byproducts of waiting on God. God is sometimes protecting us from ourselves when he does not give us the answer right away. See, patience is a process, and God knows that we are like spoiled children if we get everything we ask for. Sometimes in sports, we must also learn patience. You see, we may think that we are better than the upperclassman playing in front of us.

We cannot understand why we are not playing more or have not moved up in the lineup. The truth is that sometimes the coach is grooming us and teaching us to value hard work and patience. You see, maybe we are more talented but less mature. Maybe we are leaning too much into our own talent and not receiving the coaching and guidance that is being taught. Maybe the coach is teaching us how to be a leader. The truth is that we are all in process, and part of that process is learning to be patient in life. Remember, God will never leave or forsake you, and so he will eventually answer. And remember, if you keep playing hard, the coach will notice. So, keep your faith; you are learning patience as part of your maturation. Did you hear that the coach is calling you up? Come on, I will see you at the plate.

Dear Wonderful Counselor,

Please hear my request and teach me what your will is and what my will is. Protect me from the request that would draw me further from you. Help me to learn patience because this is what leads to faith through maturity. God, please hear me. I love you and thank you for your Son Jesus Amen.

Day 243

Following Your Dreams

We all have dreams, not nightmares or R.E.M. sleep dreams but aspirations to be something important or famous. Your dreams can only become a reality when we put in the work required to make our dreams come to life. This week we will be doing another series that revolves around dreams and how we can make our dreams come true.

Genesis 37:19 ***"Here comes that dreamer!" they said to each other.***

What do you want to be when you grow up? Is it not amazing that when you ask a child this question, there are no limitations? They want to be doctors and dancers; they want to be astronauts and professional athletes. The truth is the sky is the limit. It is funny that when we are little, we dream big, and then the older we get, we just stop dreaming altogether. This week we are going to focus on our hopes and dreams. If you do not have any dreams, that is alright because you will when we finish this week. Let me start by asking you to stop right now and think about that one big dream you have. Go ahead, take a minute, and write it down. Welcome back. Now what you wrote down may seem unattainable or may seem out of reach, but it does not have to be. The problem with attaining our dreams is not that we dream too big, but that we think too small. God wants us to dream big to achieve big.

No team goes into a season and thinks, I hope we just score one time this year. No, the truth is that no matter where you are ranked, you have dreams of lifting that trophy in the air after going undefeated. See, no matter what your record was the year before, with every new beginning comes new dreams. In the Scripture, there is a young man named Joseph; his brothers just like to call him "the dreamer." Now Joseph did not just dream big, but he boasted of the big dreams that he had. Now, as you follow Joseph's life, you will see that he never quit dreaming, no matter what happened to him. Even when he was sold into slavery, he dreamed; when he wound up in prison, he dreamed. He refused to let his surroundings squash the dreams that had been placed before him. So many of you have let the world or your surroundings squash your dreams. It is now time to redeem yourself and dream big to achieve big. Follow your dreams but do not follow them alone. Invite your Lord and Savior to go along with you. Ask God to help you remove the distractions that keep you from achieving your hopes and dreams. Tell me again how big that dream is, and I will see you at the plate.

Dear God of Big Awesome Dreams,

Help me to keep faith in my dreams and aspirations. Help me not lose hope because losing faith and losing faith is to be trapped in this self-induced wilderness. Help me to dream bigger than I could possibly achieve. You are the God of the possible, not the God of the impossible. God, through your Son Jesus, all things are possible. Help me remember that the world wants to steal and rob me of my dreams, but I stand firm on your word. Let people, when they see me say, Look, here comes the dreamer.

Day 244

Little Dreams

Proverbs 12:11 ***The one who works his land will have plenty of food, but whoever chases fantasies lacks sense.***

I know the title has you saying, Man, you are schizophrenic; you just told me yesterday to dream big, and now you entitled today's devotional "Little Dreams." But before you quit reading, let me explain what I mean. Sometimes you must dream little dreams in order to achieve big. Some dreams are not dreaming; they are just fantasies. You see, sometimes we get it in our heads to try to achieve a fantasy. A fantasy is something that is not only unattainable but does not need to be attained. Fantasies pull us away from our big audacious dream and sometimes pull us away from God. Fantasies are different than dreams in the fact that dreams originate with God. Dreams also benefit our life as well as benefit the Kingdom of God. Little dreams stem from things like trying to achieve all A's. Maybe you start practicing extra hard so you can become a starter. A little dream may also mean doing a Bible study consistently for 30 days so that you can grow in your relationship with Christ. You see, these are all little dreams that become part of your big dream. The truth is that without the little dreams, your big dreams may not get to fruition. Take, for instance, the example of your grades. I do not know how often I have heard of an outstanding athlete being academically ineligible because they did not dream little dreams about their grades. Joseph, the dreamer, dreamed of some big dreams, but he also dreamed of small dreams that he could share with people. Once while he was in prison, two people came to him with a recurring dream. Joseph was able to tell them what these dreams meant, and ultimately it was because of these little dreams he was able to save not one but two nations. (You can read this story in Genesis 40:1-23.) Remember, fantasies take you away from reality and what God wants you to achieve. But little dreams stacked together result in the big dream that you have prayed and hoped to achieve. So dream little, and I will see you at the plate.

Dear Shekinah Glory,

God, we know that you are in every small detail. We can just look at the human body and how it is put together to know that you are in every small detail. God, sometimes we need to dream small before we can dream big. God, please trust me with the small things so that I can be trusted with greater things. Sometimes just let me dream small, so I can realize how big you are.

✞

Day 245

Building a Dream

2 Chronicles 6:8-9 ***"However, the Lord said to my father David, 'Since it was your desire to build a temple for My name, you have done well to have this desire. Yet, you are not the one to build the temple, but your Son, your own offspring, will build the temple for My name.'"***

Sometimes the reality of a dream is for us to start it and then let someone else finish it. This is a really hard concept for us to understand because we want the fruits of our blood, sweat, and tears. We tend to ask the question of why someone else should benefit from our dreams and hard work? Sometimes our success is the direct result of someone's else dream. In college, I played on the first team when Campbellsville College brought back football (1987) after a ten-plus-year hiatus. I got to be a part of a brand-new dream and a brand-new team. I got to lay the foundation and the groundwork for a program that has now been competitive for the last 33 years. When I say lay the groundwork, I mean groundwork because we actually took off practice one day to lay the sod for the football field. We spent the first year practicing in the baseball field's outfield, which needed sodding after practicing on it for a year. (We let the baseball team sod it.) We had no idea or could envision what that program has grown into today, but we had a dream, and then at some point, we passed the baton on to someone else. Now in 2012, that first team was invited back, and we were all inducted into the Campbellsville Athletic Hall of Fame because of the dream that had now been achieved. It truly was a great honor, but it was also humbling to see what we had begun to build and was now being built upon by others. See, sometimes God calls us to dream the dream and then pass the dream on for someone else to achieve. This is so hard for us to fathom, but it is God's way of doing things in his different ways. In the Scripture, Moses had led the people for forty years in the wilderness. Now this walking in the desert was not a cakewalk but was a very taxing, arduous journey. Now just before Moses crosses over into the promised land, God asks him to pass the staff. Joshua then brings the people into the dream of the promised land that Moses had started. Then there is the story of David and the rebuilding of the Temple. David had dreamed of building the Temple, but because of his murderous sinful acts related to Bathsheba, God told him that not he but his Son would complete the dream of building the temple. Sometimes we may never live to see our dream completed, but it does not mean that we should not start building a dream, a program, or a foundation. The truth is that the team you are playing on was probably the result of someone else's dream. When we trust in God, we know that God will continue to build upon the dream that we started. When this comes to Kingdom building, starting the dream will have rewards that will last for all of eternity. So, let's start building a dream, and I will see you at the plate.

Dear River of Living Water,

Help me to be a part of something better than myself. Help me to make decisions from the aspect of what will build the Kingdom of God. I may not even get to see these dreams come to fruition, but I lay the groundwork for these to be built upon. You have promised that if I sow a seed, you will water them. God, I want to be a Kingdom builder so that others can come to know who you are the way I know who you are. Thank you for your Son, who built my faith with some rugged wood, some ropes, and some nails.

Day 246

God's Dreams for Us

Romans 12:1-2 (GNT) ***Offer yourselves as a living sacrifice to God, dedicated to his service and pleasing to him …. Do not conform yourselves to the standards of this world, but let God transform you inwardly by a complete change of your mind. Then you will be able to know the will of God, what is good and is pleasing to him and is perfect.***

We are sitting there in class daydreaming about what we have been given the ability to achieve when a voice calls us back into reality and asks us to answer the question that has just been put on the board. We are brought immediately back into reality. The truth is that many times we are snapped back into reality as we are daydreaming about being the hero, driving in the last run, scoring the winning goal, or hoisting the championship trophy into the air. We cannot help but daydream about what we love to do. Did you know that God daydreams about us also? He wants us to realize that we are already champions in his Kingdom because of our decision to follow his Son, Jesus Christ. Now what kind of dreams do you think that God has for our lives. The first dream is that he would be our first priority. The Scripture says, "have no other Gods before Yahweh." This means that we would put him first in everything that we do.

How do we do this? We do this by making Jesus our top relationship. I have argued with many people that how we treat our relationship with Jesus is exactly how we tend to treat our other key relationships. The next dream that God has for us is to tap into the power of the Holy Spirit that he has provided for us. So often, we are self-dependent rather than being spirit-dependent. When he left earth, he was clear that he would not leave us alone but would give us one with even greater power. Next, God drams that we will be able to handle temptation and flee from the sin that so easily ensnares us.

Finally, God dreams that our lives will be filled with passion and joy. Then we would see the world for what it is, a temporary place on our way to glory. His dream is that we will realize that the Kingdom of God is here amongst us. We must realize that by doing his will and following the example of his Son, we can be filled with joy and that we do not have to wait for the kingdom of God. The reason we do not have to wait is that the Kingdom is right in our midst. God dreams for you because he loves you and cares about you as a parent cares for a child. He not only wants you to succeed on the field, but he wants you to thrive in everyday life. Remember that God loves you and dreams the best for you. Hey, wake up from that daydream, and I will see you at the plate.

Dear Sanctified One,

God help me to realize that the victory has already been won. Your Son defeated sin and death, and they have no power over us. Bring me back to reality when I get outside of your kingdom priorities and try only to achieve what priorities I have set. God, thank you for giving me the ability to dream. Help me to dream big to achieve big. Thank you for your Son, who dreamed of a cross that would allow me to live the life I live. Amen.

Day 247

Powered by Will

Proverbs 25:28 ***Like a city whose walls are broken through is a person who lacks self-control.***

"I wish I had more willpower!" How many times have you heard someone say that after breaking off what they had vowed to achieve? Sometimes this is in direct correlation to a diet and exercise program. Sometimes it is related to knowing when not to speak; most people feel they come up short in the will-power department. The other day while working on this devotional, I saw a girl studying in the coffee shop with a shirt that had the slogan, "Powered by Will." I must admit that this statement intrigued me. What does it mean to be powered by will? The truth is that "will" is the fortitude not to give up even when all odds are against it. Now that is not the dictionary definition but my own. I have heard athletic teams say "that they willed their way to a win." I think what they are saying is that they refuse to give up. So often in life, people's will is battle-tested. It is easy for us to wave the white flag and surrender.

I heard a story the other night about a walk-on athlete that had become a star. He had walked on the team and made it but had some personal issues in his life. He then left the program but came back after a year. He then worked so hard that he received a starting position and a full scholarship. He will graduate this year with a degree. How did he get to this point? He refused to let the world break his will. He refused to let his situation define the outcome of his will. He continues to press on and work through. Listen, when we are powered by will, we have the ability to face all kinds of hurdles and obstacles. Now, willpower comes from a strong relationship with Jesus? How many times do we see Jesus push through his circumstances and situations? His willpower started with the power of prayer. You will never know how powerful prayer is till you powerfully pray. The second thing that Jesus did was he leaned upon his Father's power, who can do all things. Will power is something that has to be a constant practice and discipline. God will give you the power to will your way through the schemes of the evil one. Just keep pushing, use your willpower, and I will see you at the plate.

Dear Preeminent One,

Help me to will my way through what the world has put in front of me to break my will. Help me to tap into the power of the Holy Spirit that will help me power through what seems impossible. Help me realize that my will may not always be your will, and those are the times I need to surrender so that I can be found blameless in your eyes.

Day 248

Being My Brother's Keeper

I Samuel 18:3-4 (NKJV) ***And Jonathan made a covenant with David because he loved him as himself. Jonathan took off the robe he was wearing and gave it to David, along with his tunic, and even his sword, his bow, and his belt.***

One of the greatest lessons you will learn when you play team sports is the concept of being a team. Now some teams are just teammates that play together, but some teams become true family units. In some teams, cohesiveness and chemistry form a tight bond, leading the team to become a band of brothers/sisters. Part of becoming that family unit is when you truly respect what each one brings to the field. Although each person may have different gifts and skills, another important aspect of team cohesiveness is mutual respect through tough competition and battling for positions on the depth chart. The question here is, are you able to cheer for your team when you are on the sidelines? A third element can be identified when you look out for one another as a team. You are not only concerned with what happens on the field but what happens off the field. You become your brother's keeper. You realize that a team is a whole unit, and what happens to one ultimately affects the whole team. You help to hold teammates accountable for their behavior, grades, and how they carry themselves in public. The truth is that you do not even have to be the star of the team to be your brother's keeper. By being your brother's keeper, you will reap a lot of criticism at first, but if you are true to your walk, you will eventually gain respect and a place of leadership among your teammates.

In the Scripture, there is a great story of two friends that became each other's keepers. Jonathan was Saul's son, and he was next in line to succeed the throne, but instead of him being picked for the succession, his friend David was anointed to be king. Now, most people would respond with retaliation and a jealous spirit, but Jonathan did not. Instead, he decided that he would support and defend David through the whole process. Jonathan became his brother David's keeper and even defended him from being killed by his father. When we have that kind of honor and love for a friend, we can truly gain the respect of those around us. What would your team look like if you helped carry your brothers/sisters when they could not push on? Let me challenge you to be your brother's keeper, and I will see you at the plate.

Dear Jesus the Nazarene,

God help me to become my brother's keeper. Help me realize that you put me here to pray for and walk alongside my brothers and sisters. Help me to love my neighbor. And who is my neighbor? My neighbor is anyone you created. God help me to put aside myself and to become selfless. I am my brother's keeper because you are my keeper.

✞

Day 249

G.O.A.T.

Matthew 23:11 ***The greatest among you will be your servant.***

There is a slang term that has been going around for the last few years. The term is G.O.A.T. I have even seen this term used by several people as their Twitter handle or as a hashtag. G.O.A.T means the Greatest Of All Time. The funny thing about this term is that it is relative to who is using the term as to how relevant it really is. Many people call people the greatest of all time based on what they are doing now without considering all the others that came before and what unique challenges they may have faced. The term is also relevant to whether we are talking solely about wins and losses as compared to character and reputation. It is so funny that Jesus says that in order to be the greatest of all time, you had to be like a little child.

Now when he used this statement, children were not highly regarded. The truth is that children were treated more like property and less like gifts from God at that time. Now Jesus is saying if you want to become the greatest of all time, you have to be looked at as a servant and not a leader. That is truly a headscratcher because everyone knows a G.O.A.T is not someone who serves but on who everybody worships. Now, this is where we must interject that biblical statement I love to use. "For our ways are not your ways, and our thoughts are not your thoughts." (Isaiah 55) The truth is that the greatest of all time has already come and gone and will one day return again. His name is Jesus Christ, and the people did not think of him as the greatest of all time (The GOAT) but thought of him as a common criminal that was insane. He was a leader that came to serve and not be served. He was a leader that rather than gain military strength, brought peace, love, and mercy. He was one that, rather than gain a Kingdom here on earth, brought the Kingdom of God with him. He gave his life so that we could one day be with him in eternity, free from our own bondage. No, there will only be one that was the greatest of all time, and his name is Jesus. Now the question is, where does that leave you? You can still be a G.O.A.T . ***Giving Our Awesome Testimony***. Rather than being the greatest of all time, tell others about who was truly the best of all time. So, come on, G.O.A.T, I will see you at the plate.

Dear G.O.A.T, "God of all Things"

God, you are the God of all things. You are the God of the beginning and the end. Lord, help me realize that I am not the greatest of all time, even when other people allude to this. God help me to be humble myself and be true to the game. Help me to be as humble on the field as I am in life. Help my life be the story and testimony that will change the world. Help people to see you through me.

Day 250

I Am Redeemed

I Peter 1:18-19 ***For you know that it was not with perishable things such as silver or gold that you were redeemed from the empty way of life handed down to you from your ancestors, but with the precious blood of Christ, a lamb without blemish or defect.***

I was listening to sports talk radio the other day, and I heard one of the announcers say that one of our state teams was on a redemption mission for a brutal loss they had suffered in the last game of the previous year. I thought about the phrasing of those words, <u>redemption mission</u>. I then thought that was probably a poor choice of words and the words that should have been used where they are on a "revenge mission." When I think of redemption, I think of something that we cannot solely achieve by ourselves. I think of this is in terms of my sinful nature. There are so many days when I want to do the right thing, but I just cannot get going in the right direction. There is no way that I can redeem my sins when I cannot even do what I set out to do. There is no bar set for how good we must be to enter heaven. The only way that we can be redeemed for our sins against God is by imposing the blood of Jesus. The true meaning of redemption is to buy back something that is lost. This is exactly what Jesus did when he died for our sins. He bought us back and redeemed us by his blood. We can avenge a loss to a rival from the year before, and we may even have a revenge type of year where we go out and beat everyone that beat us the year before, but redemption is what God has already done for us. He did that when he sent his Son Jesus to save us from ourselves. To impose his precious blood so that we could be made clean. Now that you know you are redeemed, I will see you at the plate.

Dear Rabboni,

I am redeemed, and I have been set free. I am set free because your Son set me free. The heavy chains of sin that bind me have been broken, and I am washed new. I am saved, sanctified, and redeemed. Yes, your Son has set me free.

Day 251

An Aha Moment

Ephesians 5:16-18 ***Be very careful, then, how you live—not as unwise but as wise, making the most of every opportunity because the days are evil. Therefore, do not be foolish but understand what the Lord's will is. Do not get drunk on wine, which leads to debauchery.***

Sometimes in sports or life, we have what we call an "aha" moment. You will easily recognize when you come to one of these defining moments. One example of this type of moment is when you get tired of watching the game from the sidelines and not playing, so you decide to work harder. Another example could be when the coach calls you in the office and tells you that you are ineligible unless you bring up your grades in the next two weeks. Another example is when you realize that many players are outworking you in every aspect of the game. All of these should lead to an "aha moment." A realization of the fact that if things do not change then, you are headed for trouble. An "aha moment" has three distinct elements.

The first is "the awakening." This is where you realize or are shocked into a reality that something needs to be different. This is the crossroads to whether you make a change or not. You must decide to do something different here, or you will continue to make the same decision with the same results. **The second component is the "honesty component."** In order to make a change, you must want to make a change and be honest with yourself that you want to change. Many people refuse to make changes because they are not honest with themselves. The truth is that the person who lies to you the most is you. We try to convince ourselves that if we do not change, things will still change. Honesty is the most important concept of the aha moment, becoming a reality. **The third aspect of an "aha moment" is action**. This is where you sit down and plan what you must do differently and then put it into action. If you have an awakening and are honest but do not put it into action, then you will never have a complete "aha moment." <u>The harsh realization is nothing will change when nothing changes.</u> So now that you have had an "aha moment," I will see you at the plate.

Dear God of Epiphanies,

First of all, bring me to that "aha" moment, even if it is painful. Help me see that I have to quit lying to myself about being ok to change. The truth is that I am really not alright. The truth is that unless I change, I am headed for destruction. God help me not only to realize that I need the aha moment, but I must take action to change my life.

Day 252

Put Your Pride Aside

Proverbs 11:2 ***When pride comes, then comes disgrace, but with the humble is wisdom.***

I knew I did not need to say it as soon as it came out of my mouth. You have been there before, I am sure. You know how it is; there are two things you cannot take back. The first is when you hit the send button knowing you should not have sent it, and the other is speaking and then wishing you could take the words back. I recently met a very prominent high school coach, and I dropped the name of another coach I had worked with to sound like I was important. I knew immediately that this was a "hey, look at me moment." It was a moment that I wanted to be recognized for who I knew and what I had accomplished. The truth is that I was gaining fame through someone else's name. It was a very pride-filled moment. Now, this is not the good pride but the pride that got Adam and Eve in trouble. It is the pride that comes right before we commit a big sin. The kind of pride that kept David from going into the battlefield and led to the downfall of his kingdom. The pride that Peter spoke when he cursed and said, I do not know the man. Yes, pride is written upon our lips when we hope for people to honor and praise us rather than praise God. Pride always comes before the fall. The true definition of sin in and of itself is having pride that competes with God. You see, we long to be accepted and looked at in a way that we gain fame. I sometimes wonder if Paul had a hard time containing his pride. I mean, after all, what he had been through for the sake of Jesus Christ is very brag-worthy. But instead, Paul says that if we are going to be prideful, then it needs to be in the power of the cross and not in our accomplishments. I think Paul needed to keep this at his forefront to stay humble, forsaking all pride. See, we can be strong followers of Jesus Christ and still have what we call spiritual pride. The Pharisees in the Scripture were filled with spiritual pride to the point that they were the focus of their religion. You have known the person who boasts about the great things they have done and how they have done it, they are more spiritual than anyone could even imagine, but they are so full of pride that they are hard to be around. Listen, do not be prideful, boastful, or self-absorbed because it will kill your witness. Remember, do not be prideful, and I will see you at the plate.

Dear Humble Savior,

Help me to see the error of my ways as it comes to my prideful spirit. Help me to only boost of the cross and what it has done for me. Help me realize that spiritual pride is the worst kind of pride because it seeks to release us from living under grace. Help me to boast of what God has done for me that I could not do for myself. Thank you for your Son, who relinquished all of his pride and died for me and my pride. Amen.

✞

Day 253

Lose Yourself to Me

Mark 8:35 ***For whoever wants to save their life will lose it, but whoever loses their life for me and for the gospel will save it.***

Let's face it; no one likes to lose. The truth is that we do everything we can in order to not lose. I remember when my son was a little boy and played 7-8-year old baseball all-stars, and they lost to a neighboring team. I looked around and could not find my son. We finally found him sitting on a picnic table all by himself. When I asked him what he was doing, he looked up and said, "Dad, it hurts." The truth is that losing hurts. But there is a place where we do need to lose in order to win, and that is when it comes to our relationship with Jesus.

The truth is that when we lose ourselves is where we find God. We try to find peace in all the things that the world has to offer, and we keep coming up void. We try to hide, thinking that we can escape the consequences of our decisions. The truth is that when we lose ourselves and quit trying to replace God with the things of this world is where we find him. We find God in the middle of the darkest nights; we find in the storms of life and the times we have left his side. The truth is that in order to find him, we must lose ourselves. It is amazing that in the Scriptures, every time people quit trying to do things on their own and got lost in God, they truly found themselves and claimed victory. To lose yourself means that you put aside everyone and everything to find your dependence on God. God wants you to get lost in him so that he can love you in a way that he intended to love you. So, lose yourself, and I will see you at the plate.

Dear Seeker of the Lost One,

Help me to lose myself to find you. Help me to quit hiding behind all the worldly things that I think will satisfy me and save me. Help me get so lost in you that others want to be found in you and your love. You love me so much that you would leave 99 in order to just find me. Thank you for sending your Son and for allowing me to get lost in the cross so I could be found in the resurrection. Amen.

✞

Day 254

I Want the Absolute Truth

I Timothy 4:4-5 ***They will turn away from hearing the truth and will turn aside to myths. But as for you, keep a clear head about everything, endure hardship, do the work of an evangelist, fulfill your ministry.***

Do you think people believe that there is an absolute right and a wrong? I mean, is there a guideline that we must follow in order to set the bar for the moral behavior of a professing Christian? Is the Bible an absolute truth, or is it just a suggestion on how we should live and what we should do as it relates to Christian living? Are we allowed to take only certain Scriptures out of the playbook of life, and if we do not agree, we can disregard the Scriptures we do not agree with? Did you know that in 1804 Thomas Jefferson took out two Bibles and cut out with razor the parts he did not agree with? Now before we are too critical of Thomas Jefferson, we may want to ask if we have not done something similar. I think we live in a world where we follow what we agree with. I mean, Christians ought to look different than that of the world, but I am afraid they do not. I saw a picture the other day of a professional athlete who used his eye black to put crosses on his face. This usually means that you are a follower of Christianity, but that same athlete is charged with several accounts of sexual misconduct. He has also been known to be cancer to any team he has played on and has been released by at least three teams. Now I promise that I am not judgmental, but it seems as if he calls himself a Christian without absolutes. A recent survey showed that only 6% of teens believe that moral truth is absolute. Now in the sporting world, there are many (rules) truths that cannot be relative.

Could you imagine if every athlete played by their own rules? No foul balls. You can run the bases backward. A touchdown is worth 10 points, not 6. What if everyone defined winning differently—one by score, one by effort, and one by who had the best-looking uniforms? Go ahead, make up your own rules; there are no absolutes. The truth is this would be absolute chaos! Fortunately, there are absolutes in sports to keep the events from being chaotic and unfair. The truth is that God also gave us absolutes in the Scripture to keep the world from being in chaos. Look around the world today, and you will see that there is chaos because we have taken the Scripture and changed it rather than allowing the Scripture to change the way we live. So now that you know there are absolute truths, I will see you at the plate.

Dear God of Absolute Truth,

Help me pick and choose what is easy for me to follow and help me see the Scriptures as a whole moral absolute. God, when I do not follow what the Scriptures have instructed me to do, I am living in sin. To live in sin separates the distance between you and me. God, your Son, was the absolute truth because in him could be found no sin and no deceit. Help me to not only believe this but to follow this so that the world may see you through me.

Day 255

Fair-weather Follower

Deuteronomy 13:3-4 ***"For the Lord, your God is testing you to know whether you love the Lord your God with all your heart and all your soul. You must follow the Lord your God and fear Him. You must keep His commands and listen to His voice; you must worship Him and remain faithful to Him."***

Lately, a lot of radio-hosted college football talk has centered around low attendance and people not staying till the end of the games. Many times, fans leave because the game has been well decided by halftime. The second point is that where I live in the South, it is October, and temperatures are still in the 90's with unbelievable humidity. Now the problem is that some coaches and other fans call those that leave early fair-weather fans. That is kind of funny because they are not hot weathered fans. A fair-weather fan is a fan that is not truly all in with the team. They are on board if the team is winning and doing well, but one bad season or, in some instances, one bad game and social media blows up with fire the coach and boycott the team text/tweets. These fans do not stick with the team or the coaches through the rough patches. Fairweather fans do not care about extenuating circumstances; they just care about wins and, well, just wins. The truth is that some people are like those fans in their faith. They are fair-weather followers. They will follow as long as everything is going their way. These people tend to look at faith more like, God, what can you do for me? The problem with that is that they are only committed to the point of what he can do for them. A fair-weathered follower never asked the question of what can I do for the Kingdom?

I think about instances where Jesus could have been a fair-weathered savior but chose to put his true reliance on his Father. The first was in the garden when he asked if it would be possible to let this cup pass from him. He knew what he was going to endure, and he also knew that his death for some would be in vain because they would still reject him. The second time he could have wavered was when he was on the cross and felt his father had abandoned him. But he kept the faith and pushed through the physical and mental anguish so that he could save the world. He realized that he had been obedient and had never become the fair-weather savior as he said on the cross, "it is finished." Look, do not give up on your team just because things are not going as you think they should, and do not give up on your faith just because you are going through the rough waters of life. No fair-weather players are allowed here. Go all in, and I will see you at the plate.

Dear Committed Savior,

I pray that you will help me to be committed even when it seems easier to walk away. Help me always to see that there will be a test, and there will be tumultuous times. Help me to realize that fair-weather followers surround me, but if I stay the course, I might just help them in their commitment. Thank you that your Son was committed to the point of death for my sin's savior. He had times where he could have taken a lot easier road, but he always took the road less traveled. Help me to take the road less traveled also. Amen.

Day 256

One Thing to Do?

Genesis 2:17 ***And the Lord God commanded the man, "You are free to eat from any tree in the garden; but you must not eat from the tree of the knowledge of good and evil, for when you eat from it, you will certainly die."***

One of the funny sections on Sports Center is the one that is entitled, "You Only Had One Thing To Do." In this segment of the show, someone is messing up at the only job they had to do. Sometimes it is a minor gaffe or goof, but sometimes it cost their team the win. The truth is that even though it is funny, it will sometimes make you cringe as you feel for the person that is involved. You feel that way because you have been there, and you have been that person. You only had one thing to do, and you forgot, or you dropped the ball. Do you remember how you felt? You felt as if the weight of the world had just come crashing down on you. In the Scripture, God gives a similar example of: "you only had one thing to do." He tells Adam and Eve that you only have one thing not to do. The only thing you cannot do is that you cannot eat from that tree. Now, most of us look at the story, and we go; you know, I think I could have done it. I think I could have resisted the temptation and followed through with not eating from the tree. But when we remember how many times we have failed in our "you only have one thing to do scenarios," we would have also failed the test. Now, this is where grace steps in to pick up our slack and take away our embarrassment. God knew that we would fail him even before we were born, even when we just had one thing that we needed to do. God knew that no matter how hard we tried or even if we just had one rule to follow that we would fail. So, what did God do, he sent his only Son into the world, and he only had one job to do, and he successfully completed that job. Jesus only had one thing to do, and that was to die on a cross so he could provide grace for us that fail in our one thing-to-do moments. So, pick your head up and know that even though you failed, you are covered. You are covered in love and the grace that God has to offer through the sacrifice of his Son. Now listen, you only have one thing to do right now, so I will see you at the plate.

Dear Holy One True God,

Help me to follow through with the task that has been given to me. Help me realize that sometimes the weight of the world is on my shoulders, but you are helping me carry it. Help me realize that sometimes even though I only had just one thing to do, I failed. It is here that your Son's death and resurrection help me realize that it's moments like these that he came and died for me. God, I pray for those who do not have Jesus because when they have not accepted that grace, these embarrassing moments begin to define their lives rather than the love and grace of Jesus defining their life. Amen.

✞

Seeing the Whole Field

Psalms 119:18 ***Open my eyes so I can see what you show me of your miracle-wonders.***

In the sports world, being able to see the field is truly a gift. We all know that the most successful players see the whole field and that they can see what might happen even before it happens. Often, a coach can check off and do something different just by seeing the field and the other team's alignment. The truth is that the best players and coaches see what will happen before it even happens, and they respond instinctively. Some people say it is like they have eyes in the back of their head. When I first started helping with contemporary worship, one of the songs we sang almost every week was the song "Open the Eyes of My Heart Lord." Now, I sang that song but never really thought about how significant those words really were and what I was truly asking to happen in my life. The truth is that our eyes are the window to the soul.

How we see the world directly affects how we treat those that are in the world. To open the eyes of my heart is to ask God to let me see the world and see people as he sees people. God sees people differently than we do because he created all people. Most of the time, we judge people based on their skin color or what they wear. We judge people based on their zip code or their education level. You see, when we say, "open the eyes of my heart Lord," we are asking God to make us susceptible to being changed and to see the world differently than we have ever seen it before. The truth is that when we see people, God wants us to see him. He wants us to move to a place that breaks our heart for the least, the last, and the lost. God wants us to see his world as a good coach or player sees the field. He wants us to see who our neighbor is and how it is we might love them. When you see the world as God sees the world, it allows you to be more engaged with the world and the Great Commission that God called us to. Let me ask you, how do you see your team? This is a good place for you to ask God to open the eyes of your heart. I bet as you pray for your eyes to be opened, you will begin to see your teammates differently. So open the eyes of your heart, and I will see you at the plate.

Dear Jehovah-Chereb,

Open my eyes that I may see. Open my heart so that I may see. Open my soul that I may see. The reason that I pray this prayer is so that by the opening of my eyes, I will see others as you see them, and others will see you through me. Open the eyes of my heart Jehovah. Open these blind eyes to see.

Day 258

The Hay Is in the Barn

Proverbs 2:1-2 ***My Son, if you accept my words and store up my commands within you, turning your ear to wisdom and applying your heart to understanding…***

Have you ever felt like you could have done more to prepare for what you are getting ready to undertake? I remembered a few months ago I was getting ready to ride a century ride. At breakfast that morning, I was talking to a guy that was very anxious about whether he could finish the century ride or not. He was stating how he wished he had done more long rides coming into this event. He commented he wished he would have ridden more outside and less inside on his stationary trainer. Now the truth is that he could wish all of those things, but the ride was today, and the "hay was in the barn." This is a statement often used in sports to express that the preparation is finished. Towson State's head football Coach Albert used to say, "The hay's in the barn." He meant all the hard work was done, and all they had to do now was go out and compete. This statement leads to the fact that we can no linger in thought about our preparation and must shift our focus to the race or event at hand. We have to shift our thinking from what we did not do to what we have done to get to this moment. This statement is not only important to our athletic endeavors, but it is also pertinent to our spiritual life. See, in our spiritual life, "hay" is our spiritual discipline. The reading of the word, memorization of Scripture, and diligent prayer time. Now the "barn" is represented by what we have stored in our hearts. Have we treasured up those training events to be ready when asked to witness or speak out for Jesus? See, we make many excuses as to why we should have spent more time in Scripture and prayer, but none of them are good excuses. The truth is that we chose to do something else, yet nothing is more important than our relationship with our Father. Listen, in our spiritual life, just like our athletic life; we cannot skim. The truth is that our devotion to God and our training for the team are how we put hay in the barn. If there is no hay in the barns, the animals will go hungry when those cold winter days come. Maybe we are sometimes spiritually hungry because we have not put our hay in the barn. Let me ask you what you have done today to put hay in the barn, and I will see you at the plate.

Dear Jehovah-Tsori,

I cannot worry about what did or did not happen yesterday. I can only embrace today, and if today is the day of the performance, then the hay is in the barn, and it is time to put my training into effect. If I worry about my yesterdays, then I will never have accomplished my today or tomorrow. God, if I have not prepared, then I pray that you will help me through the power of the Holy Spirit to fill in the gaps. As far as my salvation, Jesus put that hay in the barn when he went to the cross for me, and so the one thing I never need to worry about is how much you love me. Amen.

Day 259

No Pain, No Gain

2 Timothy 2:8-10 (NEV) ***Remember Jesus Christ, risen from the dead, the offspring of David, as preached in my gospel, for which I am suffering, bound with chains as a criminal. But the word of God is not bound! Therefore, I endure everything for the sake of the elect, that they also may obtain the salvation that is in Christ Jesus with eternal glory.***

Several years ago, I owned a gym shirt that said, "No Pain, No Gain." It was a shirt that represented lifting weights, but it was Jesus lifting the cross with anguishing pain upon his face. The truth is that weightlifting requires that one goes through a great deal of pain. I have seen some of the ugliest faces in the world in the gym when people were pushing past the point of no return. Most of you are also familiar with this statement, "pain is just weakness leaving the body." If we are going to be the best we can be, then the truth is that we have to be willing to push our bodies past the point of our pain threshold. We are pushing harder so that we can get bigger, faster, and stronger. See, you are breaking the body down so that you can build it back up. You have to think this way one more sprint, one more rep, one more box jump. I recently saw a video of Jalen Hurts, the transfer quarterback now at Oklahoma. The video is him after a game, still in uniform, working out after the game. That is someone who embraces the pain of the game so that they can win. Now, this not only applies to sports, but it also shows up in every aspect of our life. To grow spiritually, our faith must be tested. No one ever grew in faith by things just coming up candy and rainbows. No, faith under fire is where it is refined and strengthened into true faith. We have to engage in situations that are beyond our own understanding and control. This is where we allow God to step in, which is sometimes painful but is so rewarding. In our relational life, as it relates to those around us, we must also experience pain. This pain comes from putting others first, which can be very painful as others may not reciprocate the notion. There is also the pain of saying, "I was wrong." There is also the pain of forgiving even when the other person does not deserve it. Healthy relationships are fostered through pain. What about growing mentally? This may involve the pain of learning something that is difficult or brand new. If we are going to grow mentally, we need to challenge our brains to think about new things and things that seem so challenging that they seem impossible. It is here once again that we must rely on God to help us grasp our new learning endeavors. Finally, we must grow emotionally, and we do this through the practice of empathy. Not feeling sorry for but understanding what people are going through based on their circumstances. This means connecting with someone on a different level, and it requires time, effort, and sometimes emotional pain. The truth is that to be a well-rounded person in every phase of our physiology, we have to experience pain. Listen, Jesus experienced greater pain than we will ever feel as he was beaten, scourged, and nailed to the cross. But he would still tell you today you were worth his pain. So, remember no pain, no gain, but also remember his pain was your gain. See you at the plate.

Dear Crucified Lord and Savior,

Thank you that you are there with us amid our pain. You truly set the bar for no pain, no gain as it related to the cross. Because of sin, we will always experience pain, but we know that those that believe in the name of Jesus will one day be set free from all pain and anguish. Amen.

✞

Day 260

No Pain, No Power

John 19:10-11 ***Do you refuse to speak to me?" Pilate said. "Don't you realize I have power either to free you or to crucify you?" Jesus answered, "You would have no power over me if it were not given to you from above. Therefore, the one who handed me over to you is guilty of a greater sin."***

The other day I was hanging out in my local coffee shop, and a lady walked in with a Nike shirt with the slogan across the front that reads "No Pain, No Power." Now I must admit that this was confusing because I did not know how pain and power coincide. God speaks to me in the weirdest places, but that is what makes following God so interesting. Just yesterday, we talked about no pain, no gain, but I was still stumped about how pain and power were related. So, in doing some research, I found that the slogan referred to the pain of falling, not necessarily physically falling but falling from a place of position. When we think that we are the real deal or think we have arrived, those are the times when we need to feel the pain of being dethroned so that we can once again come back to reality. This gives us the power to not just prop ourselves up on our strength, but it is where we learn that when we find ourselves in pain, we find power in Jesus Christ. Sometimes we need to use the humbling situations of losing a starting position or suffering a loss to realize that we are powerless in some situations. Some things are just out of our control, but it is there that we can find power in the cross. Yes, this is where that slogan truly hit me.

I cannot imagine the pain that was associated with the crucifixion of Jesus. But it was through that crucifixion that a greater power than had ever been seen was now available for everyone. The power of the cross extends anything that we can understand. Just before Jesus was crucified, he stood in front of Pilate. Pilate asked him who he really was and what were his true intentions. Pilate then says, "do you know that I have the power to release you." I love Jesus' response; he does not defend himself but simply says, "you do not have any power, but only my God in heaven is powerful." Jesus was saying; you have no power over me. He reminded Pilate that God had put him in this position, and there would be great power from the crucifixion. I thank God that power came from the cross and not from a throne or place of position. No Pain, No Power, keep that in mind, and I will see you at the plate.

God of the Powerless,

So often, we find ourselves powerless against some of the things that we find ourselves up against. We sometimes find ourselves powerless in our health battles. Sometimes we are powerless over how other people treat us. Sometimes we are powerless against those that are in charge or are in places of position. But when we experience pain, it is there that we find power. Our power comes from the cross. Amen.

Day 261

Under Pressure

Mark 6:30-31 ***"The apostles gathered around Jesus and reported to Him all that they had done and taught. He said to them, 'Come away by yourselves to a remote place and rest for a while.'"***

Can you imagine being 19 years old and playing a top ten SEC matchup under the pressure of 90,000 fans in a place they call the swamp? That is exactly what Bo Nix did this past Saturday night. Now, I wish I could tell you that he handled the pressure well and led the team to a big victory, but the truth is that he had a hard time handling the pressure. There was the pressure of a rancid crowd, the pressure of 300-pound linemen pressing in on him, and the pressure that comes with being the team leader at such a young age. The truth is that a quarterback in the SEC has the weight of the world on their shoulders. The pressure got to Bo Nix in such a way that he threw three interceptions. He had never thrown that many interceptions in a game. There were times during the game. I thought the coach should make a change for a few series just to allow him to breathe, but for some reason, he left him in the fire. Maybe the coach's reasoning was because he knew there would be other big games coming up with huge amounts of pressure and that being in the heat of pressure is a refiner for later games.

After the game, the dreaded social media came out in droves to criticize his play and the loss. They talked about him not being ready and being a freshman. Now all that is true, but not one of those people who made those comments can even be on the field, not to mention that many have never been under such intense pressure. It is easy to sit on the sidelines and criticize or be the armchair quarterback because you do it from comfortable conditions and not extreme pressure. The truth is that in sports, it is not only being able to manage the game, but it is being able to manage the pressure that comes from it. Now I can tell you that Bo will be alright. He will handle the negativity that will be pushed his way, coming back strong and courageous. I know this because he is more than an SEC football player, he is a follower of Jesus Christ, and his acceptance does not come from the people in the stands but comes from the Lord above.

As you read this story, have you thought about the times in life when you faced adverse pressure? Maybe you are under huge amounts of pressure right now. Here is what you need to do, you need to get by yourself, and you need to take a break; and rest and reflect. Here, you will find the strength to get through the pressure and the angst associated with poor performance. The Disciples had been out witnessing, healing, and driving out demons in today's Scripture. They had been under a great deal of pressure and even persecution from the surrounding opponents of Jesus. When they came to Jesus with a report of all the great things they had done, he immediately identified that they needed to take a break from the pressure. The truth is that even if we handle the pressure well and come out in victory, we still need to remove ourselves from the pressure for a while. God wants us to take a moment out of the pressure so he can once again remind us that the weight of the world is not on our shoulders but was taken off our shoulders when Jesus bore the cross on his shoulders. Now that you have had some rest and a break from the pressure, I will see you at the plate.

Dear God of Sabbath and Rest,

God, sometimes the pressure is just too much to handle. We love to criticize others when they fail under pressure, but we want the world to leave us alone when we are crushed under pressure. God helps us think before we criticize those who give their all but fail because of the intense pressure. God help me know when to walk away from even the limelight so that I can rest and escape the pressure of everyday life and hear you say the words, I love you, my child.

Day 262

Setting Goals

I Corinthians 9:24-26 ***Do you not know that in a race all the runners run, but only one gets the prize? Run in such a way as to get the prize. Everyone who competes in the games goes into strict training. They do it to get a crown that will not last, but we do it to get a crown that will last forever. Therefore I do not run like someone running aimlessly; I do not fight like a boxer beating the air.***

This week, we will spend some time looking at goals and why goals are vital for thriving in life, in sports, and in your walk with God. Now the first thing to realize is that goals must be realistic and attainable. Goals are real obstacles that we set in order to achieve something greater than what we think we can achieve. When we set goals, it keeps us focused on the task at hand. A few years ago, I got a call from a guy that had been in one of my previous churches. He called to tell me that he had completed the goal that I set for the church. He explained that I had challenged the congregation about eight years ago to read through the whole Bible. Now, I thought that I had specified to read it in a year, but it had taken this guy eight years. He explained that he started reading but wanted to study and not just read, so it took him eight years, but he finished the goal. To complete your goals, you must push through adversity and obstacles that will pull you away from your focus.

Another thing that is essential to achieving goals is having a short memory. This means that when you have a bad day, a bad game, or just really mess up in your spiritual walk, you do not dwell on the mistake but forget it and move forward. Now what we will be focusing on this week are these three components as it relates to goals. **Here is what we will cover: Clarity, Alignment, Movement, and Focus**. The truth is that with these four components, you can achieve your goals and go beyond what you could have imagined. Now I want you to ask yourself these questions as we start this week. What is my first and foremost goal? Have I set short-term and long-term goals? Have I prayed through my goals? This is the most essential element if you are going to achieve what you have dreamed of. So, this week set your goals, and then I will see you at the plate.

Dear All-Sufficient One,

So many times, I have failed because I took my eyes off the goal. I have also failed in my walk with you because I took my eyes off you and what it is that you had prepared for me. This week help me to focus on pushing through when things are tough. Help me to see that to give in is to give the devil a foothold in my life. Help me to see with clarity, to align my life with you, to not just talk about it but really move through it. And finally, help me focus on what you did for me and what I can do for the Kingdom of God. Let my goals align with your goals for my life. Amen.

✞

Day 263

Clarity: Seeing My Goals Before Setting Them

Jeremiah 33:3 "***Call to me, and I will answer you and tell you great and unsearchable things you do not know.***"

One of the vital things to reach any goal is knowing which direction to travel to reach it. So often, we set out without a destination or without planning. One of my favorite quotes is, "no one plans to fail, but few people plan so they do not fail." We must have clarity in our direction and our goals. Have you ever heard someone speak, and you were more confused after they tried to explain something? I often say, well, that was "as clear as mud." Clarity is not only important as it pertains to long-term goals but is also vital as it relates to short-term goals. Every day you should be getting better than you were the day before. One way about having clarity in goals is to write them down and read through them every day. Check off the ones we have achieved and then celebrate, but do not get lost in the celebration, or you will wander from your clarity of the other goals. Clarity is also praying that God will give you the vision to see as he wants you to see and not as you want to see.

There is a great story in Mark 8:22-26 about Jesus healing a man's eyes to give him clarity. He is in Bethsaida, and he runs into a blind man; then, he leads the man out of the village. Why take him out of the village? Because he wanted him to be free of all distractions. Then Jesus spits on his eyes, lays hands on them, and asks, what do you see? The man said, "He saw people, but they were not clear; they were as trees walking around." Then Jesus lays his hands on him a second time, and he is then able to see and see with "clarity." Jesus used this miracle to show his disciples and those around him that they see, but one day, they would see with absolute clarity. They would see what his sacrifice would mean for their salvation and the forgiveness of their sins. Jesus did not want them to just see but to see with clarity and vision. He did not want anything to be muddled as to how one achieves eternal life. Jesus reached his goal because of the clarity that he had as he journeyed to the cross. Clarity will also help you to reach your goals and aspirations. So it is time to see with clarity, and I will see you at the plate.

Dear God of Vision and Clarity,

Help me to see with clarity. So often, the world seems to be foggy and hazy, but your word is very clear as to how to navigate the fog. Let me follow your word as it is the direction that you would have me lead my life. God, place your hands upon my eyes so that I will not look upon those things that cloud my judgment and harden my heart. Let me see the cross with clarity as it is clear what the cross has done for me. God, I give my life to you. Amen.

Day 264

Proper Alignment

I Peter 4:1-2 ***Therefore, since Christ suffered in his body, arm yourselves also with the same attitude because whoever suffers in the body is done with sin. As a result, they do not live the rest of their earthly lives for evil human desires, but rather for the will of God.***

A few months ago, I bought a used car that my son is going to drive. When I drove it off the lot, the motor and all the mechanics were in good working order, but the front end was out of alignment, and the tires were also out of alignment. It was one of the roughest rides I had ever experienced driving it home. The next week I had all that adjusted, and the front end realigned, and it ran so smooth. I tell you this because one of the other things that a team must have in place if it is going to reach its goals is proper alignment. You can have a team of all blue-chip, 5-star athletes, but you will struggle to reach your goals no matter how talented you are if you do not have the proper alignment. Proper alignment is essential if you are going to perform at a peak level. This means that you not only have talented players, but you have players that play well together. You must have the right leadership in place and have players willing to accept their role on the team. Some people would refer to this as team chemistry. The other thing that a team must do is align themselves to the goals they want to achieve.

It truly must be an all-in concept. They must work with and towards each other, not against one another. Author and Pastor Andy Stanley calls this the Principle of the Path, which is a book that you may want to read. This path principle is summed up like this: "Direction, not desire, determines destination."[24] In other words, we are all going to end up somewhere, so we probably should go down the path that will get us to where we want to end up. Another quote that goes along with this principle is that everybody ends up somewhere, but few people end up somewhere on purpose. This means that we must align ourselves with one another to achieve the goals that have been set before us. In our daily walk, God has given us an example to align our lives with, and that example is Jesus. So, let me ask you if your life is aligned with Christ because no matter what happens in this life, you will be aligned in the one to come. So, check your alignment, and I will see you at the plate.

Dear Jehovah-Hashopet,

Thank you for giving me your Son to align my life with. I know that when I get out of balance that your Son helps to realign my priorities and values. I also know that if we are going to be successful in life and sports, we have to align ourselves with one another and not fight against one another. Jesus aligned himself with the cross that took away the sins of the whole world, so how can I not align my life with his. Lord, align my life with the cross, Amen.

Day 265

Movement Matters

Proverbs 16:27 (TLB) ***Idle hands are the devil's workshop; idle lips are his mouthpiece.***

The next concept involved in achieving goals is that you must have movement. You must be moving in order to get somewhere. You cannot be stationary and get to where you are going. Movement must also be fluid and in sync. A few years ago, they introduced a new swimming sport in the Olympics known as synchronized swimming. The synchronized swimming movements are done in the water, and every swimmer is doing the same movement together in perfect synchronization. It truly looks like poetry in motion. Now I know for a fact I could not be a synchronized swimmer because I cannot even get the movements down to the line dance, "The Electric Slide."

Now back to movement. Movement is really what propels you from one point to another. Have you ever seen a team that was struggling, and then they will get a turnover, and you hear the game announcer say, "that is going to swing the momentum?" The truth is that movement creates momentum. In the team concept, if everyone is not moving in sync, there is a breakdown in the fluid movement. Movement also keeps people moving through to reach the next level. Movement is where you get better and are inching closer to reaching the goals you have set. In the Scripture, Jesus was always in motion and constantly moving. It was essential to his ministry that he keeps moving toward the cross. On one occasion, Jesus, Peter, James, and John were led up a mountain, and there they met Moses and Elijah. Peter sees this place as the pinnacle, but Jesus knows that to reach his goal, he must keep with the movement of the Father. So they come off of the mountain to keep moving. Like Peter, we can often be tricked into thinking that we have arrived when God wants us to keep moving. Remember, when we are idle is when the evil one can attack us the most. So, let's get moving, and I will see you at the plate.

Dear God of Transfiguration,

In order to get to where we want to go, we must be moving. Movement is the sign that we are alive. Keep in mind that so many people are not truly living because they are not moving. Lord, keep my hands in your service and my lips singing your praise so that I do not find my heart idle. Thank you that your Son kept moving so that when my hands get idle, I can be reminded that he loved me so much that he died for me. I do not deserve what he did for me, but that is grace, and for that, I thank you, and I love you.

✞

Day 266

Staying Focused

Proverbs 16:3 ***Commit your work to the Lord, and your plans will be established.***

When we think about the word Focus, we often think solely in terms of eye-related vision. A few years ago, I decided to buy some new glasses. The optometrist suggested that I get progressive lenses. These are set up for people with different types of vision in each eye. They are set up to read up close and to see far away. I ordered them, and when they came in, I put them on, and everything went blurry. Not only did it go blurry, but I felt dizzy and totally out of focus. It took several weeks for my eyes to adjust and know whether I needed them for distance or reading. Eventually, my eyes learned to move to the part of the lenses that they needed so that everything came into focus. Now focus is about making sure you can see with clarity, but the true focus goes a step further than this.

Clarity means saying "no" to almost everything else so that you can achieve your goals. The world is great about pulling us away from our focus. How many times have you set down to check an email or Facebook and an hour later realize that you have been taken off task and that you have lost focus? How many times in life have you set a goal but allowed friends or life situations to pull your focus away from the task at hand? See, the sobering fact is that "distraction" is the nemesis of focus. See, in order to keep our focus on the cross of Jesus Christ, we must purposely let the things of this world fade out. How does this happen? It comes from focus because focus comes from discipline. This means we train our eyes to see where we are headed, and we do everything in our power to stay focused on goals. This means that we focus on God and not on our circumstances. It means that prayer becomes a priority, and so does getting into the Word of God. This will clarify the focus on the movement that God has aligned us with to reach our goals. Focus means saying no to everything that gets in the way of our goals on the field and everything that gets in the way of our relationship with Jesus. So, let me ask you, are you focused; I mean, really focused? If not, get focused, and I will see you at the plate.

Dear God of Light,

Help me to focus on the task at hand. The world wants to pull me away from my goals and from my relationship with Jesus. Keep me from all distractions that hinder my relationship with my Savior. So often, the devil tries to lead me into the darkness so that everything becomes dim and blurry. But you are God of light and not of darkness, and I ask that you illuminate my path. You are the God of focus, and I thank you for that. Amen.

✞

Day 267

On the Field, Off the Field

Ephesians 5:15 (ESV) ***So be careful to live your life wisely, not foolishly.***

I read an article yesterday about a college football player that led his team in sacks last year but has not recorded a sack through 7 games this year and has only played sporadically. The article also stated that he had not even seen the field in the game the day before. The article quotes his head coach as saying, "that the player must get his act together on the field as well as off of the field." One of my coaches used to say, "boys, you have to handle your business off the field so that you can handle your business on the field." I cannot tell you how many great athletes I have seen forfeit their right to play because of off-the-field behavior or poor school performance. Listen, the truth is that you are a student-athlete, not an athlete-student. The other thing is that you represent your team, whether on the field or off the field. The truth is that you must be committed to the team in every aspect. You must always remember that the butterfly effect is especially true when it comes to the team. What you do affects not only you, but it affects others. You must realize that to take care of business, you must make sure that you are doing what represents your name, your team's name, and God's name all the time. One of my favorite Scriptures in Ephesians (5:15) is a reminder of who we represent; this passage is where Paul warns the church that people are watching and learning from them. He says they should write this on their hearts, so be careful to live your life wisely, not foolishly. So often, if we would just stop and ask, how will this make my witness look, we would not make some of the decisions that keep us off the field. See, you can be a great player but make poor decisions that keep you from ever using the talents that God has given you. So, let me ask, are you making wise decisions off the field and on the field? My prayer is that you are so that I will see you at the plate.

Dear Author of Life,

I have to realize that because of my position, people are watching me. That means I have to exemplify Christ in everything I do. There have been so many times that I have tainted my witness because of not handling my business on and off the field. I have so sinned against you, but you have repaired, restored, and reaffirmed my relationship with you through the death of Jesus. God help me to be the example that you want me to be.

Day 268

Are You Willing to Sacrifice?

Hebrews 13:15-16 ***Through Jesus, therefore, let us continually offer to God a sacrifice of praise—the fruit of lips that openly profess his name. And do not forget to do good and to share with others, for with such sacrifices God is pleased.***

In order to be successful, one will have to sacrifice. I have mentioned this before in a devotional, but if you are going to reach your goals, you will have to say "no" to almost everything else. Sacrifice is just part of the process if you are going to be elite or you are going to reach what goals you have set. You may have to sacrifice time with your friend, video games, or time spent sitting watching television. You may also sacrifice sleeping in and eating anything you want. If you are going to be truly successful, you must sacrifice what the world is unwilling to sacrifice. The truth is that nothing comes easy. NBA Hall of Famer Kareem Abdul-Jabbar was quoted as saying, "I think that the good and the great are only separated by the willingness to sacrifice." The question that you must ask yourself is what I am willing to give up to reach my goals. The story of Cain and Able at the beginning of Genesis shows us the difference between one who was willing to sacrifice and one that was holding back. See, Abel brought his best and chosen animal sacrifice and presented it to God. He gave up what was pleasing to his eye so that he could give it to God. What he did was truly a sacrifice. But Cain gave what was leftover. He was not willing to sacrifice his best for God. He held back, and this is what displeased God. In this story, we see one brother willing to sacrifice and the other brother who gave it no thought. Now fast forward to the New Testament on a hill on Calvary. God did not hold back his best from us, but he sacrificed his only Son so that those who believe in him would have everlasting life. The thought of that sacrifice should give us the fortitude to sacrifice so that we can be who God has called us to be. Let me ask you what you are willing to sacrifice so I can see you at the plate?

Dear God of Love and Sacrifice,

Thank you for the ultimate sacrifice that was your Son. He was blameless and sinless, and yet he died for such a sinner as I. How can I not sacrifice after all that you have sacrificed for me? God help me to give up what hinders me from being who you have called me to be. God let me realize that the sacrifice today will reap rewards tomorrow. Amen.

Day 269

I Am the Underdog

1 Peter 2:9 (NLT) ***But you are not like that, for you are a chosen people. You are royal priests, a holy nation, God's very own possession. As a result, you can show others the goodness of God, for he called you out of the darkness into his wonderful light.***

When I was a child, a cartoon came on every Saturday entitled "Underdog." The cartoon was about a crime-fighting dog that wore a red cape with a "U" on it. Several years later, a contemporary Christian group Audio Adrenaline came out with a song entitled "Underdog." (You may want to listen to this song.) The chorus talked about being beat down and broken. It talked about being put facedown to the ground. See, when we are facedown, there is only one way to go, and that is up. The same is true of an underdog; for the underdog to gain respect, they must fight from their knees. You can call me the underdog, but God has a habit of using underdogs; just look throughout the Scripture.

The truth is that most of us love to see the underdog win. It is even better when we are the underdog. In life, most of the time, we are the underdog because of the constant attacks from the evil ones. But just like in the song, life is not about running the race but who we pick to run the race with us. See, a winner is not judged by his small size but by the substitute he picks to run the race of life, and I am a winner because of what Jesus did for me. See, you need to realize that God is running with you. He won this race a long time ago when he defeated Satan at Calvary. Yes, most people counted Moses as an underdog, but he led the people through the desert and right up to the Promise Land. Most people counted David as the underdog, but he defeated Goliath, and most of the religious leaders counted Jesus as the underdog. But no one considered that all of these men knew God, and God is always standing with the underdog. Hey, you may be the underdog, but you got someone running with you; you have the power of the Holy Spirit, so with his help, I will see you at the plate.

Dear Empowering God,

I may be an underdog, but I know someone who is not. I know someone that has already completed this race, and now they are running with me. The world is surely against me, but I have a friend that has conquered the world and has brought me out of the darkness of being an underdog and into the light of being a champion. Come, Holy Spirit, run with me and run for me.

Day 270

More than Anything Else

Psalms 16:11 ***You will show me the way of life, granting me the joy of your presence and the pleasures of living with you forever.***

If someone asks, what do you want more than anything else? What would your response be? For most athletes, it will revolve around playing at the next level or winning a championship. The truth is that in our minds, we have dreamed of the day where we would have the opportunity to be in a position to bring home the championship. But as we get older and mature, we begin to realize that what we need more than anything else is our relationship with Jesus Christ. Case Keenum led one of the greatest comebacks in NFL history. "Gun buffalo right key left seven heaven." [25]That was the name of the pass play that went to Stephon Diggs to seal the comeback victory against the Saints. Keenum still finds himself stunned by the ending of that nail-biter. "You talk about the best moment? It was an unbelievable moment," Keenum said. "I still don't believe it sometimes that it happened. It was so crazy." After the game, Case was asked about the play, and the reporter asked if this was the greatest thing that had ever happened to him. "Is this the best moment in your life?" Now Case explains this was truly a defining moment, but the greatest moment in life was when he accepted Christ. His response to the reporter was this, "The greatest day was the day I opened my heart and asked Jesus to be my Savior." He explains that loving Jesus is what he wanted more than anything else. It is so easy for us to get so caught up in the moment that we forget what we need more than anything else. The truth is that all the accomplishments that we achieve on this earth will pass away or be forgotten. That is why it is so important that we keep in perspective what we need. We need Jesus. When Jesus becomes what we want more than anything else, it centers us on when we win the big game or lose the heartbreaker. Championships and promotion at work or receiving a scholarship are things that bring joy to our life. But none of these things can replace what you need more than anything else, and that is that you pray the prayer to ask Jesus to come into your heart. SO, now you know what you need more than anything else, I will see you at the plate.

Dear God of Abundance,

Help me realize that this world's things are great achievements but that there is something so much more. Help me to remember that I must seek you daily. Help me to love you more than anything else. Help me to realize that you loved me so much that you sent your Son. Humble me to be in love with you even more than with the things of this earth.

Day 271

Playing for Encouragement

Proverbs 27:6 ***Wounds from a friend can be trusted, but an enemy multiplies kisses.***

Do you play the game because you want accolades, or do you play the game because you love it? I cannot imagine being the quarterback of a Power 5 college football team and all the criticism that comes your way when you do not play well or win a game that you were supposed to win. The addition of social media has allowed so much more criticism to come to those that lead their team. The truth is that many times if we are playing for the approval of the crowd, then we are playing for the wrong reason. I believe that many young people are incapable of turning off the noise. I think that is why it is so important to find your worth in Christ and not in the world. The truth is that this world will turn on you like a rabid animal. I tell people that you need to surround yourself with believers because they are praying people, and I would much rather surround myself with people who pray for me than people who talk about me. So often, those around us are wolves in sheep's clothing. The other thing that can center us is that we need people who will speak the truth in love. We need people to remind us of why we play and for who we play. Sometimes what will help us from playing to the beat of the applause is "tough love." We need someone who will be honest with us and still loves us at the same time. This reminds me of Jesus asking the disciples one time how much longer they were going to doubt before they got it.

In Matthew 17, the disciples are unable to heal a boy, and the father comes to Jesus, and he heals the boy. It is at this point that Jesus looks at his disciples, and he says to them, "you unbelieving and perverse generation," Jesus continued, "how long shall I stay with you? How long shall I put up with you? Bring the boy here to me." Jesus then rebuked the demon, and it came out of the boy, and he was healed at that moment. You see, we need to surround ourselves with people who will speak the truth into us and challenge us to play the game for the right reasons. We play the game so that we hear the applause of heaven and not the applause of man. So, let me ask you this, who are you playing for? I will see you at the plate.

Dear God of Heaven and Earth,

Please surround me with people that will speak the truth into me. Remind me that I play for your applause and not the applause of the crowd. The crowd will turn on me, but you will never turn on me. Help me to remember that I started playing this game because I loved it. God, I love you with all my heart so that I will play for you, and through my play, may your glory be revealed. Amen.

✞

Day 272

Grace: It Is Not Fair

Ephesians 2:8-9 ***For it is by grace you have been saved, through faith—and this is not from yourselves, it is the gift of God- not by works, so that no one can boast.***

I have mentioned this before but want to say it again. Life is not fair, and we need to thank God for that. This week we will be talking about the most unfair concept in the world but greatly benefits you. This week we will look at "Grace." Grace is unmerited and undeserved, but it cost Jesus everything.

One of the hardest concepts for athletes is the concept of "grace." The reason that this is so hard is that athletes are used to having to earn something. Athletes live under the theme that nothing comes easy or is free. We earn our way onto the team; we earn a scholarship, starting position, and all-area or all-conference honors. The truth is that sports is about earning and grace is about something being given to us. That concept is so hard because we feel like if we are going to receive something, we should have to earn it. Grace is also for everyone and not for just the select few.

Christ said that he came to die for all. In Timothy, Paul says, "Christ Jesus came into the world to save sinners – of whom I am the worst." The worst means you are not deserving; you have not earned it. Think about being the worst on the team and the coach calling out awards at the end of the season banquet and him telling you that you just received an "All-American Award." You say, 'but coach, I did not play one play this season." He then looks at you and says, "I know, but Jesus did, and it is his grace that gave you this award." The rest of the team will look at you and think it is not fair, and it is not fair. But grace does not play by our rules. Grace is what levels the playing field in the eyes of our Creator and Savior. I often tell my kids when they say life is not fair, "that I know life is not fair, and one day you will be so glad of that because what you deserve you will not receive, and what you do not deserve you will receive. See, the greatest need that we do not realize in life is our need for his grace. Christianity is truly the only religion that has grace as the premise for all of its doctrine. A Savior that came seeking us and then died for us before we were even born. This week we are going to look at five Scriptures that point us toward God's grace. Now, remember, one day, you will be so happy that life is not fair. I will see you at the plate.

Jehovah-M'gaddishcem - Lord my Sanctifier,

Life is not fair because I will not get what I deserve and what I do not deserve, I will inherit eternal life. You made sure of that through the death of your Son Jesus. I am so thankful that life is not fair because there is no way I can be good enough to earn what you have given me. What is not fair is that it cost you everything, but then again, that is how much you love me.

✞

Day 273

Grace: Sufficiently Supplied

2 Corinthians 12:9 ***"But he said to me, 'My grace is sufficient for you, for my power is made perfect in weakness.'"***

In the sports world, sometimes, we are just outmanned. I mean, we just do not match up well with our opponent. I remember my sophomore year in college, we were playing Earlham College, and the guy I would be facing all day on the defensive line was a Kodak All-American. He was bigger than I was, and he was stronger than I was; as a matter of fact, he was just better than I was. I wish I could say that I handled him, but the truth is, all day, I had trouble blocking him. Sometimes when we have a day like this, we just need to remember that God's grace is sufficient for us. So often in life, we find ourselves with our backs against the wall. Sometimes because of life's situations, we find ourselves in the midst of weakness. Sometimes it is because of a lack of preparation, but sometimes it is just because the other opponent is better. Now we have to remember that we will live to play another day, and we will have the opportunity to get better. We must also remember that God's grace is sufficient for us, and that promise in and of itself helps us get through those days when we just get whooped.

In the Scripture, we see where Paul has endured many hardships for the sake of the call and is at the point of exhaustion. As a matter of fact, Paul pleads with God to take it away. It is a thorn in his flesh that is a constant nag and aggravating issue. This is where Paul uses the phrase, "but my grace is sufficient for you." Paul is quoting the words that God gave him in his situation. See, when we find ourselves in our weakest moments, God reminds us that His grace is sufficient for us and that we will see his power in the midst of our weakness. God wants us to tap into his power when we feel as if we cannot push through. See, we may be defeated on the field, but we will never be defeated when it comes to our salvation. May God be your strength, and I will see you at the plate.

Gracious Loving God,

Your grace is sufficient in the failures of my life. Sometimes I just go in my own way and do not follow you, but your grace is sufficient. Some days I sin knowingly, and your grace is sufficient. One day I will die, and your grace will be sufficient. Thank you for the sufficient grace of your Son and my savior Jesus Christ.

✞

Day 274

Grace: It Is Justified

Romans 3:24-25 ***Being justified freely by His grace through the redemption that is in Christ Jesus, whom God set forth as a propitiation by His blood, through faith, to demonstrate His righteousness, because in His forbearance God had passed over the sins that were previously committed.***

When we think of the word justified, we tend to lean toward getting back or getting even with someone because of something they have done to us. How many times in a game have you seen a player push a player, the player retaliates, and the player that was just responding to getting pushed gets the penalty thrown against them? The truth is that we were justified in pushing them back, but it still is wrong. If we let anger harbor itself in our spirit long enough, we will eventually think that we are justified to take action against the person that wronged us. Sometimes we call this harboring anger. But in the Scripture, being justified has a very different meaning. Being justified in God's terms means that rather than God harboring his anger against us for the sins we have committed, he writes them off. It is like writing all our sins on an etch-a-sketch and then just shaking it till they all disappear. It is not that we deserve this but that we are justified from our sin because of the death of Jesus Christ. We are set free from the sins that ensnare us and keep us from moving forward in our relationship with Christ. If not for justification, it would be impossible for us to have a relationship with God; our sin prevents that relationship.

God knew we would need justification before we ever knew what sin was or had even committed a sin. **Justifying Grace** is what fills in the gaps because we can never be good enough. "Justifying faith implies, not only a divine evidence or conviction that 'God was in Christ, but that he was reconciling the world unto himself,'" John Wesley writes in a sermon entitled, "Justification is by Faith, that faith is a sure trust and confidence that Christ died for 'my' sins, that he loved 'me,' and gave himself for 'me.' And at what time soever a sinner thus believes...God justified that ungodly one."[26] See what Justifying Grace requires of us is for us to believe it and accept it. Do you realize that you have been justified? Have you accepted that amazing grace that comes in the form of justification? If not, then accept it right now, and I will see you at the plate.

Dear Jehovah-Ganan - Lord Our Defense,

So often, I feel justified in my action to respond to someone hurting me. Sometimes I feel justified to sin because I feel I have earned the right. But justification comes through your spirit and not through my actions. Thank you that the death of your Son justified me and that I was able to make the decision to follow him so I could accept that justification.

Day 275

Grace: The Practice of Sanctification

Philippians 2:12-13 ***Therefore, my dear friends, as you have always obeyed—not only in my presence but now much more in my absence—continue to work out your salvation with fear and trembling, for it is God who works in you to will and to act according to his good purpose.***

The goal of practice and repetition is to get better. The truth is that without practice, you will never get better. In the sporting world, if you are standing still, then everyone else is passing you by. Practice can sometimes seem boring and mundane, but without pain, there is no gain. Practice requires effort, and it requires real commitment. As we have already stated, grace is a free offering, but it does require something of you. You see, justifying grace is an aha moment where you realize what Christ has done for you, but sanctifying grace is a process. It is a daily dying to self.

You see, grace does not want you to stay where you are. It accepts you where you are with the expectation that it will lead you into sanctification. Sanctification is the process of becoming more Christ-like. In the Wesley tradition, we know this as moving toward perfection. What could be a great concept for practice than moving toward perfection? You have heard it said practice makes perfect, but to take it a step further says that perfect practice makes perfect. Sanctification is not necessarily that you no longer need grace; it is just that now you are justified to recognize how sin affects your life and your relationship with Jesus.

When you practice, you not only learn what to do, you learn what not to do. You see, many times, our mistakes are out of ignorance. Sanctification helps us to come to the realization of what hinders us in our relationship with God. How do we practice this process of sanctification? We do so by spending quality time with God in prayer and in the word. God speaks to us through his word, but so few people take time to look at the playbook of life. Sanctification, also like practice, takes into account your past, your present, and your future. In practice, we need to know what we have failed in doing in the past or what bad habits we have picked up. Then we must change them in the present through practice, and finally, we will put what we have learned into practice to achieve greatness. The sanctification process will not be finished until we are called home and have completed the race. So now that you are being sanctified, I will see you at the plate.

Dear God of Sanctification,

Thank you for not leaving me where you found me. God, I am always in process, and I am moving closer to you through the process of sanctification. Please continue to help me in this process of moving toward perfection until the day I find myself in your presence.

Day 276

Grace: No Arrogance Allowed

James 4:6 ***"But he gives us more grace. That is why Scripture says: 'God opposes the proud but shows favor to the humble.'"***

One of the biggest distractions that players witness these days is the art of arrogance. I call it art because it almost seems rehearsed before it is played out. I would say that arrogance has ruined more careers than anything else. I would also say that I have met people who have destroyed their witness and testimony by their arrogance. In the Scriptures, Jesus truly opposed the Pharisees which were full of arrogance. They not only were religious in their minds, but they boasted of being the best and the greatest along with being the only ones chosen by God. The truth is that arrogance is a lot easier to live out than humbleness. I remember growing up in Louisville during the highlight of Muhamad Ali's outstanding boxing career. Now I liked Ali, and I would arguably say he was the greatest boxer ever. But I would say what Ali lacked was humility. As a matter of fact, he told himself and the world that he was the greatest before he had ever had a professional fight. The reality is people loved to hate Ali because of his arrogance. (They wound up loving him because of his boxing legacy.) No one would deny how good he was; it was just that not everybody wanted to hear how great he was. In today's sports world, cockiness combined with a high salary has promoted a whole new arrogance. So often, this example is passed down to even to the recreational level of sports. Why is arrogance so opposed to grace? Simply because grace is the opposite of being proud and puffed up. Grace comes in the form of humility and the ultimate act of sacrifice. We should practice humility because it has been given to us in the form of grace. Not only has grace been given, but it also keeps being extended every time we sin against our Father. When we practice humility after we make mistakes, it helps the world to give us some grace. Humility also helps us in our witness and how we see the world and other people. When we realize that we are saved by grace, it helps us be more patient with other people's mistakes and shortcomings. Humility also helps us pattern the life of Jesus, who never once said he was the greatest of all time but instead went to the cross to prove he was the greatest of all time. So now that you know who was the greatest of all time, I will see you at the plate.

Dear Greatest of All Time,

I am not great, but I know who is great, and that is you, my Lord, and my God. There are times when I am prideful and arrogant. There are times when I puff up and times when I think more highly of myself than I should. Humble me so that I live a life of humility. Let others see your humility through my humility. The greatest to ever live was the one that came to die, not to become King of the World. Amen.

Day 277

Don't Quit On Your Team

John 6:68 (ESV) ***Simon Peter answered him, "Lord, to whom shall we go? You have the words of eternal life…***

So, this week two second-team quarterbacks from two NCAA power five teams entered the transfer portal. (This means they want to transfer to another school.) Now what makes this interesting is that there are only four games left in the regular season. The reason for the transfer is that they were not getting enough playing time and did not see more playing time in the foreseeable future. But my question is, why do you leave in the middle of the year? I really think that qualifies as quitting on your team. I also think it is a very selfish move as others on the team have been relegated to the second team. Every player wants to start, and I understand they want to get playing time, but quitting in the middle of the year does not benefit you or your team. The truth is that you are one injury away from being the starter. The other thing is that when you quit, you are no longer getting reps at practice. You have also called into question your loyalty to the team and your loyalty to the process. Jalen Hurts, a prominent quarterback for the University of Alabama, lost his job to another quarterback, and he also transferred, but he did not quit on his team. He waited until the end of the year after graduation, and then he went to Oklahoma as a graduate transfer. He did things the right way, and his next year, he had his best year ever. We live in a world where we do not encourage sticking it out and not quitting on your team. It once again is part of the me-generation instead of a team generation. In the Scripture, there is a place where Jesus allows the Apostles the opportunity to quit. He had given some hard teaching to the crowd, and it says that day many of his followers left him, they essentially quit on him. He then turns to the apostles, and he says, "are you going to leave also?" To which Peter, their leader, says, "to whom would we go?" They refused to give up on Jesus even when the going got tough. Now, were there times when they wavered? Absolutely, but their commitment was evident in that 10 out of the remaining 11 were martyred while sharing the gospel. We must not quit on our team, but more importantly, we must not quit on Jesus, the author and perfecter of our faith. Listen, things that may not be going as you planned but do not quit on your team. I will see you at the plate.

Dear Lord of All People,

Thank you for not giving up on me. I have failed you more times than I can count. So, I have wavered in my faith many times, and I have thought about quitting, but then I see the cross – the cross that was endured for me and my sin. I cannot give up on someone that loved me that much. God, I will never quit on my team, and I will never quit on you.

Day 278

Beating the Odds

Judges 3:31 ***And after him was Shamgar the Son of Anath, which slew of the Philistines six hundred men with an ox goad: and he also delivered Israel.***

The Washington Nationals won game 7 of the World Series Wednesday night to win their first World Series Championship. Now what is interesting about the Nationals is that no one expected them to win the Championship. The truth is that not only were people against them, but the numbers were stacked against them. On May 23, 2019, they only had a 3.4% chance of making the playoffs. But they refused to look at the odds. They had to come out of the wild card bracket even to make the NLDS, and they only had an 11.6% chance of winning in the bottom of the 8th of the wild card game, but persevered and won that game to move on. Then they had to once again work some magic in the National League Division title game as they had a 9.7% chance of winning in the top of the 7th inning of the final game. Once again, they pulled it off. Finally, they stood one more time against the odds as they faced a 15%-win expectancy in game 7 of the World Series, down 2-0 in the 7th inning. Once again, they made sure that they did not quit and pushed through the odds to make history, winning 6-2.

The truth is that most athletes love to play against the odds. Being told that you cannot do something will push you to dig deeper and overcome adversity. We are also told that we may not ever amount to much or that the odds are against us in life. I have served as chaplain to three high school football teams, and many kids on those teams had been told that they would never amount to anything. I cannot tell you how often the kids refused to listen to the negativity or be a statistic. They rose above what most people thought they could do or be. The Lord does not play by the percentages; he plays by his grace and faith. You see, God is for you and not against you. You get to decide; you can be a statistic or defy the odds and be an anomaly for God. You must remember that God does not play by the odds. He feeds five thousand with five fish and two loaves. The truth is that God laughs at the odds. So, let me ask you, are the odds stacked against you? I mean, you have never got a hit off of this pitcher, and the odds are against you, but I will see you at the plate.

Dear God of All Possibilities,

I can expect great things from you, Lord, so let me attempt great things for you. We live in a dark time when the evil one seems to be getting all the victories. I serve a God who is greater than the evil one and greater than the odds stacked against us. So, let me not only believe but achieve so that the world will see your victory. Amen.

Day 279

"Go 1-0"

Judges 7:4-5 ***But the Lord said to Gideon, "There are still too many men. Take them down to the water, and I will thin them out for you there. If I say, 'This one shall go with you,' he shall go; but if I say, 'This one shall not go with you,' he shall not go." So Gideon took the men down to the water. There the Lord told him, "Separate those who lap the water with their tongues as a dog laps from those who kneel down to drink." Three hundred of them drank from cupped hands, lapping like dogs. All the rest got down on their knees to drink.***

On May 23rd, 2019, the Washington Nationals had a dismal record of 19-31; they had dug a hole that would seemingly be impossible to climb out of. So, their coach Dave Martinez began to preach a new mantra; his new mantra was, today, let's go, "1-0." He was trying to get them to not focus on the record, and where they had been, he was trying to get them to focus only on today. If they could just go 1-0 then today, they would be winners for at least today. If they kept going 1-0, then at some point, their losing record would become a winning record. That mantra stuck, and as we mentioned yesterday, they became the MLB World Champions. Sometimes we just need to go 1-0 for today. In several of the churches that I have served, we have had recovery ministry. Recovery ministry is tough because most of the people we see have been defeated and have been tossed aside by family and the world. They have failed over and over, and they just need a victory. They just need to win the battle today so that they can face another day tomorrow. The truth is that when they begin to go 1-0 day after day, those victories add up, and before you know it, you are winning the war of life by winning the daily battles. Sometimes when we feel defeated, we must begin to look at simple, realistic goals. If we can just win today, we just might get to tomorrow. In Judges, Gideon is outnumbered; he doubts he can win, but God tells him to cut his numbers instead of giving him more men to fight. Gideon started with 23,000 men, but God culled it down to 300 warriors. God did this so that he could go "1-0" for today. It does not make sense, but if God made sense, then he would not be God. If you have ever been in any playoff scenario, you know you cannot look ahead but must focus on the next team because one defeat will end your season. If you can just go "1-0," then you can live to play another day. Are you ready to go 1-0? If you are, then I will see you at the plate?

Dear God of Victories,

God, thank you for being on my side. You are always for me and not against me. So often, I think I must fight this fight on my own. Many times, I give it to you, and then I take it back. Today I need to go 1-0. If I can just win today, then I can fight again tomorrow. Thank you that your Son went 1-0 on Calvary so that I can go 1-0 today.

Day 280

Get Out of the Boat

Matthew 14:28-29 ***Lord, if it's you," Peter replied, "tell me to come to you on the water." "Come," he said. Then Peter got down out of the boat, walked on the water, and came toward Jesus. But when he saw the wind, he was afraid and, beginning to sink, cried out, "Lord, save me!"***

The other day while working on this devotional book, I was listening to Kutless. In their song, "What Faith Can Do," I heard these words, "Impossible is not a word. It's just an excuse for someone not to try or to do it (paraphrase)." How true is that when it comes to the sports world? People are told all the time that they are too slow, they are too small, and they are just not strong enough. Often, people deem their dreams as impossible, so they do not even try to defy the impossible. The truth is the world loves to see people fail because it makes them feel better about their failures. I remember a few years ago finishing a triathlon at the end of the pack. Someone who did not even do triathlons began poking fun of me to come in close to the rear. The fact of the matter was that I took the step to enter the race and to finish the race.

I waded out in the water, and I finished the race while they just flapped their jaws. I have often wondered if the other 11 Apostles made fun of Peter because he looked at the waves and began to drown in Matthew 14. I have this vision that what Peter said if they did make fun of him, he looked at them and said, "Well, at least I got out of the boat." You see, it was faith in Jesus that made Peter even get the chance to take three steps on water. That is more steps than any of the others would ever take. Peter had defied the impossible because he got out of the boat. You see, the world tells us that things are impossible because they do not want to risk it. They do not want to put in the effort. They are scared, and they have little faith that God will help them get through it. Listen, do not let the word impossible define you or your situation. Remember that God is the God of "possible." The reality is that the word "impossible" is not even in the Lord's vocabulary. Faith in God tells the world you can when the world tells you that you cannot. What can faith do? It can do the impossible! See you at the plate.

Dear Lord of the Water,

Lord, let me be the one that gets out of the boat no matter how scary it seems. Help me to focus on you and not the waves that are crashing around me. Remind me daily that all things are possible through you who can do all things. For you, nothing is impossible. What can faith do? It saved me, and because of that, I will step out on the water.

Day 281

Unconditional Love and Respect

I Corinthians 1:8 (NLT) ***He will keep you strong to the end so that you will be free from all blame on the day when our Lord Jesus Christ returns.***

The Scripture refers to the highest form of love as "agape love," which means unconditional love. It is a love that loves no matter the circumstance and no matter if the love is reciprocated. There is another unconditional verbiage in the sports world that must be in place: "unconditional respect." This week the Auburn Tigers barely beat the Ole Miss Rebels. It was a game where Auburn was favored by 17 points. They only won by 6, but to look at social media, you would have thought that they lost by 6. The fans were so harsh and demeaning. This led me to think about how the fans often do not have "unconditional respect" for their team. The truth in this matter is that they are only team followers if they are winning and they are winning big. This can also bleed over into the team chemistry. The question we often need to ask is, do we have mutual unconditional respect for our teammates? Do we cheer them on and encourage them when they are not performing well? Do we listen to the voices around us bashing out teammates and join in, or do we defend our teammates? Unconditional respect is beneficial not just for a team but also to a healthy marriage and corporate chemistry in the workforce. Respect is something that we can always continue to work on and get better, but it requires that we humble ourselves and look at our own lives and where we often fall short. There are going to be times when we do question whether we can depend on a teammate. Sometimes teammates make mistakes or get into trouble. When that happens, we begin to question whether we will depend on them when the game is on the line or when we need to be picked up. In the Scripture, Peter was the ringleader for the disciples. But Peter was very impulsive and made tons of irrational decisions. There were times when the disciples questioned him, but it is apparent in the Scriptures that Jesus had unconditional love and respect for Peter. It is also apparent that Peter was the team captain of the disciples. The truth is that Jesus would build the church upon the name of a very impulsive loudmouth. I found this prayer in an FCA article by Bill Buckley, who is the Mississippi State FCA Chaplain. I think it is something that we should all pray through and recite in our hearts from time to time. Make this your prayer for the day, and I will see you at the plate.

God of the Promise (I promise God and My Teammates)

"To my teammates and coaches: I will believe in you and your potential regardless of your ability, performance, or past failures. I will trust you to grow, to rise to the occasion, to do the right thing. If you fail my trust, I will not give up on you and do whatever I can to help you succeed. If I see a weakness in you, I will honor you enough to pray for you and, if necessary, challenge you face to face to rise up to our higher calling. I commit always to treat you better than I treat myself. I will fight for your honor if you are attacked in any way. I will stick by you and stick up for you, always."

✞

Day 282

From Hurry to Worry

Revelations 22:17 ***The Spirit and the bride say, "Come!" And let the one who hears say, "Come!" Let the one who is thirsty come, and let the one who wishes take the gift of the water of life.***

The next four days, we will look at how hurry can kill your progress. Being fast is great, but hurry will be detrimental to the process. You cannot hurry through life and get what God wants you to have. You will miss so much if you are always in a hurry. So this week, we will look at how to eliminate hurry from your life so that you not only get better but you enjoy the process.

The question today is how do we eliminate hurry in our life when athletics is all about speed? You have heard it said before that speed kills, but it can also kill your life if you never slow down. The truth is that several years ago, a sociologist said that with the coming of the digital age, things would slow down. We would get more done in less time. But as you may have already experienced, life is busier with less time. It seems that we are always on the run from one place to another. We eat in the car and try to multitask on the phone and drive at the same time. (Please do not text and drive.) So, the question is how we slow down so we can enjoy life and get the most out of it.

Dallas Willard said, "that the greatest enemy in our spiritual life was hurrying." He went as far as to say that we must "ruthlessly eliminate hurry from your life."[27] See, if the evil one cannot make you sin, then he can keep you busy. Constant hurry and worry pull your focus away from connecting with God. Now some of you are saying, but "idle hands are the work of the devil." I am not saying that we should not be busy; even Jesus was busy. The problem lies not in the concept of having a lot to do; it's when you have too much to do, and the only way to keep the quota up is constant hurry and unnecessary worry. See, when we hurry through the process, we do not do things efficiently or with excellence. Jesus was busy, but he always took time to pray, and he never really got in a hurry. As a matter of fact, in one instance, he waits three days till Lazarus is fully dead before he begins to move in his direction. I mean, he was only a day's journey away, but he waited to show us what God can do when we do not hurry. For the next few days, we will look at what life might look like if we could just slow down. Ask this question of yourself, what have I missed by the constant hurry in my life? Now take a deep breath because we will slow down this week, and we will pay attention to things that we have been missing. As you slow down, pay particular attention to your stress level. You may also notice that you are spending more time talking to God. Lastly, you will notice that you are more present in people's lives. Listen, speed on the field is not the same as speeding through life. Slow down, and you just may get more done. See you at the plate.

Dear God of Peace and Tranquility.

Help me to slow down. Help me enjoy what I have been missing as I have been speeding through life; it has been passing me by. Your Son set the example of what eliminating hurry and worry looked like in life. Help us to see the importance of slowing down so that we can enjoy this short-lived life. Amen.

Day 283

Slowing Down to Love

John 13:34-35 ***A new command I give you: Love one another. As I have loved you, so you must love one another. By this, everyone will know that you are my disciples if you love one another."***

Hurry cannot live with love. The two are totally incompatible, just like oil and water. You see, love takes time, and it takes being present in someone's life. Have you ever had one of those long practices, and the coach calls everybody up and begins to recap the days' practice? You are at the point of exhaustion, so what do you do? You zone out. Then you hear the coach say to you, "did you just hear what I said." You nod, and then he says, "well, repeat it back to me." You cannot do it, and now you know that you will be running even more laps in your exhausted state. See, you were present in body but not in spirit.

Love requires that you not only be present physically but that you are also present spiritually and mentally. Love takes effort, and it requires a lot of time. Any good parent can tell you that raising kids in love requires constant effort and the ability to not just hurry through raising them. See, there are no shortcuts, apps, or hacks that allow you to love more easily. Love takes time and requires us to slow down and be with the person that we love. Jesus did not teach his Talmud in a classroom setting; he taught them in an apprenticeship where he was constantly present with them. Jesus knew that if the disciples were going to learn love, they would have to learn how to be present in people's lives.

The only way that the world will know our love is by the time we spend with them. It takes an enormous amount of time to love well. I have often hurt a relationship because I got in a hurry and was not present with someone. How many times have you known an absent parent that tries to make up for not being there with gifts or money? It does not work; I can tell you that. Nothing can take the place of being present in someone's life. That is why coaches have such a tremendous platform and ministry as they have the opportunity to be present in players' lives. These players may have never had anyone spend that much time with them. Now, as a player, you must realize how much your coach loves you and why he does what he does. So my challenge to you is to love and to love well. To love well, you must walk, not run. The Scripture never talks about running with the Lord but only about walking with the Lord. Walking with someone allows us to walk through what they are going through and give them what they need from us. If you are not present, you will never know what they need. The same is true in the athletic world; if you want to be good and a teammate, you must be present on the field and in your teammates' lives. So, this time, when the coach asks, "what did I say? You will know how to respond; I will see you at the plate."

Dear Jehovah-Magen - Lord my Shield,

Help me to slow down. Help me to take time to be present in the lives of others. Help me to be present both mentally and spiritually. I confess that I have often been absent and distant from those that needed me most. Thank you for your Son, who taught us what the new covenant of love looked like as his body was broken, and his blood poured out for the forgiveness of my sins. Thank you that the Holy Spirit is always present with me.

✞

Day 284

You Can Not Hurry Joy

Nehemiah 8:10 ***Nehemiah said, "Go and enjoy choice food and sweet drinks, and send some to those who have nothing prepared. This day is holy to our Lord. Do not grieve, for the joy of the Lord is your strength."***

What brings you joy when it comes to your life as an athlete? Is it a victory, is it getting better at the game you love to play, or is it the camaraderie of hanging out with your teammates? Whatever it is, the game that you play ought to bring you joy. Yesterday, we talked about love being incompatible with hurry, and today we will look at how hurry is also incompatible with joy. The fact is that hurry robs us of the joy that surrounds us. When you hurry, it creates worry, and worry cannot be found connected with joy. Worry and hurry keep us from experiencing joy, even in some of our greatest moments in life. We often think of joy as an emotion, but it is so much more than that.

You may remember growing up and singing the simple little song; I got the Joy, Joy, Joy, Joy, Joy to infinite and beyond way Down in my Heart. Where? (Go ahead and sing it right now.) Joy is more than an emotion; it is a condition of the heart. So how do we tap into this joy and bring back the love of the game and a love of life? Well, the key is giving away what we think we have ahold of. We often think that we are giving God our future, but God is already the author and perfecter of our future. See, "Joy" is often found at the moment. An example of Joy is when you realize who has never played just scored. It may be when one of your friends is chosen to play in an all-star game. It may be simply watching the clouds dissipate so that you can play the game. The fact is that our true joy comes from finding our strength in the Lord. How often have we felt defeated and hopeless, and then God intervenes, and we experience the joy of his love and grace? Many times, we are always in such a hurry that we do not experience the presence of joy because we do not slow down long enough to experience what God is offering. But the Scripture says, "that strength is found in the joy of the Lord." We must learn to slow down so that we can find our strength in the joy of the Lord. We must condition our heart so that it does not hurry right through the joy of the Lord. So experience the joy that the Lord has for you right now, and I will see you at the plate.

Dear Ancient of days,

I have hurried right through the joy that is so ever-present in me and around me. I say I have joy in my heart, but I often find that the world has turned my joy to hurry because of my constant worry. Let me slow down long enough to ask the Lord for his strength because it is there that I will find joy. We also know that many times we experience pain, but that joy will come in the morning. This is a direct reference to your Son conquering the grave on that Easter morning that brought a new life and joy.

Day 285

The Consequences of Hurry

Colossians 3:15 ***And let the peace of Christ rule in your hearts, to which indeed you were called in one body. And be thankful.***

I find it somewhat ironic that every time Jesus entered a room or exited a room, he used the phrase "shalom." Peace I bring to you and peace I leave with you. Jesus came to bring us peace, and yet we see a world filled with turmoil and unrest. Not only is the world filled with hostility and strife, but so often, our inner being conflicts within ourselves. Most people would tell you that they have a tough time finding peace within themselves. So why is it that so many followers of Christ find it so hard to be at peace? Once again, we can look at a hurry and how it also robs us of our peace. If you want to test this, search your soul next time you are running late and see if you can find a feeling of inner peace. One of my youths had earned his way to being a punter for the University of Alabama. One day he had forgotten his scrimmage clothes and had "no peace" about what was going to happen to him at practice because of this error. So, he jumped in his truck, and he hurried off to the dorm to get his clothes. On his way, he lost control of his truck, and he hit a telephone pole crushing several bones in his kicking leg. He would never be able to kick again. He had allowed the hurry and the worry to rob him of his peace. Sometimes, it is better to face the consequences than hurry from place to place with no peace. When we slow down in life, we reduce our stress, which helps us mentally. When we slow down in life, we enjoy more of life and really enjoy what we do. When we slow down, there may be some consequences, but they will not be nearly as damaging as if we keep the pedal to the medal going 100 miles an hour in every direction. Jesus gave us the ultimate example of how to balance life. Jesus was the most on-point person that ever lived, but he worked at God's pace and not at the pace of the world. He took time out to pray. He took time out to enjoy the people that he was training to do ministry. He took time out for the least, the last, and the lost. He took time out to pray and to commune with his Father. He took time out to love those who had been shown little or no love. Jesus was on task, but he was not in a hurry. So how can we eliminate hurry from our life?

1. Stop first and pray.
2. Plan ahead.
3. If you are behind, accept the fact and do not make matters worse by speeding or cheating.
4. Surround yourself with people that you rely on to help you slow down and enjoy life.
5. Do one thing a day out of the ordinary to change things up.

Do not let hurry rob you of the life that God intended for us to enjoy.

Dear God of Shalom,

Lord still my heart in the midst of this chaotic world. Teach me to have patience amid hurry and scurry. Help me to slow down so I can enjoy the life that God created for me. Help me accept the consequences of being in a hurry so that I do not receive even greater consequences.

Day 286

Battle Armor

Ephesians 6:10-11 ***Finally, be strong in the Lord and in his mighty power. Put on the full armor of God so that you can take your stand against the devil's schemes.***

Every Sport has essential equipment that you must wear to protect your head and your body from injury. In football, you wear a variety of protective gear to ensure that you are protected from injury. I have seen several photographs of football history where the players were wearing only leather helmets and essentially no other protective gear. Can you imagine if players did not wear equipment today? The technological advances in equipment show just how much the game has evolved into what it is today. When I played football in college, we had a guy that played linebacker that we nicknamed "Robocop" because he wore so much protective gear. He wore literally every pad he could find, and I dare to say there was not an unexposed area on this guy's body. (By the way, he was also the most injured player on the team, go figure.) He wore extra elbow and knee pads, a shield on his facemask, a padded neck brace, padded gloves, and rib and back protectors.

I honestly do not know how he moved. Now in life, we must also wear a spiritual kind of gear to protect the vital parts of our being. We must remember that our battle is not against flesh and blood but against the unseen spiritual world. Ephesians 6 tells us, "to put on the whole armor of God, that you may be able to stand against the wiles of the devil." This week we will look at each piece of armor that you must equip yourself with so that you can fight the good fight that you have been called to. You must remember that you will find yourself injured if you do not protect your soul just like you protect your body. This week we will look at wearing the belt of truth so that you can stand up against the deception of the world. We will then talk about the breastplate of righteousness that protects your heart from the fatal wounds that the world tries to inflict upon you. We will then look at how to protect your feet so that you can stand steadfast as the world tries to knock your footing out from underneath you. The next day, we will look at the shield of faith, which will help you quench the fiery arrows shot at you from a distance, and how your shield will protect you and protect others around you. Then we will look at how the helmet of salvation helps protect and guard our minds against the corruption that the world is pushing in our direction. On the final day, we will look at the sword of the spirit, which is the Word of God given to us for the everyday battles that we find ourselves amid. So get ready to study the full armor of God. So go put on your helmet, and I will see you at the plate.

Dear Ultimate Protector,

Help me to put on the full armor of God so that when I am tempted, tested, and tried, I may fight the evil forces that come against me. Thank you for providing me the protection I need to fight against the evil forces of darkness that are constantly after my soul. Thank you that your Son has already won the war as he defeated Satan on Calvary. Now give me the protection to protect his holy name as I fight the good fight of life. Amen.

✞

Day 287

Tighten Your Belt

John 8:31-32 ***To the Jews who had believed him, Jesus said, "If you hold to my teaching, you are really my disciples. Then you will know the truth, and the truth will set you free."***

A few years ago, as we were preparing to take the field, one of the starting offensive linemen came up to me and told me that he had a serious problem. He explained that he had forgotten his belt back at the school, and his pants would not stay up without a belt. We found a younger player that would most likely not play and took his belt and put it on the starter. Then we took a leather belt that someone had worn with their street clothes and put it on the non-starter to hold his pants up. Yes, the disaster of overexposure was diverted, and his pants stayed up the whole game. In Scripture, the Roman soldiers girded their midsection with a thick leather belt similar to a weightlifting belt. It was known as the "balteus," and it held the soldier's scabbard and sword. It protected their crucial midsection all the way down to almost the knees. The belt not only kept the armor together but also helped with protection and support.

Now in the Scripture, belt refers to wearing the belt of truth. See, to stay firmly grounded, we must be grounded in the truth. See the truth not only sets us free from our sin, but it also helps us to have a firm foundation. So many people have no foundation because they buy into the lie the world is selling them, and the truth does not support them. See, the evil one uses lies and deception to confuse people and to lead people astray. If we are going to stay strong and true in every aspect of life, we have to gird our waist with the truth. Why the waist? Because just like in sports, you can get fooled by arm moments, shuffles, and spins, but where the waist goes, so the whole body goes. When you teach someone to tackle in the open field, you always teach the tackler not to get fooled by deception and focus on the waist. A player may juke and jive, but the waist cannot contort. Put on the belt of truth so that you are not deceived by a world full of schemes to pull you away from what God has called you to do. So put on your belt, grab your bat, and I will see you at the plate.

Dear Author of Truth,

Help me to realize that without the truth that I am living in darkness. When I am completely immersed in the truth, God, then I have the support to stand against all opposition. God, I rebuke the schemes of the evil one, and I only want to be found in the truth. Remove all deceit from life lips. I will not fall into the world that tells me to accept a half-truth because a half-truth is a whole lie. God, you are the way, the truth, and the life.

Day 288

Cover for Righteousness

Psalms 34:15 ***The eyes of the Lord are on the righteous, and his ears are attentive to their cry.***

Now the center of who you are is not your mind but is your heart. Many people study diligently to become smarter, but few work on the condition of their hearts. You show me a person's heart, and I will show you who that person is. It is important to protect our hearts because we can even deceive ourselves if our hearts are not righteous. You know this because you have followed your heart before, only to find yourself in a mess. Righteousness is a word that the world thinks of as antiquated. The world says, "do not worry about righteousness; if it feels good, do it." "If it is fun, it must be good."

The Roman soldiers wore a breastplate that covered the heart and kept them from being fatally wounded. A few years ago, when my son played coach pitch baseball, the player that played the pitcher position had to wear a protective pullover that protected him/her if they were hit in the chest with a ball. This told me that someone had been mortally wounded when they were struck in the heart. Now many people in the world walk around with fatally wounded hearts. They have bought into the evil one's deception, and it has left them wounded. To protect our souls, we must protect our hearts with the righteousness that Jesus left for us when he empowered us with the Holy Spirit. See, Jesus was found blameless in his Father's eyes; he was actually the only one ever found blameless. He was totally righteousness, and when we ask him to come into our hearts, he brings with him the righteousness to cover and protect our hearts from our shortcomings and sin. His righteousness becomes the protection of our hearts. So, when God looks upon our hearts, he sees the covering of Jesus' righteousness. We cannot wear this protection if we live outside the will of God. The reason that there are sidelines on a field is so that we stay in bounds and that every team plays within the same boundaries. Righteousness helps create the boundaries in our lives and keeps us from allowing the evil one to destroy us from within. Guard your heart with the righteousness of Jesus Christ so that you will not fail from a fatal wound. By covering yourself with righteousness, you are readily able to thwart the attacks of Satan. Cover yourself with the breastplate of righteousness, and I will see you at the plate.

God of Jeshurun,

I am covered in the righteousness of Jesus Christ. He was the only one that was found sinless, and yet he carried my sin to the cross and made penance for me. I can only be found righteous through him and through the blood that was shed for my sin. Help me to protect my heart because I am who my heart says I am. God, my heart belongs to you because Jesus lives in my heart. Amen.

Day 289

Shalom Shoes

Philippians 4:4-7 ***Be anxious for nothing, but in everything, by prayer and petition, with thanksgiving, present your requests to God. And the peace of God, which surpasses all understanding, will guard your hearts and your minds in Christ Jesus.***

Shoes are a big deal in any sport, and there is a vast array of shoe brands to select from. Every brand promises to deliver superior performance while giving the player a stylish look that will turn heads. Some shoes are designed in the high-top form to protect the ankles, while others offer superior arch support. The truth is that most athletes pick their shoes because they prefer a brand, style, and fit. Some choose shoes because they just fit better and are more durable. Now a few years ago, before a softball game, I went out for the coin toss, and I noticed the behind-the-plate umpire wearing some interesting shoes that looked like they gave optimal protection for his feet. I asked him about the shoes, and he told me that they were specifically designed for behind-the-plate umpires. They had steel toes, and the tongue portion was protected by another shield so that a foul ball did not bounce off the top of your foot. Then he added, these shoes are super hard to run in, but they offer maximum protection. I thought about how different this type of shoe was; most shoes were designed for speed, but these were designed for ultimate protection.

Now Roman soldiers needed shoes that provided protection but also gave them the ability to move in battle. Their shoes came up to about their knees, and they were studded on the bottom like cleats for traction and secure footing while fighting. As prayer warriors, we need a firm foundation and protection from the evil schemes of the world. Having this firm foundation gives us a "shalom" brand of shoes. Shoes that offer us peace so that we can stand firm and also be protected. When the Scripture talks about "preparation," it alludes to the fact that peace has been established through the death and resurrection of Jesus Christ. But in order to receive that peace, you must walk in it with the shoes of shalom. Now the world seems to be a place in constant turmoil and a place of no peace, but when we walk with the Lord, we experience peace during chaos. See, the enemy, just like the opposing team, tries to steal our peace and keep us anxious, upset, and fearful. The enemy also wants to remind us of what happened in our past. The scheme is to take us out of our peace by reminding us of our past failures. But when we steady our prayer lives with the shoes of "shalom," we can push past the schemes of the evil one. Peace is a place where you dig your cleats in, and you accept nothing less. Yes, even when we may not understand what is going on, Jesus gave us a peace that passes all understanding. So lace up your shalom shoes, and I will see you at the plate.

Dear Peace Lily,

God help me to keep my feet planted while I reach to the heavens with my heart and my hands. Give me peace in the midst of chaos. Help me to remember that you came to bring peace, and then you left peace with the power of the Holy Spirit. God, your grace is enough for me, so I will sing hallelujah. Amen

Day 290

Faithfully Shielded

Genesis 15:1 ***After this, the word of the Lord came to Abram in a vision: "Do not be afraid, Abram. I am your shield, your very great reward."***

One of the greatest feelings in football is when you get to take the victory formation for the game's last few plays. But even when you are in the victory formation, you must have your offensive lineman serve as your shield to shield you from the other team jarring the ball loose and gaining another possession. The truth is that many times in sports, we need a shield to keep us from getting injured. In baseball and softball, we weld a leather shield on our hands, which is our glove. Our glove keeps us from being struck by a dart off of the hitter's bat. The gloves are made of leather, which reminds me of the Roman soldiers' shields made of leather, wood, and metal. The shield was known as a "scutum." It was used to protect soldiers from flaming arrows shot from a distance or from a sword used in hand-to-hand combat.

The shield was often soaked in water to immediately extinguish the flaming arrows shot at them. Now sometimes, a Roman official would have a designated shield barrier that went to battle with them for the sole purpose of protecting them. The shield-bearer was on the defense as the other fought. This shield-bearer gave the Roman more solid faith that he could fight without being struck by the opposition. Now God tells us that we should take up the shield of faith. God's word assures us that this shield of faith will be enough to protect us from the flaming arrows being shot at us daily. See, what the enemy wants to do is wear us down to lose our faith and turn toward the world and away from God.

We have all had that teammate that lost faith and left the team for another. God has given us the shield of faith so that we can protect ourselves with the faith that we have gained through our relationship with Jesus Christ. Being a Christian does not make us exempt from trials and tribulations, but our faith in Jesus Christ gives us faith that we can conquer all and that we are shielded by the faith that Christ left with us in the power of the Holy Spirit. See, faith helps us to dissipate fear and to make us more than conquers. Faith helps us to get through the process of what we do not understand. Faith helps us understand that we are not God and that we may not understand God's mind, but that God is for us and never against us. The shield of faith must be picked up daily because as sure as the day you forget will be the day that the enemy attacks. So, pick up your shield of faith, and I will see you at the plate.

Dear Faithful Father,

God, you have been faithful to me every day of my life. You have given me faith that helps when I might not understand what is going on around me. You give me faith to believe when I struggle with doubt and wonder. Help me to stable my feet so that I can stand firm when the world attacks my faith. Help me to stand firm.

Day 291

Proper Headgear

1 Thessalonians 5:8 ***But since we are of the day, let us be sober, having put on the breastplate of faith and love, and as a helmet, the hope of salvation.***

Over the last few years, there has been a lot of talk about headgear and if it fully protects or not. Helmets have changed tremendously from the old leather helmets with no face guards worn in football's beginning days. Helmets today claim to help alleviate the risk of a concussion. The other thing taught in football is that you cannot lead with your helmet, using it as a weapon instead of protection gear. Recently, there was an incident where a player ripped the quarterback's helmet off and hit him with it. In this instance, the helmet may have caused a concussion, not eliminated it. The truth is that a helmet is not a weapon but is for our head's defense and protection. Like with a Roman soldier, the helmet was used to give maximum protection from a blow to the head or face area. The helmets were known as "Galea." The helmets were molded medals and protected the ears and sides of cheeks. Some helmets even added a proactive front piece that came down the front and protected the nose. The helmets had crests and plumes on the top. (This looks like feathers on the top of the head of a bird.) These plumes were for decoration, but also the color signified rank.

In life, we must put on our spiritual helmet of salvation. This protects our minds while knowing that we are saved by the salvation Christ provided for us as he gave himself up for us as a ransom. See, the reason that we need the helmet of salvation is to protect us from the lies of the evil one. The lie that says our past will always haunt us, the lie that we will never be good enough, the lie that we cannot do it, and the ultimate lie that God does not love us. Lies surround us, but when our mind is protected, we understand that salvation tells us that all of that is just one big lie. Salvation protects us from guilt, loneliness, helplessness, and misery. See, the helmet of salvation helps us renew our mind and our ability to see who we are through Christ. Jesus had one mission on this earth: to bring salvation so that he could obliterate Satan's lies. Salvation means that the King has adopted you; it means that you are an heir to the throne. Salvation sets you free and helps you to be confident in who you are. The helmet of salvation fits more like a crown and less like a helmet. You must put on this helmet every day as you go to battle with the world. You would not play a football game without first putting on your helmet, and you would not get up to bat without first putting on your helmet. So do not go through life without the protection of the helmet of salvation. Put it on, and I will see you at the plate.

Dear House of defense,

Protect not only my heart but my head. Salvation is the knowledge of the mind in knowing that we are saved by grace. Protect my mind from believing the lies that are thrown my way daily. Salvation is the knowledge of knowing that I am saved from what I cannot save myself from. Thank you for Jesus wearing the crown of thorns so I could wear the helmet of salvation.

Day 292

Weapon in Hand

II Timothy 3:16-17 (ESV) ***All Scripture is breathed out by God and profitable for teaching, for reproof, for correction, and for training in righteousness, that the man of God may be complete, equipped for every good work.***

Almost all the protective gear we have talked about up to this point has been solely for our defensive protection. Now the sword of truth is both an offensive and a defensive form of protection. That is why in Hebrews 4:12, it is called a double-edged sword in our hands. The Romans soldier's sword was known as a "Gladius." The gladius was small, about 18 inches, and was always worn on the right side;

whether one was left or right-handed did not matter because it was always worn on the right. It was always on the right because the shield was always wielded on the left; in doing this, everyone was in the same formation, and everyone donned their weapons in the same way. This assured that everyone was in synch and that everyone was uniform as they marched into battle. It is funny that they were that meticulous about only doing it one way, but the same is true of the Scripture; it is the one way God has provided for us to be offensive against Satan. The "word of God" gives us everything we need to go into combat. Before Jesus was even born, King Herod had a plan to destroy the Messiah. He planned to put the sword to all of the babies born in Bethlehem. Some thirty years later, as Jesus starts his ministry, Satan challenges him to a duel in the desert. How does Jesus combat Satan? He uses a sword. Not a sword made of steel, but a sword made from the Word of God. The sword that we take with us into battle is the sword of the Spirit. It is the Word of God. When I first got into coaching, I did not realize how essential it was to know the playbook. The truth is not only knowing the playbook but what to do when the other team aligns differently or comes out in a different formation. The truth is that in the sporting world, you must know the playbook to make quick adaptive changes. Now the playbook that we have in life is the Scripture, the Word of God. God gave us the playbook to know how to navigate life and adjust to the schemes that the evil one throws against us. God's Word is how the Holy Spirit guides us and leads us in the direction we need to go. The truth is that the reason so many fail tests in life is because they do not know the playbook. Jesus had an answer for everything that Satan threw at him in that dual in the desert. Jesus was hungry, and Satan tempted him with food. Jesus responded, "Man shall not live on bread alone, but on every word that comes from the mouth of God." Then he was tempted with testing God to see if he had ultimate faith in him and him only. Jesus responded once again with his sword as he said, "It is also written: 'Do not put the Lord your God to the test.'" Finally, Satan challenged Jesus with the power to take over the world. But once again, the sword of truth came out, and Jesus combatted Satan with these words, "For it is written: 'Worship the Lord your God and serve Him only.'" All three battles with Satan were won with the sword of truth. So, let me ask you, what weapon do you have in your hand? No, not your bat but your Scripture. Take up "the sword of the spirit," and I will see you at the plate.

Dear True Word,

God, you have given me all I need in the Scripture, but I have often neglected to read it and memorize it. So often, I go into battle naked fighting without the words that I need from the Scripture. Your Scripture is like a two-edged sword given to me for the sake of fighting the battle from an offensive front. Thank you that Jesus set the record straight as he fought with Satan in the desert and came out victorious because he used the word of God to crush the scheme of Satan.

✞

Day 293

Tempted, Tried, Tempted

1 Corinthians 10:13 ***"No temptation has overtaken you except what is common to mankind. And God is faithful; he will not let you be tempted beyond what you can bear. But when you are tempted, he will also provide a way out so that you can endure it."***

So we ended yesterday's devotional by talking about the three temptations that Jesus faced in the desert. For the next three days, I want to look at those temptations and how they relate to us, especially to athletes in the sporting world. One of the things that playing sports does is that it puts you in the spotlight. The spotlight is a great platform for you to share Christ, but it can also lend itself to more temptations. How many times have you heard about athletes giving into temptation and ruining their chances of playing? Headlines from sports media outlets read this way every day. "Player suspended over positive drug test; Player suspended because of an altercation in a bar; Player suspended because of domestic violence with a live-in girlfriend; Player suspended over the use of P.E.D.'s" Yes, no matter what level you play at, you are going to face the temptation that is associated with being in the limelight. The question is, what are you going to do when you are tempted, and how can you reject the temptations that can so easily ensnare you? Jesus gives us the formula for combatting the temptations that we face daily. This week we will look at the three temptations that Jesus faced in the desert. Now let me say that again. He is in the desert, not surrounded by people but in the desert all alone and with the only support coming from his heavenly Father. Now, I would say that this is a vital first lesson that we realize that the world will offer you the temptation, and then they will say, "if I was you, this is what I would do." So hear this; they are not you, and they are not God, so they do not have your best interest at heart. This is where one temptation leads to another sin and begins the domino effect. Now back to the three temptations that we will discuss this week.

The physical temptation: do what feels right. (Matthew 4:3-4.)

The emotional temptation: question God's love. (Matthew 4:5-7.)

The control temptation: take over the throne. (Matthew 4:8-10.)

So as we consider these, let me first point out that no one is exempt from temptation. Everyone will face it, and most of the time, daily. Now temptation leads to sin, but it is not the same as sin. Sin is giving in to temptations. The thought of doing it is not a sin, but the follow-through is. The way to respond to temptation is by using God's Word. So put God's Word in your mind and a bat in your hand, and I will see you at the plate.

Dear Holy Provider of Hope,

Help me to fight the temptations that surround me. Help me to eliminate the things that lead to temptations. Forgive me for my past sins and show me how not to fall prey to the evil world that wants to trip me up. I pray for those seeking to be renewed because they have fallen into temptation, and temptation has cost them everything. Help them seek repentance, and then show them, your grace. God, I have failed you and have given in so many times to the snare of temptation, but you are a loving, forgiving God that restored my hope through Jesus Christ. Amen.

Day 294

But It Feels Right

Galatians 1:10 (NASB) ***For am I now seeking the favor of men, or of God? Or am I striving to please men? If I were still trying to please men, I would not be a bondservant of Christ.***

The world tells us that if it feels right that it must be the right thing to do. How many times have we been led astray by this notion? The truth is that feeling good or a good feeling can be very deceptive. Our makeup is one that responds to immediate gratification, but this is not always the right thing to do. Many years ago, I had a bulletin board in my youth room. I had a youth volunteer that was a middle school teacher help me decorate and maintain the bulletin board. I remember one of the slogans that she put on the board was, "What is right is not always popular and what is popular is not always right." Now, after research, I found out that Albert Einstein had coined that phrase – what an important statement to put into our mental toolbox.

Many times we make decisions because it is what the popular people are doing. Now, if our sole purpose in life is to please other people, we will never please God. The truth does not do something just because it feels right to do it because it is "right." The Scripture gives us the standard of what is right and what is wrong. Now so often, the world takes the Scripture and fits it into their lifestyle rather than changing their lifestyle to live by the plumb line, which is the Scripture. You cannot grow in your relationship with Christ if you only do what feels right. How many times have you said, I got a good feeling about this, and it turned out to be a disaster? We all know that this concept goes into our training and into our practice time. We know that if we are going to push ourselves, it is sometimes not going to feel good; as a matter of fact, it will hurt. How many times have you seen the star player be the last to leave the field or get the lights turned out on them in the weight room? How often do we need to study game film or get some extra rest rather than go out with friends for a good time? The truth is that it may feel right, but it may be j "so wrong." How does one decipher whether it is right or not? First, pray through it and ask the Holy Spirit to guide you. Second, have someone in authority that you can ask or go to for knowledge and accountability. Third, use your past experiences to guide you. How did this end last time? Remember, just because it feels good does not mean that it is good. The truth is, to be a champion, there is no immediate gratification. See you at the plate.

Dear God of Righteousness,

I have often made the wrong choice by choosing what feels right, not what is right. In this process, I have hurt people, and I have compromised who I am as a servant of Jesus Christ. Help me to make difficult decisions in life and to seek wise counsel. Help me to remember to pray through before going through. Thank you that your Son did not do what felt right but did what was right. I owe it all to Jesus, my Lord, and my God. Amen.

✞

Day 295

Where Are You Headed?

Matthew 7:13-14 ***"Enter through the narrow gate. For wide is the gate and broad is the road that leads to destruction; many enter through it. But small is the gate and narrow the road that leads to life, and only a few find it."***

The other day God gave me a statement that has stuck with me. The statement was this, "If you do not change your direction, then you are going to wind up right where you are headed." So the question is, where are you headed, and are you on the path you want to be on to get you to where you want to go? So often, the reason we are on the wrong path is that we are following others. A few months ago, I was riding in a charity bike ride; the ride had three different long distant options: a 60-mile ride, a 75-mile ride, and a 100-mile ride. I had signed up to do the 75-mile ride. There was a point where the road split off in two different directions based on what ride you had chosen. Now, I followed a guy straight because I had asked him if the straight path would lead me to the 75-mile destination; he responded that this was the distance he was also riding. After about seven more miles, we came to an aide/rest station, to which they said, you just have one more stop, and you are finished.

Knowing the distance on my bike computer, I knew that this would not take me to the 75-mile mark. It then dawned on me that I had followed the other biker on the 60-mile route and would now not be able to do the 75-mile route I had planned on. The truth is that I followed someone down the wrong road. So often, this is what happens to us in life. We are heading down one path, but we allow someone to influence us to the point of pulling us off the road that we need to be on. We must constantly be checking our direction and the path that we are on if we are going to get where we intend to go. So often, we wind up somewhere, but it is not where we planned on being. Often, we must spend lots of effort getting back on the path to take us where we first planned to go. Some have traveled the wrong path so long that they just give up on getting where they first planned on going. God tells us in the Scripture that narrowing the way will get us where we need to go. But he also tells us that few people travel that path because it is the road less traveled. It is not the popular way or the easiest road to travel. The road of purity is less traveled; the road to righteousness is less traveled; the road to strong moral character is less traveled. So, let me ask you again, are you on the road that will get you to where you want to go because the road you are traveling will get you where you are headed. So, stop and evaluate the road or, better stated, the roads you are traveling: the road of your studies and academics, your athletic road, and, most importantly, your spiritual road. After you have pondered that for a minute, I will see you at the plate.

Dear Jehovah-Misqabbi - Lord my High Tower,

Help me to realize that by following the world that they will lead me into destruction. Your Son did not follow the world but followed the path to Golgotha. Let me be on the path that has been less traveled. Help me to find the path that few find. I want to end up where the road of truth and righteousness leads me, and that is directly to you and your kingdom.

Day 296

Selfish Celebration

Philippians 2:3-4 ***Do nothing from selfishness or empty conceit, but with humility of mind regard one another as more important than yourselves; do not merely look out for your own personal interests, but also for the interests of others.***

Thanksgiving night, 2019, I returned to my hotel from visiting my parents and turned on the television to watch the fourth quarter of the Ole Miss/Mississippi St. rivalry game. Many know this game as the Egg Bowl. But after this night, they may change its name to the "urination bowl or toilet bowl." At the end of the game, Ole Miss was down by 7 points with under two minutes to go; they had driven the length of the field and had two ESPN SportsCenter-type plays to set them up in the red zone. With just 4 seconds left in the game, Ole Miss scored with a reception to sophomore Elijah Moore. Now, this is where we interject selfishness into the game. Elijah Moore then acted like he was a dog urinating in the end zone by lifting his leg.

Now in professional football, you can celebrate all you want, but this is an excessive celebration 15-yard penalty when you celebrate in the end zone in college. Moore was flagged, and the penalty was accessed on the field goal attempt. This moved the ball back considerably, and it was now a field goal attempt and not just an extra point. The kicker lined up, the ball sailed right, and the game ended with Old Miss losing their rivalry game. Now the repercussions of this selfish decision would not be just a loss to your bitter rivals, but it also gave Mississippi St. the win, making them bowl eligible. This means that they will get two to three additional weeks of practice. It means that they will be able to recruit against Ole Miss because they can boast that they will be in a bowl game. Two days later, the Ole Miss coach, Matt Luke, was fired, which may not have happened if they had won the rivalry game. (Now that is just speculation on my part.) See, the moral of excessive celebration is that it can have grave consequences. Not following the rules or bringing all the accolades on yourself can have dire consequences for your whole team. See, football is a team game, and what you do will affect the whole team. Often, we get caught up in the moment, but when we are prayed up and have others hold us accountable, we will not make decisions that can cause extreme damage. The correct way to celebrate a touchdown is to hand the ball back to the referee and then go back to your sidelines and celebrate. Then you will be able to also celebrate after the game and not hang your head in defeat because of a terrible decision that you or a teammate made. Remember this quote, "your decision will always affect others." This is not only on the field but in every aspect of life. The selfish celebration always leads to trouble. Jesus never did anything out of selfish ambition; he gave his life for you. Keep in mind that his winning drive culminated in his death. No need for excessive celebration, but I will see you at the plate.

Dear Humble Lord Jesus,

Help me not to think of myself as greater than I should. Help me to be humble even when I score the winning drive or hit the walk-off. Help me to realize that my decisions have consequences not just for me but for everyone. Thank you for forgiveness for those times that I have excessively celebrated instead of giving you the glory.

Day 297

Faith Tested

Genesis 22:8 ***Abraham answered, "God himself will provide the lamb for the burnt offering, my Son." And the two of them went on together.***

This week one of my police chaplain colleagues, Derrick Jordon, gave the Thanksgiving message at the community-wide Thanksgiving service. In his sermon, he used a quote that has stuck with me for days. He said, "that a faith that is not tested is a faith that cannot be trusted." Wow! I began to think about the magnitude of that statement and how true that rings my life and in the life of everyone that has ever followed Jesus Christ. Jesus said to the disciples, "come follow me." Now that is a faith that would not only be tested but would ultimately lead to a trusting faith, a trust that would lead to the Disciples' Martyrdom. I was thinking about how often we must put our faith in our leaders and our coaches. This year, the high school where my son plays football has 1/5 of its seniors playing at the next level. This led me to think about the recruiting process and how these players knew the right school to choose. It then dawned on me that the process is just like our trust in God. They are venturing into the unknown, moving away from home. They must put their faith in a coach and hope that they have made the right decision.

The truth is that over the next four or five years, they will have their faith challenged as they learn the highs and lows of college athletics. But it is through the testing of our faith that we develop a deep-rooted faith, not just a good feeling faith. How many times have you seen someone throw in the towel as soon as their faith is tested? Many people buy into what I call a weak faith. Weak faith is not really a faith but an emotion. Some people's faith is so shallow that they just think that their belief in God should just give them anything they want. They want Faith to make life easy. The reality is that even Jesus said: "that in this world we would have trouble." One of the most troubling Scripture passages occurs in Genesis 22 when the Spirit leads Abraham to the desert to sacrifice his firstborn son. The thing that grabs me about this Scripture is that Abraham never waivers in his faith. This story is a true test of faith and what a trusted faith can do. Abraham looks at Issacs and tells him God will provide. The reason that Abraham trusted was that his faith had been held to the fire for the last 80+ years. <u>A tested faith becomes a trusted faith.</u> Listen, in the sports world; there will be all kinds of tests related to our faith. My advice is to dig in deep and be tested because that tested faith will soon become a faith you can trust—time to test the faith; see you at the plate.

Dear God of Ultimate Faith,

God, I have so often settled for a cheap faith. I have used my faith to try to persuade you that I knew what needed to be done. God help my testing led to a trusting and deepening of faith. Let me have Abraham's faith to follow you even if it is not where

I want to go. Lead me, test me, and prove to me that you can be trusted like you have done so many times before.

✞

Day 298

How Big Is Your God?

Jeremiah 32:27 ***"Behold, I am the Lord, the God of all flesh; is anything too difficult for Me?"***

I wear a rubber wristband every day that reads, "God is Bigger." I wear it as a constant reminder that God is bigger than all my problems. God is bigger than my failures and my shortcomings. Some may ask why I need this constant reminder, and the answer is that sometimes I have a habit of shrinking God down to human form. That means I shrink God down to what I think he can do, not what he is capable of doing. I have been a God follower for many years, but I have never allowed him to be as big and as infinite as he is or wants to be in my life. I often tell God what I am going to do and then ask him to help. When our God is bigger, we learn to work the process in reverse. Rather than tell God what we want, we need to learn to ask God what he wants us to do. The truth is that when God is with us, we can dream bigger than what we can possibly do. Reggie White was a big man that played professional football for the Green Bay Packers. But even though Reggie White was a big man, his faith was bigger. Reggie played professional football and served as a part-time associate pastor, and loved to preach. Somedays, he would preach before going to play football. Reggie was a big man, but his God was bigger.

One story that is shared in his autobiography is the story of him being told that he could not play because of a torn hamstring. He says, "that he went into the church to pray and that his God was so big he came out healed. Another time arsonists racially targeted the church that he served by burning it to the ground. They then called the Senior Pastor and projected death threats his way. But Reggie kept praying and kept believing. See, Reggie White was a big man, but his God was bigger. When he played ball, he entered the stadium with not only his strength but the strength of a God that was so big that nothing was impossible for him. Let me ask you this question: How big is your God? Have you shrunk your God down to things that you can handle on your own, or do you pray for God to do big audacious things in your life? God is bigger, now believe that, and I will see you at the plate.

Dear Big God,

Help me to realize that I cannot shrink you down to fit my mold or thoughts. You are bigger than anything and everything. Forgive me for putting you in a box. Forgive me for praying for things that I can do on my own but neglecting the prayers that seem impossible. God, you are the God of possible, and impossible does not exist in your vocabulary. God, thank you for Jesus. Help me realize that no matter how great my accomplishments are, I will never be as big as Jesus. God, you are Bigger. Amen.

Day 299

Embracing the (Game Ball) Cross

Revelation 3:11 ***I am coming soon. Hold fast what you have, so that no one may seize your crown.***

Have you ever received the game ball? The gift of the game ball is to remember the game and perhaps our own personal performance that helped lead to a victory. This last week after Auburn beat Alabama in the Iron Bowl, which is arguably the best rivalry in sports, Bo Nix's Auburn's quarterback, was seen clasping the game ball in his post-game interview. He clutched that ball in what seemed like a death grip refusing to let go of it. The sideline reporter asked him how he got the game ball, and he said; "that he had it in his hand after the game ended and he was not letting go of it." Bo Nix had dreamed of winning the Iron Bowl since he was a small child. He was now holding on to the ball that commemorated this significant achievement in his life. He did not want to let go of the ball because he wanted to savor this memory that he had dreamed of for so long. It was truly a dream that had come true. As athletes, we all have things that remind us of our accomplishments. Some receive medals, and for others, it is the accumulation of trophies, and if you are fortunate enough, you may get to dawn a championship ring upon your finger. Now as important as these things are to our remembering the great things we have accomplished, there is one thing that we need to embrace that represents the greatest victory of all. We need to embrace the "cross." I wear a cross around my neck as a constant reminder of what Jesus did for me on that cross. He took my sins to the cross and became victorious in my battle against sin and death. The truth is that the cross is a game ball for all who trust in the Lord and confess that they need Jesus to save them from their sins. The truth is that every time we see a cross, we are reminded that this is the trophy of all trophies. The reason that we get to do what we do is because of the cross. Is it ok to embrace the game ball? Absolutely, but what is most important to embrace is the cross of our Lord and Savior, Jesus Christ. The cross has set you free, and if you ask for it, Jesus will give you this game ball. So now that you already have the game ball (cross) of eternal life, I will see you at the plate.

Dear The Barrier of My Cross,

Thank you that your Son embraced the game ball of life and went to the cross to die for my sin and shortcoming. I do not deserve it, but that is what grace is all about. Every time I see a cross, let me remember that this is the ultimate game ball of life. The game ball of eternal life, which I am eternally grateful for. The game ball covered all the sins of my life. Amen.

Day 300

Relinquishing Control

Matthew 26:42 ***He went away a second time and prayed, "My Father, if it is not possible for this cup to be taken away unless I drink it, may your will be done."***

As athletes and coaches, we love to have total control. We love to control our schedules, our diets, and our workout regimen. The truth is that any change in our ability to control leads to us becoming uneasy in our spirit. This makes us uneasy, and then we become explosive because that is the nature of a competitor. (I am not giving you permission to go off, just pointing out why we explode.) Coaches are especially taken out of their comfort when they cannot control the practice or game outcome. If you do not believe me, just watch any Saturday slate of college football games, and watch the head coaches completely lose their minds on the sideline. Now the reason that we like to have control is that usually, something in our life is out of control, or there has been a time in life when there was something that could not be controlled. But the truth is that "the greatest of all illusions is the illusion that we ever had control." The truth is that the most freeing day in your life will be the day that you realize that you never really had control. This is the day that you say there is a God, and I am not him. The truth is that everyone struggles with control, whether you are on the controlling side or the being-controlled side. So, what can we do about our issue of control? We can do what the great "AA" slogan says; "We can let go and let God." When we give God control, it helps take some of the pressure off us. It also keeps us from saying or acting out in a way that will embarrass our team and us. One of the greatest stories in the Bible involves a young teenage girl named Mary. The Holy Spirit comes to her and tells Mary that she will give birth to the Son, and he will save the world.

Now you talk about being out of control. You talk about asking questions and looking for a change in trajectory. How would you respond? Here is how Mary responds, "Behold the maidservant of the Lord! Let it be to me according to your word." And the angel departed from her. Did you get that she essentially says what Jesus says 33 years later in the garden? Not my will, but your will be done. When we relinquish control and give it to God, life becomes more controllable because we are being led and not trying to lead ourselves. So, give the strings to God, and I will see you at the plate.

God of All Control,

Help me to let go so I can let you have your will and way in my life. Help me to see I am not in control and have never really been in control. Help me control what you have trusted me with, and trust you in what I cannot control. Thank you that your Son took control and gave his life for me. Amen.

Day 301

Reckless Trust

Joshua 3:12-13 ***Now then, choose twelve men from the tribes of Israel, one from each tribe. And as soon as the priests who carry the ark of the Lord—the Lord of all the earth—set foot in the Jordan, its waters flowing downstream will be cut off and stand up in a heap."***

Let me ask you a question, does trust come easy for you, or do you struggle with trust because of previous events in your life? Many people in athletics use athletics as a gateway to forgetting about the distrust exhibited in their lives. The truth is that sports can be a great tool for teaching us how to learn to trust. I have served as Chaplain for some high school football teams, and many of these teams had several players that lived below the poverty level in some horrible conditions. We found out very quickly that these young people had a hard time with trust. Because of these trust issues, they may also have trouble with authority or even with male figures above them. But after time, trust can be built between a coach and the player if intentionality and consistency are key components. This trust is not just a lesson for the field, but it is a lesson that hopefully, they will carry through life. Last week, I read Joshua's story and how God told him that he must trust him and cross the Jordon to reach the destination of the promised land. Now, this was not a crossing the Jordon by boat or by a bridge. This was taking the Ark of the Covenant down to the Jordon (which by the way was above flood level) and step into the water with the Ark, and then the Jordon would part, and the people would cross into the Promise Land. This required a trust that surpassed one's ability. This required a trust that humanly made no sense. This would be a "ruthless trust." The same "ruthless trust" that it takes when you step on the field supremely outmatched, the same "ruthless trust" when you step up to the plate against the number one pitcher in the state, the same "ruthless trust" that puts you on the mat against the undefeated state wrestler. All of these require a trust that is outside of your ability. But you know that if you win or lose in those situations, you are learning to trust even when it does not necessarily make sense. The truth is that we all have a Jordon that we must face, and sometimes these Jordons are even bigger than anything we will face in the sports world. Remember, trust in the Lord with all your heart and lean not into your own understanding. Do you have a ruthless trust? Just trust, and I will see you at the plate.

Dear Trustworthy God,

Help me to face my Jordon with confidence. Help me to realize that rust is formed from what I cannot do with my own ability. Help me to trust even when I cannot see what is ahead. Help me to step into the Jordon even when it is at flood stage. Help me trust and obey because it is truly the way to know you most intimately.

Day 302

Fear Not, Really?

Isaiah 41:10 ***So do not fear, for I am with you; do not be dismayed, for I am your God. I will strengthen you and help you; I will uphold you with my righteous right hand.***

The Scripture says, "fear not," but the obvious question is that possible? Science has debated whether we are born with fear or whether fears are developed over time. The reality is that no matter how tough you are, you have something that you fear. Sometimes it is the fear of things like snakes, storms, darkness, or flying. Sometimes it is the fear of the unknown or fear of getting an incurable illness. We can control some fears, but some fears are totally out of our control as we do not control external forces surrounding us. Now in the sports world and in the real world, our fears establish the limits in our lives. Think about it; if you fear failure, you will not try; if you fear rejection, you will not ask; if you fear heights, you will stay low. We are limited by what we fear. So, what fear eventually leads to is paralysis. This is a state where we are frozen with fear and are scared to death to move forward. This can limit us from achieving what we were created to be or created to do. Fear is not the plan that God has for our life. God wants us to fear him so that we do not have a fear of this world. See, God says that he has conquered the world. So, what we fear the most, God has already conquered. Now the fear that God has for our life is not paralyzing fear but is empowering fear. It is the fear that God is God, and we are not. It is the same fear that we have of our coaches and mentors. This fear stems from a plan they have laid before us, and if we do not follow it, we will be disappointed in the outcome. A healthy fear of the Lord helps us understand that a higher power loves us and wants what is best for us. So how do we change our pattern of fear? It starts with us changing the way we think because that is where the origin of fear starts. The formula to removing fear is that we must no longer conform to the world's pattern before us. Then we must renew our minds so that we remove the fear that surrounds us. So how do we not "fear not?" The answer is simple; we learn to trust in the Lord with all our heart and lean not into our own understanding. "Fear not" requires that you fear the Lord and that you trust in his will and not your understanding. So, fear not, and I will see you at the plate.

Dear God of Boldness,

Empower me. Help me to fear you so that I do not have to fear the world. God, you go with me even though I travel through the valley of the shadow of death. You will always protect me and give me a spirit of boldness. Help me to realize that fear is of Satan and not of you. Help me to fear not so that I can share your love and salvation to all those that you have put in my sphere of influence. Amen.

Day 303

Rebuild Time

Isaiah 9:10 ***"The bricks have fallen, but we will (re)build with dressed stones; the sycamores have been cut down, but we will put cedars in their place."***

In the world of college sports, you hear these words thrown around all the time. This year will be a "rebuilding year" for this team. Sometimes, a team can achieve great things because of many upperclassmen or elite talent, maybe even going undefeated for a year. But then the next year, the team finds that their talent level or team chemistry may just not be as good, and they begin to struggle. It is easy to go from 11-1 to 3-9 in just one season. The truth is that we are all going to find ourselves in these "barren" seasons. These seasons can sometimes be very trying, but they can also help teach us a lot about ourselves and may even cause us to reevaluate what is important in life. Sometimes we need a time of rebuilding, and we may even need time to get back to the reliance on a team concept. During these seasons, we may realize that individual performance was the reason we achieved such greatness. In the Scripture, God's chosen people went through many barren times. They often turned their back on God and relied solely on a human presence to get them through. God used these fruitless seasons to help them realize that they forgot to focus on the most important thing. That most important thing was God. I am often reminded of how quickly God's chosen people were to forfeit his presence and try to achieve things independently. Moses had gone up Mount Sinai to get the Ten Commandments, and within 30 days, the people had turned on Moses and began to worship a calf made of gold. They had turned their back on God because things were not going exactly like they thought they should go. How many times do you hear of someone turning their back on the team because things are not going their way? The truth is that we need to be part of the rebuilding process, and sometimes that is going to be difficult and require that we roll with the changes. Other times we must accept that this year may be a rebuilding year. Sometimes it is during these rebuilding years that we grow the most. Sometimes the lesson is in the struggle and not in the victory. How many times in the Scripture do we hear of God using someone to rebuild? He used Abraham to rebuild a nation, he used Nehemiah to rebuild the wall, and he used Solomon to rebuild the temple. The truth is that you just might be building something that later will be something special. You may not get to see the fruits of your labor, but you will know that you were building something that would be honored and blessed. Let's build it now, and I will see you at the plate.

God of Rebuilding and Rebirth,

God, thank you that you help to rebuild what so often we tear down with our own hands. Thank you for letting us be part of a rebuilding process that you may bring to fruition later. Thank you that you give us a new start every day, even when the day before we failed you and failed the people that you love. Thank you for rebuilding my life through the death and resurrection of your Son Jesus.

Day 304

Leaving It All

2 Corinthians 5:18 ***And all of this is a gift from God, who brought us back to himself through Christ. And God has given us this task of reconciling people to him.***

This week, I heard an analysis ask a professional athlete if they wanted to retire while still on top? The athlete's response was, "why would I retire as long as I still have gas in the tank. The truth is, no matter where I am at in my career, I want to leave it all on the field. I do not want to go out with some still left in the tank". How often do you hear a comment like that? The truth is that many people do like to go out at the height of their career, but the question is are they wasting what God has given them. I mean, maybe they are a coach that takes a lesser job to build a new program. Maybe it is a player that comes alongside a rookie to help them develop. Maybe, it is a player that is more utilized in situations instead of every down or inning player.

The truth is that we do not want to take what we have with us. I cannot tell you how many times I have heard a player have regrets that they did not leave it all on the field. They say that they had held back or had tried to reserve but now regret that they had not just given it their all.

When they hold back, it affects not only their performance but also the game's outcome. The truth is that if we take what God has given us for granted, then we will be filled with regret instead of the fulfillment that comes from having given it our all. I think about this as it relates to God's love for us. God spared nothing in his love for us. God sent his only Son to atone for the sinners that did not deserve his love. Then his Son Jesus gave everything that he had so that we would be saved from death. The truth is that Jesus left nothing on the field; he gave everything by giving himself up as a ransom for our sin. If we just look at the example that Jesus set for us, we should never leave gas in the tank. The truth is that when we give our all, we honor what God has given us and what Jesus did for us. So let me ask you, what is holding you back from giving everything you got? Jesus gave his all, and so should we. See you at the plate.

Dear Jehovah-'Ez-Lami - Lord my Strength, (Prayer Adapted from Kristin Stanfill, Jesus Paid It All) Jesus paid it all, and I owe it all my Savior and redeemer; Sin had left a crimson stain, but my Lord and Savior washed it white as snow. Thank you, Jesus, for giving your all so that I can give my all every day in everything that I do. You paid it all and did not give up on me.

Day 305

Refuse to Play and Betray

I Chronicles 29:9 ***Then the people rejoiced at the willing response of their leaders, for they had given to the LORD freely and wholeheartedly. And King David also rejoiced greatly.***

We are in the middle of the 2019 Football Bowl season, and what a great slate of games are on hand for your viewing pleasure. This year there will be 43 bowl games starting before Christmas and ending the second week of January. A bowl game is a great reward for a team having a winning season and working hard so you can continue to play. Even though there are 43 games, many more teams will hang up their cleats rather than head to the practice field to prepare for a bowl game. One would think that making it to a bowl game would be a great honor, but the truth is that some teams turn down bowl bids because they feel they have been slighted or they did not get into the game they think they deserved. But in the past few years, there has been a new trend in college football, and I think it solidifies that we live in a generation of entitlement. I also say that many players think they will put the "I" in a team. Now, I know some will disagree because there is a lot of money involved but remember that the love of money leads to evil. So the new trend is that if you are not playing in one of the national championship-deciding bowl games and you are a projected top pro draft pick, you sit out. The players say that they are protecting their future and their career. But I would argue that what they are doing is that they are quitting on their team. Often, what they are doing is putting themselves in front of the team that helped them get where they are. As a leader, we are never supposed to quit on our team. Team is not about me; it is about us. Team is about selling out for the others that have gone to war with you week after week. There is a sad story in the Scripture about one of the apostles quitting on his team.

Judas puts "me" in front of the other eleven disciples. Judas decides that he must force the hand of Jesus because he is not getting what he wants. So, he betrays the head coach with a kiss. Judas gave up on his team and, in essence, gave up on the process. Now, I am not suggesting that not playing in a bowl game is equivalent to betraying our Lord and Savior. What I am saying, though, is that team abandonment can lead to greater bad decisions. My opinion is that finish what you started, and you do that by putting your team above yourself; I mean, after all, is that not what Jesus did? He did not just give some but went all in, and so should we. There is no "I" in team, but "I" will see you at the plate.

Dear God of All In,

Thank you that your Son put himself aside for a sinful being like me. Help me to never quit on my team, my marriage, or my faith. Help me always put the team above me or the I. Forgive me for those times before I quit for selfish reasons or gave up on someone. The truth is that quitters never get the chance to witness.

✞

Day 306

Goal: Winner's Circle

Luke 15:4 ***"Suppose one of you has a hundred sheep and loses one of them. Doesn't he leave the ninety-nine in the open country and go after the lost sheep until he finds it?***

Let's face it, the whole point of being successful in sports is being in the winner's circle and staying in the winner's circle. I mean, the truth is that we all want to be in the winner's circle in every aspect of life, not just sports. The truth is that this is what we have been taught, or maybe a better use of terms here is, "what we have been programmed to do" since we were born? I mean, are you not in the winner's circle if you live in the right house with the right zip code and drive the right car? Are you not in the winner's circle if you are in the right school or play on the right team? What about being in the right circle of friends or the right club? I would not disagree that the winner's circle is a great place to be, but there is a misconception that if you are not in the winner's circle, you cannot experience grace. I would say that believing in this concept is the exact opposite of how we experience God's grace. God's grace is usually found outside of the winner's circle. Most of the time, when we are in the winner's circle, we think that we do not need grace because we are propped up on our accolades. But sometimes, when life has left us living in Plan B is when we are most aware of God's grace. When we find ourselves struggling with death, illness, sickness, or loss, that is where God's grace is most experienced. It is almost freeing to know that we do not have to live solely in the winner's circle to experience God's grace. See, many times, the winners' circle lends itself to be a place of arrogance, self-reliance, and the feeling that you have arrived. But it can also be a lonely place because God can only be found when we let him in. God will not push himself through the door and into your life. God is found when we are so lost that we cannot find ourselves. I had heard many professional athletes talk about where they found themselves the most when they were a lot the most. I think that this explains the nonsense of leaving 99 sheep to go after just that one; that one that has been pushed out, the one that has been eliminated, the one that no longer stands in the winner's circle. There are only two places where we can be; we can be in the winner's circle or outside the winner's circle, but we can always be in God's grace. Let's not quit trying to win the game but understand that God is the God of those outside the winner's circle as much as those inside the winner's circle. Now get out of that warmup circle, and I will see you at the plate.

God of Those Outside of the Circle,

I have been in the winner's circle, and I have been outside the circle. I have been on 0-for teams, and I have been on undefeated teams. But I have always experienced your grace not because of who I am but how you are. Leaving 99 to find one does not make sense unless you are the one. Thank you that when I was that one, you came looking for me and that you found me. I have experienced your grace so many times outside of the winner's circle.

✞

Day 307

Who Are We?

Philippians 3:8-9 ***...I consider them rubbish, that I may gain Christ and be found in Him, not having my righteousness from the law, but that which is through faith in Christ, the righteousness from God on the basis of faith.***

The other night I caught the pregame speech given by Clemson's Coach Dabo Sweeney before his team took the field to play Ohio State for a spot in the National Championship Game. Here is a quote that he used that caught my attention. He said, "they can prepare for what we do, but they cannot prepare for who we are." So, the challenge that he was presenting to his team was, "who are we?" Who have we taught you to be as football players and as young men? You know, when we ask that same question of ourselves, we are quick to answer, but it is different to prove who you are both on and off the field. In sports, every opposing team can see on film what our tendencies are, see where our weak spots are, and see the areas of the field that lend to them making plays. But what they cannot prepare for is who the competitor is under the helmet.

You also cannot prepare for who they are in their heart. Sometimes the victory is a victory because of how a team believed in themselves and one another. Do you know that God asked you this same question as you go through life? He asked the question, "who are you?" What God is hoping for is that we will be a "little Jesus." I used to have a mentor who would always say, "be a little Jesus with skin on." You see, in the end, we will not be defined by how many games we won, and we will not be defined by our house or car. What we will be defined by is who we are in Jesus. You see, the world can take away your possessions, but it can never change who you are in Christ. Jesus even asked his disciples one day; who do you say I am? What is funny about that is that he really wanted to know if when people see the disciples, will they see Him? (Jesus) So be who God has called you to be, and I will see you at the plate "Little Jesus."

Dear Great I am,

Help me to be who you want me to be and not who I want to be. Help me realize that the world may attack me but cannot break who I am. Thank you that your Son never wavered in who he was and that he patterned who I can be in him. Thank you for my best friend and my Lord and Savior, Jesus Christ.

Day 308

Spitting Mad

Matthew 26:67 ***Then they spit in his face and struck him with their fists. Others slapped him.***

The other day I watched a post-season bowl game, and one of the players got ejected for a personal foul. Now, I watched the replay, and I did not see anything that malicious. I mean, there was a push, and then the player lunged toward the face of the other player but did not make contact. But then they slowed the film down, and you can see the real reason for the personal foul and the dismissal of the player. The player lunged toward the other player, and then there it was coming out of his mouth. He spits on the opposing player. Now on a personal side note, I do not think that there is anything more demeaning or flagrant than spitting on someone. I used to work at a group home with lots of boys that had behavior problems. Many days they would cuss me and yell at me, but if they spit on me, we would have serious problems. I told them upfront that you will be physically restrained if you spit on me, and it will not be gentle restraint. Now I know that in a game, a player can lose control of their temper, but there is really no excuse to ever spit on a person. Spitting just shows your lack of respect for your competitor and ultimate for yourself. I think the reason that spitting bothers me so much is because it says in the Scripture that as Jesus was being crucified, they spit on him. It was not enough to beat him, push him down and strip him naked, but they also spat upon this wounded servant. I just see this as the ultimate sign of disrespect and hatred. The truth is that we must learn to play the game without hate for any of our fellow competitors. I am not saying that we should not play to win, and we should definitely go as hard as we can every play. But we need to play the game from the aspect of respect and not the aspect of hate. See, the problem is that we carry many of these traits of hate with us off the field and throughout life. If we are not careful, this kind of hatred will ruin relationships and lead us to abuse people we love. I think right now; you just need to decide that your mouth is a no-spit zone no matter how pushed or taunted you are. So now that you are in the no-spiting zone, I will see you at the plate.

Dear God of Respect,

Help me to tame my tongue and to watch how upset I get over many trivial things. Help me to make the promise to never spit on anybody. They spit on your Son, and yet he still asks God to forgive them. Wow, what a Savior and what a lover of all people. He loved them even when they hated him. If Jesus can hold his temper in a situation where they are taking his life, then I should be able to endure when others come after me.

Day 309

Firing Monday

Deuteronomy 31:8 ***Do not be afraid or discouraged, for the LORD will personally go ahead of you. He will be with you; he will neither fail you nor abandon you."***

Today, some coaches will hear these words, "You are fired." Today is known as Firing Monday in the NFL. Yesterday, the NFL played their last regular-season slate of games, and so today is known for losing NFL teams to fire their coaches so they can make a change and hopefully get back to winning. I am typing this early this morning; it is not even 8 am yet, and two coaches have already been fired. The truth is that the coaching profession is a profession that you can be a hero one minute and be on the proverbial hot seat the next. If you want to keep coaching, you have to win, and you have to win consecutively. One bad season and the fans and administration will turn their backs on you. So, I am going to be honest. I have never been fired from a job in my life. But I can imagine that it is very demeaning, and it takes a huge toll on one's psyche. I have counseled many people who have been fired, or the soft terminology "they were let go," and I can tell you their whole lives were thrown into chaos. I am so happy that God does not fire us for our wins and losses in life. I am so glad that God's grace says, "no one gets fired." When I look at my life, I often see how often I failed God in my promises and daily walk. The great thing about God's grace is that I get a new day tomorrow and that God does not love me any more or any less. Now, this does not give me a license to sin or a spirit that says, "I quit." No, grace helps me realize that I will never be fired but that I must move on toward perfection. So, knowing that God will never fire me gives me the security of how much he loves me and that he will never let me go. Now in life, you may get fired or let go, but God will never fire you from his team because you were bought at a price, and that was the price of his Son Jesus Christ. So now you know that you have job security. I will see you at the plate.

Dear Big Boss,

Thank you that you sent your Son that through my acceptance of him, I could play on your team. That I could be a part of something bigger than I will ever understand. God, I thank you that you do not fire me based on my wins and losses. I thank you that you extend your grace even when I do not deserve it. God help me not to exercise grace by sinning on purpose. Thank you for never leaving me but going before me so that I can know the way. In your kingdom, I will never hear the words, "you are fired." Amen.

Day 310

Are You Hungry?

I Samuel 21:6 (NLT) ***Since there was no other food available, the priest gave him the holy bread—the Bread of the Presence that was placed before the LORD in the Tabernacle. It had just been replaced that day with fresh bread.***

After someone makes a great shot or a game-changing tackle, they often get up and act like they are eating (scooping food off of a plate and into their mouth). It is supposed to signify their hunger for the game and their ability to eat you up. Sometimes we are very good at feeding our appetite associated with fame and accolades, but we often neglect the deep-down God-given hunger hole that is the portal to the soul. I sometimes have this notion that we are surrounded by food, but some are starving to death. Now the food I am referring to is not substance for the body but substance for the soul. Mother Teresa once said, "that people in India were starving physically, but in America, people are starving spiritually and emotionally. See, God hard-wired us with an appetite for his spiritual love. That is why so many people reach the pinnacle of their job or career, and they say, "man, there has to be more to life than this." For others, they are bored and constantly restless even though they are always in motion. Have you ever felt like something was just missing from your life? This is our soul's way of telling us that we need nourishment to satisfy our soul's hunger. The truth is that you can be eating from the world all the time, but if you are not feeding the soul, then you can find yourself starving. This means that you may be achieving great things on the outside, but there is a longing inside, and you know that is true by the emptiness you feel.

There is a great story in the Bible about David and his warriors finding themselves upon returning from battle starving to death. They find themselves at the temple, and in order to combat their hunger, they eat the consecrated bread. This was a deliberate breaking of the law, but I think there is a significance here to David finding himself not only physically hungry but spiritually drained as he is on the run from Saul. I think this passage shows us where to run when we feel famished. We run to the cross as David ran to the temple. Jesus has told us, and we see this significance in the Lord's Supper, that his flesh and blood are the nutrients that keep us from starving to death. I just wonder what it would look like after a great small group or time of worship if we left the building acting like we had been spiritually fed. I mean after all, the spiritual food has so much more importance than physical food. So now that you are fed, I will see you at the plate

Dear Spiritual Provider,

I have often been surrounded by food and been starving to death because I refused to go to the temple or the cross. God, your Son, provided the spiritual nourishment we needed, but we often reject it. Sometimes the spiritual food is hard to digest because it calls us to make a change in our life. The truth is that sometimes we would rather starve than change. Help me to be the nourishment for others as I preach and teach your word. Thank you for providing the bread of life. Amen.

Day 311

Religion vs. Relationship

James 1:27 ***"Religion that God our Father accepts as pure and faultless is this: to look after orphans and widows in their distress and to keep oneself from being polluted by the world."***

Let me ask you, do you treat your personal and spiritual life with the same approach that you have on the field? Last week, I watched a game where the quarterback was disqualified because he pushed a player after the play was over, and his hand slipped, and he hit the referee in the face. Now you know that means he was immediately tossed from the game (not to mention it was his senior year). After the game, the quarterback issued an apology saying that this is not who he is or the example he wants to set. Now it was great that he apologized for letting down his team, the university, and the God that he serves. Now the truth is that it was great that he apologized for all those things as he should because it was wrong, but the truth is that God did not love him any less because of what he had done. (His coach and teammates may have.)

We so often are under this false theology that God rewards us or punishes us based on our behavior or actions. Poor decisions can ruin our witness, but God does not ever love us any less. See, religion says God's love for us is based solely on how we perform for him. It is all about the rules and ensuring that we are inside a denomination that does things the right way. Religion is all about doing and never about being. Now the truth is that we find God in our relationship with him and not by the rules we follow. See, religion says, "that if we obey God and do everything right that God will love us and reward us." But the Gospel of Jesus Christ says it is because God loved us that we follow and obey God. See, religion is all about putting your trust in yourself, whereas the gospel is all about putting your trust in the perfect atonement of Jesus Christ. Another way of looking at this is that religion is about what we have to do, but the Gospel of Jesus is about what we get to do. We often know that our poor performance on the field will result in us being benched, so it is easy to slip into this same mentality off the field. The truth is that we should approach the throne of God with the excitement that we get to follow a God that loved us so much that he came looking for us. Listen, do not have a religion with Jesus but have a relationship with him. Ask him to be the center of your life, and then consider it a pure privilege that you get to follow him. See you at the plate.

Dear Relationship Builder,

God, thank you that I am not judged by my doing as much as my being. Thank you that I do not have to earn your love. Thank you that I am not rewarded for what I get right and what I get wrong. I am saved by grace, and I have been created for a relationship with you. Thank you that you came looking for me and I found you. Help me to grow in my relationship and not my religion.

Day 312

Learning the Hard Way

Proverbs 21:11 (NIV) ***When a mocker is punished, the simple gain wisdom; by paying attention to the wise, they get knowledge.***

Have you ever met a friend or a teammate that had to learn everything the hard way? I was listening to the starting lineup for a professional football team a while back. This is where they have each player before their first possession introduces themselves, their position, and what school they attended before turning professional. When it got time to announce the school that he came from, one of the players announced it as having attended "the school of hard knocks." That made me wonder just what type of path he had journeyed to get to where he was now. The truth of the matter is that if we sat down with him, he would probably tell us how the decisions that he had made in his life had made this journey more difficult. I grew up very similar to that in that I had to learn everything the hard way. I would push the envelope and test boundaries to the max. The problem with learning this way is that it takes a lot longer to arrive at our destination, which may force us to miss some of the things that have been prepared for us. One of the most amazing stories in the Bible about learning things the hard way is the story of the Israelites escape from

Egypt. The whole trip, including the crossing of the sea, was supposed to be an 11-day journey. But because of their stubbornness and learning things the hard way, they turned an 11-day journey into a 40-year wandering in the desert. Wow! Now, as I look at the Israelites, I am reminded of how many times I have turned something that should have only taken a moment into a monumental task because I wanted to do it my way. The truth is that when we want to do it my way, and it is in direct opposition to what God wants us to do, there will always be a delay. So many times, our pride gets in the way of our obedience. We know we are wrong and should listen, but we insubordinately continue doing things the hard way. The truth is that we should not judge the Israelites too hard because there have been times in our life when we turned an 11-day journey into a 40-year wandering. So quit wandering, and I will see you at the plate.

Dear Mighty Leader,

Lord, help me to put aside my stubbornness. Lord, help me to put aside my pride. Lord, help me to quit saying I did it my way. Lord, help me listen to your guidance so that I do not turn an 11-day journey into a 40-year wandering. God, help me realize that you created me for a purpose and help me be obedient to that purpose.

Day 313

Time Teaches

Ecclesiastes 3:11 ***He has made everything beautiful in its time. He has also set eternity in the human heart, yet no one can fathom what God has done from beginning to end.***

There is an amazing story about a backup quarterback for the University of Florida. His name is Kyle Trask, and he has not started a football game since he was in middle school. He sat behind D. Eric King, a multi-star quarterback in high school, and then sat for three years behind others at the University of Florida. One of the Florida assistant coaches told the head coach that they could not recruit a backup to a division one elite program when he was being recruited. But the head coach was willing to take a chance because he had all the attributes that a good quarterback needed. Here is where the story gets good that willingness to take a chance paid off halfway through

Trask's junior year. The starting quarterback Felipe Franks was injured against the University of Kentucky, so Trask would finally get his chance, and he led them to a comeback victory.

As a matter of fact, Kyle Trask finished out the season with a 9-2 record. Not bad for someone that had not started a game since middle school. I read a quote the other day that helped me understand how something like this is even possible. Time is a trainer, teaching you to wait upon me, to trust me in the dark. I cannot imagine knowing you have the skills and just have to wait till the time is right to play. But so often, this is the lesson that God is teaching us in daily life. He is teaching us that by waiting, we are learning to trust in him.

By waiting, we are more thankful for the opportunity when it finally presents itself. By waiting, we can sit with him and abide solely in God. I think of Abraham in the Bible, and the time is training that he had to go through to get a son. He had to wait on the Lord and wait for many years, as a matter of fact, a lifetime of years. I am not talking about the 15-minute line out the door at Starbucks that has you cursing under your breath. I am talking about years upon years of hoping, praying, pleading, and weeping. But God came through in God's timing, and Abraham was all the more faithful for the time that he had been waiting. There may be some things in your life right now that you have been praying for, and you feel that God is absent from your request. But stay the course and let time teach you what God wants you to know. God is faithful, and he uses the time to teach us that our reliance is on him. You may be third on the depth chart right now but do not give up. For at the proper time, you will get your chance, and when you do, make the most of it. So now is the time I will see you at the plate.

Dear God of Kairos (TIME)

God help me to understand that you have set me apart, that you are the one that knows more than I do about how to time things in my life. Give me patience when I feel that you are not quick enough. God help time to teach me to love you more and to rely solely on you. God, help me remember that you will not always give me everything I asked for and that sometimes your answer to my prayer will be unknown. Who am I that I should question you on time? After all, you created all time and space. Amen.

✞

Day 314

"Anchor Down"

James 1:6 (NLT) ***But when you ask him, be sure that your faith is in God alone. Do not waver, for a person with divided loyalty is as unsettled as a wave of the sea that is blown and tossed by the wind.***

So a few years ago the Vanderbilt University adopted a new slogan for their football program. The slogan is written across the field, and even on their helmets, the slogan simply says, "Anchor Down." Now to anchor down means to secure yourself for the fight and the battle that is about to ensue. We all know that an anchor helps secure and steady a ship. An anchor keeps a ship from being sent back out to sea by the wind and the waves. But the truth is that we must also anchor down in our life. The Scripture says that we should not be blown back and forth but that we should be anchored.

If you are not anchored, the world can quickly throw you off course or blow you back into the sea. The anchor that we have in the Christian faith is the cross. It is a symbol of what we need to be anchored to. The cross helps us to remember that our faith is stabilized with the power of Jesus Christ. The cross represents grace, love, and the ultimate sacrifice. The cross that held Jesus is also what holds us to the faith. The cross, which had also been known as an instrument of death, can now be known as an instrument of life. When we are anchored to the cross, we are not blown about by society's changing waves. The cross helps us anchor ourselves to understand that we are free to receive grace even though we do not deserve grace. I once heard a pastor say, "you know it was not the nails that held Jesus to the cross; it was his love for us that held him to the cross. So, I want to challenge you to anchor down with the cross of Jesus Christ. This cross will stabilize you and keep you on the right path. So anchor down, and I will see you at the plate.

Dear Anchor of Hope,

God help me to anchor myself to the cross and not to the world. God, it is so easy for us to be blown about from place to place and from sin to sin. But when we are anchored upon the cross of Jesus Christ, we realize how much you love us and how much you gave up so that we could be with you. Your love is what held Jesus to the cross so that we could see how much he loved us. God, may I anchor down to the cross and put my faith in no one but you. Amen.

Day 315

Defeating the Undefeated

Ephesians 2:10 ***For we are his workmanship, created in Christ Jesus for good works, which God prepared beforehand, that we should walk in them.***

We have all known teams that are on an undefeated winning streak. Sometimes it is that they have not been beaten in years. Sometimes teams are undefeated at home. Oklahoma owns the longest winning streak in NCAA Football, with 40 wins in a row. Their winning streak spanned from 1953-1957. The truth is that being undefeated puts a target on your back. Right now, Auburn University's basketball team has started the 2020 season off 14-0. Being 14-0 means that every night you play, you get the opponent's best because they hope to end your streak. Now being undefeated made me think about the world as it related to Satan before Jesus came to do battle against him.

You see, Satan was undefeated when it came to causing people to sin. The Scripture says, "for all have sinned and fallen short of the glory of God." But there is one that defeated the undefeated. Jesus came and was found blameless in the eyes of God. Jesus faced every temptation that we face, but he passed every temptation that was thrown at him. Jesus defeated Satan so that our sin does not defeat us. We all know that we sin and fall short of what God has called us to do so many times. See, Jesus was the underdog that took on the impossible task of defeating one that was solely out to defeat anyone he came into contact with. The underdog not only won, but the Scriptures say that he crushed the opponent's head. Now see, because of the crucifixion, we also have an opportunity to defeat the undefeated. When you accept Jesus as your Lord and Savior, then his sinless life covers our sinful life. The truth is that this is the only way to defeat the evil one. So let me ask you a question have you adopted the game plan of Jesus Christ? The only way to defeat the sin in your life is to pray the prayer we mentioned before. Jesus, come into my heart; come into my heart today; come into my heart to stay. Come into my heart, Jesus. "Bam!" and the undefeated is defeated once again. Now that you have prayed that prayer, I will see you at the plate.

Dear Undefeated One,

I cannot do it on my own. I want to do the right thing, but I just fail to do it. I have tried forever to be good enough, but I am not even sure what is good enough. I feel defeated many times, but the truth is that I have the undefeated one on my side. His name is Jesus, and I am with him. That is what covers me and leaves me in a place where I have victory. Thank you, Jesus, that you defeated the undefeated.

Day 316

Use SOAP

Psalm 119:15-16 ***I will study your commandments and reflect on your ways. I will delight in your decrees and not forget your word.***

The sports world is always using acronyms and abbreviations to explain things. One of my favorite ones that our college football coach used to say to us is that we were going to "KISS IT." It meant we were going to "Keep It Simple Stupid." It used to make us laugh, but now that I think about it, I do not know why I laughed because he was calling us stupid. So the other day, I came across an acronym that I had not seen before. It was SOAP, and a pastor was using it to teach his congregation how to study the Scripture. SOAP stands for Scripture, Observation, Application, Prayer. So here is the formula for how you can apply SOAP to your spiritual life. The first is that you must daily be in your playbook of life, which is the Scripture. You must read your Bible or do a devotional book that includes Scripture to think about how God is speaking to you through his word. So what you do is that you write down one Scripture that is speaking to you. Make sure you write it down. Then you observe why this Scripture is speaking to you and why it is so important at this juncture of your life or current situation. Then you seek how you can apply this Scripture to your life, and you begin to apply it. It is amazing how many people read the Scripture but do not apply the Scripture to their life. It is like reading the direction on medication but never taking the medication to make yourself better. For Scripture to work, it must be applied. The final thing that we must do as it relates to SOAP is write out a prayer that tells God how we will apply this to our life and thank him for allowing us to find these Holy Words. The truth is that if you use the SOAP process in your life, you will find that the Scripture will come alive in your life. Using this method, you will feel a better connection with God and see how God is still speaking to you daily.

So use the SOAP method, and I will see you at the plate.

Dear Author of the Holy Word,

Forgive me for neglecting your Holy Word and trying to find my way. Help me observe my life and the weak areas that need the Holy Word to clean up what I have messed up on my own. God, it does me no good to read your Word but never apply it to my life. Finally, let my life become a prayer to you and how I might use your Word to change my heart. Thank you that your Son was the Word and that through him, all things have been fulfilled. Amen.

Day 317

The Perfect Season

Hebrews 10:14 ***For by one sacrifice he has made perfect forever those who are being made holy.***

So last night, the LSU Tigers won the NCAA Division I College Football National Championship for 2019. This win capped off a perfect season as the Tigers finished 15-0. It was a feat that is very rare, considering that they played one of the toughest schedules in the league. To be perfect on a season takes a huge amount of teamwork and a little bit of luck. The truth is that the Tigers are now in the conversation of being the best team of all time. This conversation got me thinking about who was the best person of all time? That person, of course, being Jesus Christ.

The truth is that even though he is the best of all time, many people do not consider him in their conversation of who has made an impact on their life or who is the greatest influence in their life. They do not consider this because they see him as a historical figure and not as the Lord and Savior of their life. You see, even though Jesus looks down upon us now, he is still very active in our daily life. He is our greatest fan, and he is constantly interceding in prayer for us. Jesus came and lived not only the perfect season but the perfect life so that we could inherit eternal life. The reason he is the greatest of all time is that he faced every temptation that we face, and yet he conquered them all. How did he live such a perfect life? He lived it through the Word of God. He was the Word, and he never deviated from the Word.

So often, we fail because we do not rely on the Word of God. So even though we will never have a perfect life, we have a Savior that gives us the ability to have the perfect life through him. So let me ask you, who is the greatest of all time? I hope that you will see that it is Jesus. I not only hope that you will see him as the best, but my hope is that you will accept him as your Lord and Savior and put your whole trust into him. So now that you know who is the greatest ever, I will see you at the plate.

Dear Perfect Spotless Lamb,

You were perfect in nature; you were perfect in life. Help me realize that you were the greatest of all time, not for your benefit but for my benefit. Jesus, come into my heart and perfect me, make me whole, and cleanse me. You are my Lord and my Savior, but you are also my friend. You have never left me or forsaken me but have always been with me. I love you so much, Jesus. Thank you for being perfect.

Day 318

Cheaters Never Win, They Get Fired

Isaiah 33:15-16 (KJV) ***He who walks righteously and speaks uprightly, who despises the gain of oppressions, who shakes his hands, lest they hold a bribe, who stops his ears from hearing of bloodshed and shuts his eyes from looking on evil, he will dwell on the heights; his place of defense will be the fortresses of rocks; his bread will be given him; his water will be sure.***

So the sports scandal of the week has to do with MLB and the stealing of signals to cheat and win. So far, there have been no less than five firings with more to come. I find it ironic that two of these teams were in the postseason this year. One of the coaches caught up in the middle of this has never even coached a game for his new team. The other reality is that this will cost those managers and coaches millions of dollars. Why is it that people feel that cheating gives them an advantage? I grew up hearing over and over that "cheaters never win." I think we ought to change that statement to "cheaters may win, but when they get caught, their character will be tainted for life."

There is never a week that goes by during the sports season that you do not hear of someone suspended because they tried to cheat by using performance-enhancing drugs. (Known as PED's) What kills me is that they know that they are going to be tested.

This cheating also occurs in life when we know what is right and wrong but still choose wrong. When we cheat Jesus by our intentional sin, we taint our witness. We sometimes even forfeit our witness. I can honestly tell you that I cheated in math every chance I got when I was in high school. This later caught up with me when I had to take college algebra four times to pass and graduate from college. I thought cheating was paying off, but soon the truth was revealed when I was not prepared for the test. The reason that Jesus was found blameless is because he did not cheat or take shortcuts. We do not cheat when we pattern our life after Jesus, so we may have to take the longer route. When we do not cheat or take a shortcut in challenging times, we learn to rely on God, not our nature. When we cheat, there is no dependence on God. In the New Testament (Acts 5), there is a story about a husband and wife who cheated on God and their community. They had made a promise, but they held back some of the money they had received from their property. The result of their cheating was that they both dropped dead. Now, I am not suggesting that you will drop dead for cheating, but I am telling you that your witness is dead when you cheat. So do not cheat; just put in the hard work, and I will see you at the plate.

Dear Jehovah-'Uzam - Lord Strength in Trouble,

I have cheated so many times, thinking that it was getting me ahead. God, by cheating, I fail not only myself but you. Cheaters are always found out, and the consequences are grave and take many years to rebuild. God, I would rather fail than cheat. Help me in those places where the challenge is great, and I am tempted to cheat my way through. Your Son did not cheat but gave his life for me so that I may one day see you face to face. Amen.

Day 319

Playing It Safe

Ecclesiastes 11:4 ***Whoever watches the wind will not plant; whoever looks at the clouds will not reap.***

I talked to one of the high school freshmen in our church the other day about not trying out for a sport he had played since he was young. His response to me was "that he did not want to try out for the team and not make it." He lamented, "that it would be better not to try out than it would to go look at the list and his name not be on it." I thought, man, I hope that this pattern does not follow you in life or you will never achieve anything great or of significant value. The truth is that we all have played it safe in life because we did not want to be disappointed. There is a story of two farmers having a conversation about planting crops. One farmer expressed that he just planted nothing because he feared the boll weevils would take over the cotton. The lack of rain would cause the corn not to produce, and the strong winds would blow away his winter wheat. So one farmer expressed to the other that he was not going to have any crops this year. He was just going to play it safe.

Now the truth is that he was not playing it safe; he was just not playing at all. Because there were no crops, there would be no yield. It would just be a wasted year. How many regrets in our life stem not from failing but from not trying? The truth is that playing it safe is just another way of expressing that we are scared to death. You do realize that because of Jesus, we do not have to play it safe. Because of Jesus, we cannot only take a risk, but we can fail and still stand in the grace of Jesus Christ. See, failure is not final, and it does not define us. The worst thing in life is the regret of never trying. So what if you fail and you have to try again. Remember, Thomas Edison failed 10,000 times, but he never called it a failure. Edison once said, "I have not failed 10,000 times – I've successfully found 10,000 ways that will not work." Someone else that did not play it safe was Jesus. If he had played it safe, he would have failed to grant us the eternal life that we do not deserve but that he has given us. So do not play it safe, and I will see you at the plate.

Dear Dangerous God,

How many times have I missed because I played it safe? How many times have I not tried because I was afraid of failure? How many times have I missed the opportunity to share my faith because I was gripped with fear? Forgive me for these shortcomings and nearsightedness. God, you give us the strength to succeed, but you also help pick us up when we fail. God, you are greater than any of our failures. God, help me to keep trying even when I want to quit.

✞

Day 320

He Is in the Little Things

Matthew 25:23 ***His master said to him, 'Well done, good and faithful servant. You have been faithful over a little; I will set you over much. Enter into the joy of your master.'***

We all know that we want to do great big things in the world. We want to do big things in school, in sports, and in our personal life. We know that there are great big things that make us known. But the truth is that it is a bunch of little things that add up to the big things. I once heard a coach say, "what matters is that we do the small things right." Why do small things matter because they help to prepare us for the great things in life? If you cannot handle the small things, how will you handle the big things in the world? You see, when we work on small things such as footwork or proper hand techniques, we are helping to prepare ourselves in a way that will give us an edge. When we focus on the small things, it shows that we care. The truth is that we all like to scrimmage and play against one another. There are many days when we show up to practice that we want to scrimmage and compete, but instead, we just drill and work on technique. Even though this seems mundane and boring, it is essential to prepare us for our next opponent.

Interestingly, the Titanic sank because the builder skimped on the rivets that held the boat together. The rivets were the smallest part of the boat, but they were the pieces that held it together. You see, the smallest detail may be what leads us to the greatest things.

Another reality is that people are often waiting for God to do the big thing in their life or ministry, but they have not been faithful with the small things, so God has yet to give them the responsibility of handling the big things. Maybe even our prayer lives should focus on the small things that keep us from being the best we can be. We often want to jump right from little league to the MLB, but we know that is impossible. You must get through all the small steps to get to the big leagues. So realize that the small stuff is as important to God as the large stuff. So take a moment to reflect on the small things in your swing that lead to the big hit, and I will see you at the plate.

Dear God of the Small Stuff,

God, you are in every detail. We know that from the intricate way that you created the world. God, there is so much detail in your creation and design. This shows us how much that you are in the smallest details. God, help me to be trusted with little so that one day I will be trusted with much. God, help me be as faithful to the small as I am to the great things you will do in and through my life. God, I love that you sent your Son for someone as small as me. God, thank you for being in the small stuff.

Day 321

Playing with Heart

Jeremiah 29:13 ***You will seek me and find me when you seek me with all your heart.***

The other day while watching a game, I listened to one of the commentators on television talk about one of the player's work ethic. He was saying that this player loved to practice as much as he loved to play. He was praising the young man by saying that everything that he did, he did with heart. Sometimes, when we play with heart, we play outside of our agenda. Playing with heart is not always about going all out, but it is about doing things that we do not want to do. It is reaching deep down inside ourselves to do what we have been called to do and not only what we want to do. Now, this is not only true in sports, but life is the same way. The truth is that in faith, many times, we are projecting our dreams onto God. But what if God has other plans for our life? How often are we frustrated with God because he is not answering what we ask him to do? The reason may be because God has different plans for our life, not the plans we have made. I think so often, rather than asking God what he wants us to do or where he wants us to go, we spend our time telling him what we want to do. You see, if you are going to live out the life that God has called you to, you will have to follow his GPS. Now, his way may cause strife and headaches, but, in the end, you will see how God has led you all along.

You must trust that God is leading your heart even when it is not comfortable or easy.

I think that it is almost second nature to take the easy way out, but that is not what Jesus did. The easy way out would have been to come and live a life of fame and popularity based on being the Savior. But Jesus led with his heart, and he gave his heart for us on Calvary. Jesus ministered with heart in everything that he did. So play with heart and follow God's lead. It will not be easy, but it sure will be rewarding. So bring your heart, and I will see you at the plate.

Dear Shepherd of the Flock,

God, thank you for sending your Son to lead me. Help me to realize that my way may not be the way that leads me to the promised land. Help me to understand that I need to submit to your will and give up my agenda. God, help me take the less-traveled path even though it will be more challenging. Lead me, Lord. Lead me all day long.

Day 322

Payback

I Peter 3:9 ***Do not repay evil with evil or insult with insult. On the contrary, repay evil with blessing because to this, you were called so that you may inherit a blessing.***

Last night in the Kansas/Kansas ST. Basketball game, there was a bench-clearing brawl at the end of regulation. It might honestly have been the ugliest fight that I have ever seen in college basketball. I just wonder if the fight was not the result of a "payback." It seems that there had been some bad blood and jawing going on before the brouhaha. So many times, when something happens to us, we feel we must respond with a payback mentality. If we do not do it ourselves, we certainly pray that payback may ensue at a later time. In sports, playing with a payback in mind may cause you to lose the game and lose your teammates and fans' respect. If your sole reason for playing against a team is to get someone back, you are playing for the wrong reason. You see, the payback mentality will not only manifest itself on the field, but you will carry it through life. Now the payback mentality is the exact opposite of what Jesus Christ taught. He not only taught us to turn the other cheek, but he patterned this in his own life. He exemplified this when as the soldiers were beating, crucifying, hurling insults, and spitting on him that he said, "Father forgive them for they know not what they do." What would we have said? What would we have prayed for? I can almost guarantee you that I would not have been at a point of forgiveness. There is an old slogan that says, "what comes around goes around." I have often prayed against someone, yet that is directly opposed to what Jesus wants us to do. What if we were a difference-maker, not a person that longs for payback? What if we were the ones that, rather than hoping for payback, used uplifting words? What if we learned to pray for our enemies? Some people would say that this would make us weak, but I would argue that this makes us strong. This is how you win with class and dignity, patterning the life of Christ at the same time. By praying for forgiveness, you practice the "shalom" that Jesus so often talked about. So do not worry about paying someone back; just play the game with all your heart, and I will see you at the plate.

Dear The Passover,

I have so often prayed to give them what they deserve. I have so often hoped that what comes around goes around. I have honestly plotted and schemed for people to get the payback they deserved. Forgive me for these thoughts and actions, as they are wrong and sinful. Help me to love and to pray for my enemies. Help me to have the mentality of one that spreads peace and love even when I have been wronged. Thank you that Jesus patterned for me the act of love and not payback. Thank you, God, that you do not pay me back because you know what I deserve.

Day 323

Gasping for Breath

Genesis 2:7 (NLT) ***Then the Lord God formed the man from the dust of the ground. He breathed the breath of life into the man's nostrils, and the man became a living person.***

We all know those days when we run so much that we feel that we cannot catch our breath. How many times have you felt you were going to die if you were made to do one more sprint or one more lap? There are times when we just want to stop and catch our breath. We just want to stop and just take a deep breath. I had a friend in high school that had terrible asthma but loved to play sports. He always had to have his bronchial inhaler with him when he was competing. He was a cross country runner, and many times when he would finish the race, he immediately would have to find his inhaler. He once told me that it was like trying to breathe through a wet washcloth when his asthma hit. The truth is that we need air in our lungs so that we can breathe.

The Scripture says that God created us, then breathed his life into us with his very breath. This is how and why we took on his image. Not so much in the way that he put us together but the way that he breathed his being into our lungs. The word here in Hebrew is "Ruach," which means wind, breath, or spirit. The last definition is what is so important to us because we are created in his image. See, the image we are created in has more to do with being created with God's Spirit. We think of our image as the way we look, but if God looks upon the heart and not the outward appearance, we know that being created in his image has everything to do with the Spirit. See, God put us here on earth to do more than survive; he put us on this earth to be a little version of him. Now just like when we get short-winded from one more lap or one more sprint, sometimes, we get winded by one more bad thing or one more disappointment hitting us in life. There are truly times in life when we feel as we cannot breathe. It is times like these that we must step away for a moment and ask God to fill our lungs with his breath once again. It is here that we ask God to breathe upon us – to fill our lungs with his Spirit. Sometimes the best thing in life is just to stop and breathe. I mean breath, to soak in the goodness that comes from your Father that loves you. I think you will be surprised how quickly you will get your breath back if you just stop and breathe. So right now, stop running, pause and breath in the breath of the creator of life. I will see you at the plate.

Dear, I Am Ever Faithful,

Breath into me, oh Breathe of Life. Fill my lungs with the holy breath of your salvation. Help me to slow my breath so that I can breathe. I mean, breathe you in. Let me breathe so that I can fill my lungs with your Holy Spirit. Jesus, quit breathing on the cross so that I could breathe your salvation, and to that, I give you all the thanks. Amen.

✞

Day 324

Mirror Image

I Corinthians 13:12 (NLT) ***Now we see things imperfectly, like puzzling reflections in a mirror, but then we will see everything with perfect clarity. All I know now is partial and incomplete, but then I will know everything completely, just as God now knows me completely.***

The truth is that we all have professional athletes or coaches that we want to emulate. The truth is that we have our heroes of the game. We have people we follow, collect their trading cards, or wear jerseys to show our allegiance. I do not know how often I have heard professional athletes say they got to meet their heroes. Here is a professional athlete that gets excited because they get to meet their lifelong hero. The truth is they are excited because they have tried to mirror the person they are meeting. Now, what if I told you that we were to mirror the image of God. The problem with this notion is that we feel that we are not worthy of mirroring the image of God.

The reason that we get that feeling is that the devil tries to change the angle of the mirror or distort the image that we see in the mirror. One of the prettiest girls I ever met had a distorted view when she looked in the mirror. She saw herself as fat and ugly, and she struggled mightily with an eating disorder. She had such a distorted view of herself. The truth is that God is for you in every way He wants you to see yourself as he sees you. He created you in his image so that you could reflect the light and love of Jesus Christ. So often, we peer into the mirror and see this distorted, blurred image.

Satan wants us to believe that it is truly our reflection that we can ever measure up or reflect the Image of God. But that is a lie straight out of the pit of Hell. The other lie that Satan tries to get to appear in our perception mirror is when he tries to show us our life's worry, pride, and self-centeredness. He tries to get us to believe that we are on our own, but all of that is just a smoke and mirror routine to turn us away from God instead of turning to him. Did you know that you are someone's hero? Someone wants to wear your jersey and wants to be just like you. But if you do not see yourself as worthy of mirroring God's image, how will they see God in you. God gave you a platform so that his glory can be seen throughout your life. You do mirror the image of God. Look in the mirror and see who God sees, not who the world sees. You are truly fearfully and wonderfully made. You reflect the image of God. So with God's image written on your life, I will see you at the plate.

Dear Imago Dei,

When I look in the mirror, I see myself as your creation—created for a purpose. I am fearfully and wonderfully made. I will not let Satan distort or turn the mirror to fool me or trick me into believing that I am anything less than your creation and that you are my Father. God, you love me, so how could I not love you back by reflecting the Image of Jesus? When I look in the mirror, let me see Jesus and when people look at me, let them see Jesus.

Day 325

The Dip

2 Chronicles 15:7 ***But as for you, be strong and do not give up, for your work will be rewarded.***

Have you ever tried to learn something new? Maybe it is a new sport or a new hobby. It could even be changing the way you swing or the way you shoot the ball. Do you remember how excited you were when you first started? You could not wait to practice or play. It was new, and you were making great progress. But then there was what we call "The Dip." This was the place where you got stuck. You are no longer making the progress that you were once made. This is a place where you feel defeated. A marketing guru, Seth Godin, wrote a small business book entitled "The Dip." He describes "The Dip" as a place where we get stuck, where the newness has worn off, and where we want to give up or move to our new venture. The Dip is where it seems that our goal is no longer attainable. It is a place that either makes us or breaks us. See, The Dip is the downturn. But Godin says, "The Dip" is essential if we are going to get to the point that we want to get to." See, most quit when they get to "The Dip," but those that push past "The Dip" are the ones that reach their goals and even exceed what they first thought was possible. These are the people who set themselves apart from the rest. You see, God never intended for us to give up or to quit. As a matter of fact, it is in The Dip that we must rely on God. In The Dip, we find that our strength is gone, so this is where we prop up on the Word of

God. This is the place where the Holy Spirit whispers to us to "push on." You see, "The Dip" is a test in perseverance, a test in life and your sporting endeavors. It is the place that separates the winners and the losers. It is the place that separates those who fail from those who excel. No matter who you are or how good you are, there will be a point in your life where you find yourself in "The Dip." What are you going to do? Are you going to push through and accomplish something that only a few achieve, or are you going to quit and move on to the next thing till you hit The Dip once again? Let's get through "The Dip," and I will see you at the plate.

Dear Jehovah-Shammah - Present,

How many times have I given up because I found myself in the middle of a dip? God, I have failed you and given up when life got scary and seemed to be too much for me. For these things, I ask your forgiveness. God help me to push through when it seems that it is too difficult. Help me to rely on you when I find myself deep within the dip. God, help me separate from the rest of the world, not only on the field but also in life. Help people see your love through my perseverance. Amen.

Day 326

Sadness and Sorrow

I Corinthians 15:51-52 ***Listen, I tell you a mystery: We will not all sleep, but we will all be changed—in an instant, in the twinkling of an eye, at the last trumpet. For the trumpet will sound, the dead will be raised imperishable, and we will be changed.***

On Sunday, January 26, 2020, the news broke after church that legendary NBA Star Kobe Bryant had been killed in a helicopter crash on his way to his daughter's basketball game. His daughter and daughter's friend were also killed in the crash, and at least seven other passengers and the pilot. There were no survivors. The cause of the plane crash was likely because of the dense fog in the area and very limited visibility. Social media and news outlets quickly picked up the news and reported anything that they could glean. For the next 4 hours, it was certainly the top news story. As I write, I am saddened by this tragic news because these lives ended way too young. I am also reminded that we must never take any moment for granted because we never know when something like this crash may happen in our lives. The truth is that life can change in the twinkling of an eye. See, the reality is that the one thing that we can never get any more of is time. If we waste it, it is gone, never to be recovered. You see, this crash also reminds us that we should always have our house in order and be ready if our card is pulled today. We have no idea when Jesus is coming back, and we have no idea when our last day on this earth will be. This is why we should not hesitate in asking Jesus to be the Lord and Savior of our life. This is why the decision to follow Christ is the most important decision you will ever make, and it is urgent.

Two different aircraft have gone down in the last three weeks, with people in the sports field being killed. Carly McCord went down in a plane crash just hours before LSU took the field to play Oklahoma. Carly McCord was Steve Ensminger's (LSU's offensive coordinator) daughter. He coached that game with a heavy heart, knowing that he had lost someone way before their time should have been up. These two stories are not to sadden or scare you, but they remind you that we are not promised another day. They are a plea for you to make sure that you know whose you are (a child of God) when your time is up. This is to help you see that you are in need of a Savior and that you need to turn to Jesus. You see, when you have Jesus written upon your heart, then death does not have the last word. So have you asked Jesus to come into your heart? If you have, then say a prayer for someone that has not? If you have not made this decision for Jesus, then I urge you today to say these words, Jesus come into my heart, come into my heart today, come into my heart to stay, come into my heart, Jesus. You have at least this at-bat; I will see you at the plate.

Dear God of Comfort,

I ask you to be with the Bryant family to surround them in your arms in this time of questions and sorrow. Give them peace that passes all understanding. Today, God, I pray for those I know who have not chosen to follow you, and I ask you to show them the way to salvation. God, so many lives have been ended before their time. God, thank you that I am ready and that even if life changes in a twinkling of an eye, I will be with you forever.

✞

Day 327

Trying to Impress the Coach

Psalms 119:9-11 ***How can a young man keep his way pure? By keeping it according to Your word. With all my heart, I have sought You; Do not let me wander from Your commandments. Your word I have treasured in my heart, That I may not sin against You.***

Have you ever seen that person that is trying to be the coaches' pet? They will stay after practice if the coach suggests it. They are always in the coach's face saying, pick me, or I will volunteer. The problem with this player is that they are only willing to go the extra mile if someone is watching. They are not doing these things to better themselves, but they do them to impress the coach in hopes of more playing time or a starting position. We all know people like this in every aspect of life. When I was growing up, we said that these people had the Eddie Haskell syndrome. Eddie Haskell was a character on the television program "Leave it to Beaver." He was a brownnoser and manipulator. He was the one that instigated all the trouble, and then he wanted everyone to think he was the righteous one. I sometimes think that we can fall into the Eddie Haskell mentality regarding our spiritual disciplines. This is where we pray God sees all the good things we are doing. So often, we study or go through our spiritual disciplines because we are trying to impress God. We think somehow that if we study, pray, and journal, we earn God's love. The truth is that God loves us, no matter what. As a matter of fact, there is nothing you can do that will make God love you more. We practice spiritual disciplines to know God better, not so that he will be impressed by our spirituality. See, the real reason that a player stays after practice is so that he/she can get better. They stay after and do extra reps because they love to do what they are doing. The truth is that when we love doing what we do, then we will work at it with all our heart. The same is true when we look at our spiritual disciplines; we do these things because we love God and want to know more about him.

We are not trying to earn brownie points or get God to answer our request; we are studying because we want to show our obedience to God by learning his Word and then following it. Another reason we do extra reps is to push the other players around us to be better. We are trying to set the bar for them. We study God's Word and practice our spiritual disciplines so that we will be prepared to share Jesus with someone. Our spiritual disciplines mean a lot more to us here than they will when we get to our final resting place. So continue to stay after practice and continue your spiritual disciplines to be at your best. It is not about the show, but it is about work. So let's get to work, and I will see you at the plate.

Dear Jehovah-Helech 'Olam - Lord King Forever,

God, you love me when I was at my best, and you have love me at my worst. You love me when I turn my back on you, and you love me when I try to impress you with my pseudo-holiness. Nothing I do will ever make you love me more or less. I practice spiritual disciplines to know you better and that my heart will be one with yours. I love you, Lord, and I give myself to you and your will. Amen.

Day 328

Corner Man

Hebrews 4:16 (NLT) ***So let us come boldly to the throne of our gracious God. There we will receive his mercy, and we will find grace to help us when we need it most.***

We often think about God in many ways, but rarely do we think about him in terms of being a "cornerman." You have probably heard this statement before, "Those people are in my corner." This statement makes me think of a boxing match where the boxer is out there fighting hard, but when the bell rings, there are people immediately there to give the fighter water, towel them off, or even repair a cut during the fight. Those people in our corner are in the fight with us. If you did not have corner people, then you would essentially be fighting alone. You sometimes see in life; we feel beat up and lying on the mat. Sometimes in life, it feels as if we cannot even breathe. We often feel that we have been left to fight this battle all on our own with no cornermen to assist us. But we have three cornermen that are there are always there to help us. We have a Father who represents our head trainer. He is the one who has given us the fight plan. He is the one who has created us to fight.

We also have Jesus in our corner; he is our water boy and cut manager. He is there not to give us just water but to give us the living water of life. The same water that he provided the woman at the well he also provides for us. He also helps to bandage our cuts because he was bruised, beaten, and crucified. Because of all the things that he endured, he can cover and bandage the cuts that the world leaves us with.

Finally, we have the Holy Spirit in our corner to give us the advice we need to make sudden changes in how we are fighting. Sometimes the Holy Spirit will even lead us in a different direction. You see, we have three cornermen, and they are truly in the fight with us. So now that you know that you are not on your own, I will see you at the plate.

Dear Holy Cornerman,

God, I am in a constant fight. I sometimes feel as if I have been beaten down and broken. Sometimes I feel that I am fighting this all on my own. But then I remembered that you are in my corner and that your Son has already been through this fight. His fight was directly for me and my salvation. Help me to know that the Trinity is always in my corner. Thank you that I have a Savior that is always petitioning and interceding on my part. Thank you that I do not fight this fight alone.

Day 329

Stepping Out

2 Corinthians 5:6-7 So *we are always of good courage. We know that while we are at home in the body, we are away from the Lord, for we walk by faith, not by sight.*

One of the hardest things we will ever do is step out in faith. So often, we let the fear of the unknown keep us from taking the first step. How many times have we regretted not stepping out in faith? How many times have we missed the opportunity because we did not step out? What keeps us from stepping out is fear. You may ask, what fear? Here is a list of some of the common fears: fear of the unknown, fear of not being able to accomplish it, fear that others will laugh at us, and the fear that we do not have the resources it takes to get it done. You can fill in the blank here with anything associated with fear. God never wanted us to be stalemated because of fear. I think about all the people in life that became pioneers because they refused to let fear keep them from moving forward. I think about David stepping out to face a giant, I think about Peter stepping out to walk on water, I think about Ester stepping out to face a King. All these individuals stepped out in faith. Remember, the reward is always greater than the risk. The Scripture reminds us that faith believes in what we cannot see.

Faith is a trust that passes our understanding. Faith is where dreams become realities. One of my favorite scenes from Indian Jones is when he must get from a small ledge in a cave to the other side to reach the stone he has been seeking. The problem is that there is no bridge or rope to get him to the other side. Indiana stands there thinking how I am going to get across this bridge. The only way to the other side was to step out on faith. So what he does is he takes a step; it is a leap of faith, and as he steps out, a rock appears. Every step he takes is a step of faith, and with every step he takes, another rock appears. He would have never known how to get to the other side if he had not taken the first step. So what about you? Are you going to take the first step and step out on faith? I hope so because it is the only way that I will see you at the plate.

Dear Jehovah-Machsi - Lord my Refuge,

God, when I cannot see, give me faith.
God, when I cannot hear, give me faith.
God, when I am numb, give me faith.
God, when I am frozen in the grip of fear, give me faith.
Give me faith. Amen.

Day 330

Expect the Unexpected

Luke 18:27 ***"The things which are impossible with men are possible with God."***

This week, we will have a series of devotionals that are to help you with the mental aspects of competition.

Most of the time, when we hear the statement "expect the unexpected," we think that the worst is about to happen. In the sports world, we know that this sentence rings true many times during the season. A season-ending injury to the starting quarterback, a player becomes ineligible because of bad decisions; a coach leaves before the season ends. We all know that the sports world is full of the unexpected. I think that is why fans enjoy it so much. It is a story that writes itself as it is unfolding. Now what I want to focus on today is what this statement means related to God, not the world. You see, when we become prayer warriors and people of extreme faith, we expect the unexpected in a positive way, not a negative way. You see, we do not have a God of possible, but we have a God of the impossible. The truth is that God can do way more than we have ever thought possible. God can show up in places where we never expected. God can perform the miracle that we prayed for, but no one else believes it could happen. God can change the hearts of people that seemed too far to be redeemed. See, God is the God of the unexpected outcome. One of my favorite missionaries is George Mueller. He moved from Germany to England in 1829; he soon became convinced to set up schools and orphanages for the poor and desolate children in Bristol. Mueller was said to have always come to believe that God would move the unexpected to the expected. The reason is that in Mueller's heart, he truly believed that. He raised 151 million dollars in donations solely through prayer. He never asked one person for a dime. Every bit of it was unsolicited. One morning they had no food in the orphanage, but he sat all the kids down and prayed for breakfast; when he said amen, there was a knock at the door, and it was the local bakery that had a loaf for every child. It was also by happenstance that a milkman's cart broke down right in front of the orphanage and left all his milk with them.[28] You see, when you expect the unexpected, then you will see God show up in a mighty way. What miracle have you been doubting? What do you need to happen right now in your life? Listen! Expect the unexpected, and I will see you at the plate.

God of the Unexpected,

With you, all things are possible. You have always used the impossible to show that through you, all things are possible. We often do not see you show up because we do not believe in what we prayed or asked for. God, our faith is so shallow, yet you said that we could move mountains with the faith of a mustard seed. God, I want to see you move those mountains, but the only way that will happen is if I expect the unexpected.

✞

Fight the Resistance

Luke 6:45 ***The good man brings good things out of the good treasure of his heart, and the evil man brings evil things out of the evil treasure of his heart. For out of the overflow of the heart, the mouth speaks.***

You have probably seen someone holding up a sign on television that says, "fight the resistance." We often think that the resistance that we are fighting is that of the world. So often, when we are going against a better team, we hear how good they are and that we will have to play a mistake-free game to beat them. So what we are running up against is resistance. If you buy into the resistance, then great deeds will remain undone. Undoubtedly, I would argue that the greatest resistance that we face is the resistance of our minds. We have up to 80,000 thoughts in a day, but more than half of them are negative. So with this in mind, I mean literally in mind, the greatest resistance that we face is the resistance of the mind. Now, this is your greatest resistance because if you choose to believe the negative voice in your head, you will be talked out of accomplishing great things. The voice in our head tells us what we cannot do, and we begin to believe the voice. The truth is that the greatest enemy that we will face is the enemy of the voice in our head. See, Jesus once stated in John 8:44 that the devil lies, "he speaks his native language, for he is a liar and the father of lies." See, the truth is that Satan cannot speak the truth.

Additionally, we must learn not to believe the lies that Satan has sown throughout our minds. You see, the mind is what transmits God's plan for your life to either fail or succeed. So the resistance that you are fighting against are the lies of the devil. Here are some examples that may have played through your mind. You will never be good enough to start. You will never win a match. You will never make the team. You will never be able to keep it in the strike zone. You will always be too small, too weak, and too slow. You see, all of these thoughts flood our minds, and we must learn to block our negative and learn to listen to God. We can fight this resistance with one sentence that I want you to put to memory. God is "I Am," so that means that "I can be." Because he is, I am, and he created you in his image you can be. You can be all the things that your mind is trying to talk you out of. So I want you to block that negative thought right now, and I want you to say, God is I am so that "I can be." Repeat, and I will see you at the plate.

Dear Still Small Voice,

I will not listen to that little devil on my shoulder. He lies and lies and lies. He tells me I cannot live without him. He tells me that he knows what is best. He tells me if I lay him down, my life will be a mess. But the way that I slay him is by listening to the Holy Spirit's voice that you have instilled in me. I will constantly remind myself that because you are, I am, I can be, and I can do it. Thank you for sending your Son to seal this statement with his death and resurrection. Amen.

✞

Day 332

Handling Burnout

John 7:37 ***On the last and greatest day of the feast, Jesus stood up and called out in a loud voice, "If anyone is thirsty, let him come to Me and drink.***

You hear someone say all the time in the sports world that they are just "burned out." They are tired, and they have lost their love for the game. I truly think that total avoidance of burnout is impossible, but I do think that there are some things that you can do that will help you get back in the game after a bout with burnout. So, what can we do to avoid walking away while in the middle of burnout? The first thing is that we may need a Sabbath, a time that we truly rest. I mean rest in every aspect. This means a true break from our sport without thinking about it, worrying about it, or practicing it. A Sabbath lets us focus on what is truly important, and it allows the Holy Spirit to speak to our hearts. Sabbath is a time of rest and reflection. It is a time to be still and know that he is the Lord.

After a predetermined Sabbath, the next thing that can pull us out of burnout is a "refocusing" on why we play the game. We started playing the game because we loved it, and we loved the competitive spirit of the game. We need to explore this question, what has changed? Have I put undue pressure on myself? Have I begun to listen to the voice of the crowd? Am I playing for my team or approval? Have I begun to focus more on wins and losses than getting better? Has the team around me changed? All of these questions will help to refocus your love of the game.

By asking these questions and similar questions, we will have more clarity about what is leading to our exhaustion. Finally, we need to ask what is it that I love doing as it pertains to this sport? See, sometimes, the thing that burns us out is trying to be what we are not geared to be. I love this statement by Andy Stanley, "to work out of your strengths and not weaknesses."[29] We often spend more time thinking about what we are not rather than what we can be. In my life, I tend to work on my strengths to make them better, and I surround myself with people that are good at and enjoy what I do not enjoy doing. If you are going to avoid burnout, then you may have to take a step back right now and re-center and re-focus your life. So, with that in mind, when you are ready, I will see you at the plate.

Dear God of Rejuvenation,

I am tired, and I am weary. I feel as if I have nothing left. My tank is empty, and my cup is dry. Come to me, Holy Spirit, and let me rest. Come and let me Sabbath. Come and bring rest to my weary soul. I know you have never left me, but I have refused to acknowledge that you are here. Help me to refocus, refuel, and restore my faith. Help me to get back into the game.

Day 333

Stay Hydrated

John 4:14 ***But whoever drinks the water I give him will never thirst. Indeed, the water I give him will become in him a fount of water springing up to eternal life."***

Because we live in lower Alabama with tons of heat and humidity, one of the challenges of outdoor sports is staying hydrated. Many times, an athlete will have to leave a game because of cramps or heat-related conditions. The truth is that hydration is something that has to take place before you dehydrate. After one is dehydrated, you can help the cramps with pickle juice and water but being dehydrated may cause a player to miss the most important part of the game. Gatorade has a slogan, "Is It In You." Powerade has this slogan, "Power Through." These two sports drinks claim that they cannot only hydrate you but give you the ability to play at an optimal level. We have seen other hydration drinks hitting the market in the past few years, promising to keep you hydrated and ready for the game. These drinks include Nuun,

Power Core, Lyteshow, Propel, and the list could go on for at least five more pages. But if you want the honest truth, even though all of these can aid in hydration, the number one hydration drink is still good old H_2O (water).

There is a truth that to stay hydrated, you must drink lots of water. There is a great story in the Bible about Jesus meeting with a woman at a community well-drawing water. She was dehydrated, but her dehydration came from a spiritual sense and not a physical sense. She asked, "Jesus to give her the water of life," in which he said, "I am the water of life." Just like in sports, if we go too long without Jesus, we will become dehydrated. We can try to replace Jesus' water of life with other things, but the proper hydration of life comes only from drinking from the living water that Jesus offers. So, let me ask if you have hydrated today? If you have not, then hydrate right now, and I will see you at the plate.

Dear Living Water of Life,

My soul thirst for you. I have neglected hydrating so long that I need your living water. You offer water that continues to well up in our souls. Help me to hydrate so I can carry your water to others who are thirsty. Holy Spirit, quench my thirst and ignite my flame. Amen.

Day 334

Do Not Focus on the Loss

I Peter 5:8 ***Be sober, be vigilant; because your adversary the devil, as a roaring lion, walketh about, seeking whom he may devour.***

So, I was in the coffee shop today, and one guy that is there almost every Friday is a guy who works for the sheriff's department. He is well known in the coffee shop because his son is a starter for the LSU basketball team. Not only is he a starter, but he is a freshman, and he is averaging over 15 points a game. Can you say rock star? Now going into last week, LSU had not lost a game, but this week they dropped one. So, another regular coffee shop walked up to the Sherriff's Dept. Officer and asked what happened the other night.

The officer did not take this question very well and ask the guy why he asked about the team's only loss but had never commented on their wins? You have never asked me about the 8 SEC wins that they had before this first loss. Is this not how the world works? The world loves to talk about when we lose. I think that it helps them feel better about their circumstances. The truth is that we have kind of been wired to think this way. I remember having this one teacher in school who would wear a red pen out on my paper. It was that she loved to point out everything wrong. What she never did was that she never marked what was right. Of course, on my paper, that would not have been much.

You know the devil is the same in our life. Satan loves to remind us of the bad we have done. He is never going to whisper in your ear when you are winning the battles of life. He will only remind you of your losses, shortcomings, and your failures. So, the question is, are you going to listen to the voice of the liar? I think that so many people feel like a failure because they only focus on the losses. If you only focus on the losses, you will never be a winner. So, block out that voice in your head that tells you that you will strikeout, and I will see you at that plate.

Dear Victorious Banner,

Help me to block out the negativity. Help me to remember that you love me, win or lose. I bind Satan to stay away from my team and me. The world will take great joy in my failures, but your grace is sufficient to cover my multitudes of sin. Thank you that what seems like a failure on Calvary turned out to be the victory that defeated the dragon.

Day 335

Sideline Focus

2 Corinthians 11:24-25 ***Five times I received from the Jews the forty lashes minus one. 25Three times I was beaten with rods, once I was stoned, three times I was shipwrecked. I spent a night and a day in the open sea.***

One of the biggest questions for athletes is how to stay focused while watching from the sidelines due to an injury. Many times, an athlete can lose focus and lose heart while watching from the sidelines. The reason they waver is that they see someone else in the spot that they once held. They are also forced to go from star player to cheerleader. Then they have to listen to all the media talk about their return and whether they will be the same when they return. This year Tua Tagovailoa the quarterback for the Alabama Crimson Tide, went down this year with a gruesome season-ending hip injury. This forced him to watch from the sidelines, but he refused just to watch. He was on the practice field, engaged in all the aspects of the game. He was in the film room, continuing to break down the film. The truth is that he is what defines a great team player. That being a player that stays connected even while injured. I have seen so many players who have gotten injured that wound up letting that injury separate them from the team, but sometimes they separate totally from the sport. See, if you play your game long enough, eventually, you are going to be injured. Then the question becomes, how will you handle that injury?

There is a man in the Bible that went through great injury and trials. You see, Paul was an early missionary of "The Way," and he was as all-in as all-in can be. You would think if God were going to bless someone and keep them from harm, then it would have been Paul. But as you read the Scriptures, you see that it is just the opposite. It says, "that Paul was beaten, imprisoned, snake-bitten and shipwrecked." I mean, after all of that happens, I would say that it would be hard for one to stay in the game. But Paul was not going to let the calamites keep him out of the game. The truth is that no matter where Paul was or what had happened, he continued to stay in the game and preach the gospel of Jesus Christ. Paul is a great example of the statement, "when the going gets tough, the tough get going." In life, you will face things that sideline you, but you get to decide how you will handle that. So, stay focused, stay in the game, and I will see you at the plate.

Dear Jehovah-Keren-Yish'i - Horn of Salvation,

God, how I respond to the things that happen to me speaks to my character. So many times, when things happen to me, I just want to give in and give up. I have struggled with not only bodily injuries but with injuries to the heart. I must remember that when I stay focused and stay part of the team, people will see me through me. How I respond to life will define who I represent. God thank you that Jesus choose the cross for me. I accept Jesus as my Lord and Savior, and when I do that, it will always help me stay focused and in the game.

Day 336

You Still Have Jesus

Philippians 4:19 **And *my God will meet all your needs according to the riches of his glory in Christ Jesus.***

I watched the end of the Super Bowl last week, as many of you did. I must admit that I missed the first half because I was at the hospital but listened to it on the radio on the way to the hospital and on my way home. I got home to catch the middle of the 3rd and 4th quarter; it was a good game. I love when we have these seesaw back and forth battles. What caught my attention about the game was at the end of the game, where the camera panned across the bench of the losing team San Francisco 49ers. The 49ers were a favorite in the game and had started the game off looking like they may just walk away with the game. I truly think that they were the better team. But the outcome was not what they wanted, and they did not hold back their emotions after the shocking loss. Many of the players were seen with bowed heads, and many tears were shed. The outcome of the game dejected these grown men. Now, the truth is that if this is all that they have in life, then this dejection may define who they are, but if they have a relationship with Jesus, then they will not be defined by a Super Bowl loss. Will this loss hurt? Absolutely, but it will not define who they are. You see, so often, we spend all of our time investing in things that will bring us temporary joy and notoriety. See, our story is not the story of us just stumbling into becoming something special. No, we were created unique because we were created by God and in his image. See, we were made to find our ultimate purpose and our destiny in the Lord.

I believe that is why all of our achievements are temporal and feel as if they do not last. The truth is that next year there will be another super bowl and likely a different winner. Now, I am not saying that we should not try to win every game that we play, but I am begging you to find your ultimate victory in your decision to follow our Lord and Savior, Jesus Christ. I love this quote by John Ortberg; he says, "At the end of the day, we do not have a program, plan, platform, or product to help the world. We have a Savior. We do not point to success, knowledge, pleasure, power. We point to a cross."[30] So now that you are pointing to the cross, I will see you at the plate.

Dear Trinitarian God,

God, help me to realize that what defines me is my relationship with you. God, we know losing hurts, but we know that when we pass from this life to the next, we win because of our relationship with Jesus. What do I need? Just give me Jesus. When I have Jesus, I truly have all I need.

✞

Day 337

Mold Me

Isaiah 64:8 ***Yet you, Lord, are our Father. We are the clay; you are the potter; we are all the work of your hand.***

I may have said this before, but I do not think you can say this enough. "What you are to become, you are now becoming." Coach Ron Finley used to remind us of this statement daily. The truth is that you are not going to wake up one day and be different from what you are now. You are being molded into what you are going to become. The question that you have to ask is what and who is molding you? Another popular statement is that "you are who you hang around." You see, it is external forces that mold our inner thoughts. Whatever you are putting into your soul is what you are molding your soul to look like. Now the interesting thing is that you can fool the world with your outward appearance. But you cannot dress up what your soul has been molded into. This is why so many people feel conflicted because they want to do what is right, but they have been molded into making the wrong decision. Now the wonderful thing about being molded is that we can be reshaped. Several years ago, I was at a youth workers convention, and they brought a professional pottery technician up on stage. I do not remember professional pottery technician as a career choice when I was in school, but this guy was great. He molded a piece of clay he worked with it for a while, and then he took it off of the potter's wheel and threw it to the floor, turning it into a big blob of muddy clay. But then he did the most amazing thing, he picked it back up, put it on the wheel, and began to reshape it. This time it was even more beautiful than the time before.

You see, this is the beauty of grace. Grace helps to reshape us and mold us into who

God wants us to be. God can take what the world has molded us to be, and he can change our shape. Think about how many people in the Scripture were molded one way, but then they met the head potter, and Jesus changed them. I think about Moses, Peter, and Paul, just to mention three. See, God wants to mold you and remold you. The truth is that God will never stop shaping you into being what he has called you to be. You just have to say God break me, mold me, and shape me. And then, after you have been shaped, I will see you at the plate.

Dear Head Potter,

Thank you for molding me, mending me, and making me into who I am. I fail you daily, but you are always reshaping me. Who I am today is who I will be tomorrow, so I must focus on being more like you. Thank you for continuing to keep your hands on me. God, if I need to be reshaped, it will be painful, but it will be rewarding. Amen.

Day 338

Godspeed

Proverbs 14:23 ***"All hard work brings a profit, but mere talk leads only to poverty."***

The other day I was sitting in my frequent coffee shop, and a group of guys came in with a shirt that read, "Godspeed: Heart, Mind, Soul, and Strength." They also scripturally back each one of these Godspeed components with Bible verse. The definition of Godspeed: a prosperous journey.[31] When I saw the shirts, I asked one of the guys what they were all about, and he explained that they go into schools and organizations to train athletes. He then told me that they have two distinct programs: one program is where they will work with your whole team, and the other is where you come to them, and they will train you on your time. He then told me that they take a holistic approach to training so that it is not just physical but that it encompasses every aspect of your being. You are only as strong as your weakest component was his tagline.

Now, I thought it was a little funny that an organization could offer all these components to their training because, as a minister/pastor, I hope to help those who sit under my teaching to develop into holistic disciples. As a matter of fact, I think that this is the goal of every church, or at least should be. This is what we are hoping to disciple our people into having a heart for God. To have a heart for God means to love the Lord your God with all your heart. To think like Jesus means having the mind of Christ. To make decisions based on what Jesus would do and not be led by our own inclination. We hope that people will be a keeper of their souls. A keeper by protecting it and guarding it, truly becoming a Soul Keeper. Finally, our prayer is that everyone will have the strength to fight against the evil one's schemes; to kill, steal, and destroy. Now, I do not know if Godspeed can really mold people into these qualities and characteristics, but I know that we should be working to train the heart, mind, soul, and strength as Christians. When we train these components, then we know that our spiritual life is growing exponentially. So, Godspeed, and I will see you at the plate.

Dear Great Advocate and Spirit,

Godspeed: we are on a prosperous journey. Not to prosper in this life but to prosper in the life that our Lord and Savior went to prepare for us. God, help me to be a holistic being created in your image to do your work and will. Give me a heart for the lost. Give me the mind of Christ, give me a soul led by the Spirit, and the strength to get through the toils and snares of this dark world. Godspeed.

Day 339

Coming Home

1 Chronicles 29:15 ***We are here for only a moment, visitors and strangers in the land as our ancestors were before us. Our days on earth are like a passing shadow, gone so soon without a trace.***

I watched the home opener for Auburn's softball team last night. They did not do very well and lost a home opener for the first time in program history. They also lost to Kennesaw State, which had never beaten them, so history was made for Auburn in a negative way. The reason Auburn lost is that the other team got more people home than they did. Now, I know that sounds like a ludicrous statement, but it is such a true statement. You realize that the object of softball/baseball is to get home. To win, you have to get on base and then find a way to get home.

The one who gets the most players to home plate wins. Simple concept, but sometimes we need a reminder of our objective. When we lose the focus of getting runs home, then we will lose the game. The more I thought about this, the more I realized that this is the same concept in our lives. Our object is to get home. One of the reasons we lose focus on our eternal home is that we sometimes think that this life is our home. The truth is that the Scripture says, "that we are aliens in this world." You see, this is not the world God intended for it to be because this world is full of sin. As long as we live in a place surrounded by sin, we have no hope of this world being our permanent home. Just last week, I was sitting with a friend that was struggling with cancer. He had just been told that he would be put on hospice and would most likely never leave the hospital again. Before we prayed, he shared with me that what bothered him the most was never getting to see his home again. It was a home that he designed and built. So, what I assured him was that he would be going to a home that would even be better than the home he built. This new home would be free from the cancer and pain that he was enduring here. Five days after our conversation, he did go home. He was welcomed home to his heavenly dwelling place. He had the victory, and he was home; yes, he was safe at home. So, are you ready to round the bases and get home? If you are, I will see you at the plate.

Dear Preparer of my Eternal Home,

So often, I have lost the focus of the game. So often, I have focused more on the temporal than I have the eternal. God, help me to realize that I am just a stranger passing through this world. I have no home here, just a place that I stay while I am here. My home is with you forever and ever. Thank you that your Son went to prepare the place for me. Jesus, I am coming home. Amen.

Day 340

In the Rearview

Philippians 3:13 ***Brothers and sisters, I do not consider myself yet to have taken hold of it. But one thing I do: Forgetting what is behind and straining toward what***

is ahead, I press on toward the goal to win the prize of God's heavenly calling in Christ Jesus.

The other night we took the youth from the church to Winter Jam, which is a concert of various Christian artists from many different music genres. During one of the music sets, one of the artists said something that was profound and caught my attention. In his testimony, the up-and-coming rapper, Zauntee said, "you will never reach the finish line if you keep looking in the rearview mirror." What made this resonate with me was that earlier that day, I had preached that you could not get past your past if you keep bringing your past into your future. If the past is in your present, then it is not really your past. See, if you keep looking in the rearview, you will never see what lies ahead; you will only focus on what is behind you. When we look in the rearview mirror, it reminds us of where we have been and how many times we have failed. When we look in the rearview, we begin to fear the competition that is sneaking up on us. When we look in the rearview too long, we forget that there are things in front of us that we must face. I often meet people who never reach their full potential because they keep looking back and reliving the past. Many people's past has been hard. Many people have been abused, neglected, and left behind, but those things do not have to define your future or who God has called you to be.

See, Satan has no future, and he has no good plans for your life, so his scheme can only be to have you look at your past and your past failures. This is his sole strategy for ruining your life because he has no future; he can never be more than he already is. On the other hand, God has a future for us; he has plans to use us and for us to prosper. He does not remind us of our past; he forgives us of our past. He not only forgives, but he forgets. You see, when we keep our eyes on the road and on the prize that has been laid before us, we will not only reach the starting line, but we will reach the finish line. So, look straight ahead, and I will see you at the plate.

Dear God of my Future,

God help me to fix my eyes on the prize which you have called me to. God, too many times, I look in the rearview for fear of getting caught or passed. Other times I look back, trying to see what I may have missed. Help me to see that the past is the past. I cannot change or control the past but what I can change and dictate is the future. So, Lord, take my eyes off of the rearview and train me to look forward to the promises you have laid before me.

Day 341

Playing Favorites

Psalms 30:7 ***I'm God's favorite. He made me king of the mountain." Then you looked the other way …***

The other day, I overheard a parent talking about how political and nepotist youth sports were in our local community. I had experienced some of that with my son when we moved here, but this parent had a legitimate complaint because their kid was an exceptional ballplayer and would never get the chance to prove how good he was. He had not made the team because he was smaller and had not been on the right travel team for the last five years. He was a newcomer, and the truth be told, the coaches had long ago selected who would play on the team. The truth is that making the team is not always based on ability but on who you know and who your parents may be. This has commonly come to be known as "daddy ball." It is truly what ruined many little league and recreational teams. The parents often begin to believe that their kids are better than they are, so they start a travel team and put all their friend's kids on the team. The travesty is that these teams do not always play the best players, but they play the favorites. Now, this can leave kids crushed and feeling as if they do not measure up. These kids often walk away from a game that they loved and have worked at for many years. If you have ever been in that situation, I want to tell you about someone who has chosen you to play on his team. I guess you could say he plays "daddy ball," but all can make his team and play for him. The truth is that you do not even have to go looking for this team because this team came looking for you. What am I talking about? I am talking about your heavenly Father, who loves to play daddy ball with you. You see, in God's eyes, there is no one more important than you. He does not pick you based on your mom and dad or how much money you have. He does not pick you based on your ability but picks you based on the fact that he loves you. He does not pick you because you are heads above the rest. He picks you because you belong to him. God plays "daddy ball" the right way. Let me ask you, have you accepted God's invitation to join his team? Because when that final day arrives, it will not matter what team you played on here on earth. The only thing that will matter is that you were on "big daddy's team," that big daddy is God, our Father, and Creator. So, is it "daddy ball?" Absolutely but this daddy is the daddy of every child. So make your daddy proud, and I will see you at the plate.

Dear Big Daddy,

Thank you for choosing me before I chose you. I thank you so much that there is room for everybody on your team. God, I am inadequate to play on your team because of my sin, but you chose me anyway. Help me realize that no matter my accomplishments here on earth, the only accomplishment that will matter at death is the accomplishment that I joined your team. How do I join? By simply saying, Jesus come into my heart and change my life. I am a sinner in need of your grace. Save me by the power of your blood.

✞

Day 342

I Got Your Six

Isaiah 58:8 (NASB) ***The glory of the LORD will be your rear guard.***

A team is more than a group of athletes that try to win together. A team is a group of people that become a band of brothers/sisters. The reality is that a team is an extended family. One of the things that you sometimes may hear a teammate say is, "Come on, I got your back." This term comes from the military statement, "I got your six." Fighter pilots used it to explain that they had one another's back. In the military, positions are labeled like the hands on a clock, which many people may not know because they cannot read an older clock with hands on it. But the six o'clock position on the clock is the position directly behind a plane. It is the area that the fighter pilot cannot see, so someone else has to look out for them, or they will be shot down from behind. This expression later was simplified to "I have got your back." This meant that they would look out for one another and protect one another. But what do we do when we do not have someone to watch our back or that person with our 6 o'clock position? It is in times like this that we feel vulnerable and alone. But the amazing thing is that we always have someone watching our "six." She when Jesus left to go to his heavenly home, he promised us that he would not leave or forsake us. He promised us that he would have our back and that he would do so with the power of the Holy Spirit. See, the devil knows that if he attacks us, his attacks must come from the back. But we have the Holy Spirit that has our six and helps us to fight off and thwart the attacks of the evil one. When we listen to the

Holy Spirit, he gives us a strategy to fight against the one that came to steal, kill, and destroy. All of these ploys are done by a sneak attack from the rear. Satan wants to catch us off guard, hoping that we do not have our back protected. That is why we must daily invite the Holy Spirit to be our wingman to help us fight off the attacks that surround us. So, who has your six, God does, and he wants you to know that he will always have your back. So, now that you know who has your six, I will see you at the plate.

Dear Holy Wingman,

Thank you for protecting my rear even when I sometimes fly right into enemy territory. God, you have sent your Holy Spirit to guard my six and to help me realize what to do when I am stumped. God, I know that this world is constantly trying to sneak up on me and ruin my joy and relationship with you. But you sent your Son, and by the strips on his back, he covered my back. Thank you that his blood covers me. Forgive me of my sin and help me to now have the back of my brothers and sisters.

Day 343

Fear Does Not Evaporate

Matthew 25:24-25 Then ***the man who had received one bag of gold came. 'Master,' he said, 'I knew that you are a hard man, harvesting where you have not sown and gathering where you have not scattered seed. So I was afraid and went out and hid your gold in the ground. See, here is what belongs to you.'***

One of the greatest inhibitors of us reaching our potential is fear. Often, the way we handle fear is that we feel as if it will just evaporate. The truth is that fear will not only evaporate, but if ignored, it will multiply. We know that we have tons of fears, but we often ignore our fear no matter who we are. The truth is that many times even the toughest athlete has tons of fear. I love it when the star of a game is interviewed, and they say, "I know we won, but I was scared to death." How many times have you felt those butterflies in your stomach telling you that you are not prepared? How many times have you feared being outmatched? How many times have you feared messing up or causing the team to lose because of your error?

We all have fears, whether we admit it or not. But, God has given us permission to fight back and not to handle fear with passivity. You see, the ultimatum is that you either combat the fear in your heart, or the fear in your heart will keep you from doing what God has prepared for you. I love this analogy by Steve Furtick; he says, "if you keep handing the bully your lunch money, don't act surprised when he keeps taking it."[32] See, you will never conquer your fears or strengthen your faith by avoiding your fears. So how do we conquer our fears? Well, it starts with fear, and this is a fear of the Lord. This is not the fear that he is out to get you. This is the fear that he is so big and omniscient that nothing is too big for him. This is the fear that leaves you in awe when you think about the works of his hand. This is the fear of not asking him to join you in your fight; because if you do not ask him, you are sure to fail. See, fear of the Lord is not the same as fear of the boogie man. The boogie man is out to steal, rob, and destroy you. But our sovereign God is for you, not against you. See, what we must be terrified of is being outside of God's will and protection. So, it is time to fear the Lord so you can face your fears. I will see you at the plate.

Dear Jehovah-Sabaoth - Lord of Hosts,

You are all-powerful, all-knowing, and ever-present, and this is why I must fear you because you are holy. The real thing in my life that I must fear is living outside of your will or protection. Many times, I create my own fear because I doubt. I often create my own fear by asking what if, even before it becomes a what if. Most of my fears will never come to fruition, so let me put my fear in you so that I may trust and obey.

Day 344

The Jezebel Syndrome

1 Kings 19:4–5 ***"I have had enough, LORD," he said. "Take my life; I am no better than my ancestors." Then he lay down under the bush and fell asleep.***

One of the hardest things to do in sports is handling success. Now handling success can be more challenging than struggling with losses. The question is, how do we keep success from going to our heads? How do we stay humble when everyone around us is telling us how great we are? Then there is the question as to can we do it again? The truth is the more you win, the greater the expectation becomes. Another thing that success does is that it puts a target on your back; this means that everyone is out to get you. It means that you get everyone's best night after night, game after game. If they can knock you off, then they can call it a successful season. Amid all these questions, we can forget what it feels like to work your way to the top. There is a strange story in the Bible about a prophet named Elijah. So, Elijah confronts all the false prophets and challenges them to have the god (Baal) they pray to burn up an altar upon their summons. They cannot do it, so Elijah steps in and calls on the Lord's name, and immediately, the altar burns up. Victory! He is not only victorious with burning up the altar, but then he single-handed wipes out every false prophet that serves under Jezebel. So, you would think that he would celebrate such a great victory, but instead, just a few verses later, it says, "Elijah was afraid and ran for his life." (1 Kings 19: 1– 3) So, what happened? "I'll tell you what happened; it was that Ol Jezebel" I borrowed a quote from "The Waterboy." When Jezebel found out what had happened, she was dead set on making him pay. But hold on a minute, this is a guy that could stop the rain for 3 ½ years and call fire from heaven, and now he is running for his life. Well, not exactly; what I perceive he is doing is running from his life. The battle has left him drained and tired. He thinks that he does not have the energy to continue to fight. So, at this time, it would be easier for him to tuck it in than it would be to put up another fight. This is a different kind of "fear." This is not the fear to face but the fear to face again, this time fearing a loss even in the midst of repeated success. You see, fear is neither logical nor linear in nature. Instead of Elijah regrouping and calling on that same Spirit that prevailed before, he retreats. He gives in to the "Jezebel Syndrome," and he runs. Now, in the end, after a bitter lesson from God, he learns to put his faith back in what had got him to the top in the first place. Let me ask you are you running for your life or from your life? Either way, I ask you to stop and put your faith back in what got you this far in the first place. Place your faith back in the God that reigns victorious. See you at the plate.

Dear Victorious Savior,

Handling success may actually be harder than handling defeat. Satan loves to work with our arrogance. He loves to let us think that we did it and are more important than we think we are. My prayer is that we would run to you when fear grips us and not run from the fear. So often, we are running from rather than facing it with your help and guidance. Thank you that I believe in the ultimate victory, and that is the victory of the Cross.

Day 345

How Much Will You Give?

Philippians 2:7-9 ***Rather, he made himself nothing by taking the very nature[a] of a servant, being made in human likeness. And being found in appearance as a man, he humbled himself by becoming obedient to death, even death on a cross!***

I saw a bumper sticker this morning that caught my attention; the sticker read, "some gave some, but some gave all." I immediately recognized that this was in reference to the military. I knew that this meant that some would never come home from their post. Just this week, I saw where three people lost their lives defending our country, and we are not even at war. But in the sports world, the same cannot be said to the level that one would die giving it their all even though Nascar comes close. But when it applies to effort and maximum output, this same slogan may ring true. Some give some, but others give all they have. In sports, the ones that give the most are the ones that usually get the most out of their effort. You can observe any practice and immediately see who the some gave all players are. They are always going all out, and they never want to quit. They are the players that show up for non-mandatory practices. They also take what they do off the field seriously. They are the ones that not only give their all for their benefit, but they give their all for the benefit of the team.

The reality is to give anything less than our all is a waste of the talent that God has given us. The question is why we should give our all, and the answer is because that is what Jesus did for us. The Scripture says that he considered himself nothing so that he could give his all for us. Why did he give his all for us? Because anything less would not have saved us from our propensity. When we go all for Jesus, we are also saying that we will give all for the sake of the call. Every day there are missionaries in the underground churches that are imprisoned or martyred for the sake of advancing the Kingdom of God. Now, most of us will never pay the ultimate price of our life, but what is holding us back from giving our all. So the next time you want to give in or give up, just remember that some gave some, but Jesus gave all. See you at the plate.

Dear Creator of All,

I confess that so many times, I have held back. Sometimes because of fear.

Sometimes because of laziness and sometimes because I just did not care, help me to remember that I do not have an excuse for not giving my all because Jesus gave nothing less than that. Thank you for loving me so much that you gave your all. I know that I am saved because I have accepted that your Son gave his all, and that is enough.

✞

Day 346

Do Not Let the Accuser in Your Head

Revelation 12:10 ***And I heard a loud voice saying in heaven, Now is come salvation, and strength, and the kingdom of our God, and the power of his Christ: for the accuser of our brethren is cast down, which accused them before our God day and night.***

Have you ever been blamed for something you did not do? Have you ever done something, but it got blown way out of proportion? In the Book of Revelation, John writes about the struggle between God and Satan. It is described as the final battle, which of course, we already know God wins. But an interesting fact is that John never calls Satan by his name in Revelation. In the book, he only uses one name for Satan, and that word is the "accuser." You see, so many times, we think of Satan as a "tempter," which is one of his tactics, but we forget that he is also an "accuser." He accuses us of all different kinds of things in hopes of getting us to believe his lie. His accusations are not merited, and they can only harm us if we begin to believe the lies. How often have temptation and accusations caused you to respond in a way that you did not want to respond to? So many times, we allow our surroundings and things out of our control to cause us to lose our minds and temper. A few weeks ago, I watched as a player on a college basketball lost his cool and started throwing punches. The coach later explained that his player was a good kid and held his faith very close. The coach explained that this was so out of character for him. But this situation resulted from where the temptation met the accusations of the accuser. The evil one whispered, do not let him treat you this way. He is embarrassing you. This is no longer about competition, but he has taken it to a personal level. You see, that is the way that the accuser gets in your head. He is not outright lying; he is just using half-truths to get you to bite. But what if you take a minute to breathe and then turn the record over to the other side. This is the side of redemption and grace. It is a place where we walk back into the grace of Jesus Christ. It is the place where the accuser loses because he cannot tell his lies in the presence of the truth. It is the place where you repeat the words; there is no condemnation in the Lord. Here is where we need to train ourselves not to listen to the lie of the accuser. So here this truth you are not condemned, you are not too far gone, no the fact is that you are loved, and you are so loved that someone gave his life so that you could defeat the accusation. Now that you know the good news, I will see you at the plate.

Dear God of Encouragement,

Help me not to let temptation and accusation cross paths in my life. Help me fight against the chatterbox in my mind that is constantly telling half-truths and outright lies. Give me the wisdom to distinguish the lies from the truth. Help me to turn off the negative voice in my head, which is not you. Thank you that Jesus could not tell a lie but that he did everything that he said he was going to do, and he gave his life for me.

Day 347

Un-sin?

Luke 24:47 ***"And that repentance and forgiveness of sins should be proclaimed in his name to all nations, beginning from Jerusalem."***

Should of, would of, could of, are all statements we like to make after we sin and fall short of the glory of God. Now here is a revelation for you. You cannot un-sin. Once the sin is committed, it is there. You have done it, and you are guilty. How many times have you booted the ball, dropped the third strike, overthrew the first base, or struck out to lose the game? You cannot un-error either. In games, we all make errors and fall short of the glory of the win. That may be a little sacrilegious, but it is funny. So, the important thing that we have to remember when we sin/error does not define us. The accuser that we talked about yesterday loves to remind you of your sin. He even tries to get that sin/error to define you. So how can we move on from this situation? The first thing you do is repent. Not just say I am sorry but truly turn and go in another direction. So often, we say sorry, but we do not do anything to change the situation. I have often heard about a player missing the last shot to lose a big game and then going in the gym after it is cleared and shooting for a solid hour. That is a great example of active repentance. The next thing you must do to move beyond your sin is that you truly have to move on. You have to put that sin in the rearview and not glance back. If we keep revisiting it, we will continue to live it out again and again. Finally, we have to let God rebuild us no matter how damaging our sin/error is. Listen, God's grace is not only sufficient to forgive us, but it is sufficient enough to rebuild us. The accuser's negative voice takes what is glorious and ruins it, but God takes what is ruined and turns it into something that is glorious. It is time to be glorious. I will see you at the plate.

Dear God of Forgiveness,

God help me to move past who the accuser says that I am. Help me to confess and then to truly repent. So often, I try to move forward, but I allow myself to believe the lie that I cannot move forward. The cross made sure that I could always move forward. The cross that stood still was truly the propellant that covered a multitude of my sins. I repent, I move forward, and I put in the rearview my sin. Amen.

Day 348

Iron Fist vs. Graceful Guidance

Ezekiel 36:26 ***I will give you a new heart and put a new spirit in you; I will remove from you your heart of stone and give you a heart of flesh.***

Let me ask you what kind of coach do you want to play for? That is a question that so many athletes face when they think about choosing a team. I have played for all kinds of coaches, I have played for the laid-back, passive teaching coach, I have played for the "rah-rah" pep them up coach, and I have played for the "in your face cussing and yelling" coach. Still, the best coach I ever played for was my college coach, and he was a combination of all the above. But one thing that separated him from the rest of my coaches was that he did not just coach us, but he helped shape us. He wanted us to win, but he also cared that we won in life. See, he understood that one day we would no longer take the field and what mattered was what we did with the lessons that we had learned on the field. See, a coach is more than a coach; they are true role models. I read a quote the other day in my devotional time that stuck out to me. "Iron fists chisel stony hearts, but graceful hands shape responsive hearts."[33] I can tell you that this spoke to my heart because I am quick to anger when it comes to parenting or coaching. When we yield to coaching with an iron fist, we may get a result, but we are not grooming athletes to be responsive in the real world. Sports are an extension of who we are in the world and not just defined by who we are on the field. I think of Jesus' example when he was here on earth; Jesus likes to exercise what I call tough love. This is what it means to have graceful hands. We often think that we must coach angrily, but the truth is that we can coach from a tough-love standpoint, and we will be amazed at how the athletes respond. Remember that we are molding young people into who they will be; we are not just coaching kids to wins and losses. You have been coached with graceful hands, so I will See you at the plate.

Dear Great And Greatly To Be Praised,

Help me to realize that I am a role model. Help me to also realize that I am shaping what tomorrow looks like through my coaching and teaching. When I teach with an Iron fist, I cannot help but create a calloused heart. But when I coach with gracious hands, I teach life and not just how to win and lose. Thank you for the tough love that your Son exhibited.

Day 349

Good or Great

Mark 10:18 ***Why do you call me good?" Jesus asked. "Only God is truly good.***

Last night, I got to listen to one of our Celebrate Recovery team members give a Lenten message for the start of Lent. The talk was very provoking and well put together. He brought up one point in particular that has been on my heart for the last 12 hours. Adam said, "that good is the enemy of great." He admitted that he did not coin this phrase, but God sure used him to deliver a powerful message around this statement. You see, we often accept being good, and we never strive to reach for great. Jim Collins wrote a book a few years ago that addresses all the reasons we are only good in his book, "Good to Great." Now I know the term great is very relative, but we can become great with work and God's help. We can become great in what we do, and we can become great in who we are. One of the greatest curses for an athlete is being good at something. When we are good at something, it often prohibits us from pushing through to the next level. So often, an athlete may never reach their full potential because they are good. This is where good becomes the enemy of great because it screams you are good enough, or even worse, it screams you are better than your competition. A few years ago, on a team where I was serving as chaplain, there was a good receiver, I mean good, but because he was really good, he relied on what he already had rather than working harder to become great. I recall that same year we had an undersized young man and a tidbit too slow, but he worked to surpass good and became great on the field. Was he the greatest? No, but he truly moved from good to great! The other thing that stuck out about Adams's talk was when he said, "that reason that Jesus died on the cross was to bring us from good to great." You see, Jesus died for one purpose, and that purpose was to make what God had created and called very good even better. You see, Jesus' death on the cross moved us from good to great because being good is not good enough. What is good enough is grace, and the only way to receive grace is to accept the death and resurrection of Jesus. See, if we want to move from good to great, we have to accept the greatest of all time. We must ask Jesus into our hearts so that we can move from good to great. So now that you know you can go from good to great, I will see you at the plate.

Dear Jehovah-Kanna - Lord Jealous,

So often, God, I am satisfied with mediocrity. To become great requires self-sacrifice and reliance on you. Why do I call you good when I should call you great? Why am I great because I follow the greatest of all time? He is my friend, and his name is Jesus. Help me to move from good to great in every aspect of my life.

✞

Day 350

That Is Who You Are

Romans 2:4 ***"Or do you disregard the riches of His kindness, tolerance, and patience, not realizing that God's kindness leads you to repentance?***

There is a new worship song that has taken over the contemporary airwaves. The song's name is "WayMaker," and I love to stand and sing this song at the top of my lungs. The song has been made and remade by no fewer than seven artists. The words in the chorus give us a list of who God is. (You may want to listen to "Way Maker" this week as you study the attributes of God.)

It says that God is the Waymaker and that he works Miracles. It says that he always keeps his promises and that he lights up the dark night. That is just who he is. A confession here is that I love to listen to music before a game, competition, or working out. Most athletes love to put on those Beats or Airpods and turn up the volume to get ready for competition. By sitting listening to our favorite genre of music, we can get focused and block out the distractions of our surroundings. My go-to genre would normally be Rock, but I can tell you that I would be listening to Waymaker if I was playing today. This music will help to give you a feeling that you could run through a wall. I think the reason is that this song is more than a song; it is a great explanation of who God is and will always be. We all have thoughts on what and who God is, but these points cannot be argued. I would even say that these traits can be applied to all of our athletic endeavors. Over the next four days, we will look at every word that explains who he is in hopes of who we can become. Say these words about God right now. "God. You are a Waymaker. You are a miracle worker. You are a promise keeper. You are a light in the darkness." Now what that means is that God is the great "I Am." God is the great "I Am" because he cannot be anything else but the great "I am." What is the great "I Am"? It is a waymaker, a miracle worker, a promise keeper, and a light in the darkness. So, now that you know the great "I Am." I will see you at the plate.

Dear, I Am and Always Will Be,

I am not because you are "I Am." You have always been great I Am, but so often, I forget that you are the I Am, and I try to be the I Am. Forgive me when I take the lead rather than allow you to lead me. When Jesus was asked who he was, he responded I Am, and that was his way of testifying that he was the incarnate God. Thank you for your Son and his love for me. Amen.

✞

Day 351

Way Maker

Acts 24:14 ***However, I admit that I worship the God of our ancestors as a follower of the Way, …***

Have you ever heard someone say if someone would just give me a chance? In sports, there are always people looking for a way maker. So many people in sports and performing arts just want a chance to try or showcase their talent. Other people just need a break so that they can prove themselves. How many dreams have been fulfilled by someone becoming a way maker? I will never forget when I wanted to get into youth ministry; I went to a guy that had been my youth minister. Now, I wish I could tell you I had been a model choir boy instead of a hellion, but I gave this youth minister fits. But he became the way maker for who I am today, and the ministry that I get to do is because he created a way for me. He gave me a chance to supervise a mission trip, and then he let me do the middle school youth ministry in the church I had grown up attending. He then went to bat for me so I could get into seminary.

I had no business going to seminary because I did not have high enough grades, and I was a horrible student. I had majored in football and minored in sinful extracurricular activities in college, so my preparation was quite inadequate. But he gave me a chance, and I made the most of it. He was my waymaker; well, he was just one of my waymakers because I can give you a list of people who were waymakers for me. But now, as I evaluate, my first true waymaker was Jesus. He gave me a chance when everyone was done with me. To be honest, I would have given up on me a long time ago. But Jesus said, when I died for you, Steve, I became your waymaker.

I created a way when everything else seemed impossible. I created a way when you thought you were finished. I made a way when your sin had buried you so deep that you did not want to carry on another day. Jesus, you were and still are my waymaker. According to the Scriptures, your way is the only way; you said, "I am the way the truth and the life" (John 14:6). Those are not my words but your words. To deny that you are the "only way" is to deny you and what you did for me on the cross. I think it is so interesting that before we coined the phrase "Christian," followers of Jesus were known as "Followers of the Way." Jesus, you are the great "I Am," and thank you for being a waymaker. Now that you know the way, I will see you at the plate.

The Narrow Gate,

You are the truth, the life, and the way. I cannot remind myself of that enough. Thank you that when everyone else was finished with me that you continued to seek me. God, you have always been by me and for me. You have been my waymaker in so many circumstances, and you will continue to open new doors for me. God help me to get still and listen to your voice. I must listen because many times, the way we hear you is through your whisper. Thank you that Jesus, for creating a way for me, and the way was the cross.

Day 352

Miracle Worker

Isaiah 35:4-6 ***Your God will come. Then will the eyes of the blind be opened and the ears of the deaf unstopped. Then will the lame leap like a deer, and the mute tongue shout for joy.***

Do you still believe in miracles? So often, we think of miracles as something that happens to someone else. Sometimes we explain away miracles as coincidence or karma. Here is a nugget for you. God is still in the miracle business, and miracles happen around us every day. We are often so busy that we miss the miracles that happen right in front of our eyes, like the miracle of a newborn baby, the miracle of totally being healed from cancer, or the miracle of an accident that is averted. Yes, miracles are all around us, but we are so busy with life that we do not see what is going on around us. The sports world is also full of miracles. What about the athlete that was never supposed to be born but now plays in the NFL? What about the player that survived a lifetime of abuse and neglect but now, as a professional athlete, has a foundation to help people who grew up the way he/she did? What about the athlete that prays through an injury and returns two games before they are scheduled for return? What about the team that had no chance at the beginning of the season, but now they are playing for a championship? These are just a few examples of miracles, and the reason that I put a question mark behind each one is so that we will question what is going on here. I am amazed that the Israelites followed God through the Red

Sea and the desert and yet kept missing the miracle. Did they not taste a miracle every day when manna appeared out of thin air? Did they not see the miracle of how their clothes did not wear out while in the desert? What about the quail that appeared even though they were not indigenous to the area? The truth is that they began to see the miracles as something expected and not as God's provincial power. In doing this, they turned a blind eye to how powerful God was. I like to find fault in the Israelites, but many days I never even give a thought of God being a miracle worker in my life and the lives around me. As I look over my life, I see miracle after miracle in place after place. Then it will suddenly dawn on me what God has done for me and that he has always been doing miracles in my life. I had no chance of ever playing football in college; I had no hope of getting in and finishing a divinity degree. But God worked a miracle in these areas and a 1000's others areas of my life. Yes, God is a miracle worker, and I am the miracle. You are also a miracle; I will see you at the plate.

Dear God of Miracles,

Help me to slow down so I can see what you are doing daily in my life. Help me to see not only the extravagant miracles but the simple miracles. The truth is that the breath in my lungs is a miracle. Forgive me for taking so many of your miracles for granted. Help me to not only see the miracle but help me to be a miracle in someone else's life. Miracle Worker, that is what and who you are. That is the only thing you know to be. Amen.

Day 353

Promise Keeper

Numbers 23:19 (NLT) ***God is not a man, so he does not lie. He is not human, so he does not change his mind. Has he ever spoken and failed to act? Has he ever promised and not carried it through?***

Let me ask you, have you ever said to someone, "I promise?" Now here is the hard question, did you keep that promise? I can say there have been many times that I have said, "I promise," and I did not carry through on that promise. Sometimes I did not follow through because I just forgot, but other times, I promised, but I had no intention of following through. I just said I promise to appease the other party. I have also been on the other side of things when someone said I promise to me and then broke that promise. In the sporting world, coaches many times make promises that they can not deliver on. I think this is one reason why the transfer portal has been so busy with 4-5-star athletes. These athletes are promised starting positions or playing time as a freshman, but that promise was not met.

Being a pastor, I do many weddings, and during a wedding ceremony, the couple takes vows and promises to love one another no matter what comes their way; I can not tell you how many times those vows have been broken. The truth is that we use the word "I promise" flippantly, and we do so with conditions. But one person that keeps their promise is our Lord and Savior Jesus. He takes the word promise to another level, and he calls it a "covenant." A covenant is sealed and cannot be broken. When God promised to make a way for you, he did so through Jesus Christ. When he promised to never leave or forsake, he meant that he would always be there for you no matter what. This does not mean that you will not have rough or trying times; it just means that you will have God with you no matter what you are going through. There are many other promises that God has for your life, but the problem is most people miss out on them because they gauge their trust in God by those around them that have broken promises. If God is a waymaker, then he has to be a promise keeper. If God has promised that he will always be with you. Then you can believe his promise. The promise is that he will provide a way for you, and he is coming back for you. You know he is the great promise keeper. So keep your promise because he kept his promise, and I will See you at the plate.

Dear Keeper of All Promises,

You have never left me. You have never failed me. You have always carried through on your promises. God, thank you for being the great promise keeper. Help me be more like you, and let me seal my word by living out your word. I promise to follow through on my promises and deliver so that people will see your promise through me. Help me to be a promise keeper.

Day 354

Illuminate the Dark

John 8:12 (NLT) ***Jesus spoke to the people once more and said, "I am the light of the world. If you follow me, you won't have to walk in darkness because you will have the light that leads to life."***

Have you ever been surrounded by darkness? Sometimes this darkness is physical darkness where you cannot see, but other times, this is spiritual darkness that clouds our soul. It is a time when everything goes dark. We often think of athletes as heroes, and we cannot imagine them going through dark times, but the truth is that they do. Almost every week, we hear of an athlete stepping away from the game because of the darkness of addiction. We hear of athletes that have made millions of dollars, and they are filing for bankruptcy. We hear of athletes who have made poor personal decisions, and now they are headed for a divorce. The truth is that if we live long enough, we will all find ourselves in periods of darkness. Sometimes these dark times are not even our own doing; sometimes, they are because of surrounding circumstances. It is times like these that God comes alongside you and offers you light during the darkness. It does not matter if the darkness is self-imposed or has been inflicted from outside influence. God will come alongside you and be the light in the darkness. I have a lady in my church that is a trail runner. She is not only a trail runner, but she is an extreme trail runner, sometimes running 40 plus miles at a time. After church a few weeks ago, she told me about a race that she had run the week before. She said, "she was running, and the light that she had to light her path was going out." (See, many of these races go well into the night.) She was worried about tripping or having to quit because of the darkness surrounding her. She said it was at this point that a young man came up beside her and offered to share his light and run along with her. This young man became a light in the darkness. This is the same way that Jesus comes alongside us and lights our path. Jesus comes alongside us and illuminates the dark places that we need to eradicate so we can move forward in life. See, being a light in the darkness does not mean that we get to stand in paralysis but means that when light is shed on the situation, we must move. Listen, your path to the plate has been illuminated so that I will see you at the plate.

Dear Bright Light,

God lights my path even where I have caused the path to go dark. Help me to see the error of my ways. Shine the light in the dark places of my life. You love me even when I have turned the light off. God help me to be a light to those who need light in the dark places of their lives. God, so many around me are suffering and are lost and broken. On the day when your Son was crucified for me, the sky went dark, but it would not stay dark because three days later, the stone was rolled away, and the light of the world shone brighter than ever. I accept that light into my life right here, right now. Thank you for being the brightest light. Amen.

Day 355

Win the Moment

Colossians 3:1 ***Therefore, since you have been raised with Christ, strive for the things above, where Christ is seated at the right hand of God.***

The other night, I watched a documentary on the University of Kentucky Basketball Team, and I noticed a sign that they all see as they are leaving their locker room to play the game. The sign was displayed right before they entered the court, and it said, "Win the Moment." We often think about winning the game, but the surest way to win the game is to win the moment. The most efficient way to win the game is to win moment by moment. See, in basketball, because of the constant spurts of scoring, the best way to win the game is to never trail in the game. When we have to play catch up, we lose moment by moment rather than win moment by moment. Now to win the moment in life is remarkably similar to the statement, "carpe diem." This means to seize the day. This is so important in life that we never know how much time we have left. We know we have this moment, but we are not promised one moment beyond this. So how does winning every moment work?

First, you must realize that this is the only moment you have and that you are not promised any other moments; this forces you to make the most of the now and block out the future.

Secondly, you must realize that a moment wasted is a moment that you do not get back. I think it is so ironic that you cannot change your allotted time here on earth. You only are given so many days, yet so many people have wasted most of their moments.

Third, you cannot let the fear of the next moment cripple you from acting at this moment. Did you know that over 90% of the things we worry about will never come to fruition? So, we must realize that worrying about something that has not happened will rob us of winning this moment.

So repeat after me. I will strive to win every moment given to me. Remember that Jesus made the most every moment that he spent on this earth. He refused to waste moments on things that would not enhance his ministry. So, do not waste a moment, and I will see you at the plate.

Dear Jehovah-Adon Kal Ha'arets- Lord of Earth,

You created all things for an allotted time. You have only given each one of us so many moments. Help me to seize every moment and to make the most of it. Let me focus more on making my moments more for you and less about me. Thank you that the defining moment in life was the moment that your Son defeated death.

Day 356

Knowing It vs. Knowing It

I John 4:6-7 ***We are from God, and whoever knows God listens to us, but whoever is not from God does not listen to us. This is how we recognize the Spirit of truth and the spirit of falsehood.***

So often, we say we know something when really, we only know about something. There is a stark difference between knowing about it and knowing it. I will be honest and tell you I have never been a good x's and o's football coach, and the reason is that I know about the game, but I do not know the game like other coaches know the game. I think part of this has to do with while I was playing, I learned enough to play my position, but I did not learn about the complete process of how things work together. The truth is that football is truly a very complicated game with many moving parts, and it is a game that is always evolving. I compartmentalized the game into what I needed to know and did not study the holistic approach to the game of football. The truth is that I have often approached many aspects of life the same way.

I know about many things, but I do not know these things as I should. The worst way to study is to cram; when we cram, we will only know about it, but we will forget the most important concepts of why we are learning it. The one thing that I feel that I know and know a lot about is that I have a relationship with Jesus. I can honestly say that it is the one thing that I have continuously worked on. There is no way to cram a relationship, all relationships, if you are going to build them, will require time and effort to master. If you know about God, you have a head knowledge of who he is, but if you know him, you have a heart knowledge of God and who he is. God wants us to know him personally, and that is why he did not hide anything from us but sent his Son to give us an example of who he is. God did not keep his distance from us but came looking for us so that we could intimately know him. I am always amazed at people who argue Scripture and God's concept, but they only know about him; they do not know him. The truth is that some people argue the Scripture but have never read or studied it. They know about it, but they do not know it, and they do not know him. See, God truly wants us to move from knowing about him to experiencing how much he loves us. So, now that you know it (Jesus), I will see you at the plate.

Dear All-Knowing God,

God, I do not want to know about you, but I want to know you. I want to know you inside and out. I want you to also know every part of me, good and bad. I want nothing to be hidden from you because I was created in your image. God, you came looking for me when I was lost and overcome with darkness. God, you love me even when I do not love myself. God, you sent your Son so that we would not just know about you but also know who you are.

Day 357

Are You Next Level?

Hebrews 6:1 ***Therefore let us move beyond the elementary teachings about Christ and be taken forward to maturity, not laying again the foundation of repentance from acts that lead to death, and of faith in God,***

Recently, I saw a travel baseball team advertising their tryouts for a team known as NXT LEVEL. The X in their logo was two baseball bats. I thought, what a clever concept. But I wondered if the 7-8-year-olds that were picked to join their team would be next-level players. I mean, what is the next level when you are 7-8 years old? Does this mean you will play in middle school or make it to the high school ranks, which gets harder every year? Maybe, it was a reference to going on to the highest level, and these kids would be playing in the MLB. Here is the probability of going on to the next level; according to the High School Baseball web page, 5.6% of boys that play in high school will play in college. That equals out to 3 in 50. Now let's go to the next level; less than 11 in a 100 will get drafted to play in the MLB. If we add these to percentages together, then the result is .05% of these young men who play baseball in high school will get a major league contract.

Now I do not want to be a killjoy or discourage these young men from pursuing their dream of playing Major League Baseball, but I want to warn parents and kids against making this your sole goal in life. See, the truth is that the odds are stacked against you even if you are really good. So, I want to suggest that you make going to the next level in your relationship with Jesus Christ your top priority. I say this is because 100% of those who put their faith in Jesus Christ will be saved. Look at the difference in those to odds. While we are pursuing the next level, we must also focus on taking our relationship with Jesus Christ to the next level. I mean, Jesus warns us against gaining the whole world and losing our souls. Now what that means is that we should put our relationship with Jesus Christ as our priority. I am really surprised at how many people take so many things in their life to the next level, but they never get out of the infancy stage in their relationship with their Maker, Savior, and Sustainer. God created you for more; God created you to be a next-level Christian, and here is what I would share with you instead of the odds being stacked against you, these odds are stacked for you. So, let's take it to the next level. I will see you at the plate.

Dear God of the Highest Level,

God, you are the highest level imaginable. You long for us to take our relationship with you to the next level. So often, I take everything in my life but my relationship with you to the next level. God, I want to be a next-level Christian not only in my relationship but in my service to you and others. Next-level sometimes means sitting at the foot and not the head. It means serving and not being served. Next-level in the Kingdom of God is upside down in comparison to the world.

✞

Day 358

It Is Not Over Yet

John 19:30 (NKJV) ***So when Jesus had received the sour wine, He said, "It is finished!" And bowing His head, He gave up His spirit.***

What keeps you from giving up? What keeps you from waving the white flag or throwing in the towel? Hopefully, your answer to that is perseverance. Webster defines perseverance as a continued effort to do or achieve something despite difficulties, failure, or opposition: the action or condition or an instance of persevering: steadfastness. Sometimes, it would be easier to just quit, but our test becomes our testimony when we push on. We can feel a sense of accomplishment when we push through. We need to just stay the course no matter how bumpy the ride. The other day I was at my sons' state semifinal wrestling match. There was one boy on the team that was not given even a small chance to win. He took it into the third period and was down in points and had almost been pinned twice. But he refused to give up and, in the last second, got a pin to win the match. Because he won that match, the team won by two points. What a great accomplishment, but it would have never happened if he had given up or given in.

You know that we should never give up because we have a Savior who never gave upon us. The Scripture that you read today is Jesus's final words on the cross. It sounds like it is over and that he has been defeated. But we know that when he said, "it is finished, he referred to his dying love for us." He had conquered death so that our sin could not be held against us. Christ endured our sin and persevered the pain of crucifixion so that we could live. Whenever you think about giving up or throwing in the towel, I want you to see Jesus there on the cross saying it is finished, and then I want you to push through and finish the race. Alright, it is time to finish this, and I will see you at the plate.

Dear Finisher of Life,

Help me to push through, to press on, to never give up, even when it would be easier to just quit. Thank you for finishing for me. Thank you that you took my sin to the cross, and then you spoke these words over it. It is finished. When the devil keeps tempting me to let me scream these words, devil, it is finished. Amen.

✞

Day 359

He Is Because I Am Not

Exodus 3:14 ***And God said to Moses, "I AM WHO I AM." And He said, "Thus you shall say to the children of Israel, 'I AM has sent me to you.'"***

The greatest demise of our existence is when we think we have arrived. The moment that we think we are 100% in control is when we lose our footing. It is so easy to get the big head or to gloat over our achievements. Often, when we listen to people tell us how good we are or that we are the main reason the team is winning, we lose focus on who gave us the ability to play. We begin to think that we created our talents. I recently read a book by Louie Giglio entitled "I Am Not, But I Know I Am." The book's premise shows that God is the great "I Am" and that everything we achieve is done through him.

When you first think about this concept, you may think that it means that we should diminish our work and our willingness to win. But the truth is that when you realize you are not, you begin to give the glory to the great "I AM." You see, knowing (God) "I Am" inspires us to excel in all areas of life. We want to excel so that God can receive the glory from our accolades and achievements. The truth is that God does not need us to show his glory. If you want proof of just how great the great "I Am" is, ask these questions. Have you ever looked into the heavens, have you ever looked down the beach, have you ever studied how complex our bodies are and how they are put together? When we study all of these things, we realize just how big "The Great I AM" really is. So that means that he also created us. Why did he create us? He created us so that we could tell the world through our achievements that we are not but that we know the great "I am." So now that you know you are not but you, "I am," I will see you at the plate.

Dear, I Am Dynamis Power,

My simple prayer today is simply this: I am not, but I know I am, and because I know I am, I can become all that I am has called me to be. Amen.

✞

Day 360

Where Does Your Strength Come From?

Psalms 121:1-3 (NLT) ***Look up to the mountains—does my help come from there? My help comes from the LORD, who made heaven and earth! He will not let you stumble; the one who watches over you will not slumber.***

I love watching athletes put their weightlifting max on Twitter. It is a good way to show your hard work, and it is a good way to show recruiters your work ethic. We all know that our physical strength comes from pushing past body limits. I have seen young people double their bench press, squat, or deadlift in one year. Some of it was due to maturity, but some of it was because they chose to work hard so that they could be strong. Now physical strength is of some value; the Bible says godliness is to be placed above all. So the question is, where does our strength come from? The other day at a wrestling match, one of our good wrestlers was in a tight point match. The guy he was wrestling reached over and smacked him; one of the parents then commented, well, here he goes. He was referring to the fact that when this boy gets angry and does not wrestle under control, he tries to use only his brute strength but forgets about proper technique.

The parent was right, and he lost a match that he should have won. When things get out of our control is when we have to seek godliness. This is when we quote today's verse and then go to work. "My help comes from the Lord. He will not let you stumble." Just saying this will help to focus us and help us to remain in control. Sure we are strong, but strength will not help when we do not focus on it or channel it. Strength that is not controlled is just out-of-control energy. So, where does your strength come from? It comes from the Lord. Now I will see you at the plate.

Dear Above all Other Gods,

I look unto the hills for my strength. I look into my strength to overcome. But I will not find my strength there. I will only find my strength in the Lord. My help comes from the Lord and the power of an empty cross. You defeated death so that I might control my strength. Make me strong in the Lord.

✞

Day 361

Are You Welcoming?

Mark 10:15 ***"Amen, I say to you, whoever does not accept the kingdom of God like a child will not enter it."***

One thing we often forget about in the recipe for success is team chemistry. We know that a team comprises people from diverse backgrounds, ethnicities, and social-economic structures. So with all that in mind, the question is, "how do we become a team that operates and works together? I would suggest that the first step to ensuring continuity is that a team is humble and hospitable towards one another. In other words, we need to be a team that does not consider ourselves as elitists or above our teammates. This means that we all know our role on the team and respect others' roles. One of the teams that I helped with always complained that the placekickers never had to work as hard as the rest of the team. They always complained about the kickers never doing anything but kicking. One day I overheard them, and I told them one day that will pay off. They just kind of shrugged it off and went on pushing the sled. But toward the end of the season, they got to see just how important it was that the placekicker had kicked all practice for every practice. With 3 seconds to go and the next round of the payoffs waning in doubt, the kicker made a 35-yard field goal to win the game. See, this lesson shows that we should be a hospitable team and count everyone with worth. We should not claw to get to the top as an individual but get to the top as a team. One of the stories that Jesus shares in Mark's Gospel is the story of two Disciples arguing about who would be the greatest when Jesus took the Kingdom. One wanted to sit at the right and the other to the left. They cared nothing about hospitality or others. They just cared about themselves. Jesus uses a strong analogy to get his point across. He brings a child and says that you will not even get in the kingdom unless you welcome one of these. Here, Jesus is sharing that heaven requires being receptive and accepting God's gift to us. See, when we practice hospitality, we become welcoming to the children who need to hear the good news of Jesus Christ. So let me ask you if you are practicing hospitality as a team or have you been clawing to get to the top. Be a hospitable teammate, and I will see you at the plate.

Dear Father of All Children,

Thank you for being hospitable to me and welcoming my sinful self into your kingdom. Help me to lead others to know Jesus. Help me to work as a team and not to focus on emphasizing myself. Help me to continually evaluate where I am in my journey to the cross. God, I give it all to you now; please take it and use it. Amen.

Day 362

No Defined Finish line

Revelation 21:2 ***And I saw the holy city, new Jerusalem, coming down out of heaven from God, prepared as a bride adorned for her husband.***

Two years ago, I decided to do a century ride. It had been a few years since I had ridden that distance, but I figured that I would give it a whirl. The day before, I looked over the map or glanced at the map and decided the course was challenging but doable. Now I guess that I skipped the part where there would be a 6-mile gradual climb through the Talladega natural forest. I started ok, but the longer the grind, the more exhausted I got. I found myself riding alongside two women, and we were all gassed. We had halted to a 4 or 5 mile an hour pace – one right behind the other.

The funny things about bike riders are that they pride themselves on never walking the bike. In other words, you do not get off the bike anywhere but at rest stops. I kept telling myself only a little more till the top. But then the girl riding behind me said, I can't push anymore, and she got off to walk for a saddle rest. I kept telling myself just keep pushing but eventually, I got off and walked with her. When we got to the top, we knew it would be downhill from here, and we were both discouraged because we had not ridden to the top. (We did, however, finish the century.) Even though I finished, I still wish I had stayed on the bike because I let that hill conquer me. So now the question is, what did I learn from this experience. First off, it revealed to me that I must get in better shape if I am going to be a warrior on the bike. It also revealed to me that I can reach the finish line and still not feel like we conquered the challenge.

The second thing it reminded me of was that I have the power and presence of God on my side. What if I had prayed and pushed on? What if I would had remembered what Christ had done for me as he went to the top of Golgotha? Do you remember

Joshua in the Bible? He took over a bunch of whiners from Moses. Now the funny thing is that he did not have a defined finish line. But he just jumped in and trusted that the Lord would lead him to the promised land. Sometimes in life, we have to do the same. We may not be able to define the finish line, but we can define who is at the finish line, and that is our Father. So you may not know where the finish line is, but you know where to start, so I will see you at the plate.

Dear Creator of the Finish line,

Sometimes the finish line is not apparent. Sometimes we have to push even though we feel as though we cannot. In the most trying moments, God, we learn the most about how much you love us. Help us to push through with your strength. Your Son made it to the finish line for me, which should help me push through even when I want to get off and walk.

Day 363

Good Advice vs. Godly Advice

I Kings 12:8 ***But Rehoboam rejected the advice the elders gave him and consulted the young men who had grown up with him and were serving him.***

You know when you are playing sports everyone is always giving you advice. I often joke by saying, "I have never made a bad call from the stands." The truth is that so many people get into the game because they are passionate about it, or it brings back memories of when they used to play. That is why they are so quick to give you advice. But we all know that the game changes and that just because that worked 20 years ago does not mean it is still applicable today. The truth is that some advice given to you is not good; it is bad advice. So we must pick and choose what we listen to and what we take with a grain of salt.

Now, this same concept is a little bit easier to decipher in the world. You see, advice from the world needs to not be simply good advice, but it needs to be Godly advice. It is advice that helps us draw closer to God and does not lead us into temptation. Misery loves company, so the world tries to get you to go along with the devil's evil schemes. That is why the advice that other people give us must match up with the

Scripture. See Scriptural advice is not simply good advice, but it is Godly advice. In the Scripture, Rehoboam wants to be a good King, so he asks for his elders' advice, and they give him Godly advice, but rather than take that advice, he rejects it and then takes the advice of his friends. But here is the ironic thing that the elders had walked with Solomon, the wisest man to ever live, but these young men had yet to even experience life. If you genuinely want to grow and take good advice, no scratch that Godly advice, then finds an older mentor with an ongoing relationship with Jesus Christ. See, if we want to be Godly, we have to seek God in the Scripture, and we have to line ourselves up with people who have already experienced what we are going through to receive the Godly advice available to us. So, how do we do that?

1. Read the Scripture. A good place to start is in Proverbs. The Godliest advice ever given is contained right here in these passages.
2. Second, pray that God will lead you to an older mentor that will help lead you in a Godly manner.
3. Approach the mentor that God has intersected our path with and ask if they would mentor you.
4. Listen to the advice that your mentor has given.
5. Live a Godly life so that others will see Jesus in you.

Dear Elder of all Elders,

Could you help me to listen? Help me to find wise counsel. Help me to not listen to the advice of the world but for me to hear the voice of God. Wise counsel leads to wise decisions, but the decisions of the fool lead to destruction. Keep me away from the advice of fools.

Day 364

Game-changing Play

John 5:24 ***"Very truly I tell you, whoever hears my word and believes him who sent me has eternal life and will not be judged but has crossed over from death to life."***

Have you ever heard a coach say, "we are going to win the game on this possession?" They have waited for the whole game for this ace in the hole. They know that if the team can pull this off, then the victory is in hand. This possession is when our preparation matches the exact moment. I have seen this happen on numerous occasions throughout my life. We must realize that timing is everything, but you must be prepared to do your part to pull this off. You know this was the same thing that happened when Christ came to earth. I have often heard people say, "why did Jesus come to earth when he did?" Then they begin to give an evaluation of why it would have been better for Jesus to come now. Here are some of the examples that I have heard. "I mean, we have satellites now so that he can broadcast his Sermon on the Mount worldwide. We have the internet so that he can do a weekly devotional and reach the ends of the earth. We have arenas that he could bring people into to do mass healing, and rather than five loaves and two fish, he could just send them to the concession stand. But the cold hard fact is that Jesus came because it was the time that God saw that he needed to be here. It was in God's timing, and God's timing is perfect. The other great advantage as to when he came is that we now know the rest of the story. We know the play that won the game, and that play was called the "three on a hill crucifixion." We already know who wins the game, and that is Jesus. He is the star of the game. And we know who receives the trophy, and that is us. So let me ask you, are you part of God's master play. The one where he said we are going to win the game on this possession. See, when you are a part of this play, you get a prize that will not fade or rust; you get to spend eternity with your Father. So get ready; this play is a game-changer. See you at the plate.

Dear Eternal Play Caller,

God, thank you for your timing and what you have done for me. I do not deserve the victory, but your grace trumps my failures. Jesus is the one player that was the eternal gamechanger. He did this so that I could inherit the prize. I accept this play the way it is called, and now it lives in my heart and in my life. God, you are my God, and Christ, you are my Savior. Amen.

✞

Day 365

How Will You Finish?

John 17:4 ***I have glorified You on earth by accomplishing the work You gave Me to do.***

On this last day of devotions, I want to encourage you not to give in to the temptation to quit. The devil loves to whisper in our ear, "it is not worth it. "You cannot finish it. Give up; it is so much easier just to give up." Here is a quote to write upon your heart. "It's not where you start; it's where you finish!"[34] How many times have you started something only to quit halfway through? This week, I talked to a lady who said she had started her Lenten fast from sweets but had accidentally broken it, so she quit. I told her that she could just start again because it was not the start that mattered but the finish that defined us. So, many times, we feel that we have failed, and we have to give up. But how many people have succeeded because they refused to give up or give in? The only regrets that you will have will be the regrets of quitting. When you quit, you have no way of redeeming yourself. When you quit, you can't finish what you started.

Another point to make here is that quitting is habitual. Every time you give in or quit, it gets easier for you to quit something else. So, your life becomes defined by stops and starts and not by persevering to the end. The truth is that grace is all about finishing strong, not about when or where you started. Redemption is a word that gives us the courage and the strength to finish. When we are redeemed, we get a second chance. Jesus was this world's second chance. Adam had started humankind in the garden but had allowed sin to define his heritage. Jesus then came into the world as a second Adam (being created by God and not from two humans), and he finished the race so that we could be redeemed. So, here is your encouragement to finish the race you have started. One of the best ways to exemplify Christ in our life is to finish the race. So, I will say this one more time, let's finish this, and I will see you at the plate.

Dear, It Is Finished,

God, you sent your Son to finish what no one else could do. You sent your Son to die for our sins, the sins that Adam cursed us with when he took the forbidden fruit in the garden. Please help me to finish what I started. The best testimony that I can have for Jesus is the testimony of finishing in spite of. Help me finish something that I have walked away from. Most importantly, if I have walked away from my relationship with Jesus, help me to realize that he is standing there with his arms wide open to receive me so we can finish this race together. Thank you for your Son, the finisher, Jesus Christ.

Names Of God

Savior
Father
Lord
Spirit
God of the Universe
God of Second Chances
Gift Giver
Humble God
Holy One
God of Divine Direction
Creator of Heaven and Earth
Christ
Great, "I Am"
Messiah
Trinity
Omniscient One
Living Presence
Holy God of Infinite Wisdom
Lord of host
Jesus
Lord of Utmost Character
God of Agape Love
Lord of Lords
Sovereign Lord
Faith Weaver
Name above all Names
Author of the Book of Life
Eternal Lord and Savior
Breath of Life
Jesus Christ Son of the One True God
The Truth, The Life, and The Way,
Great Encourager
Son of Man
Sacred Wounded One
Friend of Sinners
Awesome in Power
Heavenly Head Coach
Training Partner
Sacrificial Lamb
Comforting Father
Almighty
My Firm Foundation
God of Centering
Giver of Gifts and Talents
Savior of all Humanity
Adonia
Ultimate Controller
God of the Whole Truth
Triune Father
Holy Ghost
Bread of Life
Father, Beloved Son, and Holy Spirit
Holy of Holies
Kingdom Builder
YHWH
Creator
God of All Nations
The One: The Only One
Giver of Your One and Only Begotten Son
Creator of Night and Day
Eternal Flame
Timekeeper
Lord of the Harvest
My Fortress
God of Peace
Almighty One
Savior that Brings Shalom
Creator of Heaven, Earth and all People
Holy Servant
Messenger of Life
Holy Breath
Glowing And Radiant One
The Anointing Oil
Worthy of Praise
Altar of The Tabernacle
God of Bethel
I Am Longsuffering
Creator and Perfecter of Joy
Dunamis power
Author and Creator of My Life
Lord of My Life
Peacemaker

God of Perpetual Strength
Crucified Savior
Yeshua
Lord of the Dance
Gracious Lord and Savior
God of Abraham
Sustainer
Heart Mender
Mighty Warrior
Perfector of Faith
EL ROI, (seeing)
EL-GIBHOR, (Mighty God)
Kingdom Come Near
God of Clarity
God of Joy and Laughter
Father of the Past, Present, and Future
Heavenly Abba
Eternal Provider of Grace
Father of All Nations
Fortress of Salvation
Creator of Day and Night
Son of David
Son of Humankind
Lord and Savior of My Life
God of the Cup
Creator of the Way
Provider of Communion
Vine
Jesus Friend of Mine
Teacher of Prayer
Sweet Breath of Air
Infinite, All-Powerful Mighty God of Big Dreams
Provider
Infinite God
King of My Heart
Sacrifice for Our Sins
Good, Good, Good, God
Fountain of Israel
Ark Of The Covenant
Sword Of The Spirit
Creator of Yesterday, Today, and Tomorrow
Balm Of Gilead

Root of David
Holy Loving Lord
Prophecy Fulfilled
Perfect, Spotless, Blameless Lamb
Rock of Redemption
Patient Father
The Hearer of my Prayers
God of Triumph
God, How Majestic is Your Name
Heavenly Trainer
God of Mercy and Kindness
HOLY GPS
Prince of Peace
Bearer of My Scars
Alpha and Omega
Lord of Goodness and Mercy
God of Change
Great Power Source
Jesus is Lord
Blessed Rock
Great Overcomer
Great Provider
Creator of Visible & Invisible Things
Son of the Living God
Overseer of All
Covenant of Promise
One and Only Way
Sovereignty
Abundant Grace
Everlasting Priest
Morningstar
Yahweh
Lord God of Mount Sinai
Elohim
Authority over all Authority
Pure and Holy Lord
Creator of Kairos
Holder of the Future
Baptizer
Emmanuel
God of Eternity
Precious Stone
Rejected Stone of Builders
Noble One

Holy Spirit Jesus Christ Humble Servant Your Righteousness Voice in the Wilderness Almighty Powerful Supreme God Great Rabbi God of Love, Power, and Might The Blood Atonement Bold and Courageous Lord God of Vision Creator of Body, Soul, and Mind Soulmate My Supplication Lord Jesus Heart Healer Heart Renewer Heart Changer Healer of the Lonely and Brokenhearted Listener of the Contrite Heart Dear Song of My Heart Life Coordinator Spirit of Wisdom Divine Judge of All Things Eye in the Sky Author of all Words Holy Heavenly Father Father of Time Three in One Lord and Perfecter Speaker of Life Pain Taker Mighty Fortress Thy Staff and Comfort Precious Lord Son of the Virgin Mary Wonderful Counselor God of Big Awesome Dreams Shekinah Glory River of Living Water Sanctified One Preeminent One Jesus the Nazarene	Tabernacle Father to the Fatherless Host of Honor and Dignity Author of Life God of Love and Sacrifice Empowering God God of Abundance God of Heaven and Earth Jehovah-M'gaddishcem - Lord my Sanctifier Gracious Loving God Jehovah-Ganan - Lord Our Defense God of Sanctification Greatest of All Time God of All Possibilities God of Victories Lord of the Water God of the Promise God of Peace and Tranquility Jehovah-Magen - Lord my Shield Ancient of days God of Shalom Ultimate Protector Author of Truth God of Jeshurun Peace Lily Faithful Father House of defense True Word Holy Provider of Hope God of Righteousness Jehovah-Misqabbi - Lord my High Tower Humble Lord Jesus God of Comfort Jehovah-Helech 'Olam - Lord King Forever Holy Cornerman Jehovah-Machsi - Lord my Refuge God of the Unexpected Still Small Voice God of Rejuvenation Living Water Of Life Victorious Banner

G.O.A.T, "God of all Things"
Rabboni
God of Epiphanies
Humble Savior
Seeker of the Lost One
God of Absolute Truth
Committed Savior
Holy One True God
Jehovah-Chereb
Jehovah-Tsori
Crucified Lord and Savior
God of the Powerless
God of Sabbath and Rest
All-Sufficient One
God of Vision and Clarity
Jehovah-Hashopet
God of Transfiguration
God of Light
God of Ultimate Faith
Big God
The Barrier of My Cross
God of All Control
Trustworthy God
God of Boldness
God of Rebuilding and Rebirth
Jehovah-'Ez-Lami - Lord my Strength
God of All In
God of those outside of the Circle
Great I Am
God of Respect
Big Boss
Spiritual Provider
Relationship Builder
Mighty Leader
God of Kairos (TIME)
Anchor of Hope
Undefeated One
Author of the Holy Word
Perfect Spotless Lamb
Jehovah-'Uzam - Lord Strength in Trouble
Dangerous God
God of the Small Stuff
Shepherd of the Flock
Jehovah-Keren-Yish'i - Horn of Salvation
Trinitarian God
Head Potter
Great Advocate and Spirit
The Preparer of my Eternal Home
God of my Future
Big Daddy
Holy Wingman
Jehovah-Sabaoth - Lord of Hosts
Victorious Savior
Creator of All
God of Encouragement
God of Forgiveness
Great And Greatly To Be Praised
Jehovah-Kanna - Lord Jealous
I Am and Always Will Be
The Narrow Gate
God of Miracles
Keeper of All Promises
Bright Light
The Passover
I Am Ever Faithful
Imago Dei
Jehovah-Shammah – Present
Jehovah-Adon Kal Ha'arets- Lord of Earth
All-Knowing God
God of the Highest Level
Finisher of Life
I Am Dynamis Power
Above all Other Gods
Father of All Children
Creator of the Finishline
Elder of all Elders
Eternal Play Caller
It is Finished

Endnotes

[1] 1Batterson, Mark, Circle Maker; Zondervan Grand Rapids Mich. 2011 pg. 25.

[2] The Complete Book of the Olympics, Reader's Digest Archive.

[3] 3Old / New Testament Greek Lexical Dictionary developed by Jeff Garrison for StudyLight.org. Copyright 1999-2021. All Rights Reserved, Jeff Garrison, Gdansk, Poland.

[4] Abbott-Smith Manual Greek Lexicon of the New Testament. Copyright © 1922 by G. Abbott-Smith, D.D., D.C.L.. T & T Clarke, London.

[5] THAYER'S GREEK LEXICON, Electronic Database.Copyright © 2002, 2003, 2006, 2011 by Biblesoft, Inc.

[6] HISTORY HEIST onlinehttps://patri-x.com/theodore-roosevelts-man-in-the-arena-speech/

[7] https://www.biblestudytools.com/bible-study/topical-studies/what-does-love-the-lord-with-all-your-heart-mean-in-the-bible.html

[8] THAYER'S GREEK LEXICON, Electronic Database.Copyright © 2002, 2003, 2006, 2011 by Biblesoft, Inc.

[9] https://www.finestquotes.com/author_quotes-author-Don%20Wilder-page-0.htm

[10] https://www.gotquestions.org/pure-in-heart.html(cf. Danker et al., Greek-English Lexicon of the New Testament, 489).

[11] https://www.Sermon Illustrations.com

[12] https://www.todayintheword.org/ Today in the Word, August 30, 1993 A Moody Bible Institute Devotion

[13] https://bible.org/Bible.org 2009, February © 2021 Bible.org

[14] Stanley, Andy and Hall, Stuart The Seven Chackpoints: 7 Principles Every Teenager needs to Know.Howard publishing. West Monroe LA, 2001.

[15] https://www.selfhelpdaily.com/motivational-quotes/zig-ziglar-quotes

[16] https://www.craiggroeschel.com/leadershippodcast Part 4

[17] https://www.9news.com/

---

[18] The free dictionary .com

[19] The Blue Letter Bible - https://www.blueletterbible.org/

[20] http://faithpoetry.com/ faith12/nevercompromise.shtml Connie Campbell Bratcher-June 2005, Never Compromise

[21] Goodreads.com

[22] www.gotquestions.org

[23] Ortberg, John.Soul keeping : caring for the most important part of you. Zondervan: Grand Rapids, Michigan Pg. 66

[24] Stanley, Andy: The Principle of the Path: How to Get from Where You Are to Where You Want to Be. THOMAS NELSON Nashville 2010.

[25] Article in Star Tribune: Case Keenum offers unique breakdown of "Minneapolis Miracle" JUNE 22, 2018

[26] Wesley's Sermons: Justification by Faith Year 5

[27] http//:www.soulshepherding.org Dallas Willard's Definitions and Quotes - Soul Shepherding Copyright ©2021 Soul Shepherding

[28] https://www.George Mueller.org

[29] Stanley: Deep and Wide, Zondervan 2013

[30] Ortberg, John, The Life You've Always Wanted Zondervan; Grand Rapids Michigan Underlining edition (January 1, 2002) pg. 182

[31] https://www.Merriam-Webster Online dictionary copyright 2021

[32] Furtick Steven: Crash the Chatterbox Hardcover, pg 124 Published February 11, 2014 by Multnomah

[33] Speake Wendy Amber Lia) Triggers: Exchanging Parent's Angry Reactions for Gentle Biblical Responses Paperback – February 3, 2016

[34] Zig Zigler, Raising Positive Kids in a Negative World, Ballentine Books 1989. From azquotes.com/quote/808663

Made in the USA
Columbia, SC
01 December 2021